VISUAL QUICKSTART GUIDE

MACROMEDIA FIREWORKS MX

FOR MACINTOSH AND WINDOWS

Sandee Cohen

Peachpit Press

Visual QuickStart Guide
Fireworks MX for Windows and Macintosh
Copyright © 2003 by Sandee Cohen

Peachpit Press
1249 Eighth Street
Berkeley, CA 94710
800 283 9444 • 510 524 2178
fax 510 524 2221
Find us on the Web at http://www.peachpit.com.
To report errors, please send a note to errata@peachpit.com

Peachpit Press is a division of Pearson Education
Published in association with Macromedia Press.

Editor: Cary Norsworthy
Production Coordinator: Lisa Brazieal
Compositor & Interior Design: Sandee Cohen
Cover Design: The Visual Group
Copy Editor: Pamela Pfiffner
Indexer: Steve Rath

ISBN 0-201-79479-9

0 9 8 7 6 5 4 3 2 1

Printed and bound in the United States of America

DEDICATED TO

Terry DuPrât

Thanks for everything.

THANKS TO

Nancy Ruenzel, publisher of Peachpit Press, who gave me the time to get this book out.

Cary Norsworthy, my editor at Peachpit Press. Cary is a triple threat—an artist who can edit and write.

Pamela Pififfner of **Creativepro.com,** who took the time out of her busy schedule to copy edit the book—and did a great job!

Pattie Belle Hastings, who did the screen shots of the OS X interface. I am honored to have her as a co-author and friend.

Lisa Brazieal of Peachpit Press, who does a great job of production.

The staff of Peachpit Press, all of whom make me proud to be a Peachpit author.

Steve Rath, who does the best index in the business.

Toby Malina, my intrepid tech editor. It's always a thrill to work with you.

David Morris of Macromedia, who has kept me up to date on the latest Fireworks features.

Joe Lowery, author of *The Fireworks MX Bible.* Joe has been a great resource, and I'm honored to call him a friend.

The staff at **The Big Box of Art,** who were nice enough to provide me with a complete set of their OS X stock photography and clip art collection.

The staff at **Photospin.com,** who were kind enough to provide many of the halftone images used in this book.

Michael Randazzo, Zee Demster, Emerson Braithwaite, and the staff of the New School for Social Research Computer Instruction Center.

Pixel, my cat, who has gotten very blasé about these books and doesn't watch me work anymore.

and a very special thanks to

David Lerner of **Tekserve,** who personally helped me get my G4 Powerbook running Macintosh OS X. Tekserve (www.tekserve.com) is the best place to buy, fix, or enhance Macintosh computers.

Colophon

This book was created using Adobe InDesign 2.0. Screen shots were taken using Ambrosia SW Snapz Pro X. The computers used were a Macintosh G4 450 Mhz running Mac OS 9, and a G4 Powerbook running Mac OS X. InDesign 2 for Windows ran on the Macintosh OS X platform using Virtual PC 5 (no Intel inside). Fonts used were Minion and Futura from Adobe, Circle Negative from Myfonts.com, and a specialty "tip" font I created using FontLab from FontLab Inc.

TABLE OF CONTENTS

Table of Contents

INTRODUCTION

Welcome to learning Macromedia Fireworks MX. In a very short period of time, Fireworks has become an important tool for creating all sorts of Web graphics.

What makes Fireworks so useful? Perhaps the most important reason is that it allows designers to work visually to create not just the images for Web sites but also the special code needed to assemble graphics and create interactive elements.

Another reason is that, instead of using three or more separate programs, Fireworks combines features found in image-editing, Web optimizing, and vector-drawing programs. So instead of jumping from one program to another, Fireworks lets you use one program from start to finish.

It has been very exciting to revise this book — my fifth time! Some features that used to be covered in a page or two have now been expanded into their own complete chapters. And yet, other features have been so simplified they can be covered in just a few pages.

Using This Book

If you have used any of the Visual QuickStart Guides, you will find this book very similar. Each chapter consists of numbered steps that explain how to perform a specific technique or work with a feature of the program. As you work through the steps, you gain an understanding of the technique or feature helped along by insightful tips. The illustrations let you judge if you are following the steps correctly.

Instructions

Using a book such as this will be easier once you understand the terms I use. This is especially important because some other computer books use terms differently. So, here are the terms I use throughout the book and explanations of what they mean.

Click refers to pressing down and releasing the mouse button in the Macintosh, or the left mouse button in Windows. You must release the mouse button or else it's not a click.

Press means to hold down the mouse button or a keyboard key.

Press and drag means to hold the mouse button down and then move the mouse. In later chapters, I use the shorthand term drag; just remember that you have to press and hold as you drag the mouse.

Move the mouse or cursor means to move the mouse without pressing the mouse button.

Menu Commands

Like any application, Fireworks has menu commands that you choose to open dialog boxes, change artwork, and initiate certain actions. These menu commands are shown in bold type. The direction to choose a menu command is written like this: Modify > Arrange > Bring to Front. This means that you should first choose the Modify menu, then choose the Arrange submenu, and then the Bring to Front command.

Keyboard Shortcuts

Most of the menu commands for Fireworks have keyboard shortcuts that help you work faster. For instance, instead of choosing New from the File menu, it is faster and easier to use the keyboard shortcut.

Software companies and authors differ as to the order in which they list the modifier keys used in keyboard shortcuts. I always list the Macintosh Command and the Windows Ctrl keys first, then the Option or Alt key, and then the Shift key. In actual practice, the order that you press those modifier keys is not important. However, it *is* very important that you always add the last key (the letter or number key) after you are holding the other keys.

Rather than cluttering up the exercises with long keyboard commands, I've listed the shortcuts in Appendix A, separated by platform.

Learning Keyboard Shortcuts

While keyboard shortcuts help you work faster, you don't have to start using them right away. In fact, most likely you'll learn more about the program by using menus. As you look for one command you may see a related feature you would like to explore.

Once you feel comfortable working with Fireworks, you can start adding keyboard shortcuts to your repertoire. My suggestion is that you look at the menu commands you use a lot. Then choose one of those shortcuts each day. For instance, if you import a lot of art from other programs, you might decide to learn the shortcut for the Import command. For the rest of that day, every time you import art use the Import shortcut. (It happens to be Cmd/Ctrl-R.) Even if you have to look at the menu to refresh your memory, use the keyboard shortcut to actually open the Import dialog box anyway. By the end of the day you will have memorized the Import shortcut. The next day you can learn a new one.

Cross-Platform Issues

One of the great strengths of Fireworks is that it is almost identical in look and function on both the Macintosh and Windows platforms. In fact, at first glance it is hard to tell which platform you are working on. However, because there are some differences between the operating systems themselves, there are a few things you should keep in mind.

Modifier Keys

I always list the modifier keys with the Macintosh key first and then the Windows key second. So a direction to hold the Command/Ctrl key as you drag means that Macintosh users should hold the Command key while

Windows users should hold the Ctrl key on the Windows platform. When the key is the same on both computers, such as the Shift key, only one is listed.

In most cases, the Mac's Command key (sometimes called the Apple key) corresponds to the Ctrl key on Windows. The Option key on the Macintosh usually corresponds to the Alt key on Windows. The Control key on the Macintosh has no Windows equivalent. Notice that the Control key for the Macintosh is always spelled out while the Ctrl key for Windows is not.

Platform-Specific Features

A few times in the book I have written separate exercises for the Macintosh and Windows platforms. These exercises are indicated by (Mac) and (Win).

Most of the time this is because the procedures are so different that they need to be written separately. Some features exist only on one platform. Those features are labeled to reflect this.

Fireworks Workflow

I structured this book so that you could start with an empty document and build your skills and understanding step by step. The first two chapters deal with the basics of Fireworks's onscreen elements and the document window. The next eight chapters cover the illustration and drawing tools in Fireworks. The rest go through all of the features in an orderly fashion. So, if you tend to be a little obsessive/compulsive, you should start right with Chapter 1 and march straight through the book, one chapter after another.

However, if your client is demanding that you finish the Web site tonight you may need to skip some features and jump right into specific techniques such as optimizing and exporting existing scans.

How you use this book depends on what you need to learn, how quickly you need to learn it, and what your learning style is. This workflow guides you as to how to move around and choose the chapters that most interest you—like a buffet dinner.

Basics

Everyone needs some basics to cover the workings of the program. So whatever your ultimate goal, you should begin with:

- Chapter 1: Fireworks Basics
- Chapter 2: Document Setup

Optimizing

If you're in a hurry to get scanned images up on the Web, you can then skip directly to these chapters—this means you don't want to edit or add artwork to your images.

- Chapter 14: Importing
- Chapter 15: Optimizing
- Chapter 20: Exporting

Bitmap Images

If you are interested in working with scanned images, you should cover:

- Chapter 10: Working with Bitmaps
- Chapter 14: Importing

Interactivity

People expect to click buttons to move around Web pages. Here's a quick course if you want to know how to augment your pages with interactive elements such as buttons and links.

- Chapter 15: Optimizing
- Chapter 17: Hotspots and Links
- Chapter 19: Buttons and Behaviors
- Chapter 20: Exporting

Animations

Once you've succeeded with interactive buttons, you'll be ready to try your hand at animations:

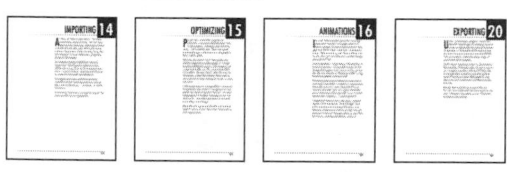

- Chapter 14: Importing
- Chapter 15: Optimizing
- Chapter 16: Animations
- Chapter 20: Exporting

Graphics Creation

Fireworks is more than just optimizing and exporting graphics for the Web. Its graphics-creation tools are among the best in the business. These are the chapters that show you how to create graphics:

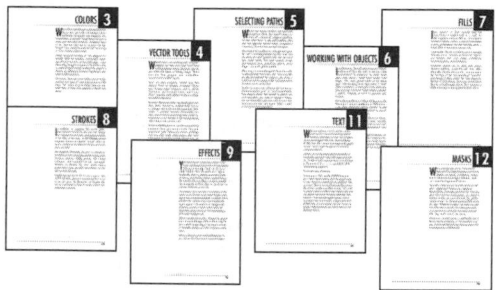

- Chapter 3: Colors
- Chapter 4: Path Tools
- Chapter 5: Selecting Paths
- Chapter 6: Working with Objects
- Chapter 7: Fills
- Chapter 8: Strokes
- Chapter 9: Effects
- Chapter 11: Text
- Chapter 12: Masks

Working Faster and Smarter

It's not enough to know how to use Fireworks—you also want to finish your projects quickly. Here are the timesavers that let you automate your process, work more efficiently, and use Fireworks in conjunction with other Macromedia products:

- Chapter 12: Automation Features
- Chapter 20: Exporting
- Appendix A: Keyboard Shortcuts

Easter Egg

Easter eggs are extra games or treats that the software engineers add to programs. (They're called Easter eggs because you're supposed to search for them and find them yourself.) However, if you want to see the Fireworks development team, here's how to get to the Fireworks Easter egg.

To see the Fireworks Easter egg:

1. Choose About Fireworks from the Apple menu (Mac OS 9), the Fireworks menu (Mac OS X), or the Help menu (Win). The Fireworks splash screen appears.

2. Opt-click (Mac) or Ctrl-click (Win) the Macromedia logo in the splash screen.

3. Enjoy the show!

TIP There is actually a practical purpose for opening the splash screen. Click the splash screen to display your Fireworks MX registration number. This can be useful if you need support from Macromedia.

Continuing Your Fireworks Education

One of the benefits of the Visual QuickStart Series is that the books are straightforward and don't weigh you down with a lot of details you don't need. However, they were never designed to be a complete reference work. So, if you need the most complete reference book on Fireworks, I recommend that you look at *The Fireworks MX Bible* by Joseph W. Lowery and Derren Whiteman.

But however you use Fireworks, don't forget to have fun!

Sandee Cohen

(Sandee@vectorbabe.com)
September, 2002

FIREWORKS BASICS 1

When I start learning a new application, I'm always in a rush to get started. I open it up and explore. It's the same way when I pick up a book about the application—I never start with the first chapter. I don't want to read about buttons, fields, and controls—especially if I'm already familiar with other programs from the same company such as Macromedia Flash, Macromedia Dreamweaver, and Macromedia FreeHand.

No, I rush right into the middle chapters of the book.

However, after a few hours of slogging helplessly through the book, I eventually realize there are many things I don't understand about the program. I recognize I'm a bit confused. So I come back to the first chapter to learn the foundation of the program.

Of course, since you're much more patient than I am, you're already here—reading the first chapter.

System Requirements *(side tab)*

System Requirements

To use Macromedia Fireworks effectively, your computer and operating system must meet the minimum system requirements for the program.

General System Requirements

- 64 MB of free system RAM (128 MB recommended)
- 800 x 600, 8-bit (256 colors) color display or better
- 80 MB of available disk space
- CD-ROM drive

Windows Requirements

- 300 MHz Intel Pentium II processor or equivalent
- Windows 98 SE, Windows Me, Windows NT 4 (Service Pack 6), Windows 2000, or Windows XP
- Adobe Type Manager Version 4 or later for use with Type 1 fonts

Macintosh Requirements

- Power Macintosh G3 processor or better
- Macintosh OS 9.1 and later, or OS X 10.1 and later
- Adobe Type Manager Version 4 or later for use with Type 1 fonts (OS 9 or later)

Running with the Minimum

The minimum system requirements are just that—just the bare minimum. Can you launch Fireworks with the minimum requirements? Absolutely! Will you be happy with the bare minimum? Most likely, no!

If you run Fireworks with the lowest-end computer, you may find it takes a while for the screen to redraw and settings to apply to objects. If you have only the minimum system RAM (memory), you may see alerts that Fireworks needs more memory to finish certain commands. This is especially true when it comes to applying special effects (*see Chapter 9, "Effects"*).

Launching Fireworks

In addition to the two methods mentioned on the facing page, you can launch Fireworks in a variety of ways.

You can launch the program by double-clicking an alias (Mac) or shortcut (Win) of the Fireworks application. You can add the application to the Windows Task bar or Macintosh OS X Dock. You can also add the application to the Mac OS 9 Apple Menu.

Consult the help files or manual for your operating system for the steps to accomplish these techniques.

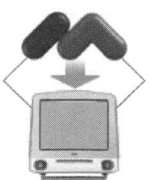

1 *The* **Fireworks Installers** *for the Macintosh.*

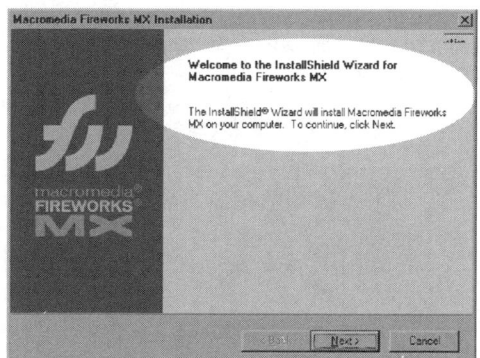

2 *The* **Windows Fireworks MX Installation** *dialog box takes you through the installation steps.*

3 *The Fireworks* **application icon.**

4 *The* **Fireworks MX application** *in the Windows Start menu.*

Installing and Launching Fireworks

When you have confirmed that your system meets the minimum requirements for running Fireworks, you can then install the application and begin to use it.

TIP Disable any virus-protection software before installing the software.

To install Fireworks (Mac):

1. Insert the Fireworks CD-ROM in the CD-drive.
2. Double-click the Fireworks Installer **1**.
3. Follow the instructions that appear.
4. After installation, restart the Macintosh.

To install Fireworks (Win):

1. Insert the Fireworks CD-ROM in the CD drive. If the installation program starts automatically, skip to step 5.
2. If the installation program does not automatically start, choose **Start** > **Run**.
3. Click Browse, and choose the Setup.exe file on the Fireworks CD. The Run dialog box appears.
4. Click OK in the Run dialog box.
5. Follow the onscreen instructions in the Fireworks Installation dialog box **2**.
6. If prompted, restart the computer.

Once you have installed Fireworks, you can then launch the application.

To launch Fireworks (Mac):

◆ Open the folder that contains the Fireworks application and then double-click the application icon **3**.

To launch Fireworks (Win):

◆ Choose **Start** > **Programs** > **Macromedia Fireworks 4**.

Onscreen Elements

When you launch Fireworks, you see the various Fireworks onscreen elements. These include the Property Inspector, the Tools panel, and the docked panels. The onscreen elements can be moved around to suit your own work habits.

TIP The positions of onscreen elements are saved when you quit the program.

To move onscreen elements to new positions:

1. Place the mouse cursor on the title bar of the docked panel, the side bar of the Property Inspector, or the top bar of the Tools panel. *(To dock and group panels, see the exercises on pages 14 and 15.)*

2. Drag the panel to the new position. A bounding box or preview shows the position of the panel **5**.

3. Release the mouse button when the panel is in the correct position.

To show or hide onscreen elements:

◆ Choose the name of the item in the Window menu. A checkmark next to the item indicates it is visible. No checkmark indicates the item is hidden.

   or

   Press the keystroke listed in the Window menu.

You can also hide items by clicking the controls on the element.

To hide onscreen elements:

◆ Click the close controller on the item **6**.

TIP Choose **Commands > Panel Layout Sets** to rearrange the onscreen panels for various monitor sizes.

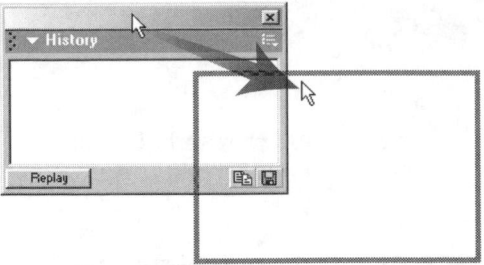

5 *You can* **drag an onscreen element** *from one position to another.*

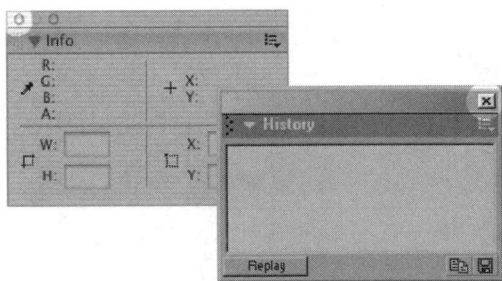

6 *Click the* **Close button (Mac) or Close Box (Win)** *to hide one of the onscreen elements.*

Presenting to a Client or Boss

If you have to present your work to a client or someone else, you might want to press the Tab key and change the view to the Full Screen mode (as discussed on the facing page). This hides all the onscreen and application elements and presents your work against a black background.

Doing this hides all indications that you are working in a graphics application. Clients are less likely to ask you to move something around, change colors, or increase the type size if they don't see the tools and menu commands.

Onscreen Elements

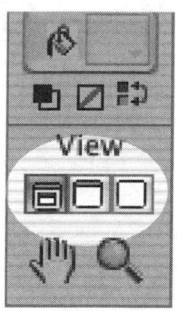

7 *The three View icons in the Tools panel (from left to right): Standard Screen mode, Full Screen with Menus mode, Full Screen mode.*

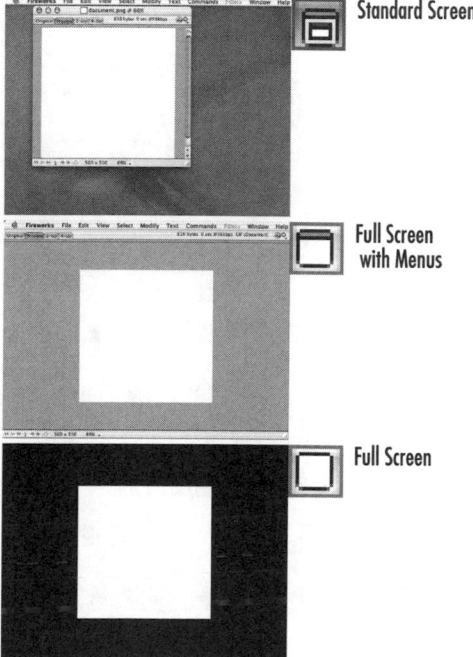

Standard Screen

Full Screen with Menus

Full Screen

8 *The* **three screen displays** *controlled by the View icons.*

Rather than hide each of the onscreen elements one by one, you can quickly show and hide all the onscreen elements with one keystroke.

To quickly hide and show all the onscreen elements:

◆ Press the Tab key on the keyboard. This hides all the onscreen elements. Press the Tab key again to show all the elements.

You can also show or hide the elements of the application itself. For instance, you can hide the application menu, the document window, scroll bars, and background elements. This lets you present your work with no distractions around it.

To change the display of the application elements:

◆ In the Tools panel, click the View icon for Standard Screen mode **7**. This shrinks the size of the document window and restores the display of all the application elements **8**.

or

In the Tools panel, click the View icon for Full Screen with Menus mode **7**. This maximizes the size of the document window, and applies a gray area around the image **8**.

or

Click the View icon for Full Screen mode **7**. This displays the image on a black background with no application elements visible **8**.

TIP You can also move through all the modes by tapping the letter "f" on the keyboard.

Onscreen Elements

Property Inspector

The Property Inspector (**Window** > **Prop-erties**) is the most versatile of the Fireworks onscreen panels. The Property Inspector displays different information depending on which items or tools are displayed 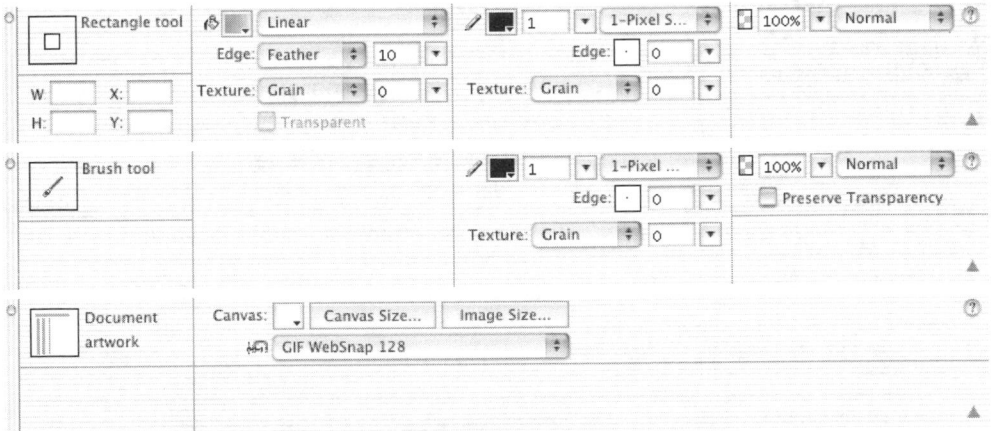❾. (This type of display is called *context-sensitive* because it changes depending on the context in which it is used.)

To see the context-sensitive displays:

◆ Use the selection tools to select an object or multiple objects. The Property Inspector shows the context-sensitive attributes for those objects.

or

With no object selected, choose one of the tools in the Tools panel. The Property Inspector displays the settings for that tool.

or

With no object selected, choose the Hand tool, the Zoom tool, or one of the selection tools. The Property Inspector displays the attributes for the document.

Property Inspector Display

I strongly recommend that you keep the Options control on the Property Inspector set to display the full-size panel (see the opposite page).

The half-size option cuts off some important features in the program. For instance, unless you are in the full-size panel, you would never know you could apply textures to objects or change the roundness of a rectangle.

All the screen shots in this book show the Property Inspector in the full-size option although some have been cropped horizontally.

---

❾ *The* **display of the Property Inspector** *changes depending on the objects or tools selected. From top to bottom: rectangle selected, Brush tool selected, and the Document artwork with no object selected.*

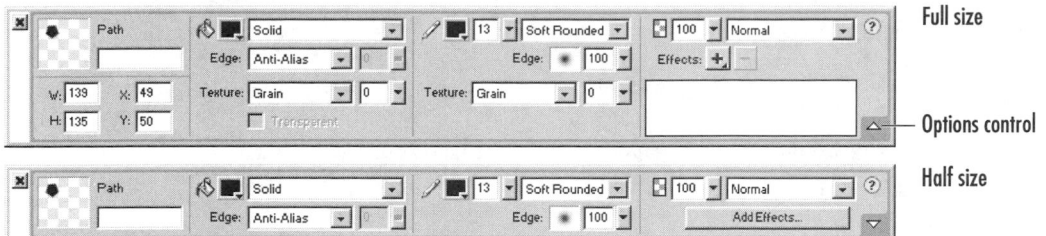

Full size

Options control

Half size

10 *Click the Options control in the Property Inspector to switch between the* **full-size option** *(top) and the* **half-size option** *(bottom).*

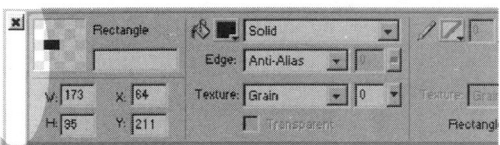

11 *Double-click the* **Property Inspector controller bar** *to dock the Property Inspector.*

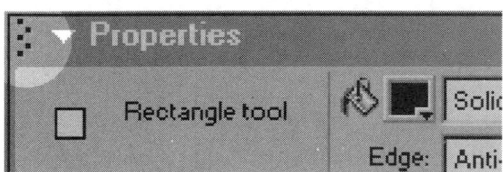

12 *Double-click the gripper dots in the Property Inspector title bar to undock it.*

13 **Collapse the Property Inspector** *by clicking the triangle next to the Properties title. This displays only the Property Inspector Title bar.*

The Property Inspector has two display options **10**. Full-size option shows the complete panel. Half-size shows only the top of the panel.

To change the size of the Property Inspector:

◆ Click the Options control triangle on the Property Inspector. When the triangle points up, it displays the full-size panel. When the triangle points down, it displays the top half of the panel.

Windows users can also dock the Property Inspector to the bottom of the window.

To dock the Property Inspector (Win):

◆ Double-click the contoller bar on the left side of the Property Inspector **11**. This docks the Property Inspector to the bottom of the window.

To undock the Property Inspector (Win):

◆ Double-click the gripper dots in the title bar of the Property Inspector **12**.

If you dock the Property Inspector, you can easily collapse and expand the panel.

To control the docked Property Inspector (Win):

◆ Click the triangle in the title bar of the Property Inspector to collapse or expand the Property Inspector **13**.

Property Inspector

The Tools Panel

The Tools panel contains the 44 tools and other controls for working with the program (*see figures* ⓮ *and* ⓯ *on the opposite page*).

To choose a tool in the Tools panel:

♦   Click the tool in the panel.

or

Tap the letter of the keyboard shortcut for the tool.

The keyboard shortcuts for the tools are displayed as part of the tool tips.

To display the tool tips:

♦   Move the mouse cursor over the tool. The tool tip shows the name of the tool and the keyboard shortcut ⓰.

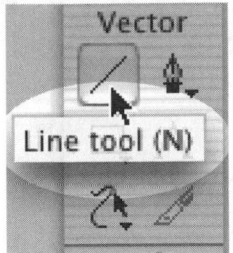

⓰ *Place the mouse button over a tool icon to see its* **tool tip**, *or name and keyboard shortcut.*

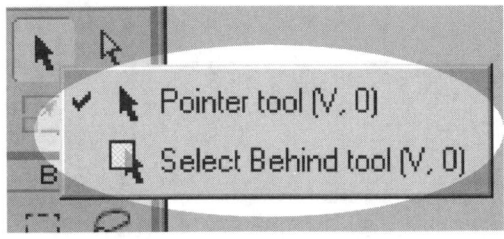

⓱ *The* **pop-up list** *displays the tools in a tool group.*

Some tools are hidden in tool groups within the Tools panel.

To choose a tool in a tool group:

1.   Press the tool icon that has a small triangle next to the tool. A pop-up list shows the tools in the group ⓱.

2.   Choose one of the tools in the group.

TIP Tools in a tool group have the same shortcut. Tap the key as many times as is necessary to choose the correct tool.

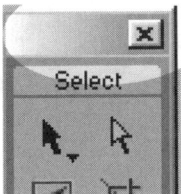

⓲ *Double-click the* **Tools panel controller bar** *to dock the Tools panel to the side of the window.*

Windows users can also dock the Tools panel to the side of the window.

To dock the Tools panel (Win):

♦   Double-click the control bar at the top of the Tools panel ⓲. This docks the Tools panel to the side of the window.

To undock the Tools panel (Win):

♦   Double-click the dots in the gripper bar at the top of the Tools panel ⓳.

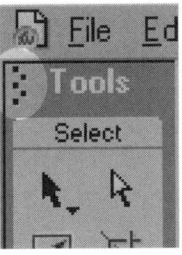

⓳ *Double-click the* **gripper dots** *in the title bar of the Tools panel.*

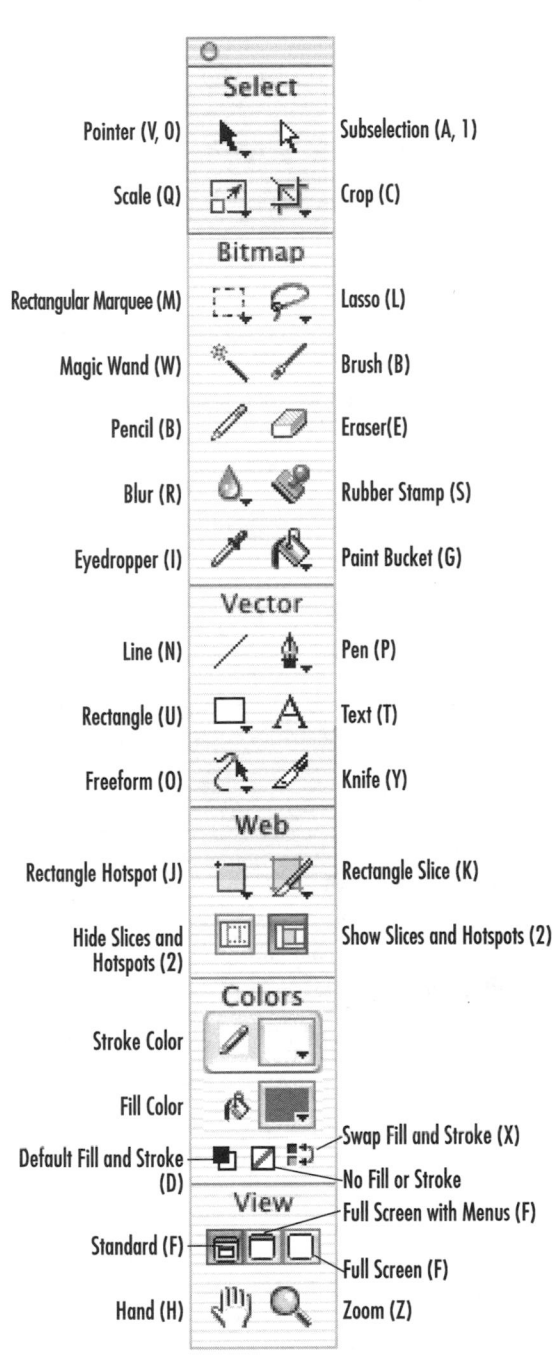

Pointer (V, 0)	Subselection (A, 1)
Scale (Q)	Crop (C)
Bitmap	
Rectangular Marquee (M)	Lasso (L)
Magic Wand (W)	Brush (B)
Pencil (B)	Eraser(E)
Blur (R)	Rubber Stamp (S)
Eyedropper (I)	Paint Bucket (G)
Vector	
Line (N)	Pen (P)
Rectangle (U)	Text (T)
Freeform (0)	Knife (Y)
Web	
Rectangle Hotspot (J)	Rectangle Slice (K)
Hide Slices and Hotspots (2)	Show Slices and Hotspots (2)
Colors	
Stroke Color	
Fill Color	
Default Fill and Stroke (D)	Swap Fill and Stroke (X)
	No Fill or Stroke
View	Full Screen with Menus (F)
Standard (F)	Full Screen (F)
Hand (H)	Zoom (Z)

⓮ *These are the* **default tools** *that are visible in the Tools panel.*

Each of the tools can be set for icon cursors or precision cursors **⑳**. Icon cursors illustrate what they do. Precision cursors, represented by a crosshair, are very useful when painting with the bitmap tools.

Choosing Icon or Precise Cursors:

◆ Press the Caps Lock key to switch between the two cursor modes.

or

Choose Precise Cursors from the Editing Preferences

Icon cursors

Precision cursors

⑳ *The difference between the* **icon cursors** *(top) and the* **precision cursors** *(bottom).*

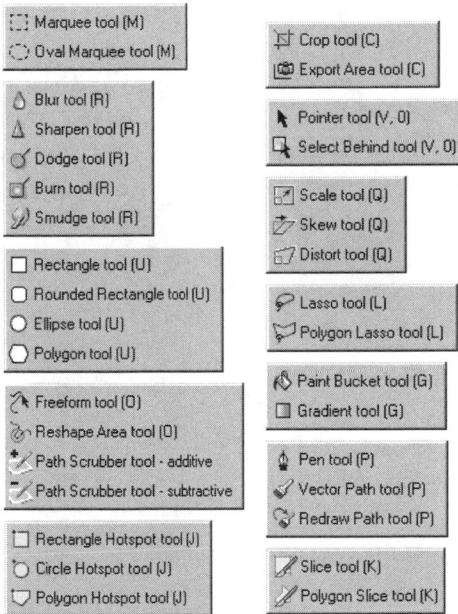

⬚ Marquee tool [M]	⬒ Crop tool [C]
⬯ Oval Marquee tool [M]	⬓ Export Area tool [C]
⬤ Blur tool [R]	▸ Pointer tool [V, 0]
△ Sharpen tool [R]	▸ Select Behind tool [V, 0]
◐ Dodge tool [R]	
⬚ Burn tool [R]	⬚ Scale tool [Q]
⬳ Smudge tool [R]	⬘ Skew tool [Q]
	⬗ Distort tool [Q]
⬚ Rectangle tool [U]	
◯ Rounded Rectangle tool [U]	⬤ Lasso tool [L]
◯ Ellipse tool [U]	⬚ Polygon Lasso tool [L]
◯ Polygon tool [U]	
	⬤ Paint Bucket tool [G]
⬚ Freeform tool [0]	⬚ Gradient tool [G]
⬚ Reshape Area tool [0]	
⬚ Path Scrubber tool - additive	⬚ Pen tool [P]
⬚ Path Scrubber tool - subtractive	⬚ Vector Path tool [P]
	⬚ Redraw Path tool [P]
⬚ Rectangle Hotspot tool [J]	
◯ Circle Hotspot tool [J]	⬚ Slice tool [K]
⬚ Polygon Hotspot tool [J]	⬚ Polygon Slice tool [K]

⓯ *These are the* **tool groups** *that contain the additional tools in the Tools panel.*

The Other Panels

In addition to the Property Inspector and Tools panel, Fireworks contains 16 other panels that control various aspects of the program.

The Layers Panel

The Layers panel allows you to control the front-to-back order in which objects appear onscreen 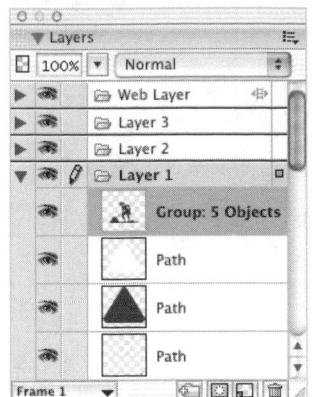. *(For more information on the Layers panel, see Chapter 6, "Working with Objects.")*

㉑ *The* **Layers panel** *displays the stacking order of the objects in the file.*

The Frames Panel

The Frames panel controls the elements used for creating rollovers and animations 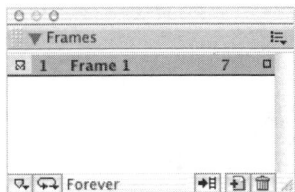. *(For more information on the Frames panel, see Chapter 16, "Animations.")*

㉒ *The* **Frames panel** *controls animations and buttons.*

The Color Mixer Panel

The Color Mixer allows you to define colors according to five different modes: RGB, Hexadecimal, HSB, CMY, or Grayscale 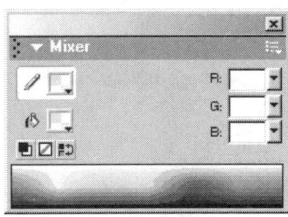. *(For more information on the color modes, see Chapter 3, "Colors.")*

㉓ *The* **Mixer panel** *lets you mix colors for fills and strokes.*

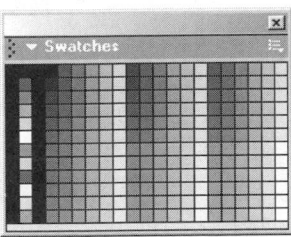

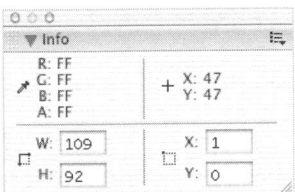

24 *The* **Swatches panel** *contains color palettes and lets you store your own colors.*

25 *The* **Info panel** *contains the coordinates, size, and color information about objects.*

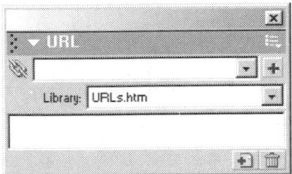

26 *The* **URL panel** *contains a record of all URL addresses used for links, buttons, etc.*

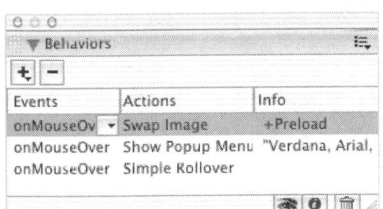

27 *The* **Behaviors panel** *lets you control JavaScript events.*

The Swatches Panel

The Swatches panel lets you work with preset palettes of color or store your own sets of colors **24**. *(For more information on the color modes, see Chapter 3, "Colors.")*

The Info Panel

The Info panel provides feedback as to the color and position of selected objects **25**. *(For more information on using the Info panel, see Chapter 6, "Working with Objects.")*

The URL Panel

The URL panel allows you to add URL links to areas on the page **26**. *(For more information on adding links to areas of your Web graphics, see Chapter 17, "Hotspots and Links" and Chapter 18, "Slices.")*

The Behaviors Panel

The Behaviors panel allows you to assign JavaScript actions to slices and image maps **27**. *(For more information on working with Behaviors, see Chapter 19, "Buttons and Behaviors.")*

The Other Panels

The Find and Replace Panel

The Find and Replace panel allows you to make changes to text and vector objects elements within a specific document or throughout many different Fireworks documents ㉘. *(For more information on working with the Find and Replace panel, see Chapter 13, "Automation Features.")*

The Styles Panel

The Styles panel allows you to save the settings for an object's appearance and then apply them quickly to other objects ㉙. *(For more information on working with styles, see Chapter 13, "Automation Features.")*

The Project Panel (Mac) or Project Log Panel (Win)

The Project panel or Project Log panel helps you keep track of the various files you are working with. You can then use the Project panel or Project Log panel to perform various actions on those files ㉚. For example, you can apply find and replace commands to all the files in the Project list. *(For more information on working with the Project panel or Project Log panel, see Chapter 13, "Automation Features.")*

TIP For convenience, I will refer to this panel as the Project Log panel for the rest of the book. This is not to slight Macintosh users in any way, just a convenience.

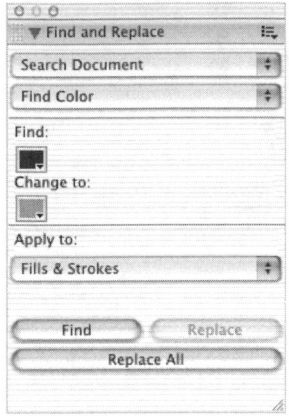

㉘ *The* **Find and Replace panel** *lets you perform global searches.*

㉙ *The* **Styles panel** *lets you store and apply graphic effects to objects and text.*

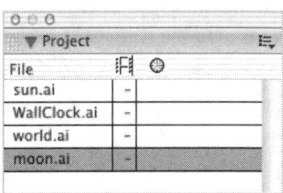

㉚ *The* **Project panel (Mac) or Project Log panel (Win)** *keeps a list of all documents you have worked on.*

31 *The Optimize panel lets you set how graphics will be converted.*

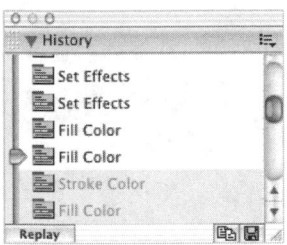

32 *The History panel keeps a record of the actions and commands performed.*

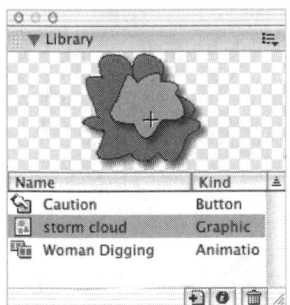

33 *The Library panel holds graphic symbols, buttons, and animations.*

The Optimize Panel

The Optimize panel allows you to control the colors and settings for exporting images **31**. *(For more information on working with the Optimize panel, see Chapter 15, "Optimizing.")*

The History Panel

The History panel records the series of actions and commands you perform within Fireworks **32**. You can then play those actions back as scripts in other documents that allow you to automate your work. *(For more information on working with the History panel, see Chapter 13, "Automation Features.")*

The Library Panel

The Library panel stores the items that you define as graphic, button, and animation symbols, so that you can easily reuse and update them throughout a single document or across many documents **33**. You can drag items from the Library panel onto your pages. *(For more information on working with the Library panel, see Chapter 16, "Animations.")*

Working with Panels

All the panels (except the Property Inspector and Tools panel) can all be grouped with other panels so they act as a unit. This is particularly helpful if you're working on a small monitor. The panel groups display the panels under a single title bar with tabs for each panel in the group.

To select a panel within a group:

◆ Click the panel tab under the title bar ❹. The tab becomes highlighted and the controls for that tab appear inside the panel.

You can move panels from one group to another.

To move panels between groups:

1. Click the panel menu control to open the panel menu.

2. Choose the name that you want to move the panel to from its Group Mixer with submenu ❺.

   or

   Choose New Panel Group to separate the panel into its own group.

Ordinarily the name of a panel group comes from the panels inside the group. You can rename the panel group to a shorter, more easily understood name.

To rename a panel group:

1. Choose Rename Panel Group from the panel menu. This clears the panel name field and leaves a blinking insertion point.

2. Type the new name for the panel group ❻.

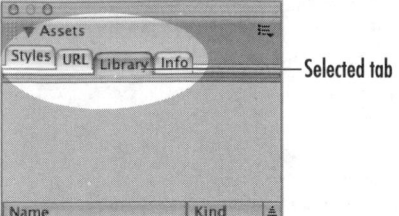

❹ *Click one of the* **panel tabs** *to select a specific panel in a group.*

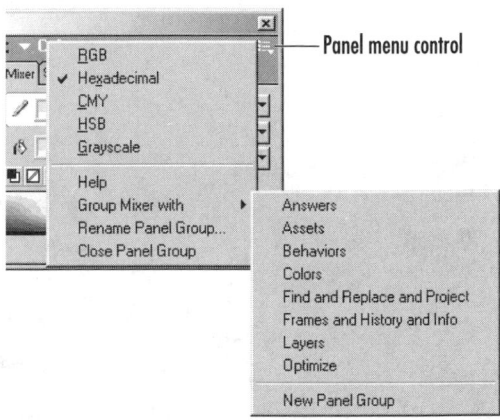

❺ *Click the* **panel menu control** *to open the panel menu.*

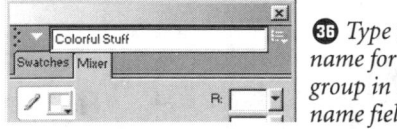

❻ *Type the new name for a panel group in the group name field.*

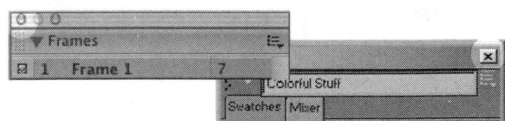

❼ *Click the* **Close icon** *to close a panel group.*

Expanded

Collapsed

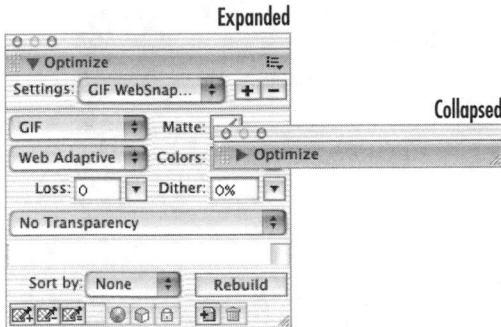

❸❽ *Double-click the panel group title bar to* **expand or collapse the panel group** *display.*

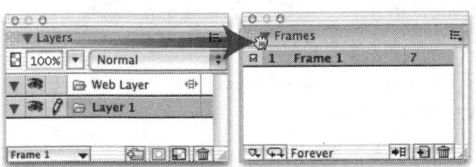

❸❾ *Drag the gripper dots to* **dock one panel with** another.

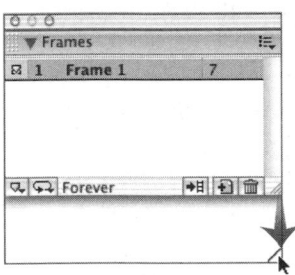

❹⓿ *Drag the corner indicator to* **resize Macintosh** panels.

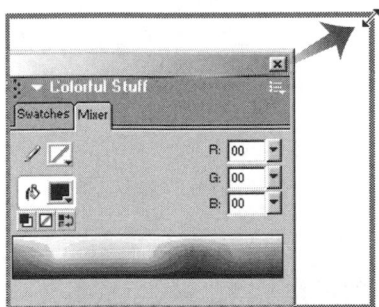

❹❶ *Drag the corners or sides of a panel to* **resize** Windows panels.

You can also open, close, or collapse and expand panel groups.

To open panels:

◆ Choose the name of the panel from the Window menu.

To close panels:

◆ Click the Close icon in the panel title bar **❸❼**.

To collapse or expand a panel group:

◆ Double-click the title bar for the panel group **❸❽**. This collapses or expands the group.

In addition to grouping panels together, you can also dock the panel groups in collections of panel groups. The docked panels can be moved together around the screen.

To dock panels together:

1. Press the gripper dots on the panel title bar.
2. Drag the panel to the top or bottom of another panel group **❸❾**.
3. Release the mouse button. The panels are docked together.

You can also change the size of a panel or panel group. This is especially helpful as you add new items in panels such as the Layers, Styles, and Frames.

To resize panels (Mac):

◆ Drag the resize icon of a panel to change the size of the panel **❹⓿**.

To resize panels (Win):

1. Move the cursor over the sides or corners of a panel. A double-headed arrow appears.
2. Drag the double-headed arrow to change the size of the panel **❹❶**.

Working with Panels

Window Elements; Windows Toolbars

Window Elements

The Window elements are contained at the bottom of a document window ❷. They allow you to display animations, see information about the file, and change the magnification of the image.

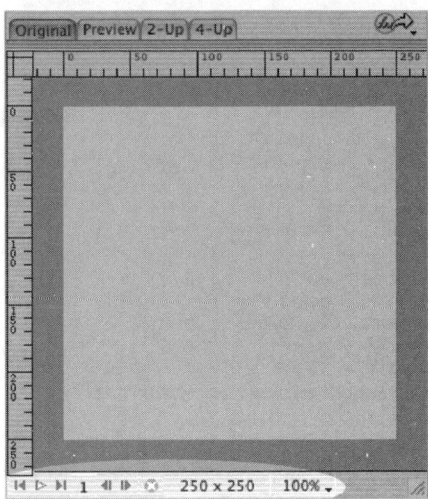

The Animation Controls

The Animation controls are at the bottom of the document window ❸. Click the controls to see how an animation will play. *(For information on playing animations, see page 281.)*

The Document Controls

The Document controls let you exit the bitmapped mode, see the document size, and change the magnification of your page ❹. *(For more information on using the Document Controls, see page 33.)*

❷ *The* **Window elements** *at the bottom of the document window.*

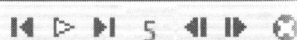

❸ *The* **Animation controls** *let you preview animations within the document.*

Using the Windows Toolbars

The Windows version of Fireworks provides two special toolbars that contain frequently used menu commands. The toolbars can be dragged to the top or bottom of the screen or positioned as a floating panel.

Exit Bitmapped mode	Document size	Magnification

❹ *The* **Document controls** *control the bitmapped mode and page view, and show the document size.*

The Main Toolbar (Win)

The Main toolbar contains commands for working with files and displaying panels ❺.

Main

❺ *Click the icons in the* **Main toolbar** *(Win) to apply the commands.*

The Modify Toolbar (Win)

The Modify toolbar contains commands for working with objects ❻. *(For more information on working with the commands in the Modify toolbar, see Chapter 6, "Working with Objects.")*

Modify

❻ *Click the icons in the* **Modify toolbar** *(Win) to apply the commands.*

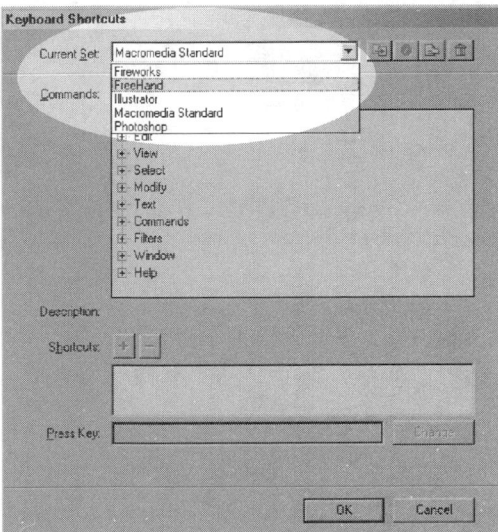

47 *Use the* **Current Set list** *in the Keyboard Shortcuts dialog box to switch to a different set of keyboard shortcuts.*

Duplicate Set

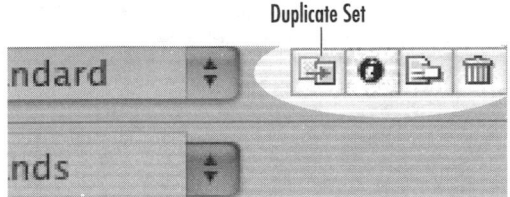

48 *Click the* **Duplicate Set icon** *to create a new shortcut set.*

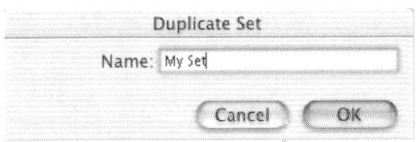

49 *The* **Duplicate Set dialog box** *lets you name a custom keyboard shortcut set.*

Customizing Keyboard Shortcuts

Keyboard shortcuts are the keys that you press to invoke commands and access tools. Fireworks lets you customize the keyboard shortcuts so that the command you use in one program is the same as the one you use in another.

Fireworks ships with different shortcut sets that let you easily switch to your favorite keyboard commands.

To change the keyboard sets:

1. Choose **Edit** > **Keyboard Shortcuts** (Mac OS 9 or Win).

   or

   Choose **Fireworks** > **Keyboard Shortcuts** (Mac OS X). The Keyboard Shortcuts dialog box appears **47**.

2. Choose a set from the Current Set list.

   TIP The Macromedia Standard set contains the shortcut list that is most similar to other Macromedia products. This set makes it easy to learn the shortcuts for all Macromedia applications.

3. Click OK to apply the set.

You can't modify the shortcut sets that ship with Fireworks. However, you can duplicate a set and then make changes to design your own shortcuts.

To duplicate a keyboard set:

1. Click the Duplicate Set button in the Keyboard Shortcuts dialog box **48**. This opens the Duplicate Set dialog box **49**.

2. Name the new shortcut set and click OK. The set appears in the Current Set list.

   TIP The duplicate set uses the shortcuts of the current set. So if you want a set that is similar to aparticular program, make that set active before you make the duplicate.

Once you have created your own custom keyboard set, you can make changes to the keyboard commands.

To change the keyboard commands:

1. Choose one of the following from the Commands list to choose what shortcuts you want to change 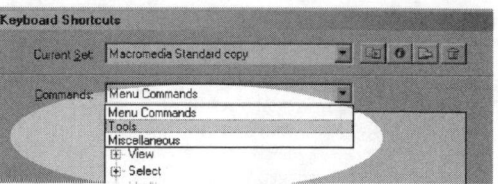:

   - **Menu Commands** displays the shortcuts found in the menu bar. These shortcuts must use one of the modifier keys.

   - **Tools** displays the shortcuts that control the tools and commands in the Tools panel. These shortcuts must consist of letters or numbers without a modifier key.

   - **Miscellaneous** displays the shortcuts for actions that do not have a list in the menu bar. For example, nudging elements up and down using the arrow keys falls under this heading. These shortcuts must use one of the modifier keys. The only exception is the up, down, left, or right arrow keys which can be used alone.

2. Choose the command you want to change in the Commands list.

3. Click the Plus Sign button to highlight the Press Key field 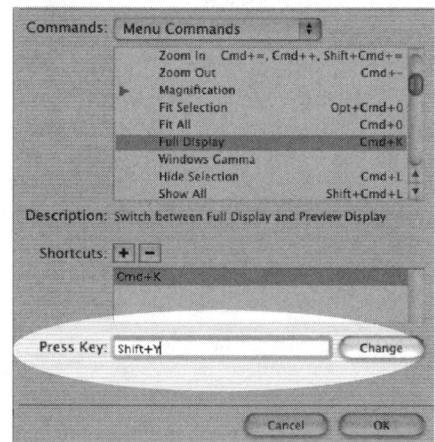.

4. On your keyboard, press the actual keys for the keystroke you want to assign. The keystroke description is entered in the Press Key field.

5. Press the Change button to assign the keystroke.

TIP If the keystroke is used for another command, an alert sign appears under the Press Key field 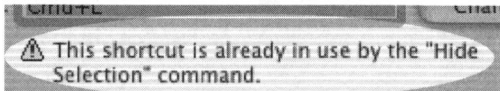. If you click the Change button, another dialog box asks you to confirm reassigning the shortcut .

TIP Cmd/Ctrl-click on the Change button to avoid the Reassign dialog box.

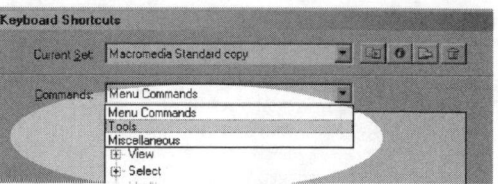

50 *The* **Commands** *list lets you choose what types of shortcuts you want to change.*

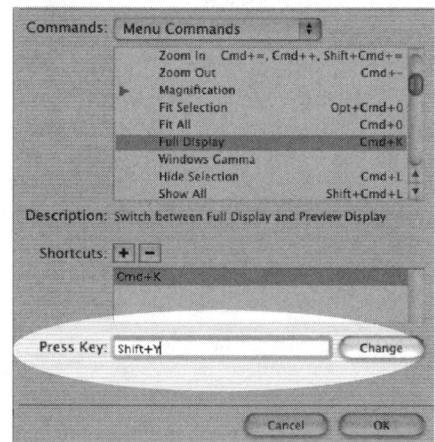

51 *Activate the* **Press Key field** *to invoke the keystroke you want to use for the shortcuts.*

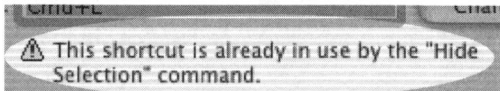

52 *The* **Alert sign** *indicates that the keystroke you have chosen is already in use by another command.*

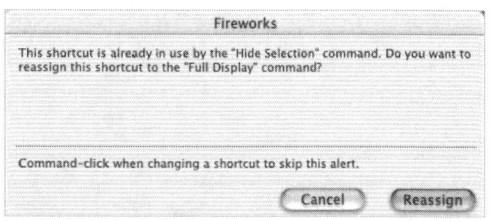

53 *The* **Reassign dialog box** *makes you confirm the choice to reassign one shortcut with another.*

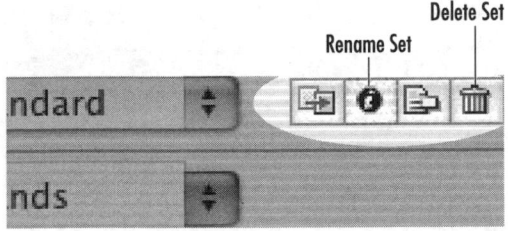

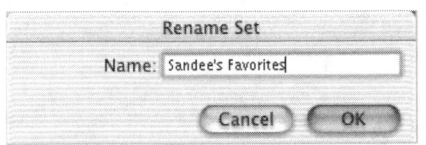

54 *The* **Current Set controls** *for modifying keyboard shortcuts.*

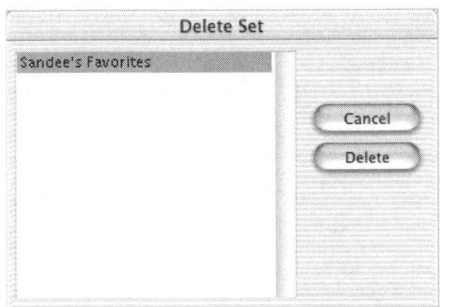

55 *The* **Rename Set dialog box** *lets you rename a custom keyboard set.*

(continued)

56 *The* **Delete Set dialog box** *lets you choose the custom keyboard sets that you want to delete.*

If you duplicate a set, the new name is listed as [original name] copy. Most likely you will want to rename the set to something that is more descriptive of its function.

To change the name of a keyboard set:

1. Select the keyboard set you want to rename from the Current Set list.

2. Click the Rename Set button from the Current Set controls **54**. The Rename Set dialog box appears **55**.

3. Enter the new name for the set and click OK.

As you create new keyboard sets, you may want to delete the old sets that you no longer use.

To delete a keyboard set:

1. Select the keyboard set you want to delete from the Current Set list.

2. Click the Delete Set button from the Current Set controls. The Delete Set dialog box appears **56**.

3. Choose the set you want to delete and press the Delete button. The Delete Set dialog box automatically closes and the set is deleted.

TIP There is no way to cancel the command once you press the Delete key.

Customizing Keyboard Shortcuts

You can also export the list of keyboard shortcuts as an HTML text file that can be opened and printed.

To export a keyboard set as an HTML text file:

1. Select the keyboard set you want to export from the Current Set list.

2. Click the Export Set button from the Current Set controls **57**.

3. Use the operating system dialog box to name the file and save it to a specific location.

TIP The Export Set command was used to create the list of keyboard shortcuts at the end of this book.

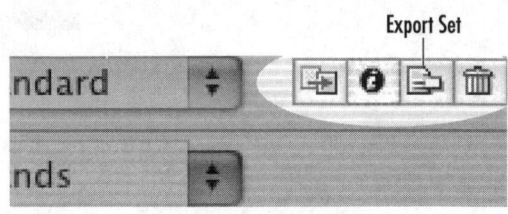

57 *Click the* **Export Set icon** *to export the current set as an HTML text file.*

DOCUMENT SETUP 2

Think back to when you were in the fourth or fifth grade. Remember how you went shopping with your mom for all your school supplies? It was really important that you got exactly the right kind of notebook, ruler, pens, and pencils. The night before the first day of school you would carefully lay out all your new school clothes for the next day. Remember how you'd spend extra time to put the paper in your notebook, neatly label the dividers, sharpen your pencils, and cover your text books?

Even in grade school you knew the importance of document setup. You knew that setting things up properly right at the beginning of the term would help you later on in the school year.

That's how it is when you start a new Macromedia Fireworks document. The time you take to organize your document setup helps you work and will help you later on.

Opening Documents

When you start a new document, you must make certain decisions about it that affect the final output. Fortunately, none of these decisions are final, and you can change your mind at any time as you work on your document.

To create a new document:

1. Choose File > New. This opens the New Document dialog box ❶.

2. Use the Height and Width fields to set the size of the document.

TIP Use the pop-up lists to change the unit of measurement from pixels to inches or centimeters.

3. Use the Resolution field to set the number of pixels per inch or pixels per centimeter for the graphics of the document.

TIP Most Web graphics are saved at 72 pixels per inch. Print graphics usually require higher resolutions.

4. Set the Canvas Color of the document by choosing White, Transparent, or Custom.

TIP The Canvas Color sets the color of the background of your document.

5. If you choose custom, click the Color Well to open the Swatches, where you can set your color. *(For more information about color swatches, see Chapter 3, "Colors.")*

6. Click OK to create the new document, which appears in an untitled document window ❷.

TIP The Original, Preview, 2-Up, and 4-Up tabs at the top of the document window are used as part of the process in optimizing files *(see Chapter 15, "Optimizing").*

Color Well

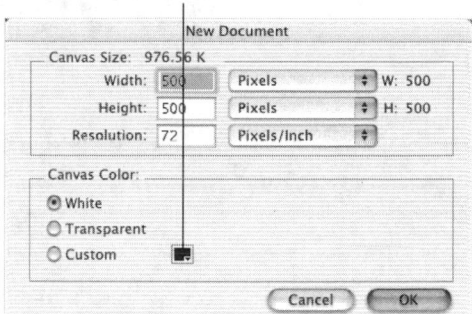

❶ *The* **New Document dialog box***.*

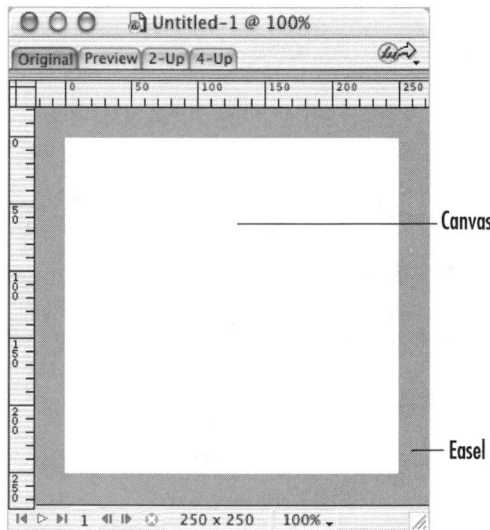

❷ *The* **document window** *is where you work on your Fireworks file.*

❸ *The* **Page Preview** *displays the size (in pixels) of the document.*

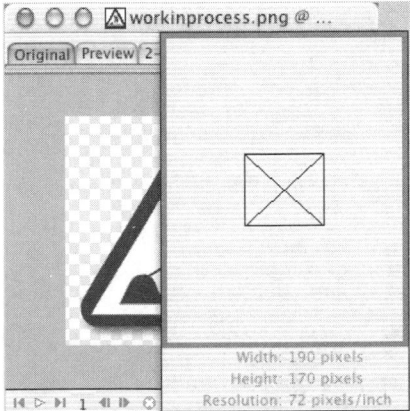

❹ *Press the* **Page Preview** *to see more information about the file and how large it would print on the paper currently selected for the printer.*

Understanding Resolution

Resolution is the number of pixels per inch. The higher the resolution, the smaller the size of the pixels.

Resampling is the technique that increases or decreases the resolution of a document. You resample up when you increase the size of an image. You resample down when you decrease the size of an image.

If you have scanned images in your Fireworks document, you should not increase the size of the document more than 50%.

However, if you only have native Fireworks objects, you can resample Fireworks documents up or down at any time.

To open a previously saved document:

1. Choose **File > Open**.

2. Navigate through your directories and folders to find the file you want to open.

3. Click OK.

When you open an existing document, Fireworks lets you protect the original file by opening the file as an untitled document. This keeps you from inadvertently writing over a document that you want to keep.

To open a document as untitled:

1. Choose **File > Open** and navigate to find an existing Fireworks file.

2. Click the Open as "Untitled" check box and then click Open. The document opens in an unsaved, untitled version.

3. Make any changes and save the document as you would any other file.

TIP (Mac) The native file format for a Fireworks file is an enhanced PNG file. If you are going to send your file to Windows users, add the PNG file extension to the file name.

To see the document information:

◆ Press the Page Preview area **❸** to see a representation of the size of the document as well as a read out of the document's size and resolution **❹**.

Opening Documents

Resizing the Image and Canvas

Having created a document, you can still make changes to it. For instance, you can change the size of the image.

To change the image size:

1. Choose **Modify** > **Canvas** > **Image Size** to open the Image Size dialog box **⑤**.

   or

   With any of the Select or View tools chosen, and no object selected, click the Image Size button in the Property Inspector **⑥**. This opens the Image Size dialog box.

2. Use the Pixel Dimensions height and width fields to change the absolute number of pixels in the document.

   TIP The Pixel Dimensions fields are not available if Resample Image is off.

3. Use the Print Size height and width fields to change the display size of the image.

   TIP Press the pop-up menu for pixels or inches to change the size of the document by a percentage.

   TIP Select Constrain Proportions to keep the image from being distorted.

4. Use the Resolution field to change the image size by increasing or reducing the number of pixels per inch.

   TIP Scanned images may become blurred if the resolution or size of the image is increased by more than 50% **⑦**.

5. Use the resampling pop-up menu to choose how the scanned imaged will be changed **⑧**. The four choices are Bicubic, Bilinear, Soft, and Nearest Neighbor.

   TIP Use Bicubic for scanned images such as photographs. Use Nearest Neighbor for images with straight lines and text such as screen shots. Use Bilinear or Soft only if you do not get acceptable results with the other two methods.

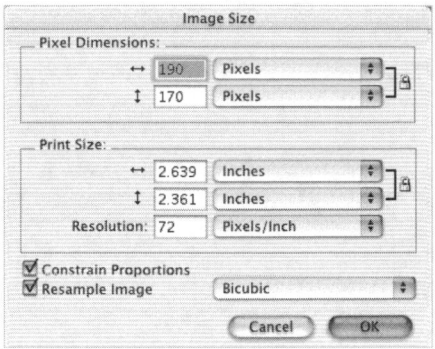

⑤ *The* **Image Size** *dialog box lets you change the size and resolution of an image.*

⑥ *Click the* **Image Size button** *in the Property Inspector to open the Image Size dialog box.*

Original   Resampled image

⑦ *The effects of* **resampling an image** *to increase its size while maintaining the resolution. Notice the blurry edges in the resampled image.*

⑧ *The* **resampling choices** *control how scanned images are changed.*

Resizing the Image and Canvas

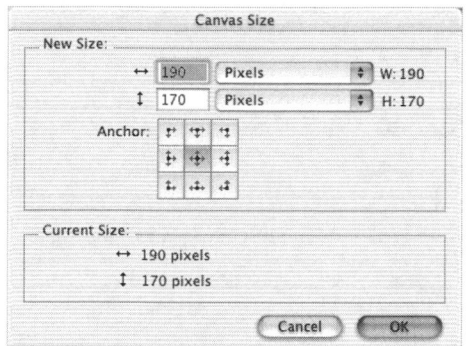

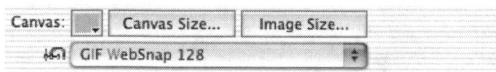

❾ *The* **Canvas Size dialog box** *lets you add space to, or delete space from, the canvas outside the image area.*

❿ *Click the* **Canvas Size button** *in the Property Inspector to open the Canvas Size dialog box.*

Original   Canvas size increased

⓫ *An example of adding a gray canvas to the right and bottom of an image.*

You can keep the image size constant while adding space to, or deleting space from, the canvas outside the image area. This changes the background relative to the image.

To change the canvas size numerically:

1. Choose **Modify** > **Canvas** > **Canvas Size** to open the Canvas Size dialog box **❾**.

   or

   With any of the Select or View tools chosen, and no object selected, click the Canvas Size button in the Property Inspector **❿**. This opens the Canvas Size dialog box.

2. Enter new amounts in the New Size height and width fields.

TIP Use the settings in the Current Size as a reference.

3. Choose one of the squares in the Anchor area to determine where the area is added to the canvas. For instance, if you click in the upper-left corner, the added area will be added to the right and bottom of the canvas **⓫**.

4. Click OK.

Resizing the Image and Canvas

You can also crop the canvas size visually by adjusting a bounding box around the image.

To change the canvas size visually:

1. Choose the Crop tool from the Tools panel 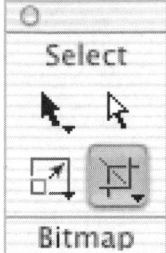.

2. Drag with the Crop tool to create the handles that define the area you want to keep inside the document **⑬**.

3. Move the handles to change the size of the cropped area.

4. Double-click inside the crop area to apply the crop.

   or

   Double-click outside the crop area or choose a new tool to continue without applying the crop.

   TIP To enlarge the canvas, extend the Crop handles beyond the area of the current canvas.

⑫ *The* **Crop tool** *in the Tools panel.*

You can use the Crop tool to work both visually and numerically.

To use the Crop tool with numerical values:

1. Drag with the Crop tool on the canvas.

2. Refer to the coordinates in the Property Inspector as follows **⑭**:

   • W controls the width of the crop area.

   • H controls the height of the crop area.

   • X controls the horizontal position of the upper-left corner of the crop area.

   • Y controls the vertical position of the upper-left corner of the crop area.

   or

   Enter numerical values in the coordinate fields in the Property Inspector.

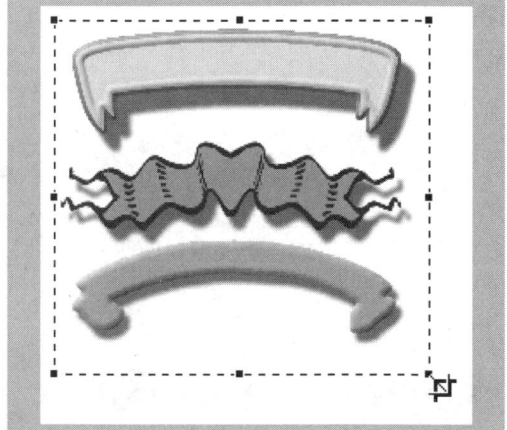

⑬ *The* **Crop tool handles** *define the final canvas size after cropping.*

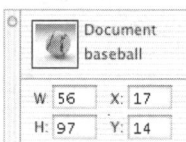

⑭ *The* **coordinates in the Property Inspector** *tell you the size and position of the crop area.*

Resizing the Image and Canvas

Original	After Trim Canvas command

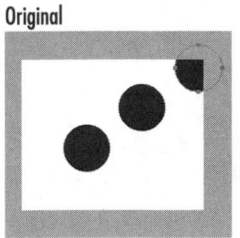 

⑮ *The* **Trim Canvas command** *crops the canvas but leaves objects on the easel untouched.*

Original	After Fit Canvas command

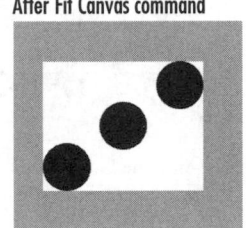

⑯ *The* **Fit Canvas command** *crops the canvas but expands it to display the object on the easel.*

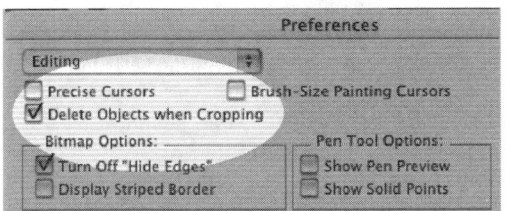

⑰ *Choose* **Delete Objects when Cropping** *from Editing Preferences to determine what happens to objects when the canvas is cropped.*

You may want to crop a document so that there is no extra canvas space around any of the objects. This helps you create the smallest possible file size.

To crop a document to the active area:

◆ Choose **Modify** > **Canvas** > **Trim Canvas**. This changes the canvas size to exactly fit the objects that are visible **⑮**.

In addition to the Trim Canvas command, Fireworks lets you crop a document so there is no excess canvas, but also adds to the canvas size if any objects are in the easel area. This is very helpful for sloppy people who may not have positioned items within the active area.

To crop so that all items fit on the canvas:

◆ Choose **Modify** > **Canvas** > **Fit Canvas**. This changes the canvas size to exactly fit all the the objects on the canvas **⑯**.

Sometimes when you reduce the size of your document, objects that were visible on the canvas end up positioned outside the canvas in the easel area. You have a choice as to whether or not Fireworks keeps those objects or deletes them.

To control objects off the canvas:

1. Choose **Edit** > **Preferences** to open the Preferences dialog box **⑰**.

   or

   (Mac OS X) Choose **Fireworks** > **Preferences** to open the Preferences dialog box.

2. Choose Editing from the menu.

3. Select Delete Objects when Cropping.

You may find it necessary to rotate the canvas along with the images.

To rotate the canvas:

◆ Choose **Modify** > **Canvas** and then choose **Rotate 180°**, **Rotate 90° CW** (clockwise), or **Rotate 90° CCW** (counter-clockwise).

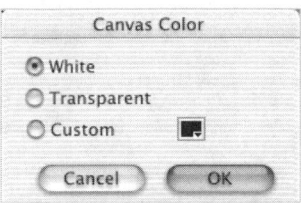

⓲ *The* **Canvas Color** *dialog box.*

The canvas color is the color automatically applied behind all the images in a document. You can change the canvas color at any time while you work on a document.

To change the canvas color:

1. Choose **Modify** > **Canvas** > **Canvas Color** to open the Canvas Color dialog box **⓲**.

   or

   Click the Canvas Color Well in the Property Inspector and then choose a specific color **⓳**.

2. Choose White, Transparent, or Custom.

   TIP The transparent background is designated by a gray-and-white checkerboard **⓴**.

3. If you choose Custom, click the Color Well to open the Swatches panel to choose a specific color. *(For more information on choosing colors from a Color Well, see page 108.)*

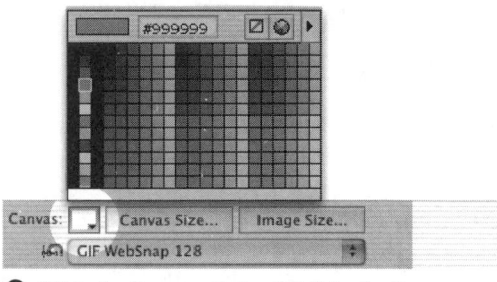

⓳ *Click the* **Canvas Color Well** *in the Property Inspector to change the canvas color.*

⓴ *The gray-and-white* **checkerboard grid** *indicates a transparent background.*

Menu Commands or the Property Inspector?

Why would anyone go all the way up to the Modify menu, then choose Canvas, and then choose Canvas Size, Canvas Color, or Image Size to modify a document when there is a Property Inspector with all those commands just a mouse click away?

Why didn't Macromedia remove those commands from the menu when they added them to the Property Inspector? Well, some people might not have the Property Inspector open. They may also have an object selected, in which case the Property Inspector shows the attributes of the object, not the document. In those cases, the menu commands are helpful.

You can assign custom keyboard shortcuts to those commands. So instead of a mouse click, you can just use the keyboard. For people like me, who are good typists, using a keystroke is always faster than either clicking with the mouse or choosing a menu command.

Horizontal ruler

Vertical ruler

21 *The* **rulers** *in the document window.*

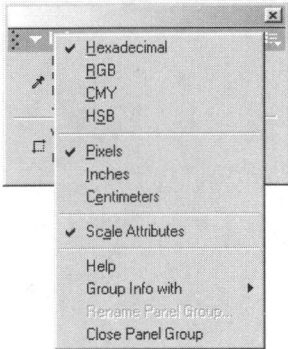

22 *Use the Info panel menu to* **change the unit of measurement**.

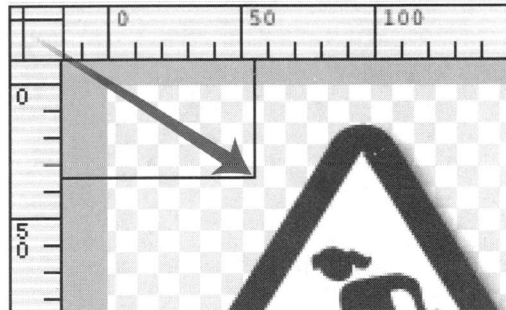

23 *Drag the* **zero point cross hairs** *onto the page to set the new zero point.*

Working with Rulers

In order to work precisely in your document, you need to work with the rulers.

To display the document rulers:

◆ Choose **View** > **Rulers**. The rulers appear at the top and left sides of the document **21**.

TIP Two lines appear on the rulers—one on the vertical ruler and one on the horizontal ruler—to track your position as you move around the document.

Fireworks ships with pixels as the default unit of measurement for the Info panel and dialog boxes. You can change that unit at any time.

To change the unit of measurement:

1. Make sure the Info panel is open. If not, choose **Window** > **Info** **22**.

2. Use the Info panel menu to choose a new unit of measurement. The choices are Pixels, Inches, and Centimeters.

TIP Even if you change the unit of measurement, the rulers are still displayed in pixels.

Fireworks uses the upper-left corner of a document as its *zero point*, or the point where the rulers start. You can change the zero point for a document. This can help you position items on the page.

To change the zero point:

1. Drag the zero point cross hairs onto the page **23**.

2. Double-click the zero point cross hairs in the corner of the document window to reset the zero point to the upper left corner.

Using Ruler Guides

The rulers also let you place additional guides that you can use to align objects.

To display the guides:

◆ Choose **View** > **Guides** > **Show Guides**. If a checkmark is next to the Show Guides command, then the guides are visible.

To create guides:

◆ Drag from the left ruler to create a vertical guide ㉔. Release the mouse button to place the guide.

or

Drag from the top ruler to create a horizontal guide. Release the mouse button to place the guide.

TIP When you drag to create a guide you automatically turn on the Show Guides command.

TIP Release the mouse button over the canvas area to create a guide. If you release over the easel area, you will not create the guide.

You may want to position guides at a precise position. Rather than try to judge by eye, you can use a numerical amount.

To position guides numerically:

◆ Drag an existing guide to move it to a new position.

or

Double-click the guide to open the Move Guide dialog box and enter the exact position of the guide ㉕.

TIP The Move Guide dialog box shows the position of the guide in pixels.

TIP Use **View** > **Guides** > **Snap To Guides** to have objects automatically snap, or align, to the guides.

㉔ **Drag a guide** *from the ruler onto the active area.*

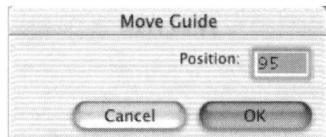

㉕ *The* **Move Guide dialog box** *lets you enter the precise pixel position of a guide.*

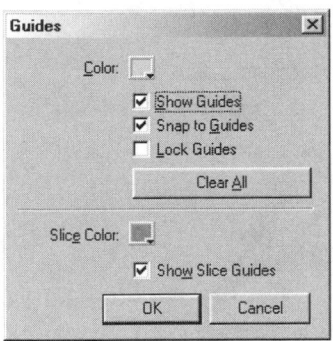

㉖ *The* **Guides (Win) dialog box**.

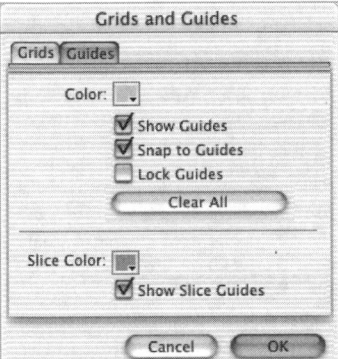

㉗ *The* **Grids and Guides (Mac) dialog box** *in the Guides mode.*

There are several ways you can edit or control the look of guides.

To edit guides:

1. Choose **View** > **Guides** > **Edit Guides** to open the Guides dialog box **㉖** and **㉗**.

2. Click the Guides Color Well to open the swatches and choose a new color. This can help make the guides look more or less obvious when positioned over the artwork in the document.

3. Click Show Guides to show or hide the guides.

4. Click Snap to Guides to turn this feature on or off.

5. Click Lock Guides to keep the guides from being moved.

TIP You can also lock the guides by choosing **View** > **Guides** > **Lock Guides**.

6. Click Clear All to delete all the guides from the document.

7. Click OK to apply the changes.

TIP (Mac) Click the Grids tab to switch from editing the guides to editing the grids (*see the steps on the next page*).

Working with Snap to Guides

The Snap to Guides feature means that as you move objects or anchor points, they will automatically jump or snap to a guide as you get near it.

Most people leave the feature turned on when they want to keep things aligned to guides.

However, you may want to turn off the features, especially if you are trying to move an object slightly away from a guide.

Using Ruler Guides

Using the Document Grid

Ruler guides are terrific because you can manually insert them at variable positions. If you need guides at repeated intervals, you should use Fireworks's document grid. The grid can also be used to align objects.

To view the document grid:

◆ Choose **View** > **Grid** > **Show Grid** to display the document grid **28**. You can use the grid to arrange your images into certain areas, or to make sure objects are aligned, or are the same size.

TIP You can use **View** > **Grid** > **Snap to Grid** to have objects automatically snap, or align, to the grid.

TIP When Snap to Grid is turned on, objects snap to the grid even if the grid is not visible.

You can also change the size of the grid. This makes it easy to create many different buttons or other objects that are all the same size or shape.

To edit the document grid:

1. Choose **View** > **Grid** > **Edit Grid** to open the Grids and Guides dialog box **29** and **30**.

2. Click the Color Well to open the swatches and choose a new color for the grid.

3. Use the Horizontal slider or type values in the field to increase or decrease the horizontal spacing.

4. Use the Vertical slider or type values in the field to increase or decrease the vertical spacing.

5. Click Snap to Grid to turn this feature on or off.

6. Click Show Grid to show or hide the document grid.

28 *The* **document grid** *shown over the art.*

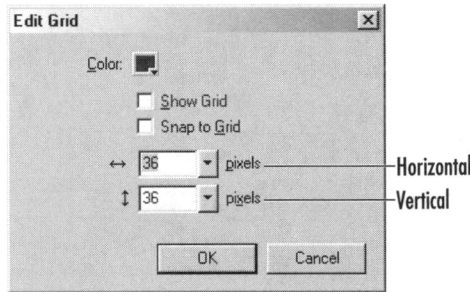

29 *The* **Edit Grid (Win) dialog box**.

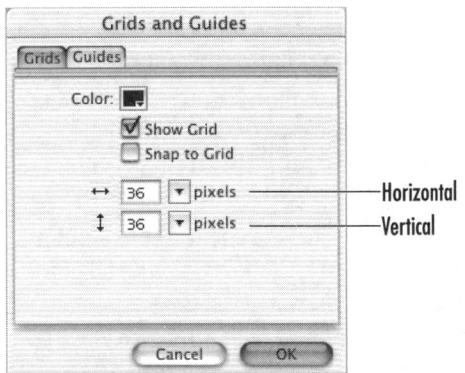

30 *The* **Grids and Guides (Mac) dialog box** *in the Grids mode.*

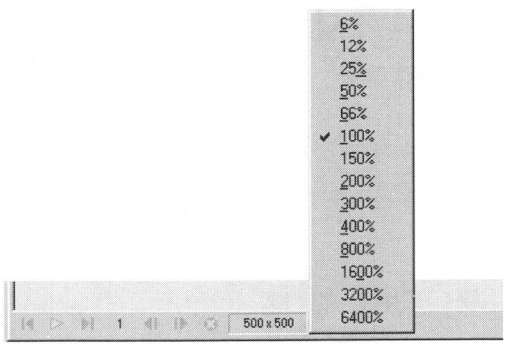

 The **Magnification control menu** *at the bottom of the document window.*

Don't Sweat the Details . . . Yet!

Unlike print graphics, you don't have to worry too much about tiny details of your graphics as you lay out your Web graphics and pages.

That's because the process of optimizing your graphics, which is covered in Chapter 16, "Optimizing," can drastically change the look of colors and details.

Just relax and set up your graphics the way you want. There's plenty of time later to sweat out the details.

Magnification

You may need to zoom in or out to see specific areas of the big picture.

To use the magnification commands:

◆ To zoom to a specific magnification, use the Magnification control ㉛. Fireworks lets you view your artwork from 6% to 6400%.

or

Choose **View** > **Magnification** and then choose a specific magnification.

or

Choose **View** > **Zoom In** or **View** > **Zoom Out** to jump to a specific magnification.

or

Choose **View** > **Fit Selection** to display the object selected.

or

Choose **View** > **Fit All** to display the entire document.

TIP If you want to zoom into a magnification amount that is not listed in the Magnification control, you need to drag with the Zoom tool *(see the next exercise).*

You can use the Zoom tool to jump to a specific magnification and position.

To use the Zoom tool:

1. Click the Zoom tool in the Tools panel ⓷.

2. Click the Zoom tool on the area you want to zoom in on. Click as many times as you need to get as close as necessary to the area you want to see.

   or

   Drag the Zoom tool diagonally across the area you want to see. Release the mouse button to zoom in ⓷ and ⓷.

TIP Each click of the Zoom tool changes your view using the amounts listed in the Magnification control menu.

TIP When you drag with the Zoom tool, you change the view to amounts not listed in the Magnification control menu.

TIP Press the Option/Alt key while in the Zoom tool to zoom out from objects. The icon changes from a plus sign (+) to a minus sign (–).

Honestly, I haven't touched the Zoom tool in the Tools panel in years. Does that mean I don't zoom in and out? No, it means I zoom in and out by using the following keyboard shortcut. I've used this shortcut so often that I can do it in my sleep. In fact, the shortcut is so important, it's got its own exercise.

To access the Zoom tool using the keyboard:

1. Press Command/Ctrl and the Spacebar. The currently selected tool is replaced by the Zoom tool.

TIP Add the Opt/Alt key to Zoom out.

2. Continue to hold the modifier keys as you drag or click with the Zoom as described in the previous exercise.

3. Release the modifier keys to return to the currently selected tool.

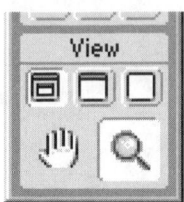

⓷ *The* **Zoom tool** *in the Tools panel.*

⓷ *Use the* **Zoom tool** *to zoom in on a specific area by dragging a marquee around that area.*

⓷ *After dragging, the* **selected area** *fills the window.*

Magnification

㉟ *The* **Full Display** *mode shows all the fills, brushes, and effects for the objects.*

㊱ *The* **Draft Display** *mode shows only the paths for the objects.*

Using the Display Options

Fireworks lets you work in two different display modes. The Full Display mode **㉟** shows all the objects in the document with their fills, brushes, and effects. It gives you the best idea of what your final image will look like.

The Draft Display mode **㊱** shows only the paths for objects. Switch to the Draft Display to improve the speed of your monitor's screen redraw. The Draft Display can also help you select objects located behind others.

To change the display options:

◆ Choose **View** > **Full Display** to switch between the two display modes.

TIP A checkmark next to the Full Display listing indicates that you are viewing the document in the Full Display mode. No checkmark indicates that you are in the Draft Display mode.

Using the Display Options

Using the Hand Tool

If you have used a computer for any type of graphics or publishing program, you should be familiar with the scroll bars of a window that let you reposition the document so you can see horizontal and vertical areas that are outside the view of the window. You should also be familiar with the Hand tool that lets you move around the window without using the scroll bars.

❸ *The* **Hand tool** *in the Tools panel.*

To use the Hand tool:

1. Choose the Hand tool in the Tools panel **❸**.

2. Position the Hand tool inside the document window and drag in any direction **❸**. This reveals the areas of the image that were previously hidden.

TIP Press the spacebar to access the Hand tool without leaving the tool that is currently selected.

TIP Once again I admit that I haven't chosen the Hand tool from the Tools panel in years. I press the spacebar to access the Hand tool without leaving the tool that is currently selected.

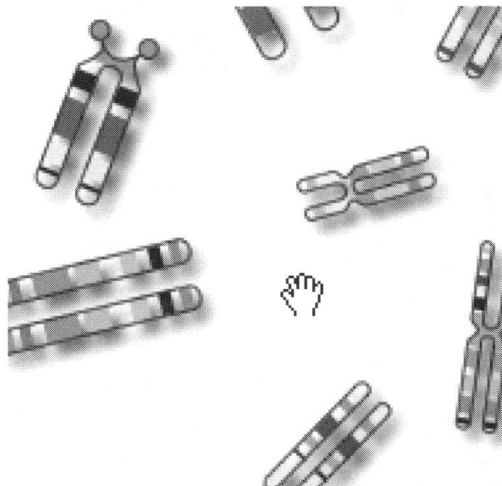

❸ *The* **Hand tool** *allows you to move an image within the document window.*

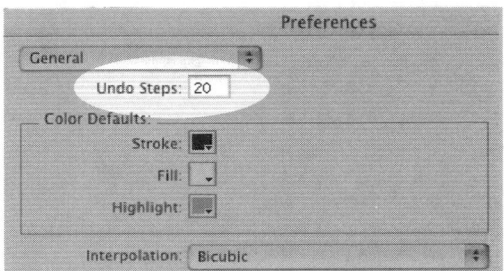

③ *The* **Undo Steps field** *allows you to set how many actions can be reversed.*

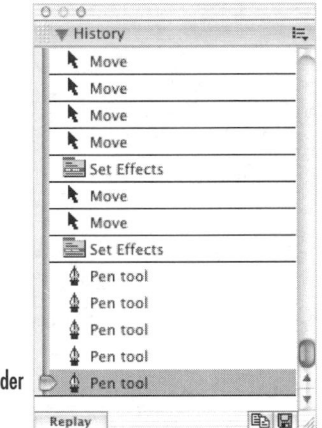

Slider

④ *The* **History panel** *shows a list of the undo steps.*

Controlling Actions

Like most applications, Fireworks lets you undo or reverse actions and commands. The number of steps is defined by the user.

To undo actions:

1. Choose **Edit** >**Undo**. This reverses the most recent action or command.

2. Choose **Edit** >**Undo** again to reverse the next most recent action.

TIP You'll work faster if you use the keyboard shortcut Cmd/Ctrl-Z.

You can undo the undo (which is a redo).

To redo actions:

◆ Choose **Edit** >**Redo** to reverse the previously chosen Undo command.

To set the number of undo steps:

1. Choose **Edit** >**Preferences ③**.

 or

 (Mac OS X) Choose **Fireworks** > **Preferences**.

2. Enter the number of steps in the Undo Steps box, which is in the General Preferences options.

TIP You must relaunch Fireworks for the change in the number of undo steps to take effect.

To jump to a previous action:

1. Choose **Window** >**History** to open the History panel **④**. The panel shows the commands that can be reversed.

2. Drag the slider up to the point where you want to reverse the actions. You can then continue to work from that point on.

TIP The History panel can also be used to make scripts that automate commands. *(For more information on working with the History panel to create scripts, see Chapter 13, "Automation Features.")*

Saving Your Work

Computers are nasty beasts. Just as you've worked several hours on an important project, they can suddenly quit or freeze on you. Any work that you haven't saved will be lost—totally lost. That's why it's an excellent idea to save your work often.

The first time you save a new file, there are several steps you have to perform.

To name and save a file:

1. Choose **File** > **Save** or **File** > **Save As**. This opens the Save or Save As dialog box **❹**. There is no difference between the two commands when working on an untitled file.

2. Use the navigation controls to choose a destination disk and folder for the file.

3. Use the Name or File name field to name the file.

TIP Mac users should add the .png extension to the name of the file, especially if they will be sending files to their Windows friends.

4. (Mac) Click Add File name Extension to automatically add the .png extension to the name of the file.

TIP The Windows operating system automatically adds the extension to the file name.

5. Click Save to save the file and return to the Fireworks application.

Once you have named a file, it is very simple to save additional changes.

To save changes:

◆ Choose **File** > **Save**. The previous version of the file will be replaced by the current version.

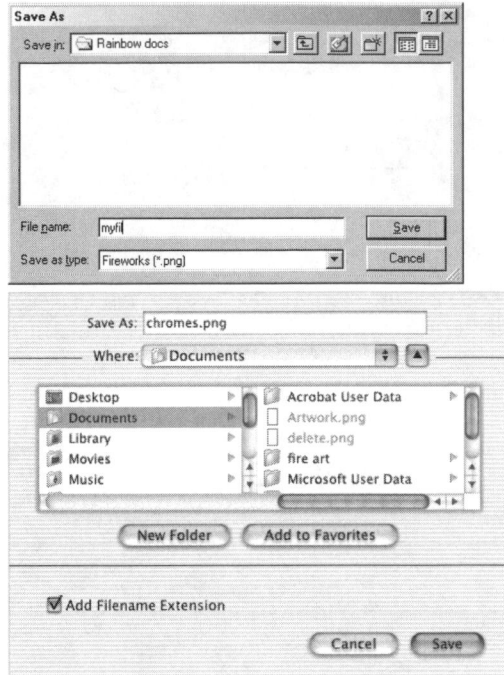

❹ *The* **Save dialog boxes** *for Windows (top) or Macintosh (bottom).*

A Special PNG

The Fireworks native file format has the extension .png. Although it has the same file extension, this is not the same as the PNG file type that can be created for the Web.

A Fireworks PNG is considered an enhanced PNG. This means that added information appears within the code for the file that is not found in a regular PNG.

You shouldn't publish a Fireworks PNG to a Web site. It will be far too big. You should export it as an optimized PNG. *(For more information on optimizing PNG files, see Chapter 15, "Optimizing.")*

COLORS 3

When I first started in advertising, the junior teams were given the low-budget, black-and-white newspaper and magazine ads. (Sometimes, if we were really lucky, we got to design, write, and produce a two-color brochure.) However, most of the time we didn't get to work on the big-budget, four-color jobs until we had moved up to be the senior creative team.

Today, designers working on Web graphics are luckier. Even the smallest, low-budget clients can afford to use color in their Web pages — just like the big-budget companies. I think that's why so many designers enjoy creating Web graphics. There's no difference between big-budget and small-budget graphics.

Of course, there are some limitations as to the number and types of colors you can use in Web pages. But, unless it's your design decision, you don't have to limit your graphics to black and white.

Setting the Color Modes

Fireworks supplies five different color modes to help you select, apply, match, or reuse colors. You choose from these modes using the Color Mixer panel.

To use the Color Mixer:

1. If you do not see the Color Mixer, choose **Window > Color Mixer**.

   or

   Click the title bar of the Color Mixer panel to bring it in front of other onscreen elements.

2. Use the Color Mixer Options menu to choose one of the five different color modes ❶.

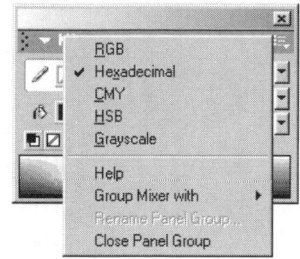

❶ *The* **five color mode choices** *of the Color Mixer Options menu.*

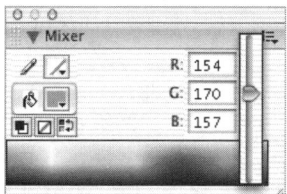

❷ *Drag the slider to* **set the value for each RGB color component** *or enter a number in the fields. RGB values range from 0 to 255.*

One of the most common ways of defining colors for Web graphics is to use the RGB (red, green, blue) color system, also called additive color. (See the color pages for a diagram that shows how additive colors can be mixed.)

To define RGB colors:

1. Make sure the Color Mixer mode is set to RGB. If not, use the Options menu to change it.

2. To choose the R (red) component, drag the slider or enter a value in the R field. Do the same for the G (green) component and the B (blue) component ❷.

   or

   Click anywhere along the RGB color ramp at the bottom of the Color Mixer to choose colors by eye, rather than by numeric values.

TIP You may want to define your colors using hexidecimal values so you can match the colors in your Fireworks file with the colors on your HTML page layout.

Understanding RGB Colors

RGB colors are called additive colors. They are formed from light such as the light from the sun, a movie projector, or a scanner, as opposed to pigments as in printer's inks. In the RGB additive color system, all three colors (red, green, and blue) combine to create white.

When all three colors are taken away, you get black. (Think about what happens when you turn off the lights in a room.)

Each of the RGB components is given a number between 0 and 255. So, for example, the color yellow could have the RGB values of R: 250, G: 243, and B: 117.

Another way of defining colors is to use the hexadecimal color system. This is the same system used in HTML code.

Setting the Color Modes

3 Hexadecimal colors *use combinations of letters and numbers to define colors.*

Understanding Hexadecimal Color

Text, links, and background colors of Web graphics are defined in HTML documents using a color system called hexadecimal.

Hexadecimal colors are defined using the numbers from 0 to 9 and the letters A through F. So, the yellow mentioned in the sidebar on the previous page would be defined in hexidecimal code as R: FA, G:F3, B: 75. It is not, however, a Web-safe color.

Web-safe colors *(covered on pages 44 and 47)* are limited to those colors whose hexidecimal values include matched pairs of numbers or letters (00, 11, 22, 33, 44, 55, 66, 77, 88, 99, AA, BB, CC, DD, EE, FF). For example, the values R: FF, G: 00, B: 99 indicate a Web-safe color. The values R: 34, G: AA, B: F3 do not.

There is no difference in download speeds if you define colors using hexadecimal values. However, you may find it easier to match the colors in HTML documents if you use hexadecimal values.

To define hexadecimal colors:

1. Make sure the Color Mixer mode is set to Hexadecimal.

2. To choose the R (red) component, drag the slider or enter a value in the R (red) field. Do the same for the G (green) component and the B (blue) components **3**.

   or

   Click in the color ramp at the bottom of the Color Mixer to choose colors by eye rather than by numeric values. The hexidecimal values appear in the R, G, B fields.

TIP The color ramp in the hexadecimal mode limits you to working with the 216 Web-safe colors *(see page 47)*.

TIP The hexadecimal system uses one or two combinations of the following numbers or letters: 0, 1, 2, 3, 4, 5, 6, 7, 8, 9, A, B, C, D, E, F. Other characters are ignored.

TIP You can also use the hexadecimal codes from your Fireworks graphics as part of the HTML code for your Web pages.

Setting the Color Modes

Fireworks also lets you define colors using CMY mode. CMY is not a typo; it is a variation of the subtractive CMYK colors used in process-color printing. *(See the color pages for a diagram that shows how subtractive colors can be mixed.)* The special CMY mode in Fireworks mixes cyan, magenta, and yellow to create colors.

To define CMY colors:

1. Make sure the Color Mixer mode is set to CMY. If not, use the Color Mixer Options menu to switch to the CMY mode.

2. To choose the C (cyan) component, drag the slider or enter a value in the C (cyan) field. Do the same for the M (magenta) component and the Y (yellow) component 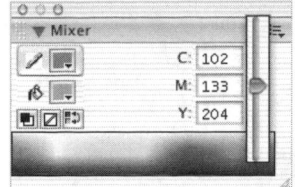.

    or

    Click anywhere along the CMY color ramp at the bottom of the Color Mixer to choose colors by eye, rather than by numeric values.

④ CMY colors *use the numbers from 0 to 255 to set the amount of each color component.*

Understanding CMY Colors

The CMY colors in Fireworks are not the same as the CMYK colors used in printing.

Theoretically (and in Fireworks), combining the three pure CMY—cyan, magenta, and yellow—colors produces black. They are called subtractive colors because when you take away each of the colors you get white. (The way I remember the colors are subtractive is if you take away—subtract—the ink from a page, you're left with white.)

In actual printing, combining the three CMY inks produces a muddy brown-black so an extra black printing plate is added to create real black.

Fireworks provides the CMY mode as a convenience for those designers who (like your humble author) find it difficult to think in RGB. We can't remember that you add green to red to make orange. Our finger-painting experiences make it easier for us to remember that magenta plus yellow make orange.

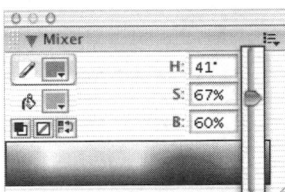

⑤ HSB colors *combine the degrees of hue and the percentages of saturation and brightness to define colors.*

⑥ Grayscale colors *use percentages of black to define colors.*

Understanding HSB Colors

The most classic form of defining colors is the HSB—hue, saturation, and brightness—system.

Hue uses the principle of arranging colors in a wheel. Changing the colors from 0° to 360° moves through the entire color spectrum. Saturation uses percentage values, where 100% is a totally saturated color. Lower saturation values create pastel versions of a color. Brightness uses percentage values, where 100% is a color with no black. The lower the brightness percentage, the more black is added to the color.

You can also define colors using the classic HSB, or hue, saturation, and brightness, system.

To define HSB colors:

1. Make sure the Color Mixer mode is set to HSB. If not, use the Color Mixer Options menu to switch to the HSB mode.

2. To choose the H (hue) component, drag the slider or enter a degree value in the H (hue) field ⑤.

3. To choose the S (saturation) component, drag the slider or enter a percentage value in the S (saturation) field. Do the same for the B (brightness) component.

or

Click anywhere along the HSB color ramp at the bottom of the Color Mixer to choose colors by eye, rather than by numeric values.

Although all Web graphics are exported in RGB or indexed colors, you may need to match colors used in grayscale images. So, the Color Mixer also lets you define colors using values of a single black (K) color.

To define Grayscale colors:

1. Make sure the Color Mixer mode is set to Grayscale. If not, use the Color Mixer Options menu to switch to the Grayscale mode.

2. To choose the K (black) component, drag the slider or enter a value in the K (black) field ⑥.

or

Click anywhere along the Grayscale color ramp at the bottom of the Color Mixer to choose colors by eye, rather than by numeric values.

Using the Swatches Panel

It would be cumbersome to have to go to the Color Mixer every time you needed a color. The Swatches panel lets you store commonly used colors so they are always available.

To use the Swatches panel:

1. If you do not see the Swatches panel, choose **Window > Swatches**.

   or

   If the Swatches panel is behind another panel, click the title bar of the Swatches panel to bring it in front of any other onscreen elements.

2. Click the Swatches panel menu to access the Swatches commands ❼.

One of the most important considerations in creating Web graphics is using Web-safe colors. You can access the 216 Web-safe colors via the Swatches panel. There are two arrangements of the Web-safe colors.

The Color Cubes palette displays the Web-safe colors in groups of related colors.

To choose the Color Cubes Swatches:

◆ Open the Swatches panel menu and choose Color Cubes. The color swatches appear in the panel ❽. *(See the color pages for a color display of the palette.)*

The Continuous Tone palette displays the Web-safe colors so that the colors flow from one color to another.

To choose the Continuous Tone Swatches:

◆ Open the Swatches panel menu and choose Continuous Tone. The color swatches appear in the panel ❾. *(See the color pages for a color display of the palette.)*

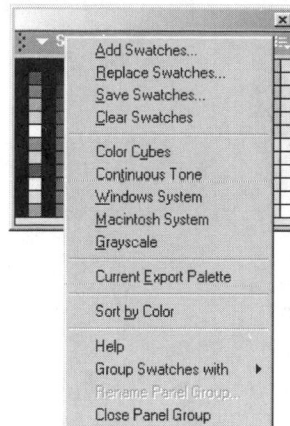

❼ *The* Swatches panel menu.

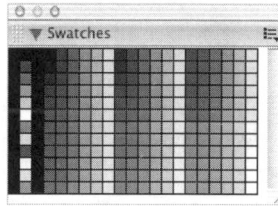

❽ *The* Color Cubes arrangement *of the Web-safe colors.*

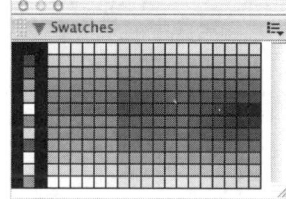

❾ *The* Continuous Tone arrangement *of the Web-safe colors.*

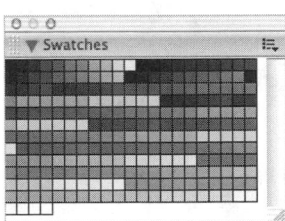

❿ *The* Macintosh System colors *in the Swatches panel.*

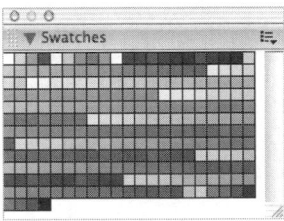

⓫ *The* Windows System colors *in the Swatches panel.*

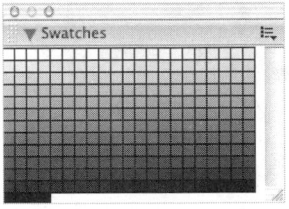

⓬ *The* Grayscale colors *in the Swatches panel.*

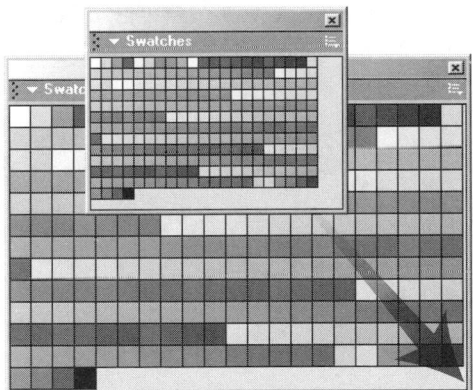

⓭ *As you* increase the size of the Swatches panel *you also increase the size of the color chips.*

You can also limit your colors to those found in the Macintosh operating system. This can be helpful if you are designing graphics for an intranet Web site to be viewed only on Macintosh computers that display 256 colors.

To choose the Macintosh System Swatches:

◆ Open the Swatches panel menu and choose Macintosh System. The 256 color swatches appear in the panel ❿. *(See the color pages for a color display of the palette.)*

You can also pick colors using the Windows System colors. This can be helpful if you are designing graphics for an intranet Web site to be viewed only on Windows computers that display only 256 colors.

To choose the Windows System Swatches:

◆ Open the Swatches panel menu and choose Windows System. The 256 color swatches appear in the panel ⓫. *(See the color pages for a color display of the palette.)*

You can also limit your colors to grayscale colors. This is done by choosing the Grayscale swatches.

To choose the Grayscale Swatches:

◆ Open the Swatches panel menu and choose Grayscale. The 256 grayscale color swatches appear in the panel ⓬.

If you find the color chips in the Swatches panel too small to use, you can make them bigger by enlarging the Swatches panel.

To change the size of the Swatches color chips:

◆ Use the resize control of the Swatches panel to increase the size of the Swatches panel. The color chips change their size accordingly ⓭.

Using the Swatches Panel

You can use the Swatches panel to store colors that you create in the Color Mixer. This makes it easy to maintain consistent colors in all your graphics.

To add colors to the Swatches panel:

1. Use the Color Mixer to define a color that you want to store.

2. Move the mouse over to the gray area at the bottom of the Swatches panel where there are no swatches. A Paint Bucket cursor appears ⓮.

3. Click the mouse button. The new color appears in its own color swatch.

You can also delete colors from the Swatches panel.

To delete colors from the Swatches panel:

1. Move the cursor over the swatch for the color you want to delete.

2. Hold the Command/Ctrl key. A Scissors cursor appears ⓯.

3. Click to delete the color from the Swatches panel.

You can also delete all the colors from the Swatches panel at once.

To delete all the colors from the Swatches panel:

◆ Choose Clear Swatches from the Swatches panel menu.

If you keep adding colors to the Swatches panel, you may want to arrange the swatches so that similar colors are grouped together.

To sort the swatches by color:

◆ Choose Sort by Color from the Swatches panel menu.

TIP The color swatches are sorted, first by hue and then from light to dark ⓰.

⓮ *The* **Paint Bucket cursor** *indicates that you can store a color in the Swatches panel.*

⓯ *The Command/Ctrl key displays the* **Scissors** **cursor** *which allows you to delete a color from the Swatches panel.*

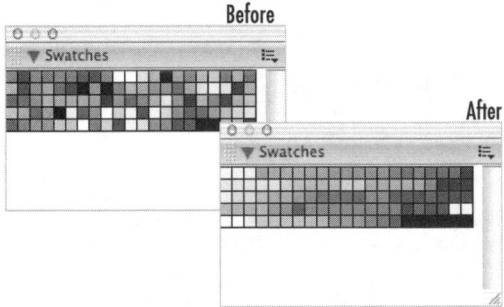
⓰ *The Swatches panel before and after* sorting the colors.

Using the Swatches Panel

When to Use Web-safe Colors

At the risk of starting a controversy, let me try to explain when (or if) you should limit your colors to only the Web-safe palette.

Some people have monitors that can display only 256 colors. There are 256 colors for Windows monitors and 256 colors for Macintosh monitors. But only 216 colors appear on both platforms. These are the 216 Web-safe colors.

If you limit your Fireworks graphics to only those 216 colors, you ensure that the colors of your document do not change when they are displayed on different monitors using different browsers.

These days, though, most people have monitors that can display more than 256 colors—most likely millions of colors. The question is: Should you limit yourself to designing Web sites for the oldest, most backward monitors or should you design for the majority?

My own opinion is that, unless you have a very good reason, you should design for the most advanced audience. The Web-safe palette is far too limiting to create sophisticated effects such as shadows, highlights, and bevels.

However, if you are designing a site with maps or financial charts, you might want to limit those images to the Web-safe colors. This guarantees that the images are displayed the same on all monitors.

Once you have created a custom Swatches panel with your own colors, you can save that Swatches panel to use at other times.

To save swatches in the Swatches panel:

1. Choose Save Swatches from the Swatches panel menu.

2. Give the file a name and then save the file wherever you want. The saved file can be loaded into the Swatches panel at any time.

To load swatches to the Swatches panel:

1. Open the Swatches panel menu and choose Replace Swatches.

2. Navigate to find a saved Swatches panel file.

3. Click Open. This replaces the current set of swatches with those from the saved file.

To add swatches to the Swatches panel:

1. Open the Swatches panel menu and choose Add Swatches.

2. Navigate to find a saved Swatches panel file.

3. Choose Open. Unlike the Replace Swatches command, this adds the new swatches to those already in the Swatches panel.

Using the Swatches Panel

Using the Default Colors

Fireworks has a set of default colors for the Stroke and Fill colors. The default color for Stroke is black. The default color for Fill is white. These are simply the colors that the folks at Macromedia thought you would like to have when you first open Fireworks. However, the default colors can be accessed easily and changed to suit your needs.

To work with the default colors:

1. Click the Default Colors icon in either the Tools panel or the Color Mixer to set the Stroke and Fill colors to their default settings ⑰.

TIP Press the letter D to apply the default colors to an object.

2. Click the Swap Colors icon in either the Tools panel or the Color Mixer to reverse the Stroke and Fill colors ⑱.

TIP Press the letter X to swap the Stroke and Fill colors applied to an object.

To change the default colors:

1. Choose **Edit** > **Preferences** to open the Preferences dialog box ⑲.

   or

   (Mac OS X) choose **Fireworks** > **Preferences**.

2. Click the Color Well in the Color Defaults section for the Stroke or Fill colors.

3. Use the swatches to choose a new default color.

4. Click OK to apply the changes.

TIP The Color Defaults also lets you change the highlight color, which is the color used to indicate that an object is about to be chosen.

⑰ *Click the* **Default Colors icon** *in the Color Mixer to reset the Stroke and Fill colors to their default setting.*

⑱ *Click the* **Swap Colors icon** *in the Color Mixer to reverse the Stroke and Fill colors.*

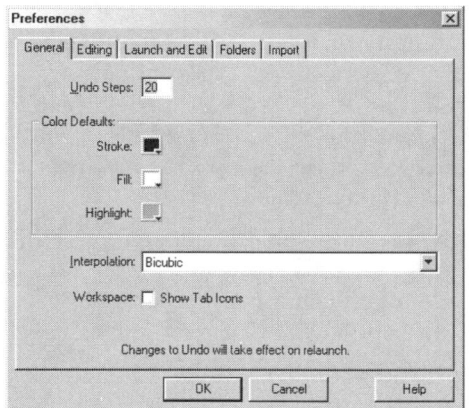

⑲ *The* **Color Defaults** *of the General Preferences lets you change the colors used for the default Stroke, Fill, and Highlight colors.*

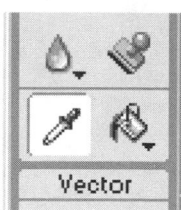

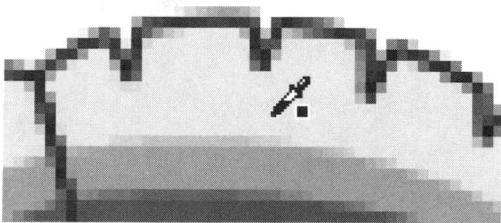

20 *The* Eyedropper *in the Tools panel.*

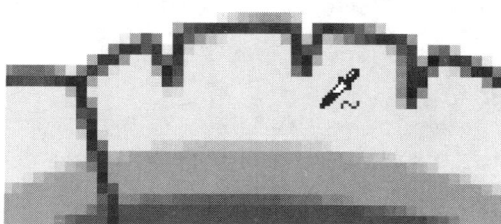

21 *The* Eyedropper **sampling a Fill color.**

22 *The* Eyedropper **sampling a Stroke color.**

Sampling Colors

The Eyedropper tool lets you pick colors from objects or images that you then can apply to the fill or stroke of other objects.

To sample colors with the Eyedropper:

1. Choose the Eyedropper in the Tools panel **20**.
2. Position the Eyedropper over the color you want to sample.
3. Click. The color appears as either the Fill or Stroke color, depending on which you have selected. *(For more information on working with fills and strokes, see Chapter 7, "Fills," and Chapter 8, "Strokes.")*

TIP When the Fill color is chosen, a black square appears next to the Eyedropper cursor **21**.

TIP When the Stroke color is chosen in the Tools panel, a tilde (~) appears next to the Eyedropper cursor **22**.

Using the Info Panel for Colors

Fireworks lets you see the details of an image in the Info panel. For instance, you can move your cursor around the image to see which colors are used.

To change the Info panel settings:

1. Make sure the Info panel is open. If not, choose **Windows** > **Info**.

2. Click the triangle to open the Info panel menu ㉓.

3. Choose a color mode to change how the Info panel displays color values.

As you are working, you may want to know the exact composition of the color of an object or image.

To determine the color of an object:

◆ Pass the pointer over the object. The color area shows the values for the color underneath the pointer ㉔.

TIP Changing the way the Info panel displays colors does not actually change the colors in the file. Colors in Fireworks are not set until they are exported as a finished file *(see Chapter 20, "Exporting")*.

You can also find the alpha or transparency value of an object or image. *(See Chapter 9, "Effects," for information on applying transparency values to artwork.)*

To determine the transparency of an object:

◆ Pass the pointer over the object. The alpha value is listed next to the letter A ㉕.

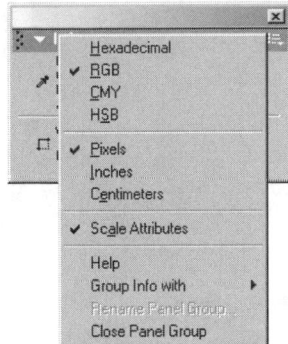

㉓ *The* **Info panel menu** *lets you choose the color mode for the display of sampled colors.*

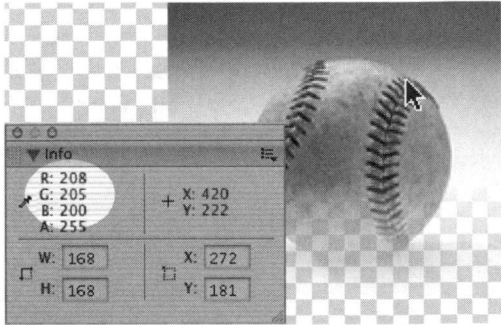

㉔ *The* **color values of the Info panel** *show the RGB values for the area under the pointer.*

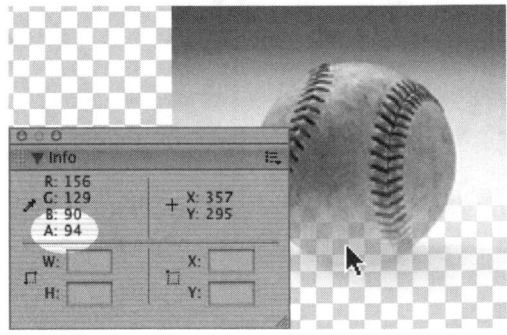

㉕ *The* **alpha value of the Info panel** *shows the transparency values for the area under the pointer.*

VECTOR TOOLS 4

When I started out working with computer graphics, the rules were clear. There were paint programs such as MacPaint that let you work with pixels in bitmap images. There were also draw programs such as MacDraw that let you draw with objects.

Later on, these programs evolved into two distinct types of graphics programs. There were bitmap-image programs such as Adobe Photoshop and Procreate Painter and vector-object programs such as Macromedia FreeHand and Adobe Illustrator.

However, Fireworks defies the simple paint and draw labels. Instead of working with vectors or bitmaps, Fireworks lets you work with both modes. In previous versions of Fireworks, the line between vectors and bitmaps was confusing. Sometimes a tool worked in the bitmap mode, other times it was a vector tool.

In Fireworks MX, the tools have been completely separated. When you choose a vector tool, you only create paths. When you choose a bitmap tool, you only create pixel images. *(For more information on working with the bitmap tools, see Chapter 10, "Working with Bitmaps.")*

If you are familiar with a vector program, you will feel very comfortable working with Fireworks's vector tools. If you have never used a vector program, pay attention to this chapter because creating paths is the primary source of images in Fireworks.

Differences Between Vectors and Pixels

The vector tools in Fireworks allow you to create vector objects—also called *paths*—such as rectangle, ellipses, polygons, or irregularly shaped objects. All the vector tools are under the Vector category in the Tools panel. All the bitmap tools are under the Bitmap category 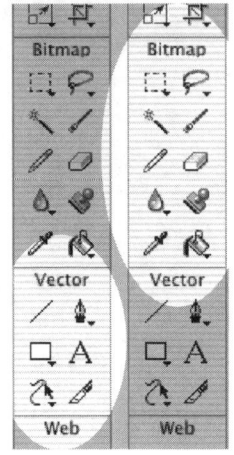.

When you select objects created with the vector tools, they display points and lines that show the shape of the path. When you select the images created with the bitmap tools, they display a bounding box around the image ❷.

❶ *The* **Vector tools** *(left) and the* **Bitmap tools** *(right) in the Tools panel.*

Benefits of Vector Objects

One of the benefits of using the vector tools to create objects is that they can easily be modified. You use the selection tools to select the points and move them to new positions ❸. As you move the points, the shape of the path changes. You can also change the colors of vector objects very easily.

You should always try to create objects for buttons, navigation bars, and other graphic objects using the vector tools. When you use these tools you have more choices for changing the objects, applying effects, or animating the objects.

Vector object   Bitmap image

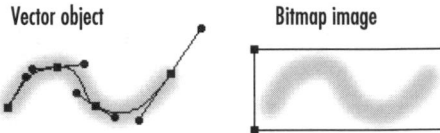

❷ **Vector objects** *take their shape from the points along the path.* **Bitmap images** *are contained within a bitmap area.*

❸ *You can* **reshape a vector object** *by moving the points along the path.*

Benefits of Bitmap Images

Bitmap tools let you do things like blur or sharpen the details in photos. You can also use bitmap tools to do things like erase scratches and dust in scanned images or copy the image from one part of a photo to another ❹. *(For more information, see Chapter 10, "Working with Bitmaps.")*

❹ *You can* **erase bitmap images** *by using tools such as the Eraser.*

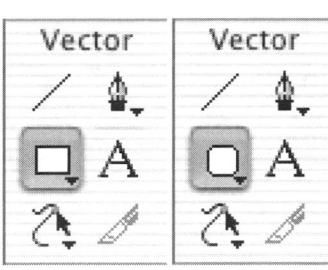

⑤ *The* **Rectangle tool** *and* **Rounded Rectangle tool** *in the Tools panel.*

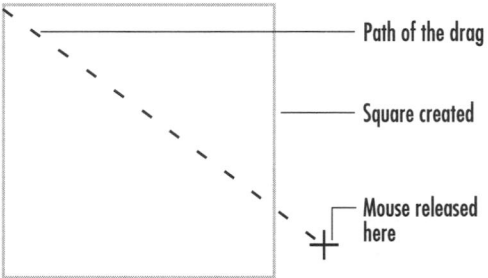

— Path of the drag

— Square created

— Mouse released here

⑥ *Holding the Shift key* **constrains the Rectangle tool to create a square.** *As long as you press the Shift key, the sides remain equal.*

Rectangle or Rounded Rectangle?

All rectangles created by either the Rectangle tool or the Rounded Rectangle tool can have a roundness setting applied to them from the Property Inspector.

The main difference between the two tools is that the Rounded Rectangle tool remembers the last setting of roundness applied to the rectangle. If you increase the roundness to 80% with no rectangle selected, all new rectangles drawn with the Rounded Rectangle tool will have a roundness of 80%. The ordinary Rectangle tool does not remember any roundness applied to the rectangles it creates.

Creating Basic Shapes

There are four tools that allow you to quickly make a variety of basic shapes: rectangles, ellipses, polygons, stars, and straight lines.

Both the Rectangle tool and the Rounded Rectangle tool create rectangles, squares, and rounded-corner rectangles. One of the most common uses for these tools is to create the shapes for buttons and banners for your Web graphics.

To create a rectangle:

1. Click the Rectangle tool or the Rounded Rectangle tool in the Tools panel **⑤**. If the Rounded Rectangle tool is not visible, click the pop-up group to choose the Rounded Rectangle tool.

2. Move the pointer to the Canvas area. The cursor changes to a plus sign (+) indicating that you can draw the rectangle.

3. Press and drag diagonally from one corner to the other of the rectangle you want to draw.

TIP Hold the Shift key as you press and drag to constrain the Rectangle tool into creating a square **⑥**.

TIP Hold the Opt/Alt key as you press and drag to draw from the center point outward.

4. Release the mouse button to create the rectangle.

Creating Basic Shapes

A rectangle with rounded corners is a very popular look for buttons and other interactive Web elements.

To create a rounded-corner rectangle:

1. Use either the Rounded Rectangle or the Rectangle tool to create a rectangle as described in the previous exercise.

2. Use the Roundness slider in the Property Inspector to change the corners of the rectangle 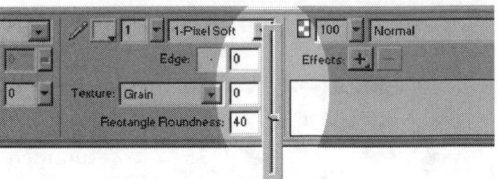. The corners are rounded according to the percentage set for the corner radius ❽.

TIP You can change the roundness interactively as you drag by pressing the up or down arrow keys on the keyboard.

TIP You can select the rectangle and use the Property Inspector to change the roundness of the rectangle at any time as long as you don't ungroup the rectangle.

❼ The **Roundness slider** *lets you round the corners of a rectangle. You can also enter a precise number in the Roundness field.*

You can create ellipses, ovals, and circles using the Ellipse tool.

To create an ellipse:

1. Click the Ellipse tool in the Tools panel ❾. If the Ellipse tool is not visible, click the pop-up group to choose the Ellipse tool.

2. Move the pointer to the Canvas area.

3. Press and drag a line that defines the diameter of the ellipse.

TIP Hold the Shift key as you drag to constrain the ellipse into a circle.

TIP Hold the Opt/Alt key as you drag to draw from the center point outward.

4. Release the mouse button to complete the ellipse.

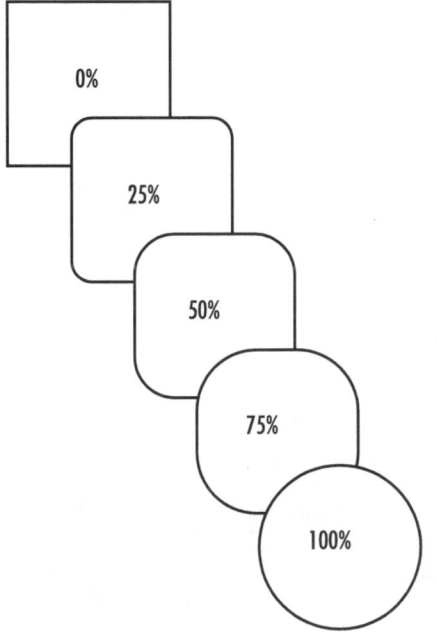

❽ *Squares drawn with different percentages for the corner radius.*

❾ *The **Ellipse tool** in the Tools panel.*

Creating Basic Shapes

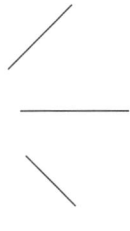

⑩ *The* **Line tool** *in the Tools panel.*

⑪ *The results of* **holding the Shift key** *while drawing with the Line tool.*

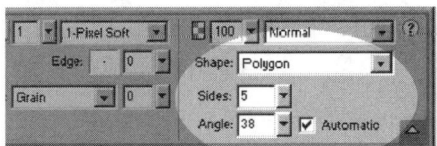

⑫ *The* **Polygon tool** *in the Tools panel.*

⑬ *The* **Polygon tool options** *in the Property Inspector.*

You can use the Line tool to quickly create straight line segments.

To create a line:

1. Click the Line tool in the Tools panel **⑩**.

2. Move the pointer to the Canvas area. The cursor changes to the plus sign.

3. Drag to set the length and direction of the line.

TIP Hold the Shift key to constrain the angle of the line to 45° increments **⑪**.

4. Release the mouse button to complete the line.

Polygons give your Web graphics a special look. The Polygon tool can create both polygons and stars.

To create a polygon:

1. Click the Polygon tool in the Tools panel **⑫**. If the Polygon tool is not visible, press the pop-up group to choose it. The Property Inspector changes to display the options for the Polygon tool **⑬**.

2. Choose Polygon from the Shape menu in the Property Inspector.

3. Use the slider or enter a number from 1 to 360 in the field to set the number of sides for the polygon.

TIP The more sides to the polygon, the closer it gets to a circle.

4. Move the pointer to the Canvas area and press and drag. The point where you start the drag is the center of the polygon.

5. Release the mouse button to create the polygon.

TIP The Angle field and Automatic check box do not do change anything when Polygon is selected in the Shape menu.

Creating Basic Shapes

The same tool that you use to create polygons can be used to create stars. Stars with many points are sometimes called bursts and are useful for calling attention to special information.

To create a star:

1. Click the Polygon tool in the Tools panel. If the Polygon tool is not visible, open the pop-up group to choose it. The Property Inspector changes to display the options for the Polygon tool.

2. Choose Star from the Shape menu in the Property Inspector 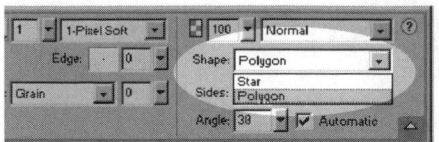.

3. Use the slider or enter a number from 1 to 360 in the sides field to set the number of external points for the star.

4. Check Automatic to create stars with parallel line segments **⑮**.

   or

   Use the slider to set the angle of the points. Low settings create acute angles. High settings create obtuse angles **⑯**.

⑭ *The* **Shape menu** *in the Property Inspector lets you create polygons or stars.*

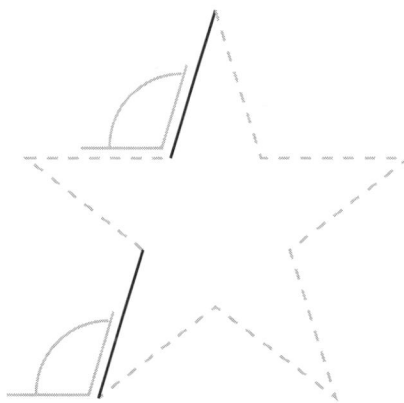

⑮ *The two black segments are parallel as a result of setting the star to Automatic.*

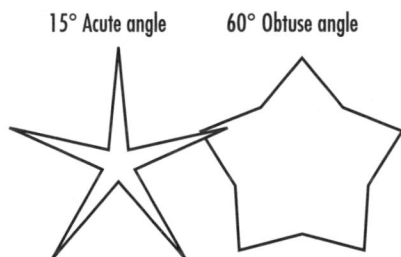

⑯ *Choose low angle values to create* **acute-angled stars** *with sharp points. Choose high angle values to create* **obtuse-angled stars** *with broad points.*

Working with the Pen Tool

One of the most important tools in any vector program is its Pen tool. The Pen tool allows you to precisely create a wide variety of shapes. The Fireworks Pen tool is similar to those found in Macromedia FreeHand and Adobe Illustrator. Before you learn to use the Pen, you should understand the elements of paths.

Anchor points define places in a path where the path changes direction or curvature. *Segments* are the paths that connect anchor points. *Control handles* extend out from anchor points; their length and direction control the shape of curved segments.

The best way to learn to use the Pen is to start by creating straight segments.

⓱ *The* **Pen tool** *in the Tools panel.*

⓲ *The* **start icon** *for the Pen tool.*

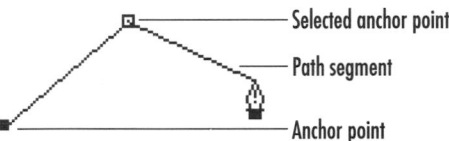

— Selected anchor point

— Path segment

— Anchor point

⓳ *Click with the Pen tool to create* **straight** **segments**.

To create a straight path segment:

1. Click the Pen tool in the Tools panel **⓱**.

2. Move the pointer to the Canvas area. The Pen cursor displays an X next to it. This indicates the start of the path **⓲**.

3. Click to create an anchor point which defines the beginning of the segment of the path.

4. Move the cursor to where you want to position the next anchor point of the path. The Pen cursor changes so there is nothing next to it. This indicates that you can create a second point, connected to the first.

TIP If you use Precise Cursors *(see page 9)*, you do not see the Pen cursor. Rather you see a cross-hair cursor.

5. Click. This connects the two anchor points with a straight line segment **⓳**.

6. Continue to create straight segments by repeating steps 4 and 5.

7. To finish the path, hold the Cmd/Ctrl key, and click.

Further Pen Lessons

If you would like more practice for working with the Pen tool, I suggest two resources. The first is my own Web site, **www.vectorbabe.com**. There you'll find a few pages that take you through exercises to create objects such as a heart and flower.

If you would like a set of electronic lessons that you can purchase and download from the Web, I recommend **www.zenofthepen.org**. This is a set of Acrobat files that contains movies and instructions for working with the Pen tool in a variety of programs including Fireworks, FreeHand, Illustrator, and InDesign. There are also electronic templates that you can use to practice in Fireworks.

Working with the Pen Tool

You can also use the Pen tool to create curved segments. Think of a curved segment as the shape that a roller coaster follows along a track.

To create a curved path segment:

1. Click the Pen tool in the Tools panel.

2. Move the Pen cursor to the Canvas area. The Pen cursor displays an X next to it.

3. Press and drag to create an anchor point with control handles.

4. Release the mouse button. The length and direction of the handle control the height and direction of the curve **20**.

5. Move the cursor to where you want the next anchor point of the path.

6. Press and drag to create the curved segment between the two anchor points.

7. Continue to create curved segments by repeating steps 3 and 4 **21**.

8. To finish the path, hold the Cmd/Ctrl key, and click.

Curves do not have to be smooth. A corner curve has an abrupt change in direction. Think of a bouncing ball. Where the ball hits the ground, its path is a corner curve.

To create a corner curve:

1. Press and drag to create an anchor point with control handles. Do not release the mouse button.

2. Hold the Opt/Alt key and then drag to pivot the second handle **22**.

TIP The longer the handle, the steeper the curve.

3. Release the mouse button when the second handle is the correct length and direction.

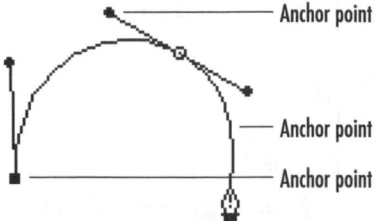

20 *Dragging with the Pen tool creates* **curved segments**.

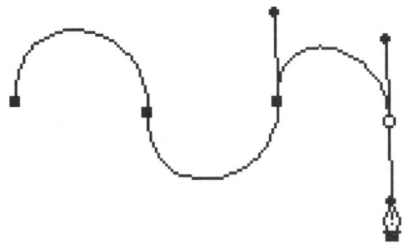

21 *A path with a series of curved segments.*

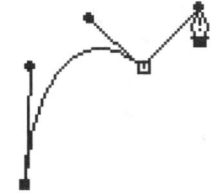

22 *Hold the Option/Alt key to pivot the handles and create a* **corner curve**.

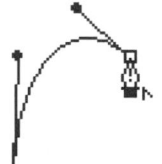

23 *Move the cursor back over a point and click to* **retract a handle** *along a curve.*

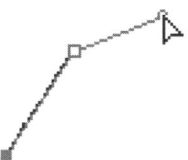

24 *Hold the Cmd+Opt keys (Mac) or Ctrl+Alt keys (Win) to* **extend a handle** *out from an anchor point.*

Father of the Pen Tool

You may have heard people refer to the curves in computer graphics as Bézier curves. This is in honor of Pierre Bézier, a French mathematician who created the mathematics for interactive free-form curves. This is the basis for the control handles used in the Pen tool found in Fireworks and other vector illustration programs.

Monsieur Bézier originally applied his mathematics as part of the designs for for the Renault car company in France. Later the same mathematics was used by Adobe as part of the PostScript drawing language.

Pierre Bézier was born in 1910 and died in 1999.

Once you have created a curved segment with two handles, you can retract the second handle back into the anchor point. This allows you to make the next path segment a straight path.

To retract the handle into a point:

1. Press and drag with the Pen tool to create an anchor point with two control handles.

2. Move the cursor back over the anchor point. A small caret appears next to the Pen cursor **23**.

3. Click. The handle retracts back into the anchor point.

4. Continue the path with either a straight segment or a curved segment.

TIP Click to make the next path segment straight. Drag to make the next path segment curved.

Once you click to create an anchor point with no control handles, you can extend a single handle out from that anchor point. This allows you to make the next path segment a curved path.

To extend a handle out from a point:

1. Click to create an anchor point with no control handles.

2. Move the pointer back over the anchor point you just created. A small caret appears next to the Pen cursor.

3. Press Cmd+Opt (Mac) or Ctrl+Alt (Win). The Pen cursor changes to a white arrow head.

4. Press and drag out from the anchor point. A single control handle extends out from the anchor point **24**.

5. Continue the path with a curved segment.

There are two ways to finish a path in Fireworks. The first way is to leave the end points of the path open. An open path is like a piece of string.

To create an open path:

1. Move the Pen tool away from the last point of the path.

2. Hold the Cmd/Ctrl key, and click. This leaves the path open and allows you to continue using the Pen tool .

   or

   Switch to another tool in the Tools panel. This leaves the path open.

㉕ *An* **open path** *has two endpoints that are not connected.*

The second way to finish a path is to join the last point of the path to the first. This creates a closed path. A closed path is like a rubber band. *(See page 70 for how to close an existing path.)*

To create a closed path:

1. Move the cursor to the first anchor point of the path. A small circle appears next to the Pen cursor. This indicates you are about to close the path **㉖**.

2. Click to close the path.

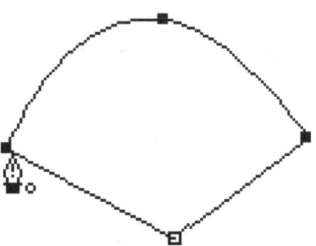

㉖ *The* **closed path icon** *next to the Pen tool indicates that you are about to create a closed path.*

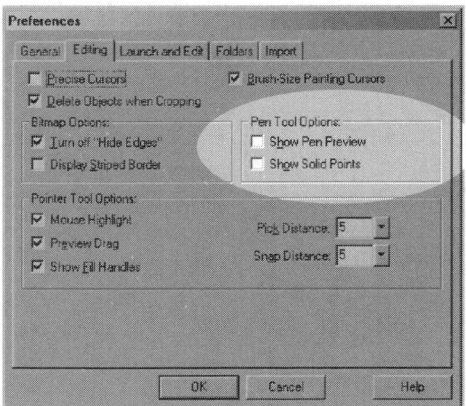

㉗ *The* **Pen Tool Options** *in the Editing Preferences dialog box control the display of the path segment drawn with the pen.*

㉘ *Turn the* **Pen Preview** *on to show the path between the last point and the next click of the Pen.*

Setting the Pen and Points Display

Fireworks contains preference settings that let you customize how you work with the Pen tool. The Pen Preview helps you see what the next path segment will look like as you position the Pen cursor.

To set the Pen preview:

1. Choose **Edit** > Preferences to open the Preferences dialog box.

   or

   (Mac OS X) Choose **Fireworks** > **Preferences**.

2. Click the Editing tab (Win) or choose Editing from the menu (Mac) to display the editing preferences **㉗**.

3. Select Show Pen Preview to see a continuation of the path as you move the Pen tool to the next point **㉘**.

   or

   Deselect Show Pen Preview to leave a gap between the Pen tool and the previous point on the path **㉘**.

TIP I always work with the Show Pen Preview turned on. It helps me judge what the next curved path will look like. It also helps me remember that my Pen cursor is still connected to the path I have drawn.

Setting the Pen and Points Display

The Pen tool options also control the display of selected points on a path.

To set the points preview:

1. Choose **Edit** > **Preferences** to open the Preferences dialog box.

   or

   (Mac OS X) Choose **Fireworks** > **Preferences**.

2. Click the Editing tab (Win) or choose Editing from the menu (Mac) to display the editing preferences.

3. Select Show Solid Points to display unselected points as filled squares and selected points as hollow squares 🠮.

   or

   Deselect Show Solid Points to display unselected points as hollow squares and selected points as filled squares 🠮.

TIP When Show Solid Points is deselected, Fireworks displays points similarly to the way Adobe Illustrator and other Adobe products display points. It is also the way early versions of Fireworks displayed points.

TIP The Show Solid Points option changes the display of all points, regardless of the tool that was used to create them.

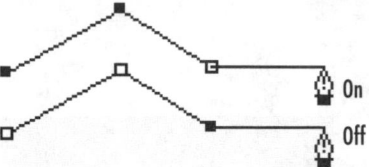

🠮 *The* **Show Solid Points** *preference setting changes how selected points are displayed.*

Setting the Pen and Points Display

🕉 *The* **Vector Path tool** *in the Tools panel.*

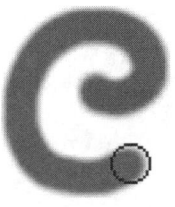

🕉 *The Vector Path tool allows you to draw free-form paths without placing anchor points.*

The Pen Versus the Vector Path

The Vector Path tool offers a quick and easy way to draw paths. You don't have to worry about where the anchor points go or pulling control handles out. All you have to do is drag. Unfortunately, the Vector Path tool tends to make paths that are not as smooth as the ones created with the Pen tool. Even if you drag very quickly, and very smoothly, you'll see that the Vector Path tool leaves all sorts of extra points on the paths. My own preference is to use the Pen tool to create smooth paths.

Using the Vector Path Tool

Fireworks also has a Vector Path tool that lets you draw more freely, without worrying about how and where you place points.

TIP The Vector Path tool displays feedback as to its mode when it is shown as a tool cursor. *(See pages 8–9 for how to display the tool cursor.)*

To draw with the Vector Path tool:

1. Click the Vector Path tool in the Tools panel **🕉**. If the Vector Path tool is not visible, click the pop-up group to choose the Vector Path tool.

2. Move the pointer to the Canvas area.

3. Drag to create a path that follows the movements of the mouse **🕉**.

4. Release the mouse button to end the path.

TIP To make a closed path with the Vector Path tool, move the mouse close to the starting point of the path. A small square next to the tool cursor indicates that you will close the path.

TIP Hold the Shift key to create straight lines with the Vector Path tool.

TIP The paths created with the Vector Path tool are not as smooth as those created with the Pen tool. If you need smooth paths, apply the Simplify command to the path *(see page 95)*.

Using the Redraw Path Tool

The Redraw Path tool is like the Vector Path tool except that, instead of just drawing paths, it allows you to modify selected paths that it comes near to.

TIP The Redraw Path tool provides visual feedback as to how it works when the tool cursor is visible. *(See pages 8–9 for information as to how to display the tool cursor.)*

To create paths with the Redraw Path tool:

1. Choose the Redraw Path tool in the Tools panel **32**.

2. Follow the steps in the previous exercise for the Vector Path tool.

To reshape paths with the Redraw Path tool:

1. Select a path. *(See Chapter 5, "Selecting Paths.")*

TIP Rectangles, ellipses, and polygons must be ungrouped *(see page 81)* before they can be reshaped.

TIP Paths are left selected after you finish drawing them with the Redraw Path tool.

2. Choose the Redraw Path tool in the Tools panel. If the Redraw Path tool is not visible, click the pop-up group to choose the Redraw Path tool.

3. Move the tool to the part of the path that you want to redraw. If the tool is in the middle of the path, a small caret appears next to the Redraw Path cursor **33**. If the tool is on the end of the path, a plus sign appears next to the Redraw Path cursor.

4. Press and drag to create the new shape of the path. A red line appears that indicates the part of the path that is modified **34**.

5. Release the mouse. The path is reshaped.

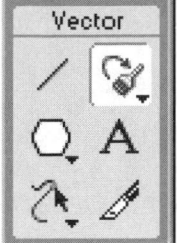

32 *The* **Redraw Path tool** *in the Tools panel.*

33 *The Redraw Path cursor indicates that the path will be reshaped by the Redraw Path tool.*

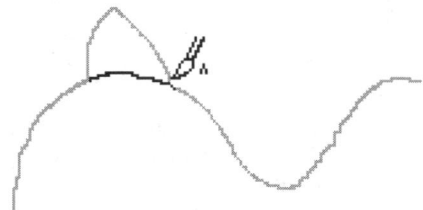

34 *A red line shows the original path as the Redraw Path tool creates the new path.*

Using the Redraw Path Tool

35 The **Freeform tool** *in the Tools panel.*

36 *The* **Freeform tool options** *in the Property Inspector.*

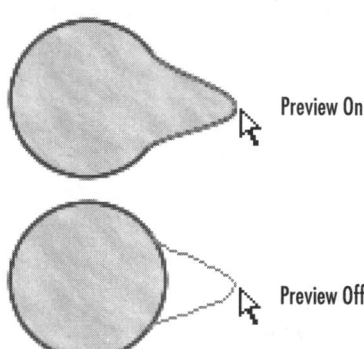

Preview On

Preview Off

37 *The* **Freeform Preview** *displays the artwork as you change its shape.*

Reshaping Objects

Once you have created an object, you may find it difficult to work with the control handles to reshape the path. Fireworks gives you several other ways to easily change the object's shape.

The Freeform tool allows you to change the shape of an object without worrying about adding or modifying points.

TIP You must ungroup a rectangle or rounded-corner rectangle before you can use the Freeform tool *(see page 81)*.

To set the Freeform tool options:

1. Choose the Freeform tool in the Tools panel **35**. If the Freeform tool is not visible, open the pop-up group to choose the Freeform tool. The Freeform tool options appear in the Property Inspector **36**.

2. Use the slider or enter a numeric value in the Size field to set the size of the tool. This controls how large an area (in pixels) is manipulated by the tool.

3. If you have a pressure-sensitive pen and tablet, click Pressure to allow your pressure on the tablet to affect the size of the effect.

4. Choose Preview to see the artwork change as you use the Freeform tool **37**.

   or

   Deselect Preview to see only the outline of the path change **37**.

TIP Deselect Preview if you have a slower computer.

TIP To decrease the size of the Freeform tool effect, press the left arrow, left bracket ([), or 1 key as you drag.

TIP To increase the size of the Freeform tool effect, press the right arrow, right bracket (]), or 2 key as you drag.

The Freeform tool has two modes: Push and Pull. In the Push mode the Freeform tool acts like a rolling pin to modify the shape of the path.

To use the Freeform tool in Push mode:

1. Set the Freeform tool options, as described on the previous page.

2. Move the cursor near, but not on, the edge of a selected object. The cursor displays the Push Freeform tool icon, an arrow with a circle next to it ③⑧.

3. Drag around the edge of the object. The shape of the object changes accordingly ③⑨.

TIP As you drag, the Push Freeform tool icon changes to a circle that indicates the size of the effect of the tool.

TIP The Push Freeform tool can work from either the inside or the outside of an object.

In Pull mode the Freeform tool acts like a magnet that pulls out new segments from the path.

To use the Freeform tool in the Pull mode:

1. Set the Freeform tool options, as described on the previous page.

2. Move the cursor to the edge of a selected object. The cursor displays the Pull Freeform tool arrow icon ④⓪.

3. Drag in or out from the edge of the object. The shape of the object changes accordingly ④①.

③⑧ *The* **Push Freeform tool cursor.**

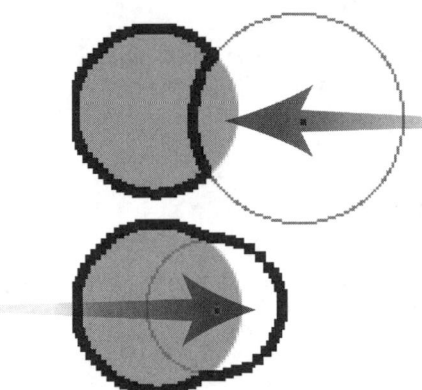

③⑨ *The* **Push Freeform tool** *allows you to push on the edges of an object to reshape it.*

④⓪ *The* **Pull Freeform tool cursor.**

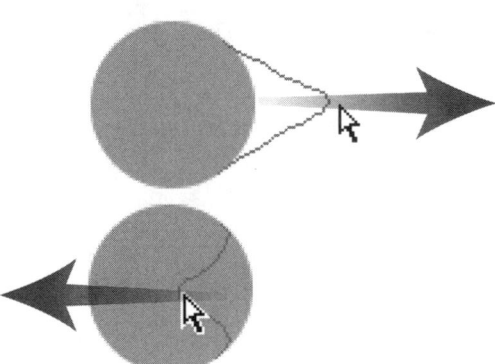

④① *The* **Pull Freeform tool** *allows you to pull segments into or out from an object.*

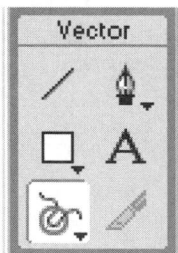

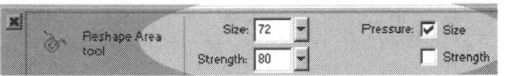

42 *The* **Reshape Area tool** *in the Tools panel.*

43 *The* **Reshape Area tool options** *in the Property Inspector.*

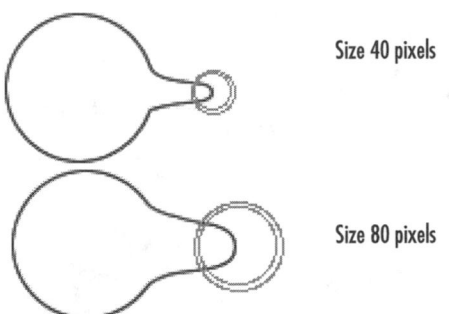

Size 40 pixels

Size 80 pixels

44 *The effect of changing the* **size of the Reshape Area tool.**

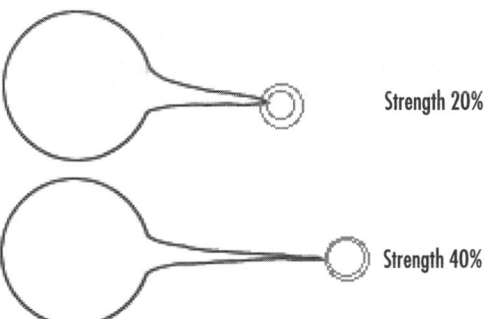

Strength 20%

Strength 40%

45 *The effect of changing the* **strength of the Reshape Area tool.**

Reshape Area Tool

The Reshape Area tool also lets you distort paths without manually adding or modifying anchor points or handles.

To set the Reshape Area tool options:

1. Choose the Reshape Area tool in the Tools panel **42**. If the Reshape Area tool is not visible, open the pop-up group to choose the Reshape Area tool. The Reshape Area tool options appear in the Property Inspector **43**.

2. Use the slider or enter a numeric value in the Size field to set the size of the Reshape Area tool. The higher the number, the larger the area that the tool distorts **44**.

3. Use the slider or type in the Strength field to set how long the tool will work during a drag—the higher the setting, the longer the tool distorts the path **45**.

4. If you have a pressure-sensitive tablet, check the Size or Strength boxes to set how the pressure on the tablet affects the tool.

TIP If you do not have a pressure-sensitive tablet, press the 1, left bracket ([), or left arrow key as you drag to decrease the size of the Reshape Area tool effect.

TIP If you do not have a pressure-sensitive tablet, press the 2, right bracket (]), or right arrow key as you drag to increase the size of the Reshape Area tool effect.

Reshape Area Tool

The Reshape Area tool modifies paths as if they were taffy. The size of the tool controls the amount that is pulled. The strength of the tool controls the length of the pull.

To use the Reshape Area tool:

1. Choose the Reshape Area tool.
2. Position the tool either inside or outside the path.
3. Drag to reshape the path **46**.

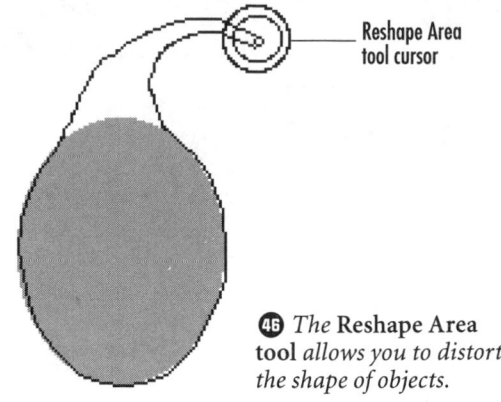

Reshape Area tool cursor

46 *The* **Reshape Area tool** *allows you to distort the shape of objects.*

Knife Tool

You can also reshape paths by cutting them with the Knife tool.

To use the Knife tool:

1. Select a vector path.

TIP The Knife tool is not available in the Tools panel unless a vector path is selected.

1. Choose the Knife tool in the Tools panel **47**. (Be careful, it's very sharp.)
2. Drag the Knife tool across a path. This cuts the path **48**.

TIP Segments created by the Knife tool can be moved away from the other objects with any of the selection tools.

47 *The* **Knife tool** *in the Tools panel.*

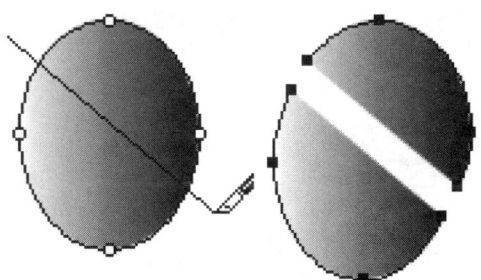

48 **Cutting an object** *with the Knife tool. (The objects were separated after cutting to show the effect of the Knife tool.)*

49 *Click with the Pen tool on a path segment to* **add a point to a path**.

50 *Click with the Pen tool over a point to* **delete a point from a path**.

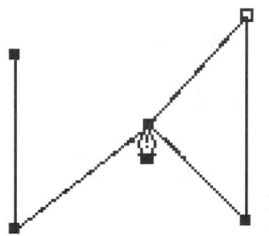

51 *Hold the Shift key as you use the Pen tool to* **continue drawing a path without adding or deleting points**.

Using the Pen to Modify Paths

As you draw paths, you may find that you need to add or delete points. You may discover that you need to change a straight line into a curve or vice versa. Fortunately, the Pen tool not only creates points, it can also modify them—even as you are still drawing the path.

TIP You can't use these techniques on rectangles unless you first ungroup them *(see page 81)*.

To add points to a path:

1. Select the path. *(For more information on working with the Subselection tool, see Chapter 5, "Selecting Paths.")*

2. Choose the Pen tool and position the cursor on the segment where you want to add the point. A plus sign (+) appears next to the cursor **49**.

3. Click. A new point appears.

To delete points from a path:

1. Select the path.

2. Choose the Pen tool and position the cursor over the point that you want to delete. A minus sign (-) appears next to the cursor **50**.

3. Click. The point is deleted.

TIP You can also delete a point from a path by selecting it with the Subselection tool *(see page 76)* and then pressing the delete/backspace key.

TIP If the anchor point has control handles, you must first click to delete the handles, then click again to delete the point.

TIP If you do not want to add or delete points on a path, hold the Shift key before you click with the Pen. This overrides the add points or delete points features of the Pen tool **51**.

You can also use the Pen tool to change between the two types of anchor points: corner and curved. For instance, you can change a curve point into a corner point.

To convert a curve point:

1. Position the Pen tool over the point you want to convert. A small caret (^) indicates that the point will be converted **52**.

2. Click. The Bézier handles of the point retract.

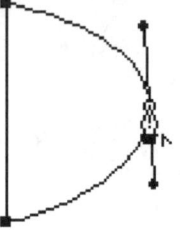

52 *Click with the Pen tool to* **convert a curve point to a corner point**.

It's a little trickier to convert a corner point into a curve point.

To convert a corner point:

1. Position the Pen tool over the point you want to convert. Although the minus sign appears, ignore it.

2. Press and drag with the Pen tool. Bézier handles appear as the point is converted into a curve point **53**.

TIP Hold the Shift key to prevent the Pen tool from converting or deleting points. Rather, you can click or drag to add one point directly on an existing point.

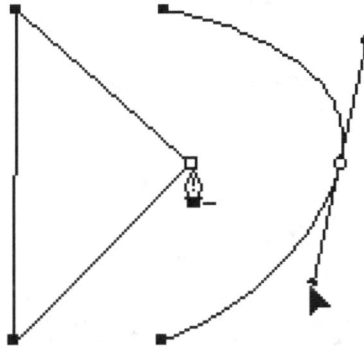

53 *Drag with the Pen tool to* **convert a curve point to a corner point**. *(Ignore the minus sign.)*

You can also use the Pen tool to close an existing open path.

To close an existing open path:

1. Use either the Pointer or the Subselection tool to select the path.

2. Position the Pen tool over one of the end points of the path. A small caret (^) appears next to the Pen cursor **54**.

3. Click or drag with the Pen tool.

4. Move the Pen tool over the other end point. A small circle appears next to the Pen cursor **55**.

5. Click or drag to close the path.

54 *Click the Pen tool over an endpoint to* **begin closing an open path**.

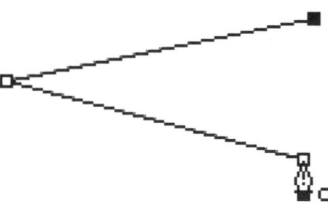

55 *Click the Pen tool over the second endpoint to* **finish closing an open path**.

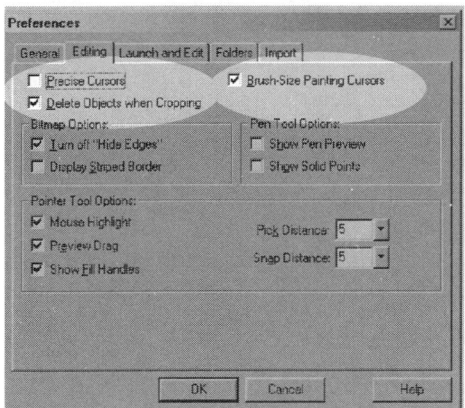

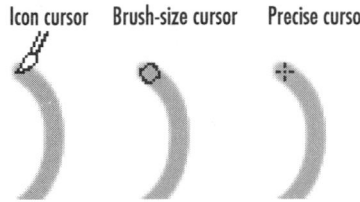

⑤ *The* **Precise Cursors** *and* **Brush-Size Painting Cursors** *in the Editing preferences control the appearance of the brush cursors.*

Icon cursor   Brush-size cursor   Precise cursor

⑤⑦ *An example of the cursors for the Vector Path and Redraw Path tools.*

Setting the Cursor Displays

You can control the appearance of the cursors for the Vector Path tool and the Redraw Path tool. This also controls the appearance of the cursors for the bitmap tools *(see Chapter 10, "Working with Bitmaps.")*

To change the cursor displays:

1. Choose **Edit** > **Preferences** to open the Preferences dialog box.

   or

   (Mac OS X) Choose **Fireworks** > **Preferences**.

2. Click the Editing tab (Win) or choose Editing from the menu (Mac). This shows the Editing preferences **⑤**.

3. Select Brush-Size Painting Cursors to display the tool cursor as the size of the stroke width **⑤⑦**.

   or

   Deselect Brush-Size Painting Cursors to display the tool cursor as the icon for the tool **⑤⑦**.

4. Select Precise Cursors to change the icon cursor into a cross-hair cursor.

   or

   Deselect Precise Cursors to see the icon cursor for the tool.

   TIP Press the Caps Lock key to change the setting of the Precise Cursors preference without opening the Preference dialog box.

SELECTING PATHS 5

When I was young, we didn't have personal computers. (Hey, that doesn't make me *that* old!) Instead of computer graphics, we had other types of arts and graphics. (Yes, arts and graphics existed before computers.) One of my favorites was nail-and-string art.

You started with a plywood rectangle and spent the entire morning hammering thin nails into the wood in a grid pattern. This was the noisy part. After lunch, you took colored strings and wrapped them around the nails to create shapes—a much quieter activity.

That's why I enjoy working with the vector paths in Macromedia Fireworks. The anchor points are like the nails and the paths are the string. I could say that the mouse is like the hammer, but it's much too quiet for that.

Unlike the nails of my old art projects, however, Fireworks anchor points are much more flexible. This chapter shows that instead of pulling out each nail when you want to change a design, you use Fireworks's selection tools to select and move anchor points and objects. (That's bound to save you a few headaches.)

Selecting Entire Objects

The main selection aid in Fireworks is the Pointer tool. The Pointer tool selects objects as complete paths, not individual points.

To use the Pointer tool:

1. Click the Pointer tool in the Tools panel ❶.

TIP Hold the Cmd/Ctrl key to temporarily access the Pointer tool while working in any other tool. Release the key to return to the original tool.

2. Position the Pointer arrow over an object and click. A highlight color appears along the path indicating that the object is selected ❷. *(See page 80 for how to turn off or change the higlight color.)*

TIP If the object has no fill color, you must click the path or stroke color to select the object.

TIP If you are working in the Draft Display mode *(see page 35)*, you must click the path directly to select the object.

You can also select many objects at once by dragging a marquee with the Pointer tool.

To select objects with a marquee:

1. Place the Pointer tool outside the area of the objects you want to select.

2. Drag diagonally with the Pointer tool to create a rectangle that encloses your selection.

3. Release the mouse button. All objects inside the rectangle are selected ❸.

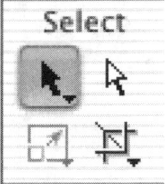

❶ *The* **Pointer tool** *in the Tools panel.*

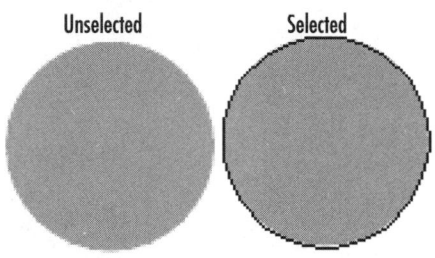

Unselected   Selected

❷ *A highlight color appears on the path of a selected object.*

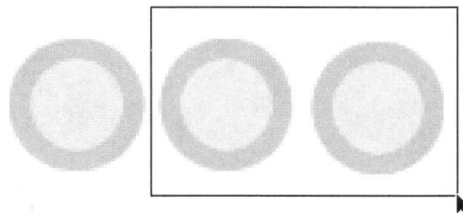

❸ *Drag with the Pointer tool to* **select objects within the rectangular marquee.**

Selecting Methods

With all the different ways to select objects, you might ask: Which one is the best way?

The best way depends on where your hands are, what tool is currently chosen, and how many objects you want to select. And there's an element of personal preference.

For instance, if you want to select all the objects on a page except one, it might be easier to use the Select All command and then Shift-click to deselect an individual object.

If you want to select all the objects on the left side of the page, it may be quicker to drag to select the objects within a rectangular marquee.

There are many times I see my students laboriously clicking, one-by-one, to select objects. Before you start clicking, consider the selection options, then think about what would be the most efficient way to select the objects.

Once you have a selection of objects, you can add objects to, or subtract from, the selection.

To add objects to a selection:

◆ Hold the Shift key and click to select any additional objects.

To subtract objects from a selection:

◆ Hold the Shift key and click to deselect any objects.

TIP Sometimes it is easier to select a group of objects within a marquee and then use the Shift key to deselect the one or two you do not want as part of the selection.

In addition to the selection tools available from the Tools panel, you can use the commands from the Select menu to select and deselect objects.

To select objects using menu commands:

◆ Choose **Select** > **Select All** to select all the objects in a file.

TIP The Select All command does not select objects on locked or hidden layers or if the Layer is set to Single Layer Editing. *(See pages 103 – 106 for information on working with layers.)*

To deselect objects using menu commands:

Choose **Select** > **Deselect** to deselect any selected objects.

TIP The menu commands can also be used when working with the bitmap selection tools *(see Chapter 10, "Working with Bitmaps")*.

TIP You can also deselect any objects in a file by clicking the empty space in a document with the Pointer tool.

Selecting Entire Objects

Selecting Points

Instead of selecting an entire object, you can also select individual points. You can then manipulate or delete them to change the shape of the path. The Subselection tool is used to select individual anchor points.

To use the Subselection tool:

1. Click the Subselection tool in the Tools panel ❹.

2. Click the object to select it. The anchor points will be displayed but not selected ❺.

TIP The Pen tool options determine the appearance of selected and unselected points *(see page 61)*.

3. Click a specific point or marquee-drag to select multiple points. The anchor points of the object will be selected.

4. Hold the Shift key and click to select additional points.

5. Use the Subselection tool to move the selected points ❻.

TIP If you switch from the Pointer tool to the Subselection tool while an object is already selected, you see the unselected anchor points for that object.

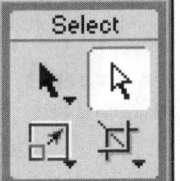

❹ *The* **Subselection tool** *in the Tools panel.*

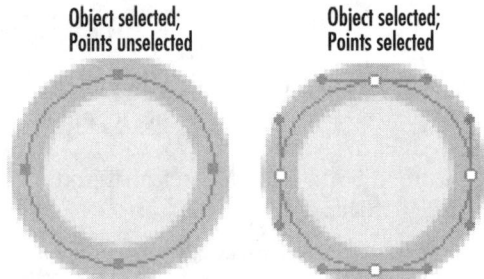

Object selected; Points unselected   Object selected; Points selected

❺ *The Subselection tool allows you to see the anchor points and handles of a selected object. Click to select the specific points.*

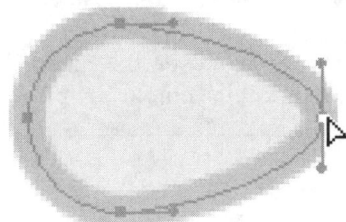

❻ *Drag with the Subselection tool to change the position of anchor points.*

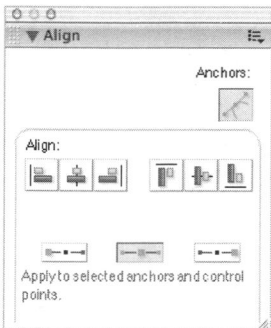

➐ *The* **Align panel** *set to aligning anchor points and control handles.*

Preceeding handle   Anchor point   Succeeding handle

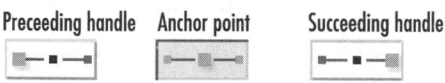

➑ *Click one of the* **handle control icons** *to choose which elements should be aligned.*

| Left Edge | Horizontal Center | Right Edge | Top Edge | Vertical Center | Bottom Edge |

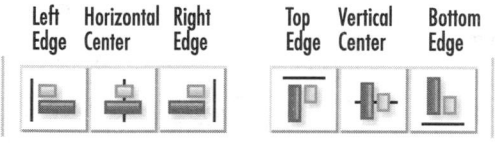

➒ *The* **Align icons** *for aligning points and handles.*

Aligning Points and Handles

As you select and move points and handles, you may want them to be neatly lined up with each other. Rather than drag guides all over your page, you can use the Align panel.

To align points and handles:

1. If the Align panel is not visible, choose **Window > Align**.

2. Click the the Anchors icon in the Align panel to display the options for aligning points and handles **➐**.

   TIP Click the Anchors icon again to return the Align panel to the options for aligning objects. *(See pages 97–101 for how to align objects using the Align panel.)*

3. Use the Subselection tool to select the points you want to align.

   TIP Drag a marquee around the points or use the Shift key to select multiple points.

4. Click one of the three handle control icons to choose which elements will be used as the basis for alignment **➑**:

   - **Preceeding handle** aligns the control handle that goes into the anchor point. This can change the length of its handle.
   - **Anchor point** aligns the anchor point but does not change the length of its control handle.
   - **Succeeding handle** aligns the control handle that extends out from the anchor point. This can change the length of the handle.

5. Click one of the Align icons in the panel **➒**. The points are aligned.

Aligning Points and Handles

Selecting Objects Behind Objects

Because transparency often figures into creating Fireworks graphics, you may find that your artwork consists of many objects stacked on top of each other. This can sometimes make it difficult to select an object behind the rest. The Select Behind tool makes it easy to select through other objects to one at the back.

To use the Select Behind tool:

1. Choose the Select Behind tool from the Tools panel ⑩. If the Select Behind tool is not visible, click the pop-up group to choose the Select Behind tool.

2. Click with the Select Behind tool over the objects you want to select. The first click selects the object on top of the others.

3. Click as many times as necessary to select the object you want ⑪.

TIP Hold the Shift key as you click to add each object to the selection. (In case you were wondering, no—you can't use the Select Behind tool to deselect behind.)

TIP The Select Behind tool was very important when working in the early versions of Fireworks that did not have a Layers panel. Today you can use the Layers panel to select objects behind others *(see page 103)*.

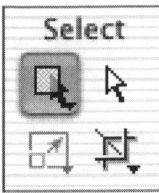

⑩ *The* **Select Behind tool** *in the Tools panel.*

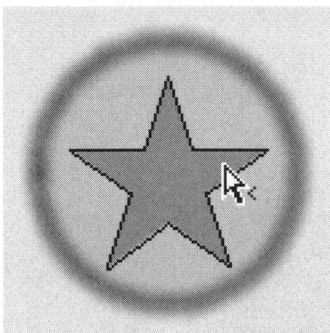

⑪ *The* **Select Behind tool** *was used to select the star behind the other two objects. The first click selected the square. The second click selected the circle. The third click selected the star.*

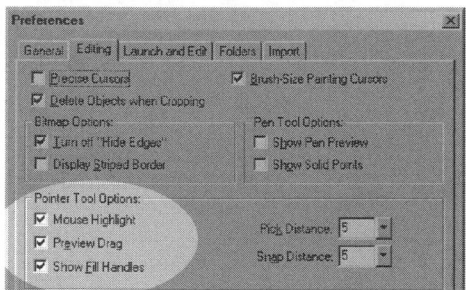

⓬ *The* **Pointer Tool Options** *in the Editing Preferences.*

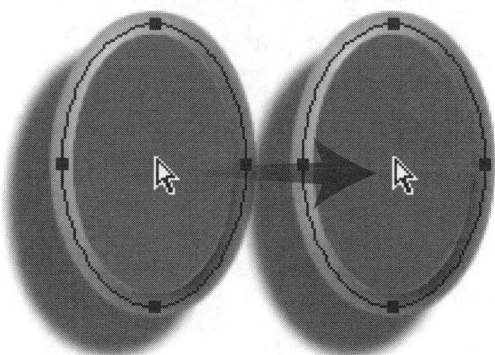

⓭ *When the* **Preview Drag option is turned on** *you can see the fill, stroke, and effects applied to an object as you move it.*

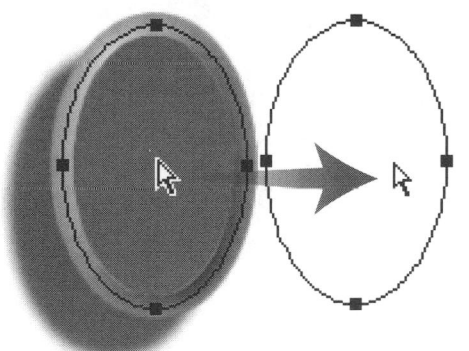

⓮ *When the* **Preview Drag option is turned off** *you only see the shape of an object as you move it.*

Controlling Selections

Fireworks gives you several options for the Pointer tool, Subselection tool, and Select Behind tool that make it easier to select and move objects. The Mouse Highlight feature helps you know which object is about to be selected with the next click.

TIP The final option for the Pointer tool, Show Fill Handles, is used when working with gradients *(see Chapter 7, "Fills")*.

To set the Mouse Highlight:

1. Choose **Edit** > **Preferences** to open the Preferences dialog box.

   or

   (Mac OS X) Choose **Fireworks** > **Preferences.**

2. Click the Editing tab (Win) or choose Editing from the menu (Mac) to display the editing preferences **⓬**.

3. Select Mouse Highlight. This adds a highlight around the object that will be selected with the next mouse click.

The Preview Drag option controls what the object looks like as you move it.

To set the Preview Drag:

1. Choose **Edit** > **Preferences** to open the Preferences dialog box.

   or

   (Mac OS X) Choose **Fireworks** > **Preferences.**

2. Click the Editing tab (Win) or choose Editing from the menu (Mac) to display the editing preferences **⓬**.

3. Select Preview Drag in the Options panel. This enables you to see the fill, stroke, and effects applied to an object as you move it **⓭**. With Preview Drag turned off, you see only the object's shape **⓮**.

If you find that the highlight effect interferes with your work, you can hide the highlight while keeping the object selected.

To control the highlight of selected objects:

◆ Choose **View** > **Hide Edges**. This hides the highlight along the path of an object.

or

To reveal the highlight, choose **View** > **Hide Edges** when there is a checkmark in front of the command.

TIP Anchor points and control handles are still visible when the Hide Edges command is applied **⑮**.

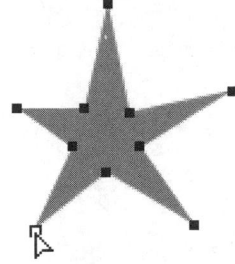

⑮ *The* **Hide Edges command** *hides the highlight along a path but keeps the anchor points and control handles visible when you use the Subselection tool.*

You may not be able to see the path highlight color if it is too similar to the color of the brush stroke around an object or the color of the canvas. You can use the Preferences to change the path highlight color.

To change the highlight color:

1. Choose **Edit** > **Preferences** (Mac OS 9 or Win) to open the Preferences dialog box.

or

Choose **Fireworks** > **Preferences** (Mac OS X).

2. Click the Highlight Color Well. The swatches appear **⑯**.

3. Choose the color for the highlight.

4. Click OK to close the dialog box.

TIP The highlight color is an application preference. Changing it changes the highlight color for all Fireworks documents.

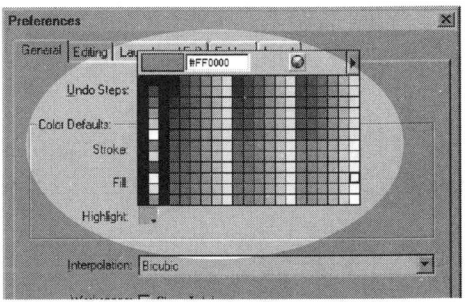

⑯ *Use the* **Highlight color well in the Preferences dialog box** *to change the color of the path highlight.*

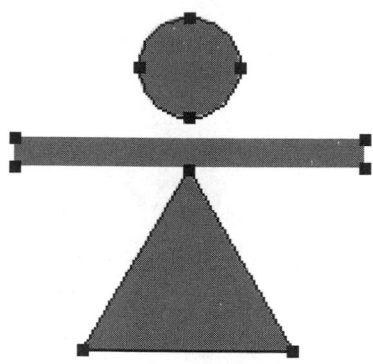

⑰ Selected **ungrouped objects** *display their individual anchor points.*

⑱ Selected **grouped objects** *display four points around the items in the group.*

Automatic Groups

The rectangles created by the Rectangle and Rounded Rectangle tools are automatically grouped. This is so you can change the roundness of the corners at any time.

If you ungroup them, you will not be able to change the roundness of the corners. The round corners will be converted into anchor points with handles.

Working with Groups

If you have a graphic that consists of several objects and text, you may find it easier to select them all together as a unit, or group.

To group selected objects:

1. Select two or more objects. Anchor points appear around the individual objects indicating they are not in a group **⑰**.

2. Choose **Modify** >**Group**. Small anchor points appear around the objects indicating that they are grouped together **⑱**.

To ungroup objects:

1. Select the grouped objects.

2. Choose **Modify** >**Ungroup** to release the objects from the group.

TIP (Win) You can also use the Group/Ungroup icons on the Modify toolbar.

Grouped objects are considered a single object. However, you do not have to ungroup to select a specific object within the group.

To select objects within groups:

1. Choose either the Pointer, Subselection, or Select Behind tool.

2. Hold the Opt/Alt key and click the individual object of the group.

TIP Hold the Shift and Opt/Alt keys to add other items to the selection.

TIP If you want to move the object, be sure to release the Opt/Alt key before you start to drag or you will make a copy of the object *(see page 85).*

Working with Groups

Groups can be nested within other groups so that one group contains subgroups. The Subselect and Superselect commands then make it easy to work with nested groups.

To create a nested group:

1. Select two or more groups or one group and some other objects 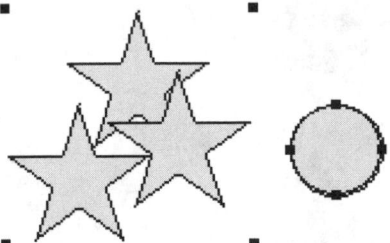.

2. Choose **Modify** > **Group**. The original selections are now subgroups of the new group ⑳.

3. Continue to select additional objects and choose the Group command to create more nested groups.

⑲ *The group of stars on the left is selected along with the circle on the right.*

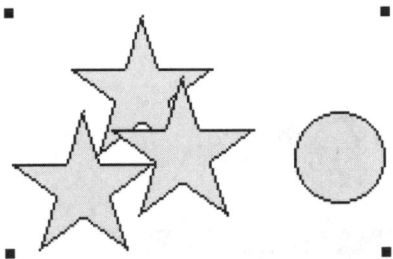

Once you group objects, you don't have to ungroup them to select the members of a group. The Subselect command lets you select a group and then easily select the individual members of the group.

To use the Subselect command:

1. Select a nested group.

2. Choose **Select** > **Subselect**. This lets you see and work with the original objects of the nested group.

TIP You can also use the Subselect tool to select individual objects within a group.

⑳ *When the group of stars and circle are grouped, a nested group is created.*

The Superselect command lets you select an individual object in a group and then easily select the entire group. This makes it easy to select different objects within a nested group.

To use the Superselect command:

1. Select a single item in a nested group.

2. Choose **Select** > **Superselect**. This selects the group that contains the selection.

TIP You can reapply both the Subselect and Superselect commands to further select groups within nested groups.

WORKING WITH OBJECTS 6

In addition to the nail-and-string art I played with as a child, I also had an art toy called Colorforms®. It consisted of shiny black pages onto which I could place cutout vinyl shapes. The vinyl pieces stuck to the black pages without any glue or tape, which I found quite remarkable. I could put them down and pick them up and move them around however I wanted, creating all sorts of patterns and pictures.

Forty plus years later, as I play with Macromedia Fireworks, I see how similar it is to Colorforms. I can place Fireworks objects together in any combinations. They can be stacked on top of each other to create new shapes.

However, unlike the plastic Colorforms pieces, Fireworks objects are slightly more versatile. Objects on my Fireworks pages can be stretched, distorted, and otherwise transformed into unlimited variations.

Hundreds of pieces came in my Colorforms set but with Fireworks I can duplicate objects over and over. There is no limit to how many objects I can have on the page. Not only that, Fireworks objects don't ever get lost under the cushions of the couch!

Moving Objects

It's not critical where you originally create an object. You can always select it and move it to a new position. Or you can change its numeric coordinates in the Info panel.

To move an object by eye:

1. Use any of the selection tools to select the object.

2. Drag the object to the new position.

TIP Place your cursor anywhere on the object — except on a point to avoid reshaping the object.

TIP Once you have selected an object, you can move it by pressing the arrow keys on the keyboard.

To move an object numerically:

1. Select the object.

2. Choose **Window > Info** to open the Info panel **1**.

   or

   Choose **Window > Properties** and view the information fields **2**.

3. Change the number in the X field to set the position of the left edge.

4. Change the number in the Y field to set the position of the top edge.

5. If necessary, press Return/Enter to apply the new settings.

TIP The Info panel also gives you readouts of the color and alpha transparency settings under the current cursor positions. *(For more information on using the Info panel to display color and alpha transparency settings, see page 50.)*

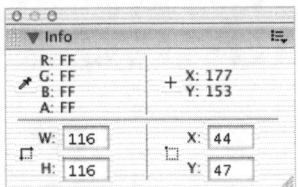

1 The **Info panel** *gives you the numerical coordinates for the position and size of objects.*

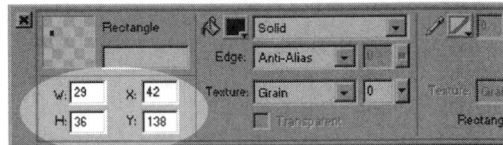

2 The **Info area in the Property Inspector** *also contains the object coordinates.*

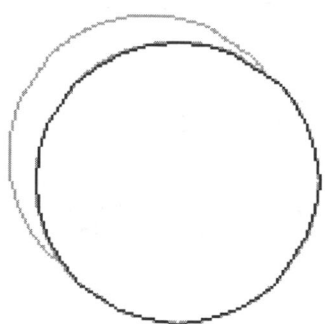

③ *The* **Duplicate command** *copies the selected object significantly offset from the original. But the Clone command places a copy right on top of the original.*

The Computer Clipboard

The Copy and Cut commands place objects into an area of the computer memory called the Clipboard. The contents of the Clipboard stay within the memory until a new object is copied or the computer is turned off.

The Clipboard can only hold one set of information at a time. So, if you copy one item, and then later copy another, the first object is flushed from the Clipboard and replaced by the second.

Using the Clone, Duplicate, Drag and Drop, and Opt/Alt-Drag techniques allows you to make copies of objects without losing the current contents of the Clipboard.

Duplicating Objects

You can easily duplicate objects in a variety of ways. Like many other programs, Fireworks lets you duplicate objects using the Copy and Paste commands.

To copy and paste an object:

1. Select the object.

2. Choose **Edit > Copy**.

3. Choose **Edit > Paste** to paste the object into the same position as the original.

4. Move the object to a new position.

The Clone command creates a duplicate of the object in the same position as the original.

TIP The Clone command is similar to using the Copy and Paste commands. However, the Clone command works in one step and does not replace the contents of the clipboard *(see the sidebar on this page).*

To clone an object:

1. Select the object.

2. Choose **Edit > Clone**.

The Duplicate command creates a duplicate of the object slightly offset from the original. This makes it easy to see the duplicate.

To duplicate an object:

1. Select the object.

2. Choose **Edit > Duplicate**. The duplicate appears offset from the original **③**.

Duplicating Objects

Perhaps the fastest and easiest way to duplicate an object is to copy it as you move it. This is commonly called an Option-drag or an Alt-drag.

To copy an object as you move it:

1. Choose any of the selection tools.

2. Hold the Opt/Alt key and drag the object. A small plus sign (+) appears next to the cursor ❹.

3. Release the mouse button. The copy appears.

❹ *Hold the Opt/Alt key as you move an object to* **create a copy of that object while leaving the original in place**.

You can also drag and drop objects from one Fireworks document to another.

TIP You can also drag and drop between other applications. However, this may convert Fireworks objects into non-editable images.

To drag and drop an object:

1. Position two document windows so that both are visible.

2. Use any of the selection tools to drag an object from one document to the other.

3. Release the mouse button. A copy of the object appears in the new document ❺.

TIP Clone, Duplicate, Drag and Drop, and Opt/Alt-Drag leave the contents of the Clipboard unchanged. *(See the sidebar on the previous page for a discussion of working with the Clipboard.)*

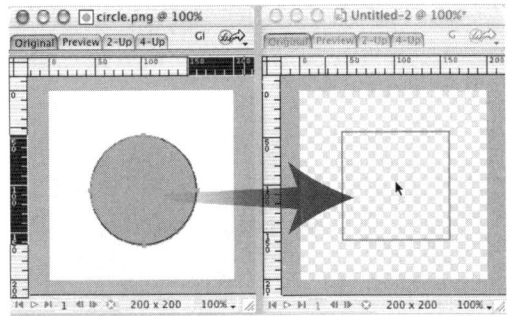

❺ *You can* **drag and drop an object** *from one document to another.*

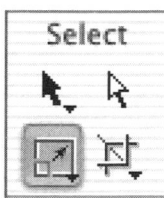

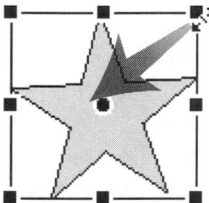

6 *The Scale tool in the Tools panel.*

7 **Drag a corner handle with the Scale tool** *to change the horizontal and vertical dimensions of an object.*

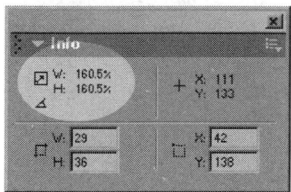

8 *The Info Panel displays the scaling percentages as you drag with the Scale tool.*

Cancelling a Transformation

If you change your mind in the middle of using the bounding box handles, you can exit the transformation mode by pressing Command/Ctrl-period.

Transforming Objects

Transformations change the size, shape, or orientation of an object. Fireworks provides many different ways to transform objects.

The Scale tool changes an object's size.

To scale an object:

1. Choose the Scale tool in the Tools panel **6**.

   or

   Choose **Modify > Transform > Scale**. The transformation handles appear on a bounding box around the object.

2. Place the cursor directly over any of the handles. A small double-headed arrow appears.

3. Drag a handle toward the object to reduce it or away to enlarge it **7**.

   TIP Drag one of the corner handles to scale both the horizontal and vertical dimensions of the object.

   TIP Drag an edge handle to change just the horizontal or vertical dimension.

4. Double-click within the bounding box to apply the transformation.

   or

   Press Return/Enter.

   TIP As you use the Scale tool, the Info panel shows the percentage amount of the scaling **8**.

   TIP You can use the W and H fields in the Info panel to change the width and height of an object.

   TIP You can also click the Match Size buttons in the Align panel to make two objects the same size *(see page 100)*.

   TIP You can also use the bounding box handles to rotate an object *(see page 90)*.

Transforming Objects

Transforming Objects

The Skew tool distorts an object by moving two sides of the bounding box together or two control handles in opposite directions. Skewing creates a perspective effect for objects or for text *(see page 189)*.

To skew an object:

1. Choose the Skew tool in the Tools panel ❾.

   or

   Choose **Modify > Transform > Skew**. The transformation handles appear around the object.

2. Place the cursor directly over any of the handles.

3. Drag one of the corner handles in or out to move that handle and the one opposite it. This changes the dimension of that side of the object ❿.

4. Drag one of the side handles to change the angle of that side of the object ⓫.

5. Double-click within the box created by the transformation handles to apply the transformation.

   or

   Press Return/Enter.

TIP As you use the Skew tool, the Info panel shows the length of distortion along the X and Y axes ⓬.

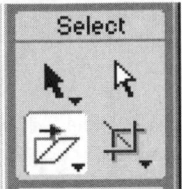

❾ *The* **Skew tool** *in the Tools panel.*

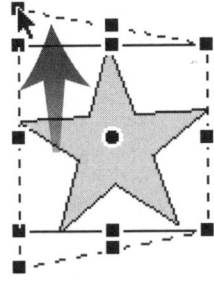

❿ **Drag a corner handle with the Skew tool** *to change the dimension of that side of the object.*

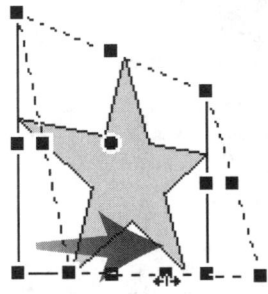

⓫ **Drag a side handle with the Skew tool** *to change the angles along that side of the object.*

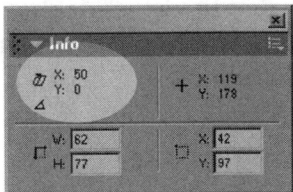

⓬ *The* **Info Panel** *displays the skew amounts as you drag with the Skew tool.*

⓭ *The* **Distort tool** *in the Tools panel.*

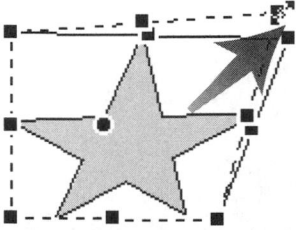

⓮ **Drag a handle with the Distort tool** *to change the shape of an object.*

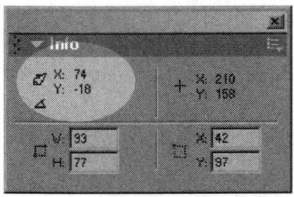

⓯ **The Info Panel displays the x and y coordinates** *of the distorted points as you drag with the Distort tool.*

The Distort tool allows you to modify the proportions of an object by changing the shape of the box that defines it. Unlike the skew transformation, a distort transformation lets you manipulate each corner handle individually.

To distort an object:

1. Choose the Distort tool in the Tools panel ⓭.

   or

   Choose **Modify > Transform > Distort**. The transformation handles appear around the object.

2. Place the cursor directly over a handle.

3. Drag to change the shape of the object ⓮.

4. Double-click within the bounding box to apply the transformation.

   or

   Press Return/Enter.

TIP As you use the Distort tool, the Info panel shows the new coordinates of the points ⓯.

Switching Transformation Tools

You can apply more than one transformation tool at a time. Instead of pressing Return/Enter to apply the transformation, switch to a different tool. Then manipulate the handles as desired.

This means you can scale an object, skew it, and distort it all at once. When you finally like the effect, you can then apply the transformation by pressing Return/Enter.

Transforming Objects

When you use any of the transformation tools, you have an additional transformation option available: rotation.

To rotate an object:

1. Choose any of the Transformation tools.

2. Position the cursor outside the handles. A rounded arrow appears.

3. Drag either clockwise or counterclockwise to rotate the object 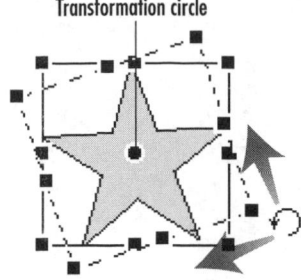.

TIP Move the small circle inside the bounding box to change the point around which the object rotates.

4. Double-click within the box created by the transformation handles to apply the transformation.

    or

    Press Return/Enter.

TIP As you use the rotation cursor, the Info panel shows the angle of the rotation ⑰.

⑯ Drag with the Rotation cursor *to change the orientation of an object.*

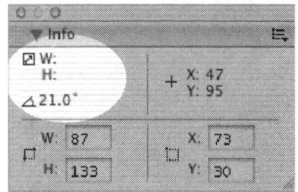

⑰ The Info Panel displays the angle of rotation *as you use the rotation mode of the transformation tools.*

You can also move an object while in the transformation mode.

To move an object in the transformation mode:

1. Position the cursor inside the box created by the transformation handles. A four-headed arrow appears ⑱.

2. Drag to move the object.

3. Continue working with the transformation tools or apply the transformation by double-clicking within the box created by the transformation handles.

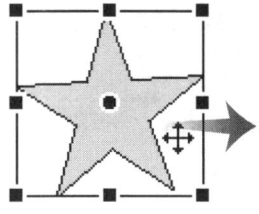

⑱ The four-headed arrow *appears when you move an object in a transformation mode.*

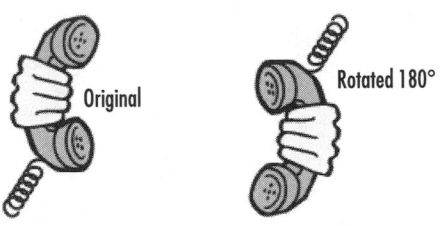

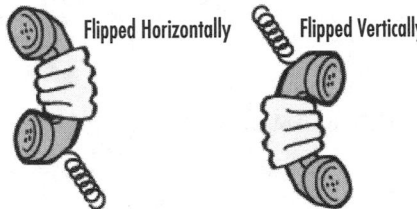

Fireworks also gives you a set of Transformation menu commands that make it easy to rotate or flip objects ⑲.

To use the Transform menu commands:

1. Select an object.

2. Choose one of the following commands to rotate the object:
   - **Modify** > Transform > Rotate 180° turns the object upside down.
   - **Modify** > Transform > Rotate 90° CW rotates the object 90 degrees clockwise.
   - **Modify** > Transform > Rotate 90° CCW rotates the object 90 degrees counterclockwise.

3. Choose one of the following commands to flip the object:
   - **Modify** > Transform > Flip Horizontal flips the object along its horizontal axis.
   - **Modify** > Transform > Flip Vertical flips the object along its vertical axis.

(Win) To use the Transform menu commands:

◆ Use the rotate buttons on the Modify toolbar to apply rotations ⑳.

⑲ *The effects of the* **Transform menu commands** *on the original object.*

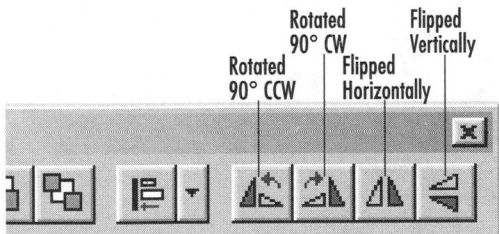

⑳ *The* **Modify toolbar** (Win) *contains icons that rotate and flip objects.*

Transforming Objects

The Numeric Transform dialog box makes it easy to scale, resize, or rotate an object using precise values, rather than by judging by eye.

To use the Numeric Transform dialog box:

1. Select an object.

2. Choose a command from the **Modify > Transform > Numeric Transform**. The Numeric Transform dialog box appears **㉑**.

3. Use the menu to choose Scale, Resize, or Rotate.

4. In Scale mode, enter the percentage of change in the width or height fields **㉑**.

   or

   In Resize mode, enter the pixel amount in the width or height fields **㉒**.

   or

   In Rotate mode, use the wheel or enter the angle in the field **㉓**.

5. In Scale or Resize modes, select Constrain Proportions to keep the horizontal and vertical dimensions in proportion to the original object.

6. Check Scale Attributes to scale any fills, strokes, or effects applied to the object **㉔**.

   TIP Choose Scale Attributes in the Info panel menu to control how attributes are transformed by the Scale, Skew, or Distort tools.

7. Click OK to apply the transformation.

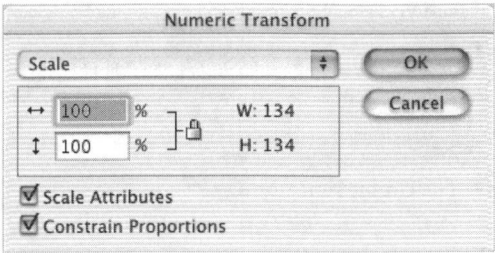

㉑ *The* **Scale controls** *in the Numeric Transform dialog box.*

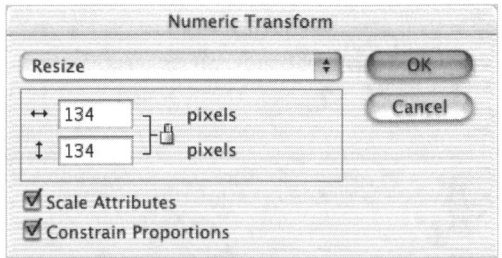

㉒ *The* **Resize controls** *in the Numeric Transform dialog box.*

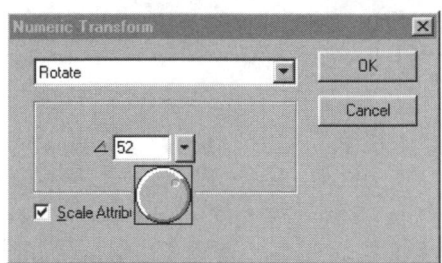

㉓ *The* **Rotate controls** *in the Numeric Transform dialog box.*

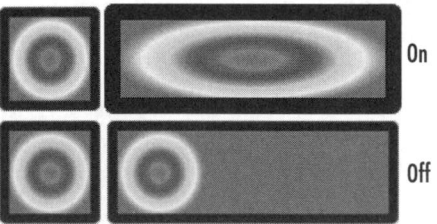

㉔ *The* **Scale Attributes option** *controls whether attributes, such as the stroke and gradient fill, scale during transformations.*

Transforming Objects

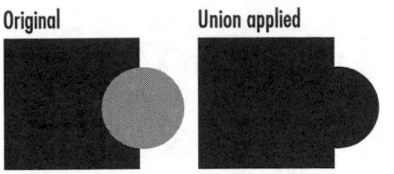

25 *The* **Union command** *forms one object from two or more overlapping objects.*

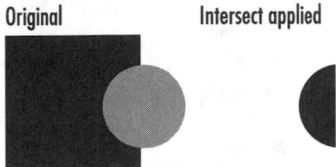

26 *The* **Intersect command** *creates an object just where two or more objects overlap.*

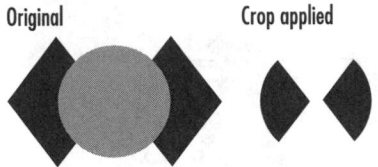

27 *The* **Crop command** *trims away all the area outside the top object.*

Combining Vector Objects

One of the secrets to working with vector objects is to combine simple paths into more complex shapes. In Fireworks you use the Combine Paths commands.

TIP The Combine Paths commands are similar to the Path Operations found in programs such as Adobe Illustrator or Macromedia FreeHand.

The Union command lets you unite objects into a single path.

To unite objects:

1. Select two or more overlapping objects.

2. Choose **Modify** > **Combine Paths** > **Union**. The path of the new object follows the path of the overlapping objects **25**.

The Intersect command creates a new object where objects overlap.

To form the intersection of objects:

1. Select two or more overlapping objects.

2. Choose **Modify** > **Combine Paths** > **Intersect**. The path of the new object follows the shape where the paths overlap **26**.

The Crop command trims objects based on the shape of the topmost object.

To crop objects:

1. Select three or more overlapping objects.

2. Choose **Modify** > **Combine Paths** > **Crop**. This trims away parts of the paths that were outside the original top object **27**.

TIP The objects created by the Combine commands take their appearance from the bottommost object.

Combining Vector Objects

The Combine Paths menu contains two commands that let you use one object to punch a hole in another so what's behind shows through.

To create a hole:

1. Place one object so that it is completely inside the path of other objects below it.

2. Choose **Modify** > **Combine Paths** > **Punch**.

   or

   Choose **Modify** > **Combine Paths** > **Join**. The top object punches holes in all the objects below it 🔢.

🔲 The difference between Punch and Join has to do with what happens when the top object is not completely contained inside the objects below it.

The Punch command uses the top object to carve out a shape from the objects below 🔢. The Join command creates a hole only where the objects overlap but keeps the rest of the path visible 🔢.

Once you have created holes using the Punch or Join commands, you must split them to move or modify the individual objects.

To split objects joined together:

1. Select the objects joined together by the Punch or Join commands.

2. Choose **Modify** > **Combine Paths** > **Split**. The object that created the hole is separated from the object below.

🔲 The Split command does not restore objects to their original colors. Objects that were joined and then split will have the same attributes.

🔢 *The* **Punch or Join commands** *create holes that let you see through one object to the canvas and objects below.*

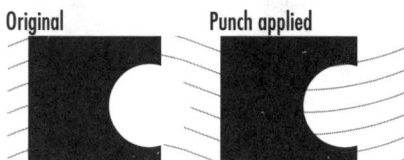

🔢 *When two objects are partially overlapped, the the* **Punch command** *carves a shape out of the bottom object.*

🔢 *When two objects are partially overlapped, the the* **Join command** *creates a hole only where the objects overlap each other.*

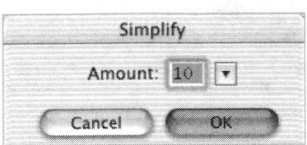

31 *The* **Simplify** *dialog box.*

Original object

After Simplify command

32 *The* **Simplify** command *reduces the number of points on a path.*

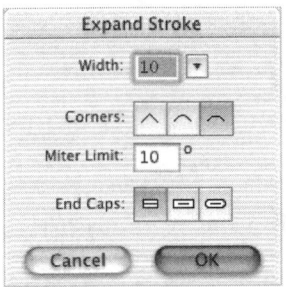

33 *The* **Expand Stroke** *dialog box.*

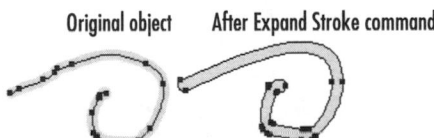

Original object   After Expand Stroke command

34 *The* **Expand Stroke** command *converts an open path into a filled shape.*

Using the Alter Path Commands

You can also change the shape of paths using the two Alter Path commands, Simplify and Expand Stroke. The Simplify command lets you reduce the number of points on a path. Fewer points makes it easier to reshape objects.

To simplify the shape of a path:

1. Select a path.

2. Choose **Modify** > **Alter Path** > **Simplify**. The Simplify dialog box appears **31**.

3. Enter an amount of simplification in the dialog box and click OK. Fireworks removes as many points as possible to simplify the path **32**.

TIP The higher the number, the greater the distortion that may occur.

You can also convert an open path into a closed path. This lets you apply a fill such as a pattern or a gradient *(see Chapter 7, "Fills")*.

To expand a path:

1. Select a path.

2. Choose **Modify** > **Alter Path** > **Expand Stroke**. The Expand Stroke dialog box appears **33**.

3. Enter the desired width or thickness of the path (in pixels).

4. Set the shape of the corners.

5. Enter an amount for the Miter Limit to control the length of the points of any corners.

6. Set the shape of the ends of the path.

7. Click OK. The path is converted into a filled shape **34**.

TIP The Expand Stroke command punches a hole in a closed path.

Fireworks also lets you increase or decrease the size of a path using the Inset Path command.

To inset a path:

1. Select a path you want to inset.

2. Choose **Modify** > **Alter Path** > **Inset Path**. The Inset Path dialog box appears ③⑤.

3. Choose the direction of the inset. Inside moves the contours of the path inside the original object. Outside moves the contours of the path outside the original object.

4. Enter the width or amount that the path should be changed.

5. Set the shape of the corners.

6. Enter an amount for the Miter Limit to control the spikes of any corners.

7. Click OK. The path is converted into a filled shape.

TIP Use the Clone command before applying the Inset Path. This keeps the original image and moves the object created by the Inset Path command inside or outside the original.

TIP While it might seem like Inset Path is the same as the Scale command *(see pages 87 or 92)*, it actually allows you to create a smaller or larger path that follows the contours of the original.

For example, the Scale command could never have created a path that fit inside the original object shown in ③⑥.

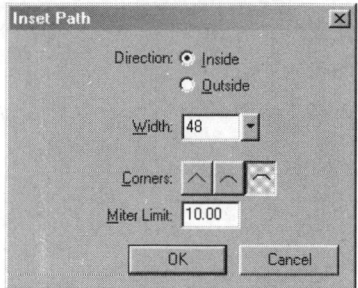

③⑤ *The* **Inset Path dialog box**.

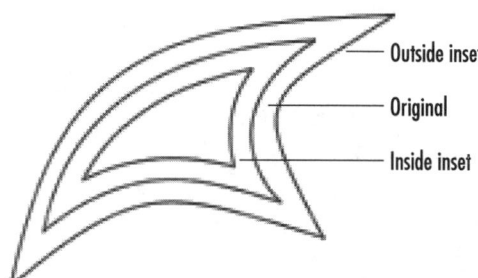

Outside inset

Original

Inside inset

③⑥ *The* **Inset Path command** *changes the shape of the object so that it lies inside or outside the original.*

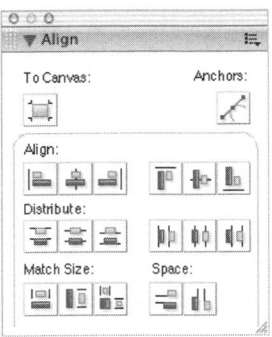

❸ *The* **Align** *panel.*

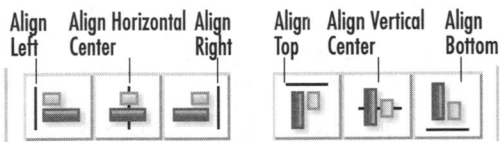

❸ *The* **Align icons** *in the Align panel.*

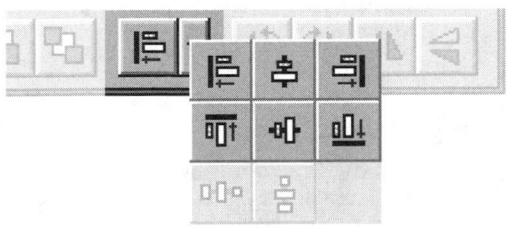

❸ *(Win) The* **alignment icons** *in the Modify toolbar.*

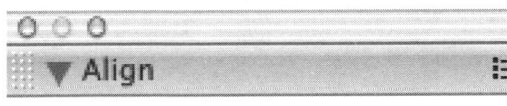

❹ *Select the* **To Canvas button** *to change the align panel so that objects are aligned or distributed to the canvas.*

Aligning Objects

Fireworks has a very handy Align panel that makes it easy to arrange objects so they all line up with their edges or centers along the same line. This is very helpful when creating navigational elements. See page 101 for a chart **❹** that displays how each of the align panel commands positions objects.

To align objects to each other:

1. Choose **Window** > **Align** to open the Align panel **❸**.

2. If the buttons for To Canvas or Anchors are selected (indicated by an orange highlight) deselect them.

3. Select two or more objects to align.

4. Click one of the Align icons in the panel **❸**. The objects are automatically aligned.

TIP Fireworks uses the left-most object as the point to align to on the left. It uses the right-most object to align to the right.

TIP Fireworks uses the topmost object to align to the top. It uses the bottommost object to align to the bottom.

TIP You can also choose a command from the **Modify** > **Align** submenu — for example, **Modify** > **Align** > **Left**.

TIP Windows users can choose the alignment icons in the Modify toolbar **❸**.

You can also use the canvas as an object that other objects can be aligned to.

To align objects to the canvas:

1. Click the To Canvas button so that it has an orange highlight **❹**.

2. Select one or more objects to align.

3. Click one of the Align icons in the panel. The objects are automatically aligned to the edges or centers of the canvas.

Fireworks also lets you distribute objects so they are neatly arranged with equal space between them.

To distribute objects evenly:

1. Choose **Window** > **Align** to open the Align panel 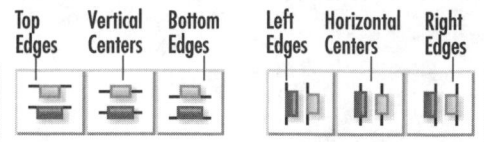.

2. If the buttons for To Canvas or Anchors are selected (indicated by an orange highlight) deselect them.

3. Select three or more objects to distribute.

4. Click one of the Distribute icons in the panel. The objects are automatically moved so they are equally distributed.

Fireworks also lets you distribute objects so they fill the entire canvas area with equal space between the edges or centers of the objects.

To distribute objects within the canvas:

1. Select the To Canvas button.

2. Select three or more objects to be distributed.

3. Click one of the Distribute icons in the panel. The objects are automatically distributed within the canvas area.

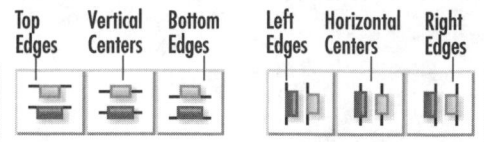

Top Edges Vertical Centers Bottom Edges   Left Edges Horizontal Centers Right Edges

41 *The* **Distribute icons** *in the Align panel.*

What's So Special About the Align Panel?

Have you noticed that the Align panel looks different from the other Fireworks panels? Unlike the other panels, the Align panel doesn't have the colors for the Windows or Macintosh operating systems.

That's because the Align panel is actually a Flash SWF movie running inside the Fireworks application. When you click one of the Align panel icons, the Flash SWF movie sends out a command to Fireworks to move or position the objects. This is similar to clicking buttons in a Flash SWF movie in a Web site. However, instead of moving to a new page, your objects are moved.

If you know JavaScript or ActionScript, you can create your own Fireworks panels. For more information see the PDF document *Extending Fireworks MX* on the Fireworks installation CD.

Aligning Objects

Space Evenly Vertically   Space Evenly Horizontally

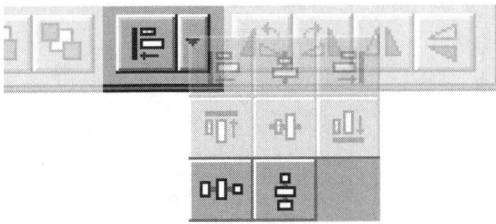

42 *The* **Space icons** *in the Align panel.*

43 *(Win) The* **distribute icons** *in the Modify toolbar.*

Align Panel Undos

There is no reset button on the Align panel. However, each click of the align panel counts as a single action. If you have clicked the wrong Align panel icon, choose **Edit** > **Undo** to get back to the original artwork.

Anchors Icon of the Align Panel?

The Anchors icon of the Align panel lets you align anchor points and control handles. For more information on working with the Anchors icon see page 77.

The distribute commands arrange objects so that there is equal space between the edges or the centers. However, if the objects are not the same size, they may not look evenly distributed on your page. That's when you need to distribute the objects by the space between the objects.

To distribute objects by space:

1. Choose **Window** > **Align** to open the Align panel **42**.

2. If the buttons for To Canvas or Anchors are selected (indicated by an orange highlight) deselect them.

3. Select three or more objects to distribute.

4. Click one of the two Space icons in the Align panel. The objects are automatically moved into the correct position.

TIP You can also choose choose **Modify** > **Align** > **Distribute Heights** or **Modify** > **Align** > **Distribute Widths**.

TIP Windows users can also choose one of the two distribute icons in the Modify toolbar **43**.

You can also distribute objects by space so they are evenly arranged within the canvas area.

To distribute objects by space within the canvas:

1. Select the To Canvas button.

2. Select three or more objects to be distributed.

3. Click one of the two Space icons in the Align panel. The objects are automatically moved into the correct position.

Aligning Objects

Strictly speaking, the next three options in the Align panel do not align objects. Rather, they resize objects so that they have the same width or height. However, since it is very helpful to have objects match their width or height when aligning objects, the icons were wisely added to the Align panel.

To match the size of objects:

1. Deselect the Canvas or Anchors icons in the Align panel.

2. Select two or more objects.

3. Click one of the Match Size icons in the Align panel ⓓ. The objects are automatically resized.

TIP Match Size always changes the smaller size for width and height to the larger size. This means that if you choose Match width and height, one object may increase its width but another object may increase its height.

You can also use the Match Size icons to force an object to the size of the canvas.

To match the size of the canvas:

1. Select the To Canvas button.

2. Select one or more objects.

3. Click one of the Match Size icons in the Align panel. The objects are automatically resized to the width or height of the canvas.

TIP The Align panel works with more than just vector objects. You can align or change the size of bitmap images, hotspots, or slices.

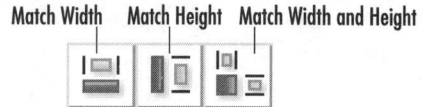

Match Width   Match Height   Match Width and Height

ⓓ *The **Match Size icons** in the Align panel.*

Aligning Other Than Objects

The Align Panel can be used to align, distribute, or resize any type of object on the Fireworks page. This includes vector objects, bitmap images, hotspots, and slices. The only things it can't affect are the marquee selections created with the bitmap selection tools *(see Chapter 10, "Working with Bitmaps")*.

Aligning Objects

Icon	Name	Objects Before Command	Objects After Command
	Align left edge		
	Align horizontal center		
	Align right edge		
	Align top edge		
	Align vertical center		
	Align bottom edge		
	Distribute top edge		
	Distribute vertical center		
	Distribute bottom edge		

Icon	Name	Objects Before Command	Objects After Command
	Distribute left edge		
	Distribute horizontal center		
	Distribute right edge		
	Space even vertically		
	Space even horizontally		
	Match width		
	Match height		
	Match width and height		

⑤ *This chart shows each of the icons in the Align panel and how they change objects.*

Arranging Objects

The order in which overlapping objects appear depends on the order in which they were created. Objects created first are at the back of their layer. Objects created later are in front. You can change the order of objects using the Arrange menu commands **46**.

To send objects to the front or back of a layer:

1. Select the object.

2. Choose **Modify** > **Arrange** > **Bring to Front** to move the object in front of all the other objects on that layer.

or

Choose **Modify** > **Arrange** > **Send to Back** to move the object behind all the other objects on that layer.

TIP (Win) You can also use the Front/Back icons on the Modify toolbar to easily move objects within a layer **47**.

Objects can also be moved forward or backward one place at a time in their layer.

To move objects forward or backward in a layer:

1. Select the object.

2. Choose **Modify** > **Arrange** > **Bring Forward** to move the object in front of the next object in the layer.

or

Choose **Modify** > **Arrange** > **Send Backward** to move the object behind the next object in the layer.

3. Repeat as necessary to put the object where you want it.

TIP (Win) You can also use the Forward/Backward icons on the Modify toolbar to easily move objects in front or behind each other.

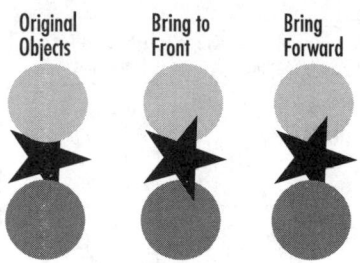

46 *The results of applying the **Arrange** menu commands to the star.*

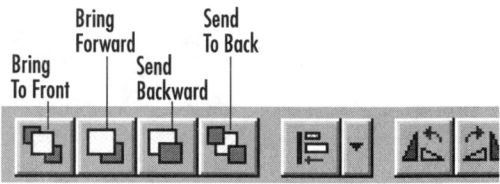

47 *(Win) The **Arrange icons** in the Modify toolbar.*

Show/Hide icon
Active layer

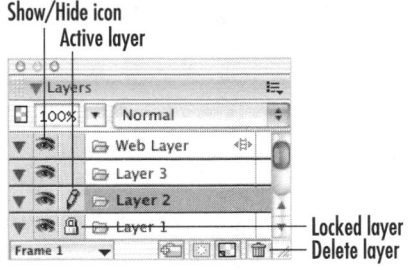

Locked layer
Delete layer

48 *The* **Layers** panel.

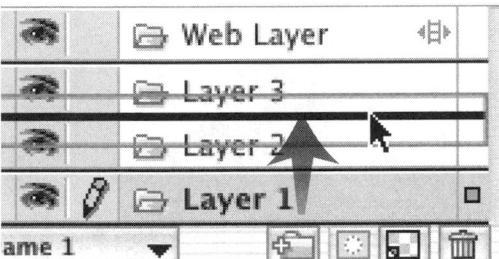

49 Drag a layer *from one position to another to change the order of the layers.*

Working with Layers

As you add more objects to your documents, you may want to take advantage of the Fireworks Layers panel. This panel lets you show and hide objects on each of the layers, lock the layers from changes, and change the order in which objects appear.

To work with the Layers panel:

1. Open the Layers panel by choosing Window > Layers **48**.

TIP The Web Layer holds objects used to add Web addresses to images and to slice them for exporting. *(For more information on working with Web addresses and HTML information in Fireworks, see Chapter 17, "Hotspots and Links," and Chapter 18, "Slices.")*

2. To make all the objects on a layer invisible, click the Show/Hide icon for that layer.

TIP To make all the layers invisible, hold the Opt/Alt key as you click the Show/Hide icon for any layer.

3. To prevent any objects on a layer from being selected, click the space in the lock area. A Padlock icon appears indicating the layer is locked.

TIP Click the layer's Padlock icon to unlock the layer.

4. Click the name of a layer to make that layer the active layer. New objects are automatically created on that layer.

5. Drag the name of a layer up or down to a new position in the panel to move that layer to a new position **49**.

The Layers panel menu controls additional features of the Layers panel.

To use the Layers panel menu:

1. Press the controller at the top of the Layers panel to view the panel menu 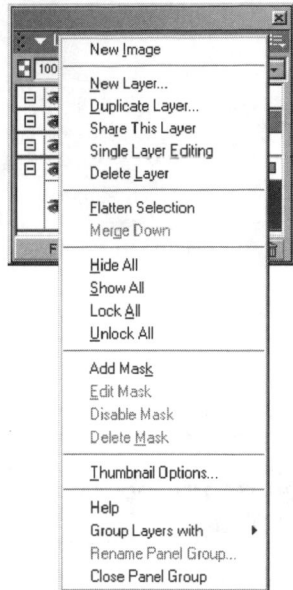.

2. Choose New Layer or click the New Layer icon to add a new layer.

3. Choose Duplicate Layer to duplicate the layer currently selected along with its contents.

4. Choose Share This Layer to display the objects on a layer on all the frames of a document. *(For more information on working with frames, see Chapter 16, "Animations.")*

5. Choose Delete Layer or click the Delete Layer icon to delete a layer.

6. Choose Hide All or Show All to change the display status of all the layers in the document.

7. Choose Lock All or Unlock All to change the protection applied to all the layers in the document.

🔟 *The* **Layers panel menu**.

To change the name of a layer:

1. Double-click the name of the layer. This opens the Layers Options 🔟.

2. Type the new name for the layer.

3. Click OK to apply the name change.

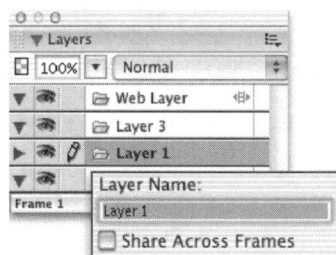

🔟 *The* **Layer Name** field *lets you change the name of a layer.*

The Single Layer Editing mode makes it easy to work only with the objects on one layer.

To use Single Layer Editing:

◆ Choose Single Layer Editing from the Layers panel menu. The currently selected layer becomes the only layer you can work on. Objects on other layers can't be selected.

Working with Layers

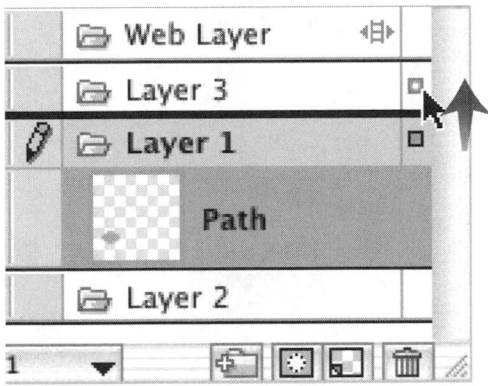

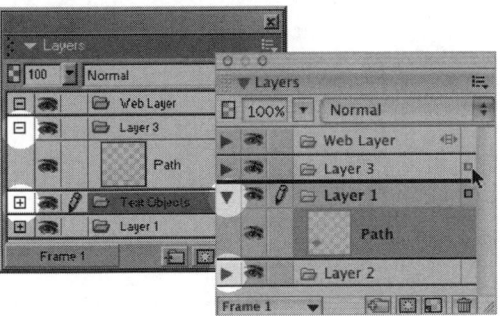

❺❷ Drag the small object square *to move an object from one layer to another.*

❺❸ Click the plus sign *(Win) or the triangle (Mac) to display the the objects on a layer.*

You can use the Layers panel to move objects from one layer to another.

To move an object between layers:

1. Select the object. A small square appears next to the name of the layer that the object is on.

2. Drag the small square to the layer where you want to place the object **❺❷**.

3. Release the mouse. The object appears on the new layer.

TIP Hold the Opt/Alt key as you drag the square to copy the object from one layer to another.

The Layers panel can also display the individual objects on each layer.

To change the display of objects on layers:

1. Click the plus sign (Win) or right-pointing triangle (Mac) to see the a thumbnail displays of the objects on the layer **❺❸**.

2. Click the minus sign (Win) or the down-pointing triangle (Mac) to close the thumbnail display of any objects on the layer.

You can also change the size of the thumbnail displayed in the Layers panel.

To change the thumbnail options:

1. Choose Thumbnail Options from the Layers panel menu. The Thumbnail Options dialog box appears ⑤⑭.

2. Choose None to display the objects with no thumbnail.

3. Click one of the thumbnail sizes to change the display in the Layers panel.

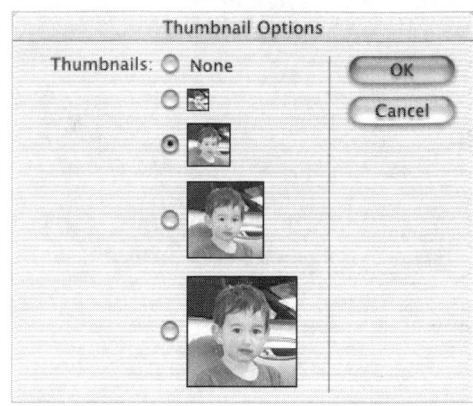

⑤⑭ *Use the* **Thumbnail Options dialog box** *to choose the size of the thumbnails dsiplayed in the Layers panel.*

FILLS 7

I was amazed to find recently that the Colorforms® I played with as a child are still popular—even in this age of computer and video games. In fact, a box of Colorforms is great preparation for any budding artist. I found them at www.areyougame.com.

Great as the objects in Colorforms are, though, they are not as versatile as Fireworks objects. For instance, you can't change Colorforms colors with just a click of a mouse.

Fireworks objects can be filled with colors, textures, patterns, gradients, and even other Fireworks objects. Even better, once an object has one type of fill, you can still go back later and change it. Also, unlike the vinyl shapes in the box of Colorforms, Fireworks objects don't have to be hard-edged objects. They can have a slight softening or fade applied to their edges.

Creating Basic Fills

Fills are the colors, patterns, and gradients that are applied inside paths. Perhaps the most basic of fills is a solid color applied inside objects. Fireworks gives you plenty of places where you can apply a solid fill color.

To apply a solid color fill:

1. Choose one of the vector drawing tools or select a vector object. The Property Inspector displays the Fill options ❶.

2. Choose Solid from the Fill category menu. This displays the options for solid fills ❷.

3. Click the Fill Color Well in the Property Inspector to open the Swatches to pick a color ❸.

   or

   Use the Color Mixer to mix a color or click the Color Well in the Color Mixer. *(For more information on working with the Color Mixer, see Chapter 3, "Colors.")*

   or

   Click the Color Wells in the Tools panel or Color Mixer to open the Swatches panel.

   or

   Choose one of the colors in the Swatches panel.

   TIP Move the eyedropper cursor outside the Swatches panel to choose colors anywhere on the screen. This allows you to sample colors from other documents, such as Dreamweaver and Flash pages.

To choose non–Web-safe colors:

◆ Click the Color icon in one of the Swatches panels ❸ and then choose from the Macintosh Color Picker or the Windows Color dialog box ❹.

TIP The Color icon is not available in the regular Swatch panel, only the panels opened through the Color Wells.

❶ *The* **Fill options** *in the Property Inspector.*

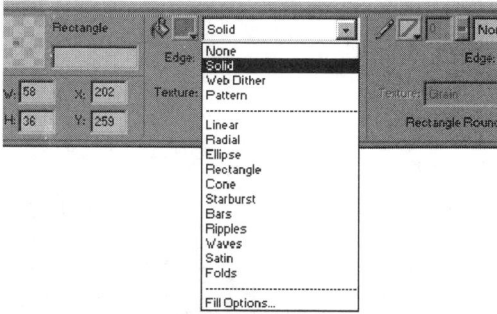

❷ *The* **Fill category menu** *lets you choose the type of fill for the object.*

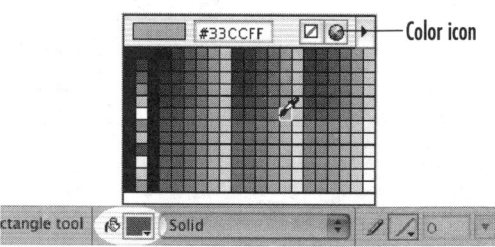

❸ *Click the* **Fill Color Well** *to select a color from the Swatches panel.*

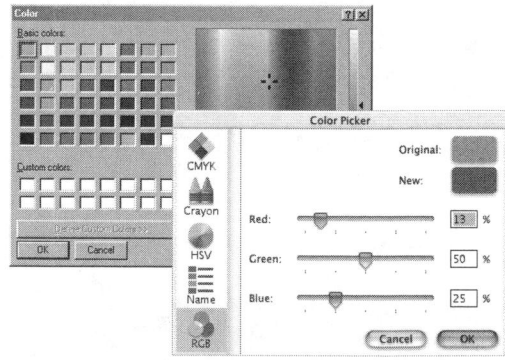

❹ *The* **Windows Color dialog box** *(top) and the* **Macintosh Color Picker** *(bottom) let you choose colors other than the Web-safe colors.*

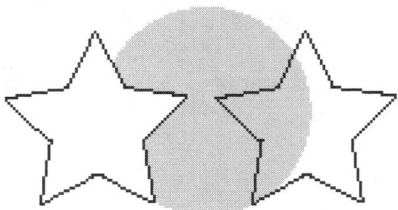

⑤ *The difference between a white fill and a fill of None becomes obvious when the objects appear over another image.*

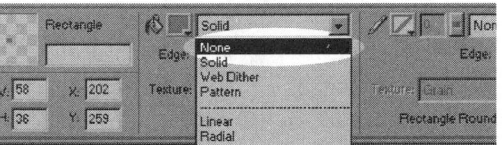

⑥ *Choose None from the* **Fill options menu** *in the Property Inspector.*

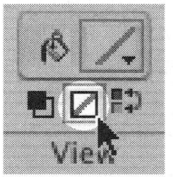

⑦ *Click the* **None icon** *in the Tools panel.*

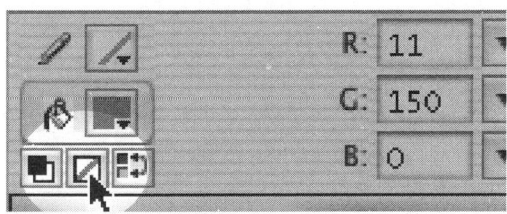

⑧ *Click the* **None icon** *in the Color Mixer panel.*

⑨ *Click the* **None icon** *in one of the Swatches panels.*

In addition to filling an object with a color, you can also set an object to have no fill. This makes the inside of the object completely transparent ⑤. You can use no fill to show just the outside path of an object. There are many different places where you can apply no fill to an object.

To set a Fill to None:

1. Choose one of the vector drawing tools or select a vector object. The Property Inspector displays the Fill options.

2. Choose None from the Fill category menu in the Property Inspector ⑥.

   or

   With the Fill icon highlighted, click the None icon in the Tools panel ⑦.

   or

   Click the None icon in the Color Mixer ⑧.

   or

   Click the None icon in any of the Swatches panels ⑨.

TIP The None icon is not available in the regular Swatch panel, only the panels opened through the Color Wells.

TIP When an object has no fill, you must click the edge of the path to select the object.

Creating a Web Dither Fill

In addition to a solid color fill, Fireworks offers a Web dither fill. This allows you to choose two colors that are combined together in a checker-board pattern (also called a *dither*) to simulate a third color. This gives you more control over the number of colors in your document. *(For a color print-out of a Web dither fill, see the color pages.)*

To apply the Web Dither Fill setting:

1. Choose one of the vector drawing tools or select a vector object. The Property Inspector displays the Fill options.

2. Choose Web Dither from the Fill category menu **10**.

3. Click the Fill Color Well in the Property Inspector. This displays the controls for Web dither fills **11**.

4. Use one of the Color Wells to set the first of the two dithered colors.

5. Use the other Color Well to set the second of the two dithered colors. The Dither preview shows how the combination of the two colors will look.

6. Select Transparent to set one of the colors as transparent. This lets any objects behind the color show through the fill.

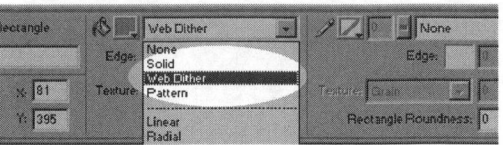

10 *Choose* **Web Dither** *from the Fill category menu.*

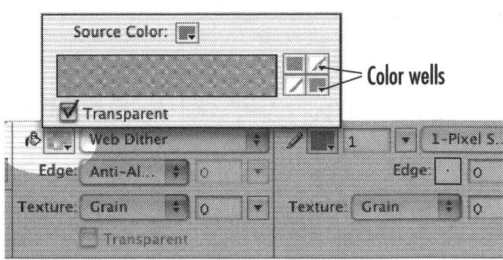

11 *Click the Color Well in the Property Inspector to open the* **Web Dither controls.**

The Benefits of a Web Dither Fill

One of the benefits of the Web dither fill is that you can limit the number of colors in your document. This keeps the file size down, but still has areas that simulate the look of other colors.

For instance, if you use only four colors—black, white, red, and blue— the Web dither fill lets you combine them into others. The black and white combine together to create gray; the white and red create pink; the black and red create dark red; the black and blue create dark blue; and the red and blue create purple.

So, although the final GIF image uses only four colors, you can design your page with nine different colors.

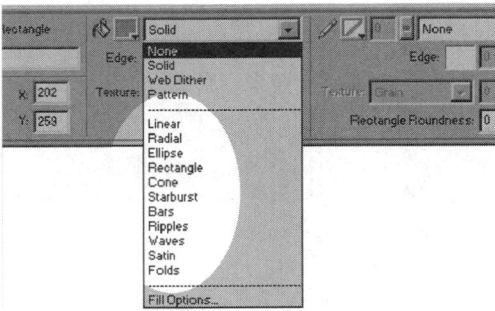

⑫ *Choose one of the types of gradients from the* **Fill category menu**.

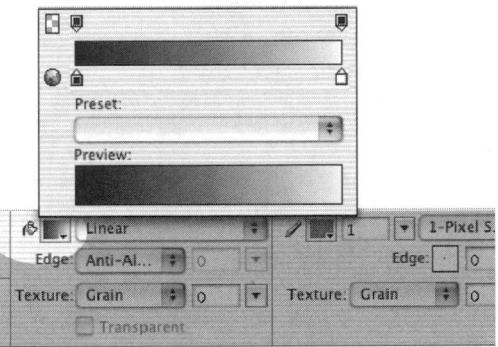

⑬ *Click the Color Well in the Property Inspector to open the* **Gradient controls**.

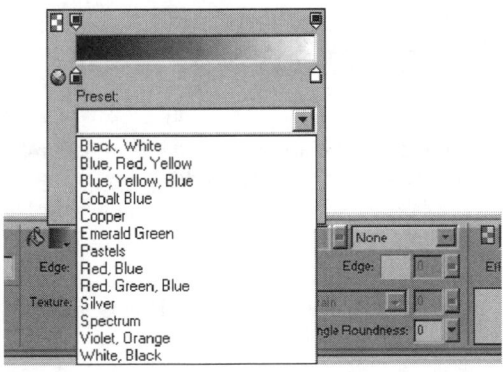

⑭ *Choose one of the preset gradient color combinations from the* **Preset Colors menu** *in the Gradient controls.*

Creating Gradient Fills

In addition to solid colors, Fireworks lets you fill objects with gradients, which gradually blend one color into another. There are two parts to applying a gradient fill: choosing the type of gradient and setting the colors.

To apply a gradient fill:

1. Choose one of the vector drawing tools or select a vector object. The Property Inspector displays the Fill options.

   or

   Choose the Gradient tool in the Tools panel *(see page 114)*.

2. Choose one of the types of gradient fills from the Fill category menu ⑫. If you have chosen the Gradient tool, the Fill category menu displays only the gradient fill choices.

TIP Each type of gradient changes how the colors of the gradients are manipulated. For instance, Linear creates a gradient that changes the colors along a line.

3. Click the Fill Color Well in the Property Inspector. This displays the Gradient controls ⑬.

4. Choose one of the preset color combinations from the Preset Colors menu ⑭. *(See the exercise on the next page for how to set your own color combinations.)*

5. Click inside the Property Inspector or on the canvas area to close the Gradient controls.

Creating Gradient Fills

The preset color combinations are just the starting point for working with gradients. Most likely, you will want to create your own color combinations.

To edit the colors in a gradient fill:

1. With a gradient selected in the Fill options menu *(see the previous exercise)*, click the Fill Color Well in the Property Inspector. This displays the Gradient controls.

2. Click one of the gradient color stops in the Gradient controls. A Swatches panel appears where you can choose a color **15**. *(See page 108 for a description of choosing colors in the Swatches panel.)*

3. To add a new color to the gradient, click in the empty area between the color stops. A new color stop appears **16**.

4. To change the position of a color, drag the Gradient color stop along the top ramp **17**.

5. To duplicate a color stop, hold the Opt/Alt key as you drag the stop to a new position.

TIP As you modify the colors, the Preview area at the bottom of the Gradient controls shows the effect of changing the colors.

6. To delete a Gradient color stop, drag it off the Gradient controls **18**.

TIP You must have at least two color stops in the Gradient colors.

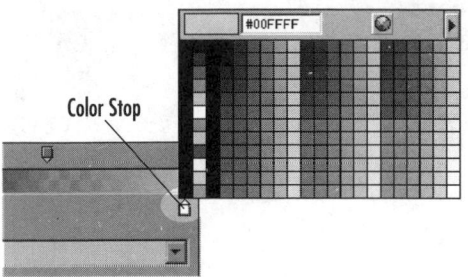

Color Stop

15 *Click the color stop in the Property Inspector to open the* **Gradient controls**.

16 **Click in the color stop area** *to add a new color stop to the gradient.*

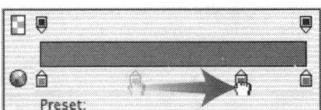

17 **Drag the color stop** *to change the position of the color in the gradient.*

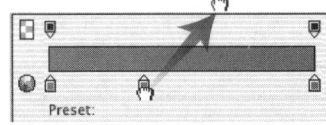

18 **Drag the color stop off** *the Gradient controls to delete the color from the gradient.*

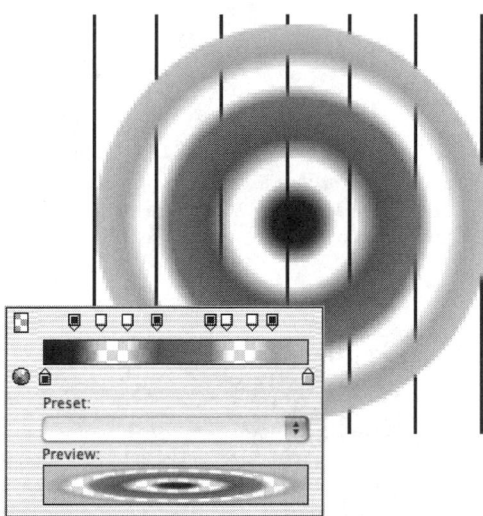

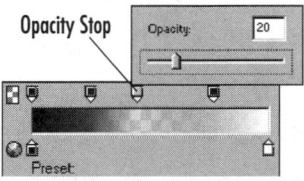

19 *An example of how the opacity settings in the Gradient controls affect the appearance of the gradient in the circle. As the color changes from gray to black, the transparent rings let you see through the circle to the stripes underneath.*

Opacity Stop

20 *Click the opacity stop to open the Opacity controls for a gradient.*

In addition to setting the color stops for a gradient, you can also set the opacity stops. This allows you to create an area of the gradient that fades to transparent.

TIP The transparency in a gradient is not readily apparent unless you put the artwork that contains the gradient over another piece of art **19**.

To add colors to a gradient:

1. Click one of the opacity stops in the Gradient controls. The Opacity controls appear **20**.

2. Drag the Opacity slider or type a number in the Opacity field to change the transparency of that area of the gradient.

TIP Use any of the techniques described in the previous exercise to add new opacity stops, move the opacity stops, duplicate the opacity stops, or delete the opacity stops.

TIP Once you have created a gradient, you will probably want to save it to use in other objects. In earlier versions of Fireworks, you could save the gradient as its own preset. Starting with Fireworks MX, you need to create a style. *(For more information on working with styles, see Chapter 13, "Automation Features.")*

Warning: Gradients Use Tons of Colors

Watch out when you apply gradients to your Fireworks documents. Even though you use only two or three colors in the Gradient Color controls, the gradient itself requires many colors to display properly.

A gradient that blends black into white may require as many as 256 colors to look smooth on screen. Add another Gradient Color control and you may find it difficult to optimize the file using the 256 colors in a GIF image.

In addition to controlling the colors in a gradient, you can also change the appearance of a gradient by changing its direction, length, and center.

To change the appearance of a gradient:

1. Select an object filled with a gradient.

2. Click the Pointer tool or the Paint Bucket tool in the Tools panel **㉑**. The Vector controls appear in the object **㉒**.

TIP If you don't see the Gradient Vector controls when you choose the Pointer tool, check Show Fill Handles in the Pointer Tool Options under the Editing Preferences.

TIP Some gradients provide two control handles to control two separate axes of the gradient.

3. Move the circle control to change the start point of the gradient **㉓**.

4. Drag the square control to change the end point of the gradient **㉔**.

TIP If a control has two handles, hold the Shift key as you drag a square control to move the other one at the same time.

5. Drag the line of the control to change the rotation of the gradient **㉕**.

TIP Double-click the circle control to reset the Vector controls to the default setting.

㉑ Select the Gradient tool, the Paint Bucket tool, or the Pointer tool to work with the Gradient Vector controls.

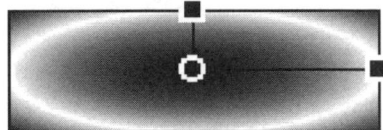

㉒ The Gradient Vector controls at their default setting within the object.

㉓ Move the Circle Vector control to change the start point of a gradient.

㉔ Drag the Square Vector control to change the end point of the gradient. A short gradient repeats to fill the object.

㉕ Drag the angle of the Vector controls to rotate the gradient.

26 *Examples of* **four patterns** *inside objects.*

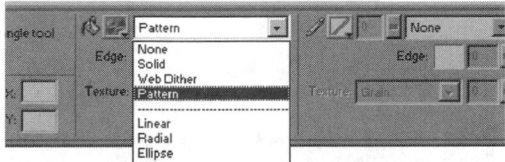

27 *Choose* **Pattern from the Fill menu** *in the Property Inspector.*

28 *Click the Fill Color Well to open the* **Pattern controls.**

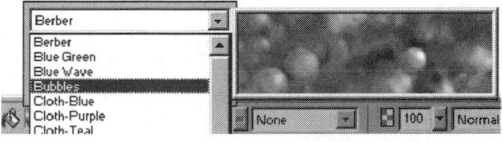

29 *Choose one of the patterns from the Pattern menu. A preview of each pattern is displayed.*

30 *An individual pattern imported from a file is displayed inside an object.*

Working with Patterns

Another way to fill objects is to apply a pattern. Patterns are images that have been specially created so that they can repeat within an object without showing an obvious repeat tile. Fireworks ships with 45 preset patterns that you can apply to objects **26**.

To apply a pattern fill:

1. Choose one of the vector drawing tools or select a vector object. The Property Inspector displays the Fill options.

2. Choose Pattern from the Fill category menu **27**.

3. Click the Fill Color Well. This opens the Pattern options **28**.

4. Choose one of the patterns in the Pattern menu.

TIP A preview box appears as you move through the list **29**.

TIP The Vector controls can also be used to modify the appearance of patterns as well as gradients *(see previous page)*.

In addition to the patterns that ship with Fireworks, you can use your own images to use as patterns.

To add individual patterns:

1. Choose Other from the pattern list.

2. Navigate and select the file you want to use as a pattern.

3. The name of the file appears at the end of the pattern list and can be applied to any object **30**.

TIP Individual patterns are contained in that document only.

TIP You can transfer an individual pattern from one document to another by copying an object containing the pattern to another file.

Working with Patterns

Fireworks ships with default patterns that appear in the Fill panel. You can add to the patterns that ship with Fireworks or create your own pattern folder.

To add to the pattern folder:

1. Scan or create artwork that can be tiled as a pattern.

2. Give the file a name and save it as any file format Fireworks can read. *(See the "Adding Patterns and Textures" sidebar on this page for a list of those file formats.)*

3. Put the file in the Patterns folder (Fireworks: Configurations: Patterns). The name of the file appears as the name of the pattern in the pop-up list.

TIP Use the same technique to add files to the Textures folder (Fireworks: Configurations: Textures). *(See the next page for information on working with textures.)*

To add a second pattern folder:

1. Place the files that you want to be patterns in a folder (directory).

2. Choose **File** > **Preferences**.

   or

   (Mac OS X) Choose **Fireworks** > **Preferences**.

3. Click the folders tab (Win) or choose Folders from the menu (Mac). The Folders preferences appear **31**.

4. Choose Patterns and then use the Browse button to navigate to the folder that holds the files.

TIP The patterns are not available until the next time you launch Fireworks.

TIP Use the same technique to add a second folder for textures. *(See the next page for information on working with textures.)*

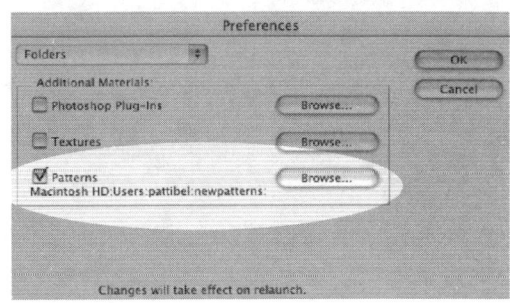

31 *Use the* **Folders Preferences** *to specify a second folder to hold patterns.*

Adding Patterns and Textures

Fireworks supports any file format that it can export as the file format for patterns and textures. So, if you use Fireworks to create your patterns or textures, you can save the file as a PNG or any of the other bitmap formats Fireworks uses for exporting.

If you use another program, such as Adobe Photoshop, you can save the file as a PNG, TIFF, or other bitmap formats that Fireworks can export.

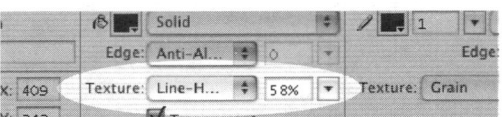

32 *The* **Texture controls** *in the Property Inspector.*

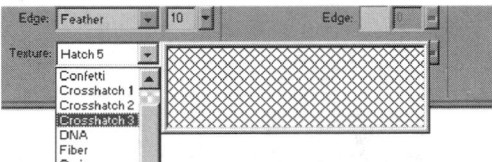

33 *The* **Texture menu** *with the preview area.*

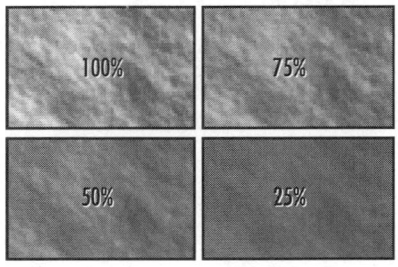

34 *Different settings of the* **Parchment texture** *on a solid fill. As the intensity is lowered, less texture is visible.*

Transparency off

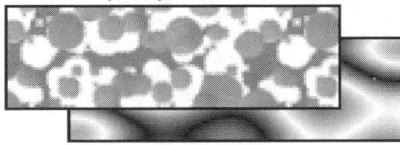

Transparency on

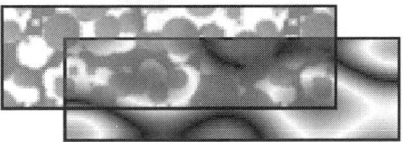

35 *When transparency is turned on, you can see one texture behind the other.*

Using Textures

Textures are one of the most overlooked features in Fireworks. They allow you to vary the appearance of solid colors, patterns, or gradients. The organic textures add the appearance of paper, stone, leather, and other natural surfaces. The grid textures apply lines, dots, crosshatches and other highlights to fills. Once a texture is applied to a fill, you can then change the intensity of the texture.

To apply a texture to a fill:

1. Choose one of the vector drawing tools or select a vector object. The Property Inspector displays the Texture controls in the Fill options **32**.

2. Choose one of the textures from the Texture menu. A preview box shows the texture **33**.

TIP There is always a texture applied to every fill. However, with an intensity of 0% the effect of the texture is not visible.

3. Use the slider or enter a number in the Intensity field to see the effects of the texture on the fill **34**.

4. Check Transparent to allow background objects to appear in the light-colored areas of the texture **35**.

Using Textures

Modifying Fill Edges

Once you have filled an object, you can control how the edges of the object display that fill.

To change the edges of a fill:

1. Choose one of the vector drawing tools or select a vector object. The Property Inspector displays the Fill options.

2. Use the Edge menu to change the edge treatment of the fill . Choose one of the following settings 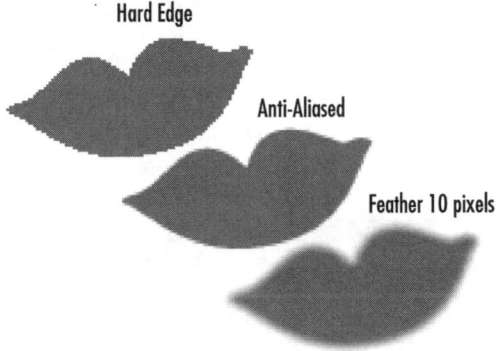:

   - **Hard** leaves the edge of the object as single-colored pixels.
   - **Anti-Alias** softens the edge of the object by changing the color of the pixels so they blend into the background or other objects.
   - **Feather** blurs the edge of the object. Use the slider to set the amount. The higher the feather, the greater the amount of blurring .

TIP The feather amount is in pixels and is applied equally to both sides of the edge.

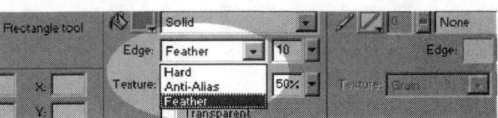

36 *The* **Edge menu** *in the Property Inspector controls the appearance of the edges of filled objects.*

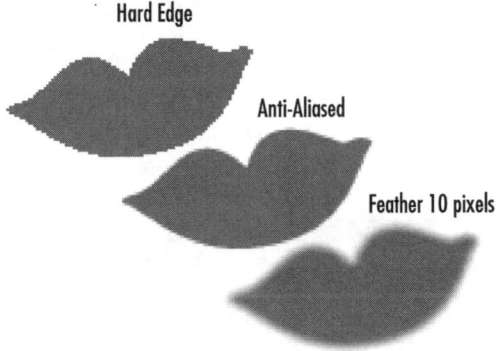

37 *The three different edge choices.*

38 *Feathering allows you to create softer, more blurred edges than anti-aliasing.*

Anti-Aliasing Adds Colors

Anti-aliasing smooths out the harsh edges of objects. Remember, though, that when you apply anti-aliasing you also add colors to the object.

Those extra colors can add to the size of your file. You can reduce the number of colors by selectively changing the anti-alias setting to a hard edge when objects have similar colors.

For instance, a yellow object with a hard edge is very noticeable over a blue background—and needs anti-aliasing to avoid looking jagged. But a light yellow object over a gold background may not need anti-aliasing.

STROKES 8

In addition to applying fills inside paths, Macromedia Fireworks also lets you change the appearance of objects by applying a stroke to the edge of the path. In an ordinary vector program, strokes are limited to just colors or dashes. In Fireworks, however, strokes are much more versatile.

For instance, Fireworks lets you set strokes to resemble all sorts of natural media such as paint brushes, crayons, chalk, pencils, oils — even toothpaste and confetti! You can also apply textures to strokes for even more varied appearances. You can add arrowheads to the start or end of a path.

Finally, you can set strokes in Fireworks so that they work with pressure-sensitive tablets — the harder you press, the thicker the stroke gets. You can also simulate the effect of drawing with a tablet, even if you work with a mouse.

Setting Stroke Attributes

Fireworks organizes strokes into categories. The categories then have submenus that contain preset variations. You can apply the various presets to quickly change the appearance of a path.

To apply a stroke preset:

1. Create an open path with one of the vector drawing tools. The Property Inspector displays the Stroke options **1**.

TIP When you create a path with the Vector Path tool or the Line tool, the fill automatically changes to None. This makes the path look like a simple brush stroke, rather than a vector object.

TIP Although strokes can be applied to closed paths, such as rectangles, it is easier to understand strokes by creating open paths.

2. Choose one of the stroke presets from the stroke category menu **2**. The stroke changes its appearance according to the category and preset chosen **3**.

The Stroke Categories and Presets

Each of the stroke categories is named after traditional drawing tools such as pencil, air brush, calligraphic pen, charcoal, crayon, felt-tip pen, oil, and watercolor. The presets have submenus that contain variations such as Creamy and Pastel under the Charcoal category. There are also strokes in non-traditional categories such as Random and Unnatural. These have variations such as Toothpaste and Toxic Waste under the Unnatural category, for example.

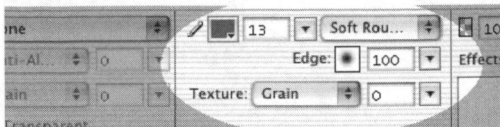

1 *The* **Stroke options** *in the Property Inspector.*

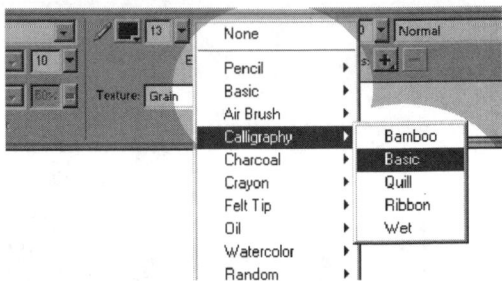

2 *The* **Stroke category menu** *and* **a preset submenu** *in the Property Inspector.*

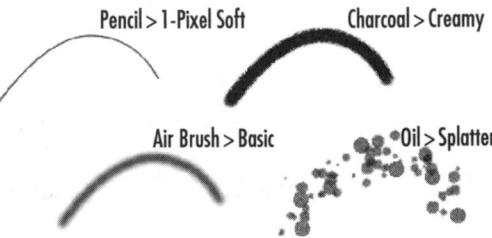

3 *Four different stroke presets applied to the same path shape.*

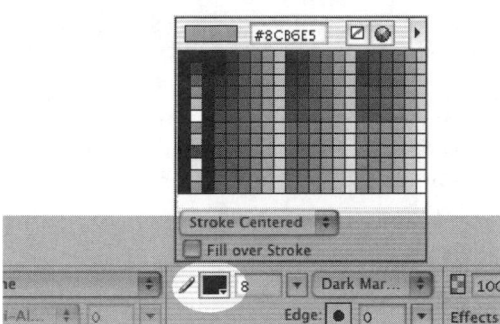

4 The **Stroke Color Well** *displays the swatches panel and additional stroke controls.*

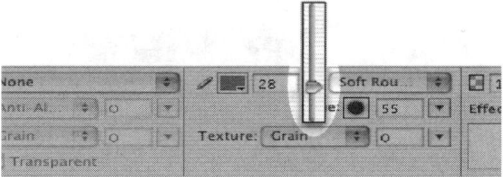

5 The **Size slider** *lets you control the thickness of the stroke.*

6 *The difference between setting the same stroke to two different sizes.*

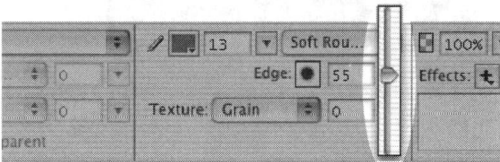

7 The **Edge slider** *lets you change the softness of the stroke.*

8 *The difference between setting the same stroke to two different edge softness amounts.*

You can modify the stroke by changing any of the Stroke options in the Property Inspector.

To change the stroke color:

1. Click the Stroke Color Well to open the Swatches panel **4**.

2. Use the Swatches panel to change the stroke color. *(For more information on using the Swatches panel, see Chapter 3, "Colors.")*

TIP You can also use the Color Well in the Color Mixer or the Tools panel to set the stroke color.

To change the stroke size:

◆ Drag the Size slider or enter an amount in the field to change the width of the stroke **5**. The larger the number, the thicker the stroke **6**.

To change the stroke edge hardness:

◆ Drag the Edge slider to blur the edge of the stroke **7**. The higher the number, the softer the stroke edge **8**.

TIP You may need to increase the size of the stroke to see the difference in the edge softness.

Setting Stroke Attributes

To change the stroke edge textures:

1. Choose one of the textures from the Texture menu in the Stroke options **❾**.

TIP You don't have to choose the same texture for your stroke that you used as the fill for the object.

2. Use the slider or enter a number in the Intensity field to see the effects of the texture on the stroke **❿**.

TIP As with patterns, you can create your own textures to use within Fireworks *(see page 116)*.

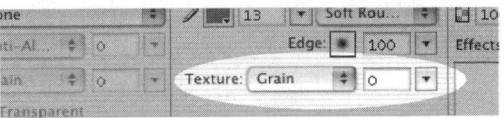

❾ *The Stroke Texture menu and Intensity slider in the Property Inspector.*

❿ *Two different textures applied to the same stroke.*

Fireworks gives you a choice as to whether your stroke will be displayed on the inside, outside, or center of your path **⓫**.

To change the position of a stroke on a path:

1. Click the Stroke Color Well to open the Swatches panel.

2. Choose one of the options from the Stroke Position menu **⓬**.

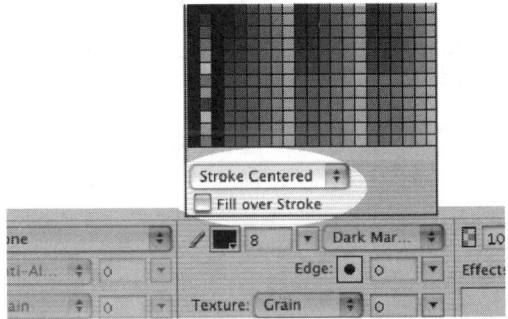

⓫ *The Stroke position menu and Fill over Stroke check box let you refine the appearance of strokes.*

When a path has both a stroke and a fill, you have a choice as to how the fill interacts with the stroke.

To change how the fill meets a stroke:

1. Click the Stroke Color Well to open the Swatches panel.

2. Check Fill over Stroke to have the fill of the object extend over the path **⓭**.

⓬ *The three choices for the position of a stroke on a path.*

Difference Between Paths and Strokes

Paths are the objects that you create in Fireworks. A stroke is an effect applied to the edge of paths. You might have a path that doesn't contain a stroke but you'll never have a stroke that isn't applied to a path.

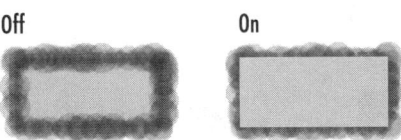

⓭ *The effects of changing the Fill over Stroke setting.*

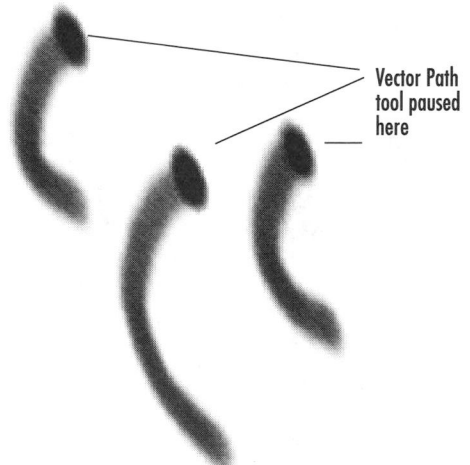

Vector Path
tool paused
here

⑭ *The effect of pausing while creating three brush strokes.*

Working with a Pressure-Sensitive Tablet

Many years ago I heard the statement that "drawing with a mouse is like drawing with a bar of soap." The solution is a pressure-sensitive tablet. I can't think of a better investment for any computer artist or graphic designer.

Fireworks uses the pressure settings in the tablet to create more natural-looking brush strokes. However, there's more than just artistic reasons to use a tablet.

Using a stylus keeps your hand in a much more comfortable position than working with a mouse, so you are less likely to develop hand strain or other problems.

Creating Pressure Effects

Pressure means more than just meeting tight deadlines. It can be a good thing, too. If you work with a pressure-sensitive tablet, you can see how Fireworks strokes respond to changes in how you press with the stylus.

Even if you draw with a mouse, you can still make a more natural stroke based on how you drag with the mouse.

To draw a path using a pressure-sensitive tablet:

1. Select the Vector Path tool.

TIP You can also choose the Brush tool in the bitmap tools. *(See Chapter 10, "Working with Bitmaps.")*

2. Choose a stroke setting such as Airbrush set to Basic or Calligraphy set to Quill.

TIP These stroke presets respond very well to pressure-sensitive tablets.

3. Drag along a path and pause without releasing the mouse button. The width of the stroke increases where you pause as you drag **⑭**.

Even after you've applied a stroke to a path, you can still alter it by by using the Path Scrubber tool. This tool allows you to increase or decrease the effect of pressure on a path. The Path Scrubber has two modes: Path Scrubber Plus and Path Scrubber Minus.

TIP If you have a pressure-sensitive tablet, you can use the Path Scrubber to further refine the look of the path. If you do not have a pressure-sensitive pen and tablet, you can use the Path Scrubber to simulate those effects.

To use the Path Scrubber tool:

1. Select a path with a stroke.

2. Choose the Path Scrubber Plus tool in the Tools panel ⓯. If the Path Scrubber Plus tool is not visible, open the pop-up group to choose the Path Scrubber Plus tool.

3. Drag along the path. The width of the stroke increases as you drag ⓰.

4. Choose the Path Scrubber Minus tool in the Tools panel ⓱. If the Path Scrubber Minus tool is not visible, open the pop-up group to choose the Path Scrubber Minus tool.

5. Drag across to intersect the path. The width of the stroke decreases as you drag ⓲.

TIP Hold the Opt/Alt key to switch between the Path Scrubber Plus and Minus modes.

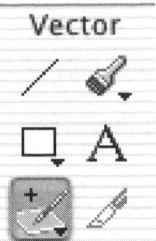

⓯ *The* **Path Scrubber Plus tool** *in the Tools panel.*

Original Path

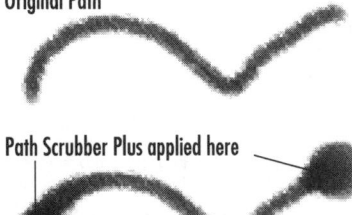

Path Scrubber Plus applied here

⓰ *The effect of the Path Scrubber Plus tool on a stroked path.*

⓱ *The* **Path Scrubber Minus tool** *in the Tools panel.*

Original Path

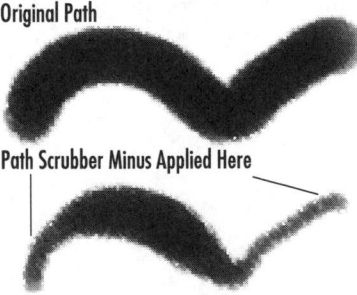

Path Scrubber Minus Applied Here

⓲ *The effect of the Path Scrubber Minus tool on a stroked path.*

Creating Pressure Effects

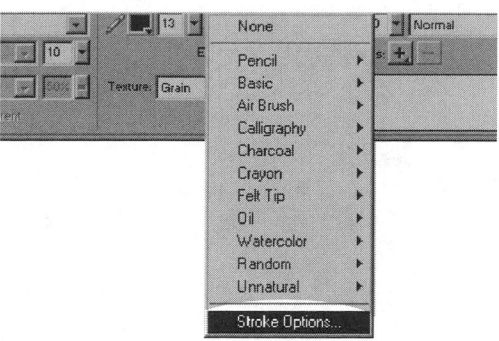

⓳ *Choose* **Stroke Options** *from the Stroke category menu to open the Stroke Options panel.*

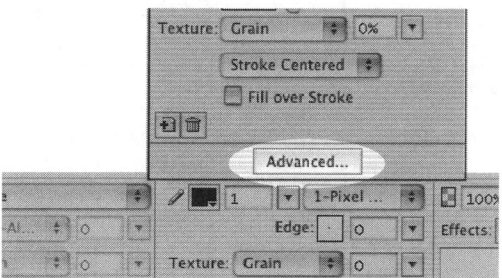

⓴ *Click the* **Advanced button** *in the Stroke Options panel to open the Edit Stroke dialog box.*

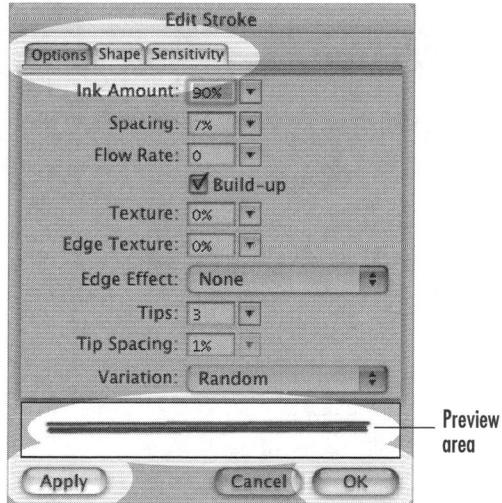

㉑ *The* **tabs, preview area, Apply, and OK buttons** *in the Edit Stroke dialog box.*

Editing Strokes

In addition to the settings in the Stroke area of the Property Inspector, the Edit Stroke dialog box lets you create your own custom stroke appearances. This is where you can create strokes that resemble leaky pens, chalk, or multi-colored streamers.

TIP Draw a sample path and keep it selected to see how the settings affect the path.

To use the Edit Stroke dialog box:

1. Choose Stroke Options from the Stroke category menu in the Property Inspector **⓳**. The Stroke Options panel appears.

2. Click the Advanced button in the Stroke Options panel **⓴**. The Edit Stroke dialog box appears.

3. Click each of the tabs in the Edit Stroke dialog box **㉑**:

   • Click Options to control the appearance of the stroke. *(See the following page for details on the Options controls.)*

   • Click the tab for Shape to control the size, edge softness, shape, roundness, and angle of the stroke. *(See the exercise on page 127 for details on the Shape controls.)*

   • Click the tab for Sensitivity to control how the stroke reacts to changes in the mouse or stylus movements. *(See the exercise on page 127 for details on the Sensitivity controls.)*

4. Click Apply to see how the settings appear on the selected path.

   or

   Watch the Preview area to see how the settings affect the path.

5. Click OK to apply the settings to the stroke and close the Edit Stroke dialog box.

Editing Strokes

To use the Edit Stroke Options settings:

1. Click the tab for Options to control the appearance of the stroke 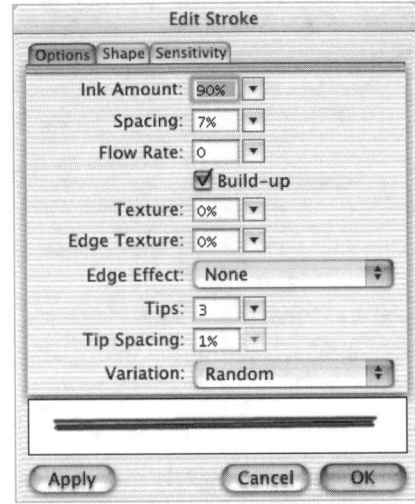.

2. Set each of the Options controls as follows:

   - **Ink Amount** changes the opacity of the stroke color.
   - **Spacing** breaks the solid lines into dots and dashes.
   - **Flow Rate** adds to the size of the stroke if the cursor remains pressed over time. This is similar to the setting of an airbrush.
   - **Build-up** allows separate stroke tips to interact with each other.
   - **Texture** makes the stroke more responsive to the texture set in the Stroke area of the Property Inspector.
   - **Edge Effect** applies one of the special edge effects to the stroke 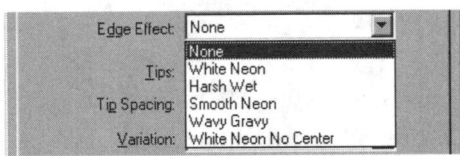.
   - **Edge Texture** makes the Edge Effect more apparent.
   - **Tips** lets you apply more than one stroke to each path.
   - **Tip Spacing** increases the distance between multiple tips.
   - **Variation** controls the colors of multiple tips 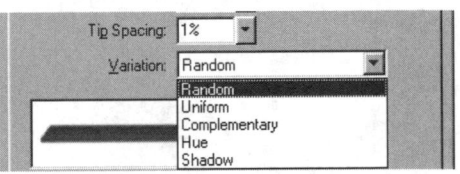.

*The **Options panel** of the Edit Stroke dialog box.*

*The **Edge Effect menu** lets you apply special effects to the edges of a stroke.*

*The **Variation menu** controls how multiple tips are colored.*

Dotted and Dashed Lines

Once you understand the Edit Stroke dialog box, it is possible to use it to create a dotted or dashed line in Fireworks. But it's too much work; and the dashed lines don't go around the corners of rectangles in the right direction.

I recommend using Fireworks text-on-a-path features *(see page 189)* to add a series of bullets or hyphens to the path. That's a much easier way to make dotted or dashed lines.

Editing Strokes

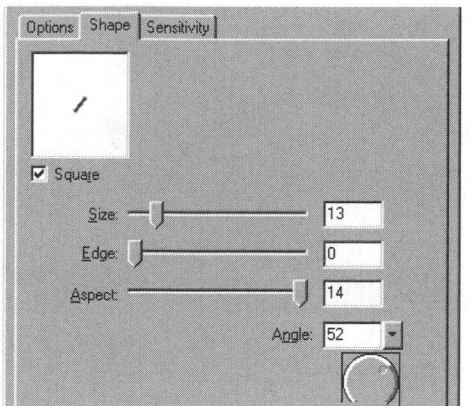

㉕ *The* **Shape panel** *of the Edit Stroke dialog box.*

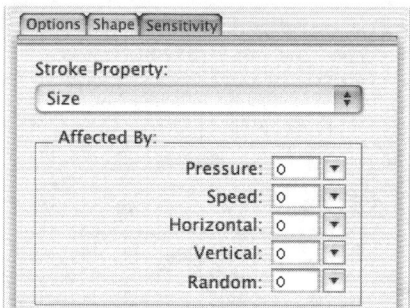

㉖ *The* **Sensitivity panel** *of the Edit Stroke dialog box.*

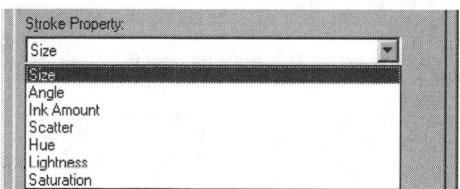

㉗ *Choose from the* **Stroke Property menu** *of the Sensitivity panel to change which attributes of the stroke are affected by the sensitivity controls.*

To use the Edit Stroke Shape settings:

1. Click the tab for Shape to control the shape of the stroke **㉕**.

2. Set each of the Shape controls as follows:
   - **Square** changes the stroke tip from an ellipse to a rectangle.
   - **Size** increases or decreases the size of the stroke.
   - **Edge** softens the edges of the stroke.
   - **Aspect** changes the appearance of the ellipse or rectangle used to create the stroke. The lower the Aspect value, the flatter the ellipse or rectangle appears.
   - **Angle** changes the orientation of the stroke tips.

TIP Changing the Aspect creates strokes that resemble calligraphy pens.

To use the Edit Stroke Sensitivity settings:

1. Click the tab for Sensitivity to control how the mouse or pressure-sensitive tablet stylus affects the stroke **㉖**.

2. Choose one of the attributes from the Stroke Property menu **㉗**.

3. Use the Affected By settings to control what type of action will vary the selected property:
   - **Pressure** makes the stroke responsive to a pressure-sensitive tablet.
   - **Speed** varies the attribute based on how fast or slow the mouse or tablet stylus is moved.
   - **Horizontal** changes the stroke along a horizontal axis.
   - **Vertical** changes the stroke along a vertical axis.
   - **Random** changes the stroke according to the whim of the computer gods.

Saving Stroke Settings

Any changes you make to the Stroke panel, such as the size, edge softness, or texture, are modifications of the original stroke preset. You can save those changes as your own stroke preset.

To save a custom stroke:

1. Make whatever changes you want to the Stroke options in the Property Inspector or create a custom stroke in the Edit Stroke dialog box.

2. Choose Stroke Options from the Stroke category menu in the Property Inspector. The Stroke Options panel appears **28**.

3. Click the Save Custom Stroke button in the panel **29**. The Save Stroke dialog box appears **30**.

4. Type the name of the new stroke and click OK. The new stroke appears as one of the stroke presets **31**.

To delete a custom stroke:

1. Choose Stroke Options from the Stroke category menu in the Property Inspector. The Stroke Options panel appears.

2. Choose the custom stroke from the Preset menu.

3. Click the Delete Custom Stroke button in the Stroke Options panel **32**.

4. In the dialog box that appears, confirm that you want to delete the stroke.

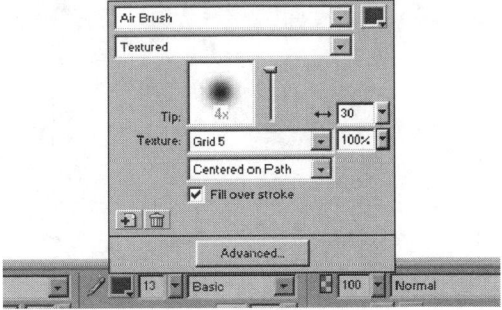

28 *The* **Stroke options panel** *lets you save custom stroke settings.*

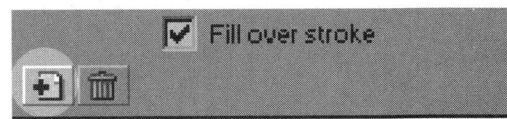

29 *Click the* **Save Custom Stroke button** *to name and save the stroke settings as a preset.*

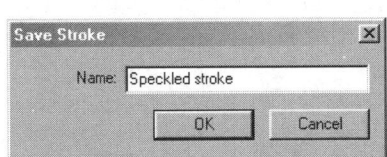

30 *Enter a name for a custom stroke in the* **Save Stroke dialog box**.

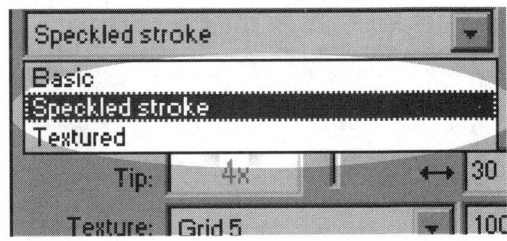

31 *Custom strokes appear in the* **Preset menu** *in the Property Inspector.*

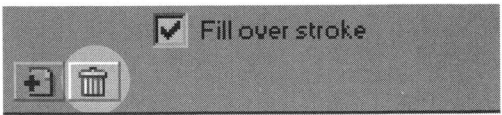

32 *Click the* **Delete Custom Stroke button** *to delete a stroke preset from the menu.*

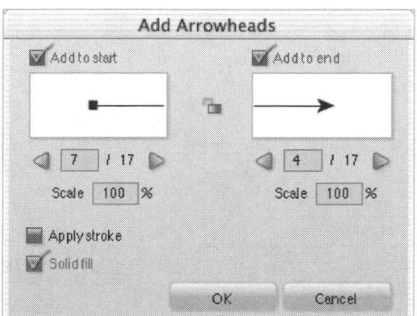

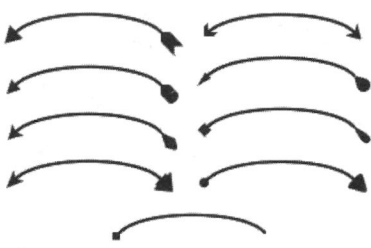

Adding Arrowheads

Strictly speaking, arrowheads aren't strokes; they're little filled paths sitting at the end of stroked paths. However, since arrowheads are linked so often to strokes, it seems as good a time as any to cover them now.

To add arrowheads to open paths:

1. Select an open path.

TIP The Add Arrowhead command does not work on closed paths. *(See page 60 for the difference between open and closed paths.)*

2. Choose **Commands > Creative > Add Arrowheads**. The Add Arrowheads panel appears ③③.

TIP Like the Align panel *(see page 97)*, the Add Arrowheads panel is actually a Flash SWF movie running within Fireworks.

3. Click the Add to start or Add to end check boxes to choose where to add the arrowhead.

4. Use the numbered controls to choose the arrowhead style.

5. Click the Lock icon to link both the start and end arrowheads to the same style.

6. Use the Scale controls to set the size of the arrowheads in relationship to the size of the stroke.

7. Click the Apply stroke check box to add a stroke to the arrowhead.

8. Click the Solid fill check box to fill the arrowhead with the same color as the stroke.

9. Click the OK button to apply the settings to the open path ③④.

③③ *The* **Add Arrowheads panel** *lets you add arrowhead elements to open paths.*

③④ *An example of the various arrowheads applied to open paths.*

Adding Arrowheads

EFFECTS 9

You could think of fills and strokes as the basic utilitarian features for styling objects. Effects, on the other hand, are the razzle-dazzle features that alter the look of objects. Unlike fills that are limited to just the inside of objects, and strokes that are limited to just the outside, effects in Macromedia Fireworks can change the look of either the inside or the outside of objects — or both.

For instance, you can add a bevel effect to the inside or the outside of an object to give it the appearance of dimensionality. A shadow effect added to the outside of an object makes the object appear to float above its background. However, a shadow effect added inside an object will make it look as if it is punching a hole in the background.

Effects can also be used to enhance the appearance of scanned images. These effects may be just a subtle sharpening of the image's details or dramatic changes in color, brightness, and tones.

Effects allow you to give added flourishes to your Fireworks objects and scanned images.

Transparency and Blend Modes

Transparency—or lack of opacity—allows you to see through an object to the other objects or canvas underneath.

To change an object's opacity:

1. Choose one of the vector drawing tools or select an object. The Opacity controls are displayed in the Property Inspector ❶.

TIP The Opacity controls are also displayed in the Layers panel ❷. *(See pages 103–106 for information on using the Layers panel.)*

2. Drag the Opacity slider or type a new percentage in the Opacity field. The lower the opacity value, the more transparent the object becomes ❸.

TIP The Opacity controls in Fireworks are similar to the layer opacity controls in Adobe Photoshop. However, in Fireworks, each object on a layer can have its own opacity setting. In Photoshop all objects on a layer share the same opacity setting.

The Effects area also lets you change the blend mode, which is how the colors of one object interact with objects below.

To change the object's blending mode:

1. Choose one of the vector drawing tools or select an object. The Blend Mode menu is displayed in the Property Inspector.

2. Choose one of the blend modes in the menu ❹. The chart on the facing page shows the effects of each blend mode. *(For a color print-out of the blending modes shown here, see the color pages.)*

TIP The Blend Mode menu is also displayed in the Layers panel.

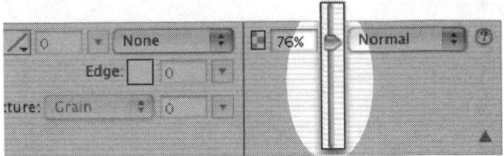

❶ *The* **Opacity slider** *in the Property Inspector.*

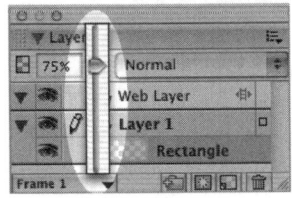

❷ *The* **Opacity** slider *in the Layers panel.*

❸ **Lowering the opacity** *lets you see through the circle to the object below.*

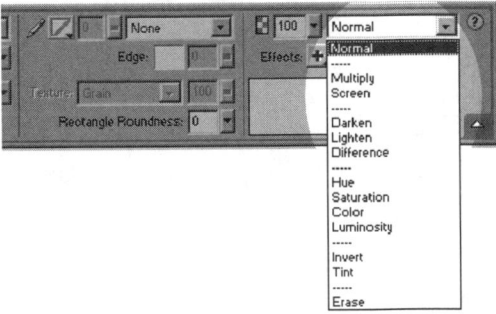

❹ *The* **Effects menu** *in the Property Inspector.*

Mode	Description	Example
Normal	In the Normal mode, the top object does not interact with the objects below it.	
Multiply	In the Multiply mode, the colors of the top object are added to the objects below. The effect is similar to the result of overprinting one object on top of another	
Screen	In the Screen mode, the colors of the top object are subtracted from the objects below. The effect is similar to the result of bleaching out one image from the other.	
Darken	In the Darken mode, the colors of the top object are visible only where they are darker than the objects below.	
Lighten	In the Lighten mode, the colors of the top object are visible only where they are lighter than the objects below.	
Difference	In the Difference mode, the colors of the top object are reversed where they pass over the objects below. The greater the difference, the lighter the color.	
Hue	In the Hue mode, the hue of the top object is applied to the objects below.	
Saturation	In the Saturation mode, the saturation of the top object is applied to the objects below.	
Color	In the Color mode, both the hue and saturation of the top object is applied to the objects below.	
Luminosity	In the Luminosity mode, the lightness information of the top object is applied to the objects below.	
Invert	In the Invert mode, the shape of the top object reverses the colors of the objects below. For instance, black becomes white and green becomes red. The object's color has no effect on the Invert blend.	
Tint	In the Tint mode, the color of the top object tints the objects below.	
Erase	In the Erase mode, the top object hides the objects below. Only objects outside the top object are visible. The color of the top object has no effect on the results.	

Transparency and Blend Modes

Applying and Modifying Effects

You apply effects to objects and images by adding effects to the the Effects list in the Property Inspector. Although each of the effects is different, they all are applied in the same way.

Add Effects button

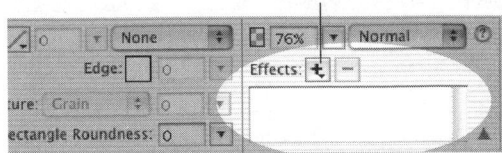

⑤ *The* **Effects area** *in the Property Inspector.*

To apply effects:

1. Select an object. The Effects area appears in the Property Inspector **⑤**.

TIP Unlike the Fill, Stroke, and Transparency controls which are available when the drawing tools are chosen, the Effects area is only available when an object is selected.

2. Click the Add Effects button. The Effects menu appears **⑥**.

3. Choose one of the effects from the submenus for each category. The controls for that specific effect appear as a panel on top of the Effects area.

4. Use the exercises on the following pages to set the controls for each of the effects.

5. Click anywhere on the canvas or in the Property Inspector to apply the effect to the object. The effect appears in the Effects area in the Property Inspector **⑦**.

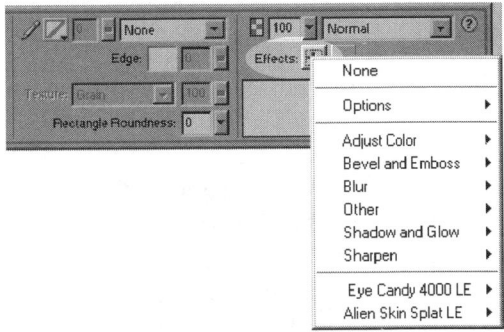

⑥ *The* **Effects menu** *displays the effects categories.*

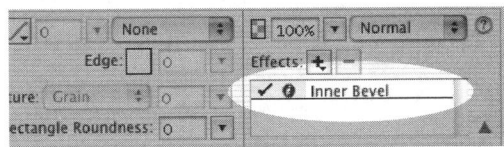

⑦ *The* **Effects area** *shows which effects are applied to any object.*

Once you have applied effects, you use the listing in the Effects area to modify them.

To change the effect setting:

1. Select an object. The effects applied to the object appear in the Effects area.

2. Click the info icon next to the name of the effect **⑧**. This opens the panel for the effect.

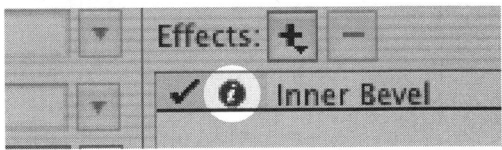

⑧ *Click the* **Info icon** *to modify the settings of an effect.*

3. Modify the effect using the options displayed in its panel.

4. Click anywhere on the canvas or in the Property Inspector to apply the effect.

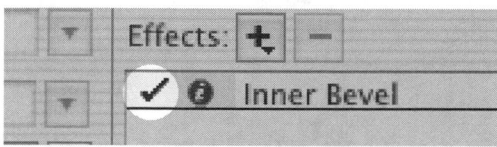

9 *The Effects* **preview column shows a** checkmark *to indicate that the effect is displayed.*

You may want to see what an object looks like without the effect applied to it. Fireworks lets you temporarily disable the appearance of an effect applied to an object. Turning off the display of an effect can also help speed the screen redraw as you work with objects.

To change the display of an effect:

◆ Click the Preview column in the Effects list. A checkmark means the effect is visible **9**. An X mark means the effect is not visible.

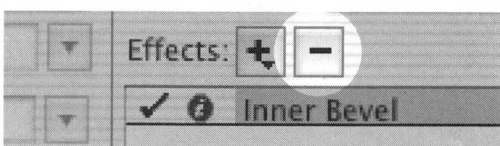

10 *Click the* **Delete Effect icon** *to remove the effect assigned to an object.*

To delete an effect:

1. Click the name of the effect in the Effects area.

2. Click the Delete Effect button **10**. The effect is deleted from the list.

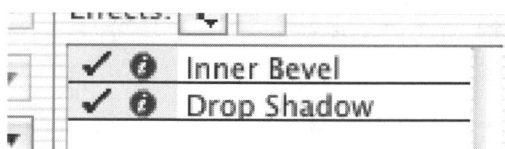

11 *Multiple effects are listed in the Effects list.*

To apply multiple effects:

1. Click the Add Effects icon to choose additional effects. Each effect is listed in the Effects List **11**.

2. Drag the effects up or down in the list to change the order in which the effect modifies the image **12**.

12 **Drag an effect to a new position** *in the Effects list to change how the effect is applied.*

TIP Each effect is applied in the order that it appears in the Effects list. When you change the order of the effects, you may change the appearance of the object **13**.

TIP If you have many effects, use the All On or All Off commands in the Effects menu to turn all the effects on and off at once.

TIP Rather than replicate intricate effects settings over and over, you can save the settings in the Effects area as a style that can be easily applied to other objects *(see page 213).*

13 *The difference between positioning the* **Drop Shadow** effect above the Inner Bevel in the Effects list (left) *or positioning the* **Drop Shadow** below the Inner Bevel (right).

Applying Bevel Effects

The Bevel effects simulate the look of 3D objects such as chiseled letters or carved forms . Fireworks lets you apply bevels to either the inside or outside of objects.

⓮ *Different looks that can be created using the* **Outer Bevel** *(left) and* **Inner Bevel** *(right).*

To apply a Bevel effect:

1. Select an object.

2. Choose Outer Bevel from the Effects list. The Outer Bevel controls appear **⓯**.

   or

   Choose Inner Bevel from the Effects list. The Inner Bevel controls appear **⓰**.

3. Choose one of the bevel shapes from the Bevel shape list **⓱**.

4. Use the Size control to change the pixel size of the bevel.

5. If you have chosen Outer Bevel, use the Color Well to change the color.

TIP The color of an inner bevel comes from the color of the original object.

6. Use the Contrast control to change the intensity of the light creating the bevel highlights and shadows.

7. Use the Softness control to change the hardness of the edges of the bevel.

TIP If the bevel around curved objects appears bumpy, increase the softness to smooth the bevel.

8. Use the Angle control to change the angle of the light on the beveled edge.

9. Use the bevel presets to quickly apply changes to the bevels **⓲**.

   • **Raised** leaves the object as styled.
   • **Highlighted** lightens the object as if a 25% white tint were applied.
   • **Inset** reverses the lighting of the bevel to invert the 3D effect.
   • **Inverted** reverses the lighting and lightens the object with a tint.

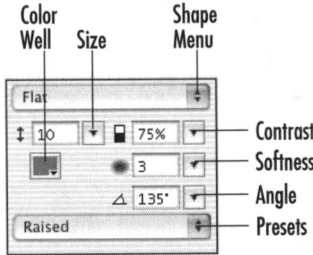

⓯ *The* **Outer Bevel** *controls.*

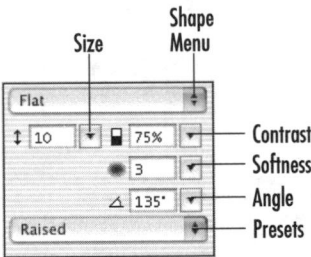

⓰ *The* **Inner Bevel** *controls.*

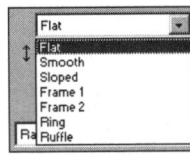

⓱ *The* **Bevel Shape** *menu.*

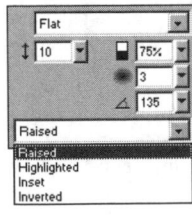

⓲ *The* **Bevel Presets.**

Applying Bevel Effects

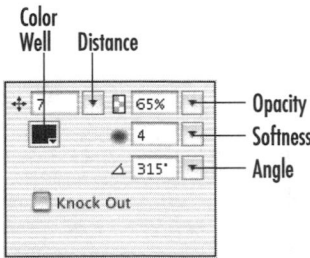

⑲ *Different looks that can be created using the* **Inner Shadow** *(left) and* **Outer Shadow** *(right).*

Color Well — Distance

Opacity
Softness
Angle
Knock Out

⑳ *The* **Drop Shadow** *and* **Inner Shadow** controls.

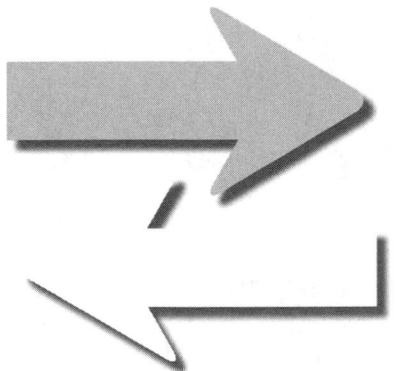

㉑ *The difference between a regular drop shadow (top) and a drop shadow set to Knock Out (bottom).*

Applying Shadow Effects

The shadow effects simulate the look of objects casting a shadow on a wall or cutting out a hole in a background **⑲**.

To apply a Shadow effect:

1. Choose Drop Shadow from the Effects menu. The Drop Shadow controls appear **⑳**.

   or

   Choose Inner Shadow from the Effects list. The Inner Shadow controls appear.

   TIP There is no difference between the controls for the Drop Shadow and Inner Shadow effects.

2. Use the Opacity control to change the transparency of the shadow. The lower the number, the more transparent the object.

3. Use the Softness control to change the softness, or feathering, applied to the edge of the shadow.

4. Use the Angle control to change the angle of the light casting the shadow.

5. Use the Distance control to change how far the shadow falls from the object.

6. Use the Color Well to choose a color for the shadow.

7. Select Knock Out to have only the shadow appear, not the object casting the shadow **㉑**.

Applying Shadow Effects

Applying Emboss Effects

The emboss effect pushes the shape of one object into another object or out from the background 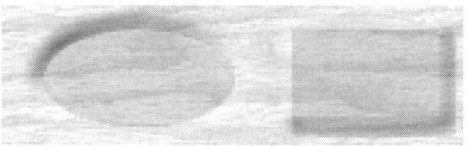.

To apply a Raised Emboss or Inset Emboss effect:

1. Choose Raised Emboss from the Effects list. The Raised Emboss controls appear ㉓.

    or

    Choose Inset Emboss from the Effects list. The Inset Emboss controls appear ㉓.

2. Use the Size control to change the width or size of the embossed edge.

3. Use the Contrast control to change the intensity of the light creating the embossing highlights and shadows.

4. Use the Softness control to change the sharpness of the edges of the embossing.

5. Use the Angle control to change the angle of the light on the embossing.

6. Choose Show Object to see any fill or strokes that are applied to the object ㉔ and ㉕.

    or

    Deselect Show Object to display the background color or any other objects seen within the emboss effects ㉔ and ㉕.

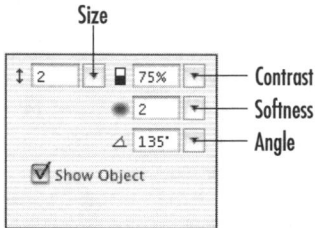

㉒ *Different looks that can be created using the* **Inset Emboss** *(left) and* **Raised Emboss** *(right).*

㉓ *The* **Raised Emboss** *and* **Inset Emboss** controls.

㉔ *A Raised Emboss effect with* **Show Object** turned on *(top).* **Show Object** is turned off *for the bottom text.*

㉕ *An Inset Emboss effect with* **Show Object** turned on *(top).* **Show Object** is turned off *for the bottom text.*

Applying Emboss Effects

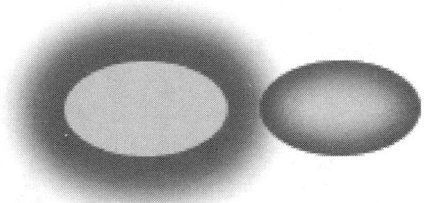

㉖ *Different looks that can be created using the* **Glow** *(left) and* **Inner Glow** *(right).*

Color
Well   Width

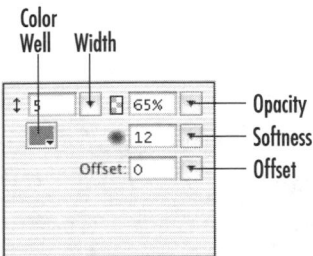

Opacity
Softness
Offset

㉗ *The* **Glow controls** *for both a Glow effect and an Inner Glow effect.*

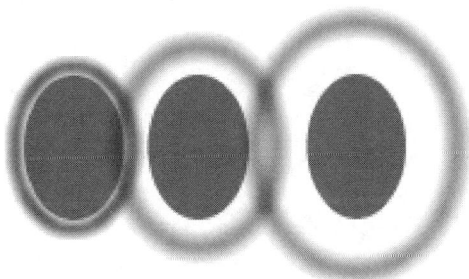

㉘ *Increasing the* **Offset amount** *adds space between the glow and the object.*

Applying Glow Effects

The glow effect lets you add a color all around the edges of an object **㉖**.

To apply a Glow effect:

1. Choose one of the following from the Shadow and Glow category in the Effects menu:
   - **Glow** applies a glow outside the object.
   - **Inner Glow** applies a glow inside the object.

TIP The Glow effect choices are the same for both the Glow and Inner Glow **㉗**.

2. Use the Opacity control to change the transparency of the glow. The lower the number, the greater the transparency.

3. Use the Softness control to change the softness, or feathering, applied to the glow.

4. Use the Width control to change the size of the glow.

5. Use the Offset control to add a space between the object and the glow **㉘**.

6. Use the Color Well to choose a color for the glow.

Applying Effects to Bitmap Images

You can apply effects to bitmap images, but the effect will be applied to the entire image. This means that a bevel, shadow, or glow will be seen only on the outside edge of the image. For most images, that means the effect is applied to the rectangle around the image. However, if the image has any transparent areas, then the effect is visible around the transparent area.

If you want the look of an effect inside a portion of an image, you should use the filters in the Filter menu *(see page 174)*.

Applying Blur Effects

The blur effects soften the details in objects. They can be used to make one object appear as if it is behind others. The effects are most obvious when applied to pixel-based images, but they also affect patterns, textures, and gradients applied to objects.

TIP The blur effects work by changing some of the blacks and whites in an image to shades of gray. This means that some of the details of an image are lost.

To apply the Blur effects:

◆ Choose Blur or Blur More from the Effects category pop-up list. The name of the effect appears in the Effects list.

TIP The Blur ㉙ and Blur More ㉚ effects each apply a fixed amount of blur and do not have a dialog box to let you control the amount of the blur.

You can also apply a Gaussian Blur, which unlike the other Blur effects, lets you control the amount of blur in mathematical increments.

To apply the Gaussian Blur effect:

1. Choose Gaussian Blur from the Effects category pop-up list. The Gaussian Blur dialog box appears ㉛.

2. Use the slider to increase or decrease the amount of the blur.

3. Check Preview to see the effects of the blur on the selected object.

4. Click OK. The name of the effect appears in the Effects list as the effect is applied ㉜.

Original　　　　Blur effect applied

㉙ *The results of applying the* **Blur effect** *to an image.*

Original　　　　Blur More effect applied

㉚ *The results of applying the* **Blur More effect** *to an image.*

㉛ *The* **Gaussian Blur dialog box**.

Original　　　　Gaussian Blur effect applied

㉜ *The result of applying a 4-pixel setting of the Gaussian Blur effect to an image.*

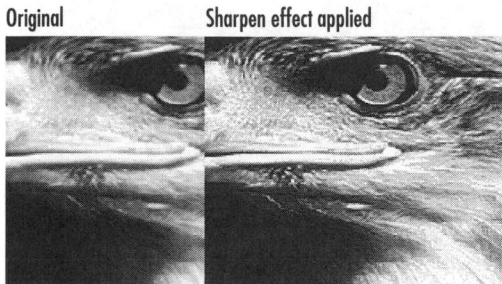

Original   Sharpen effect applied

33 *The results of applying the **Sharpen** effect to an image.*

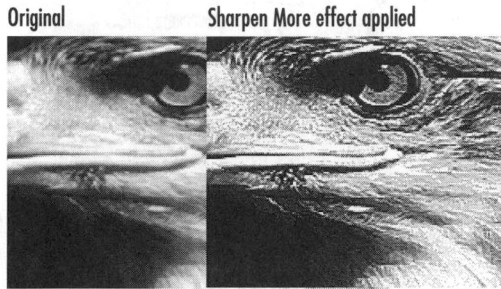

Original   Sharpen More effect applied

34 *The results of applying the **Sharpen More** effect to an image. Note the added detail around the eye and under the mouth.*

Applying Sharpening Effects

Just as you can blur images, so can you sharpen them. This is especially useful when working with scanned images that tend to look a little soft, or out of focus.

TIP The sharpen effects work by changing some gray pixels in the image to black or white. Although it may seem that more detail is revealed, strictly speaking some of the original scanned information is lost.

To apply the Sharpen effects:

◆ Choose Sharpen or Sharpen More from the Effects category pop-up list. The name of the effect appears in the Effects list.

TIP The Sharpen **33** and Sharpen More **34** effects each apply a fixed amount of sharpening and do not have a dialog box to let you control the amount of the blur.

Applying Sharpening Effects

Why We Sharpen

If I had to say what is the number one flaw in Web graphics, it would be everything is too soft or needs sharpening. There are plenty of reasons why images need to be sharpened.

First, I don't care how good your scanner is: I've yet to see a scan from a desktop scanner that doesn't need a little bit of sharpening applied. The very act of scanning softens images. Sharpening fixes that softness.

Even if you start with the most perfect scan in the entire world, most likely you have scaled it down to fit your Web page. The act of scaling also softens images. So, once again, a little sharpening is needed.

As you can see on these pages, the Sharpen and Sharpen More effects are quick and easy ways to fix soft images. However, the best way to sharpen an image is to use the Unsharp Mask effect *(covered on the next page)*. I know the name sounds like it unsharpens (blurs) images. Trust me, it doesn't.

The Unsharp Mask effect is exactly what you need to make your scanned images and stock photos look better.

The other type of sharpening effect goes under the unlikely name Unsharp Mask. This comes from a traditional photographic technique.

To apply the Unsharp Mask effect:

1. Choose Unsharp Mask from the Effects category pop-up list. The Unsharp Mask dialog box appears 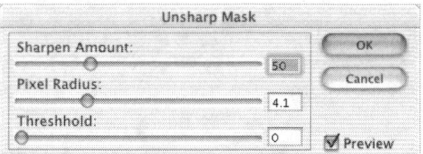.

2. Drag the Sharpen Amount slider to change the amount of contrast that is applied. The greater the amount, the greater the sharpening ⑯.

3. Drag the Threshold slider to set how different the pixels must be before they are sharpened.

TIP A threshold of 0 means that all the pixels in the image are sharpened.

TIP A high threshold means that only those pixels that are very different in brightness are sharpened. For instance, in illustration ⑯, a high threshold means that only the sharp line in the beak would be sharpened. A low threshold means that the gray feathers in the lower right corner would also be sharpened.

4. Drag the Pixel Radius slider or type in the field to set how many pixels in proximity to the edge that have the sharpening effect applied.

5. Check Preview to see the effects of the unsharp mask on the selected object.

6. Click OK. The name of the effect appears in the Effects list as the effect is applied.

TIP High Unsharp Mask settings with a high sharpen and low threshold settings can cause an unwanted halo or glow around objects ⑰.

⑮ *The* **Unsharp Mask dialog box.**

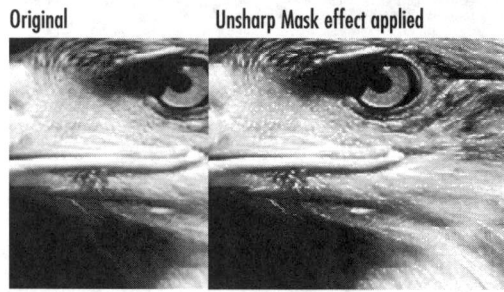

⑯ *The result of applying the* **Unsharp Mask** **effect** *to an image.*

⑰ *The Unsharp Mask effect at a high sharpen and low threshold can create an* **unnatural glow** *around details in an image.*

Original | Find Edges and Invert effects applied

③ *The effect of applying the* **Find Edges effect** *and then the* **Invert effect** *to an image.*

Original | Convert to Alpha effect applied

③ *The effect of applying the* **Convert to Alpha** **effect** *to an object containing a linear gradient.*

Applying the Find Edges Effect

The Find Edges effect changes the colors of the pixels of an image so that a line appears where there was an edge.

To apply the Find Edges effect:

◆ Choose Find Edges from the Other menu of the Effects pop-up list. The image is converted and the name of the effect appears in the Effects list.

TIP Use the Invert effect *(see page 146)* after the Find Edges effect to convert the image to black on white **③**. This simulates the look of a pen-and-ink sketch.

Using the Convert to Alpha Effect

The Convert to Alpha effect converts an object or image into a grayscale or alpha channel version. This lets you create see-through effects based on the colors of an image.

To apply the Convert to Alpha effect:

◆ Choose Convert to Alpha from the Other menu of the Effects pop-up list. The image is converted and the name of the effect appears in the Effects list.

TIP Alpha areas that are white allow the images underneath to be seen. Alpha areas that are dark hide the images underneath.

TIP The Convert to Alpha effect is very similar to masking using the grayscale values of an image **③**.

Applying the Adjust Color Effects

Fireworks also has a set of effects that alter certain aspects of the appearance of colors in objects and images, such as brightness, contrast, and tonal relationships. These effects are similar to those found in image-editing programs such as Adobe Photoshop.

To apply the Auto Levels effect:

◆ Choose Auto Levels from the Adjust Color menu of the Effects category pop-up list. This applies a preset adjustment of the Levels effect *(see page 146)* to the tones of the object ⓯.

TIP Because there are no user controls for the Auto Levels effect, the command is not often used except for those unwilling to learn the other commands.

Original   Auto Levels effect applied

⓯ *The result of applying the* **Auto Levels effect** *to an image.*

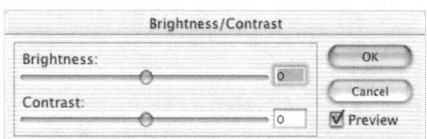

⓰ *The* **Brightness/Contrast dialog box.**

Brightness and Contrast are the simplest ways to adjust the light and dark areas in an image. The brightness and contrast settings shift all the values of the image.

To apply the Brightness/Contrast effect:

1. Choose Brightness/Contrast from the Adjust Color menu of the Effects category pop-up list. The Brightness/Contrast dialog box appears ⓰.

2. Use the Brightness slider to increase or decrease the lightness of the image.

3. Use the Contrast slider to increase or decrease the contrast of the image.

4. Check Preview to see how the controls affect the image.

5. Click OK. The name of the effect appears in the Effects list.

TIP Brightness and Contrast are extremely rudimentary controls. Most designers use the more sophisticated Curves *(see next page)* and Levels *(see page 146)* controls.

Modification point   Eyedroppers

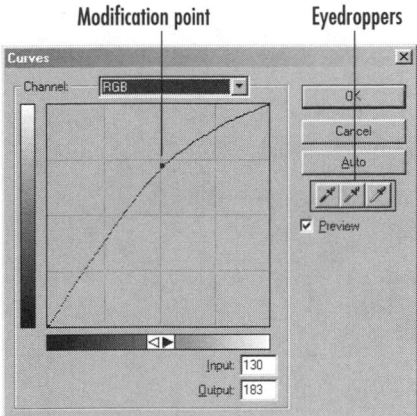

④② *The* **Curves dialog box.**

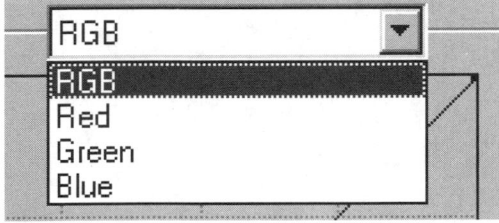

④③ *The* **Channel menu** *in the Curves dialog box.*

Color Well   Blending Mode menu

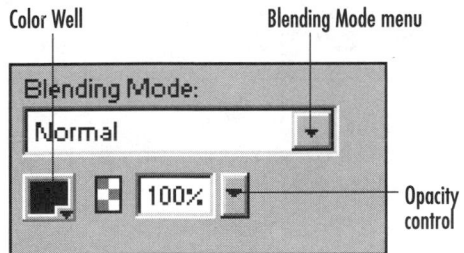

④④ *The* **Color Fill panel.**

The Curves effect uses a tonal graph to change the appearance of an image. Each position on the graph corresponds to a value in the red, green, or blue channels of the image. Moving points on the curve changes those color values in the image.

To apply the Curves effect:

1. Choose Curves from the Adjust Color menu of the Effects category pop-up list. The Curves dialog box appears **④②**.

2. Set the channel menu to RGB to change the red, green, and blue channels together **④③**.

   or

   Choose a specific channel to change.

3. Drag a point on the graph to change the straight line to a curve. Move the curve up to lighten the area. Move the curve down to darken the area.

4. Use the Eyedroppers to choose the image's black, neutral, and white points.

5. Check Preview to see how the controls affect the image.

The Color Fill effect allows you to easily tint or change the color of scanned images.

To apply the Color Fill effect:

1. Choose Color Fill from the Adjust Color menu of the Effects category pop-up list. The Color Fill panel appears **④④**.

2. Use the Color Well to choose a color.

3. Use the Opacity control to set the transparency of the color.

   TIP If you want to change an object's color, it is easier to just change the fill color. However, the Color Fill effect is helpful when animating objects so they change from one color to another. (*See Chapter 16, "Animations."*)

Applying the Adjust Color Effects

The Invert effect reverses selected images, turning them into negatives.

To apply the Invert effect:

◆ Choose Invert from the Adjust Color menu of the Effects category pop-up list. The colors of the image are reversed **45** and the name of the effect is added to the Effects list.

TIP The Invert command can be used if you want to turn photograph negatives into positive images. It can also be used for dramatic interactive effects.

Original   Invert effect applied

45 *The effect of applying the* **Invert effect** *to an image.*

The Levels effect gives you a set of controls for changing the values of an image. These controls let you move the black, white, and midpoint values of the image.

To apply the Levels effect:

1. Choose Levels from the Adjust Color menu of the Effects category pop-up list. The Levels dialog box appears **46**.

2. Set the channel list to RGB to change the red, green, and blue channels together.

   or

   Choose a specific channel to change.

3. Drag the Black point, Midpoint, or White point sliders to adjust the tonal range of the image.

   or

   Use the Eyedroppers to select the black point, white point, and midpoint on the image.

4. Drag sliders for the output ramp to change the appearance of the image.

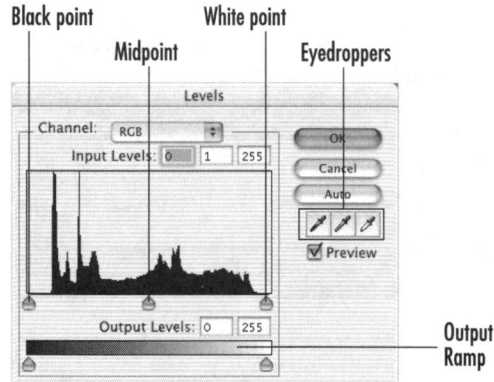

Black point   White point
   Midpoint   Eyedroppers
               Output Ramp

46 *The* **Levels** *dialog box.*

⓸ *The* Hue/Saturation dialog box.

The Hue/Saturation effect lets you shift the color values as well as tint images.

To apply the Hue/Saturation effect:

1. Choose Hue/Saturation from the Adjust Color menu of the Effects category pop-up list. The Hue/Saturation dialog box appears **⓸**.

2. Use the Hue slider to change the range of colors in the image. As you move the slider, the colors shift.

3. Use the Saturation slider to increase or decrease the saturation of the colors in the image. The higher the saturation, the more intense the colors appear.

4. Use the Lightness slider to increase or decrease the lightness of the image. Increasing the lightness is similar to adding white to the image.

5. Click Colorize to convert the image to monotone. The Saturation slider can then be used to tint the image with a specific color.

6. Click Preview to see the effects of the controls on the image.

7. Click OK. This applies the Hue/Saturation effect to the image.

Applying the Adjust Color Effects

Third-Party Plug-ins

Fireworks also supports many third-party plug-ins such as the sample filters of the Alien Skin Eye Candy and Splat filters. These appear in the Effects menu and the Filters menu *(see page 174)*.

To add third-party plug-ins using the Effects list:

1. Choose Locate Plugins from the Effects list menu **48**.

2. Use the dialog box to navigate to the folder that contains the plug-ins.

3. Select the folder. An alert box informs you that the next time you launch Fireworks, the plug-ins will be available in the Effects list.

TIP This technique also adds plug-ins to the Filters menu *(see page 174)*.

To add third party plug-ins using Preferences:

1. Choose **Edit** > **Preferences** to open the Preferences dialog box **49**.

   or

   (Mac OS X) Choose **Fireworks** > **Preferences** to open the Preferences dialog box.

2. (Mac) Choose Folders from the pop-up menu.

   or

   (Win) Choose Folders from the tab at the top of the Preferences dialog box.

3. Choose Photoshop® Plug-ins.

4. Click the Browse button.

5. Use the dialog box to navigate to the folder that contains your Photoshop plug-ins.

6. Select the folder.

7. Quit and re-launch Fireworks to see the plug-ins in the Effects list.

TIP Fireworks MX does not use Photoshop plug-ins from Adobe Systems Inc.

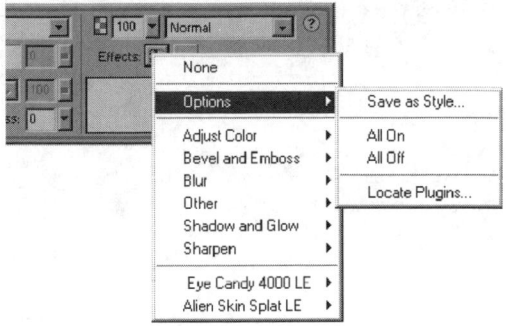

48 *The* **Options submenu** *lets you choose to locate third-party plug-ins.*

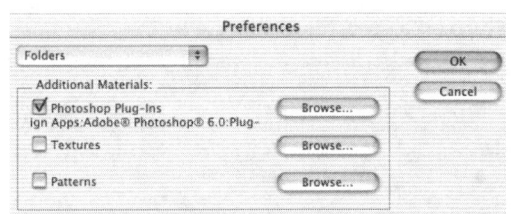

49 *Use the* **Preferences dialog box** *to select the folder that contains the additional plug-ins.*

WORKING WITH BITMAPS 10

The vector tools in Macromedia Fireworks make it easy to create objects. But that's not the only artwork it can produce. What if you want to use images such as photographs or scanned art that cannot be created by vector objects?

Fortunately there is an alter ego to the vector side of Fireworks—a complete set of features for creating, importing, retouching, and working with pixel-based artwork. These are similar to the pixel-editing features found in programs such as Adobe Photoshop, Jasc Paint Shop Pro, and Procreate Painter.

Although technically the correct term for this type of graphic is pixel-based or raster images, Macromedia calls them bitmap images.

Please note that when I write about pixels in images, I am not writing about Pixel, my cat. An image pixel is a small square of color that, together with other pixels, creates a scanned image. Pixel, the cat, is a lazy beast who hisses at strangers, doesn't create anything, and couldn't care less about scanned images.

Importing Bitmap Images

Bitmap images, such as those created by programs like Adobe Photoshop or Procreate Painter can be inserted into Fireworks files.

To import bitmap images:

1. With a Fireworks document open, choose **File > Import**. The operating system dialog box opens.

2. Navigate to find the file you want to import.

3. Click OK. The corner-shaped, import cursor indicates the file is ready to be placed on the currently selected Fireworks layer ❶.

4. Click on the canvas area to place the image at its original size.

   or

   Drag the import cursor to draw a rectangle that scales the image to fit ❷.

To open bitmap images:

1. Choose **File > Open**.

2. Navigate to find the bitmap image file and click OK.

3. Select Open as "Untitled" to open the file as a new document.

   or

   Leave the option Open as "Untitled" deselected to open the file under its original name.

4. Click the Open button. The file opens as a Fireworks document.

TIP If the Photoshop file contains layers, each of the layers appears in its own layer as a bitmap image ❸.

❶ *The* import cursor *for imported artwork.*

❷ *Drag the import pointer to place the imported artwork at a specific size. (The arrow indicates the direction of the drag.)*

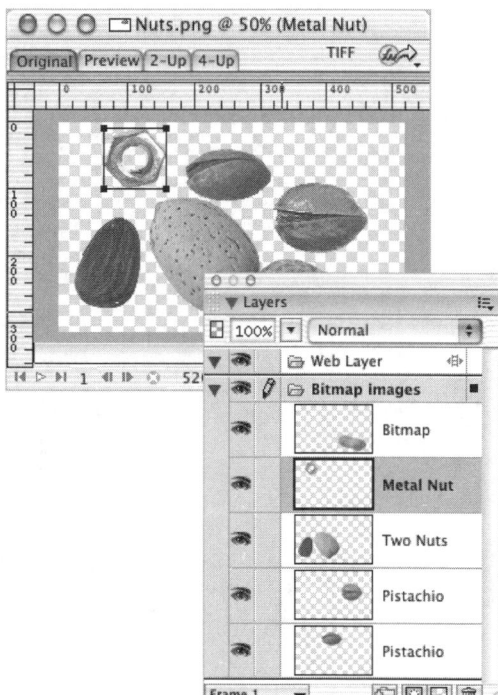

❸ **Photoshop images are imported into Fireworks** *with each of the Photoshop layers as their own bitmap image.*

Exit Bitmap Mode

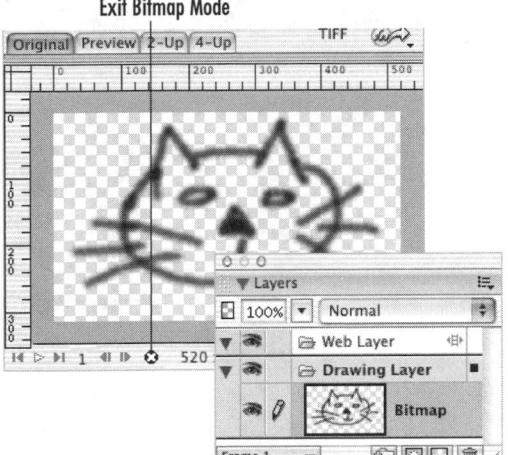

❹ Using the bitmap drawing tools *automatically creates a new bitmap object.*

When you use any of the bitmap tools, you create a new bitmap object.

To create a new bitmap object:

◆ Use one of the bitmap drawing tools. Fireworks automatically creates a new bitmap area on the canvas ❹ *(see page 52).*

   or

   Choose **Edit** > **Insert** > **Empty Bitmap** to create a new bitmap object.

TIP You can leave the bitmap mode by clicking the Exit Bitmap Mode icon at the bottom of the document window.

If you have a scanner, you can scan images directly into Fireworks.

To scan an image directly into Fireworks:

1. Choose **File** > **Scan** and then use the TWAIN module or Acquire plug-in that matches your scanner.

2. Follow the scanner software instructions to scan the image. The image opens as a native Fireworks document.

Switching to the Bitmap Mode

The first version of Fireworks made you consciously switch into the bitmap mode in order to edit bitmap images. Later versions made it a little easier to switch between bitmap and vector mode.

Today's Fireworks make it even easier to work in the bitmap mode. All you have to do is choose any of the bitmap tools and Fireworks automatically switches to the bitmap mode. Choose a vector tool, and you're back in the vector mode. It's so easy you don't even have to think about it.

How do you know if you're in the bitmap mode? It doesn't really matter. Fireworks automatically switches to the correct mode. If the Exit Bitmap Mode icon is red, you're in the bitmap mode. You can also set the bitmap preferences to display a striped line around the canvas that indicates when you are in the bitmap mode *(see page 173).*

Working with Photoshop Files

Fireworks makes it easy to work with Photoshop files. Almost all the features in a native Photoshop file are kept when the file is opened in Fireworks. Objects on Photoshop layers are imported as their own Fireworks objects. Text layers in Photoshop are converted to Fireworks text.

However, there are some features in Photoshop that have no equivalent in Fireworks. *(For more information on importing Photoshop files, see page 235.)* You may want to experiment opening Photoshop files in Fireworks to make sure the files are translated correctly.

Manipulating Bitmap Images

If you include bitmap images in your Fireworks files, you may want to crop those images to eliminate pixels you don't need.

To crop bitmap images:

1. Select a pixel image.

2. Choose **Edit** > **Crop Selected Bitmap**. A bounding box with handles appears around the image ❺.

3. Drag the handles so that they surround the area you want to keep.

4. Double-click inside the bounding box. The excess image is deleted.

❺ *The* **crop handles** *let you discard portions of imported images.*

You can also combine multiple bitmap objects into a single bitmap, convert vector objects into bitmaps, or add vector objects to bitmaps. Although it is easier to edit vector objects, you can use the Dodge, Burn, Blur, and Sharpen tools only on bitmap images.

TIP Although you may think of this technique as Merge Bitmaps or Convert Vector objects, Macromedia has named the command Flatten Selection.

To combine or convert objects into a single bitmap:

1. Use the Pointer tool to select the objects you want to combine or convert ❻.

TIP If you select a single vector object, you can use the command to convert it to a pixel-based image object.

2. Choose **Modify** > **Flatten Selection**. Vector objects are converted to pixels and separate bitmap images are combined into a single bitmap ❼.

❻ *Two bitmap images selected as separate images.*

❼ *The* **Flatten Selection** **command** *combines the two bitmap images into one bitmap object.*

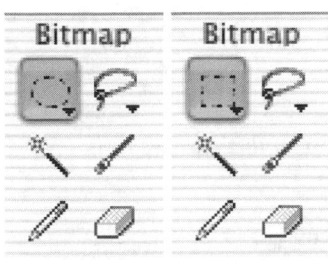

8 *The* **Marquee tools** *in the Tools panel.*

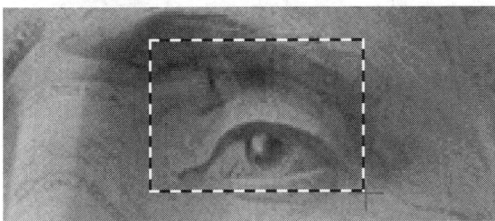

9 *The* **marching ants** *of the marquee surround the selected area.*

Width   Height

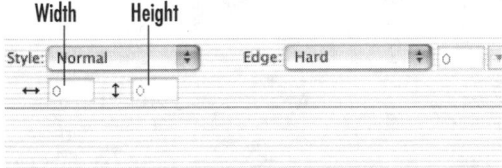

10 *The* **Marquee tool options** *in the Property Inspector.*

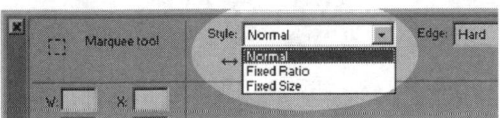

11 *The* **Style menu** *for the marquee tools.*

Selecting Pixels

The two basic bitmap selection tools are the two Marquee tools (rectangle and ellipse) and the two Lasso tools (regular and polygon).

To use the Marquee tools:

1. Choose either the Marquee tool or Oval Marquee tool in the Tools panel **8**.

2. Move the cursor over the image area and drag diagonally to create a selection. A series of moving dashes (called *marching ants*) indicates the selected area **9**.

   TIP Press the mouse and then hold the Opt/Alt key to draw the selection from the center outward, instead of from the corner.

   TIP Hold the Shift key to constrain the selection to a square or circle.

The marquee tool styles let you set specific sizes or proportions for the selected area.

To change the Marquee tool constraints:

1. Select either of the Marquee tools in the Tools panel. The Marquee tool options appear in the Property Inspector **10**.

2. Choose one of the following from the Style menu **11**:

   • **Normal** creates a marquee without any constraints on its size.
   • **Fixed Ratio** constrains the marquee to the ratios specified in the width and the height fields.
   • **Fixed Size** constrains the marquee to the pixel amounts in the width and height fields.

3. If you have chosen Fixed Ratio, enter the ratios in the width and height fields.

   or

   If you have chosen Fixed Size, enter the amounts (in pixels) in the width and height fields.

You can also change the appearance of the edges of a marquee selection.

To change the Marquee tool edges:

1. In the Marquee Tool Options panel, choose from the Edge menu 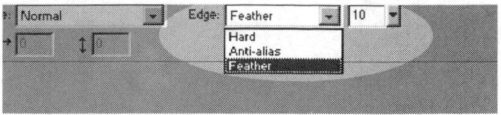.
   - **Hard** gives the selection a solid or jagged edge .
   - **Anti-Alias** gives the selection a smoother edge .
   - **Feather** blurs the edges of the selection .

2. If you choose Feather, set the amount of the blur with the control slider or type the amount of the feather (in pixels) in the field.

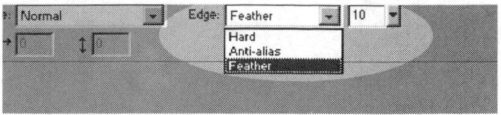

⑫ *The **Edge menu** for the Marquee tools.*

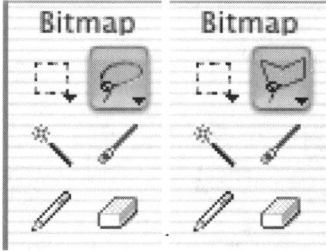

⑬ *The effects of **changing the edge choices** of a selection.*

You might want to select shapes besides rectangles and ellipses. To do so, you can use either of the Lasso tools.

To use the Lasso tools:

1. Choose either the Lasso tool or the Polygon Lasso tool in the Tools panel 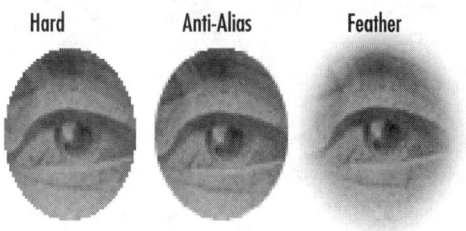.

2. Use the Edge menu in the Property Inspector to choose Hard Edge, Anti-Alias, or Feather. *(See the previous exercise for explanations of the choices.)*

3. With the Lasso tool, drag around the area you want to select 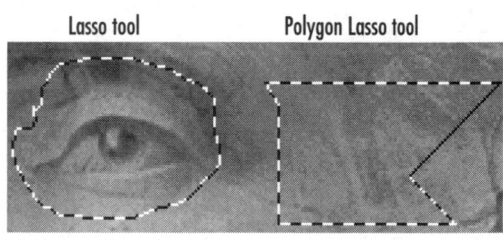.

   or

   With the Polygon Lasso tool, click the cursor around the area you want to select. Each click creates a point of the polygon that selects the area .

TIP The Lasso tool is useful for following the curved contours of images. The Polygon Lasso tool is best for creating selections with straight sides.

⑭ *The **Lasso and Polygon Lasso** tools in the Tools panel.*

⑮ *A comparison of the Lasso tool and the Polygon Lasso tool.*

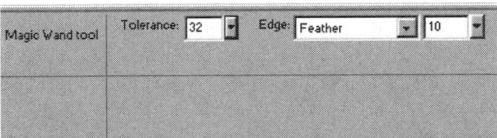

16 *The* **Magic Wand** *tool in the Tools panel.*

17 *The* **Magic Wand tool options** *in the Property Inspector.*

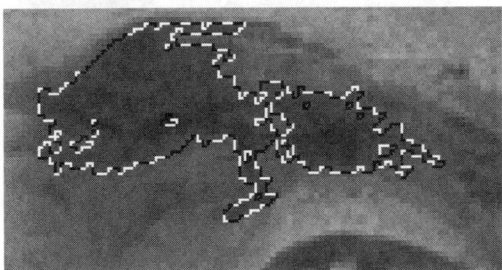

18 *The area selected with the Magic Wand tool.*

You can also select areas by their color. To do this, you use the Magic Wand tool.

To use the Magic Wand:

1. Choose the Magic Wand in the Tools panel **16**. The Magic Wand tool options appear in the Property Inspector.

2. In the Magic Wand tool options, use the Tolerance control to set how many colors the Magic Wand selects **17**. *(See the sidebar on this page for more information on setting the Tolerance controls.)*

3. Use the Edge list in the Tool Options panel to choose among Hard Edge, Anti-Alias, or Feather *(see the exercise on the previous page).*

4. Click the area you want to select. The marching ants indicate the selected area **18**.

After you finish working with a selection, you can deselect the selected area.

To deselect a selected area:

◆ Click outside the selection with one of the Marquee or Lasso tools.

or

Choose **Select > Deselect**.

TIP You cannot deselect with the Magic Wand tool by clicking outside the selection. This only selects a different area.

To hide the marching ants around a selection:

◆ Choose **View > Hide Edges** to hide the display of the marching ants around a selection.

TIP The Hide Edges command keeps the selection in effect — you just don't see the marching ants.

Setting the Tolerance

Tolerance controls how many similar colors the Magic Wand selects that are adjacent to the original point where you click. The lowest tolerance, 0, selects only one color, the exact color of the pixel clicked with the Magic Wand. If any pixels next to that one are the same color, then those pixels are also selected. But as soon as any pixel is different, that color is not selected. As you increase the tolerance, up to 255, the Magic Wand selects a greater range of colors.

You can change a selected area by using modifier keys with any of the selection tools.

To change the shape of selections:

1. Use any of the selection tools to select an area.

2. Hold the Shift key to add to the selected area. The plus (+) sign indicates you are adding to the selection **⑲**.

   or

   Hold the Opt/Alt key to delete from the selected area. The minus (–) sign indicates you are subtracting from the selection **⑳**.

TIP You can switch tools at any time. For instance, if the original selection was created by the Magic Wand, you can use the Lasso to modify it.

TIP The additional selection does not have to touch the original. For instance, you can select the top and bottom of an image, leaving the middle untouched.

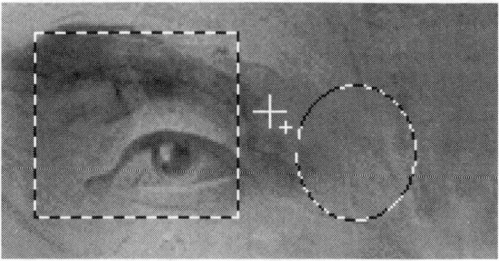

⑲ *Hold the Shift key to* **add to a selection**.

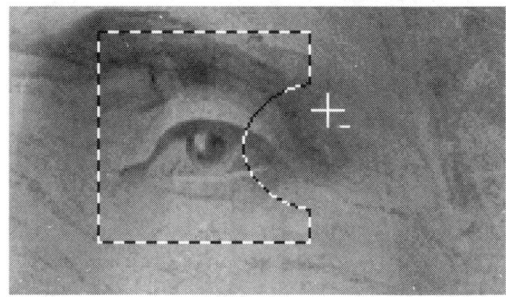

⑳ *Hold the Opt/Alt key to* **delete from a selection**.

Rather than use Marquee, Lasso, or Magic Wand tools, you can also use menu commands to select pixels. Because these commands have keyboard shortcuts (shown next to their commands in the menu), the shortcuts make it easier to select and deselect areas.

To use the Selection commands:

◆ Choose **Select** > **Select All** to select all the pixels in the image.

   or

   Choose **Select** > **Deselect** to deselect the pixels enclosed by the marching ants.

   or

   Choose **Select** > **Select Inverse** to swap the status of the selected pixels, that is, deselect the selected pixels and select everything else.

Selecting Pixels

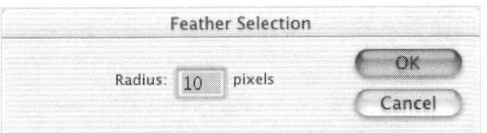

㉑ *Before the* **Select Similar command** *(top), only the color in the letter K is selected. After the Select Similar command is applied (bottom), other areas with a similar color are selected.*

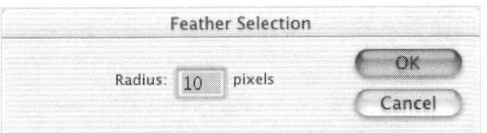

㉒ *The* **Feather Selection dialog box**.

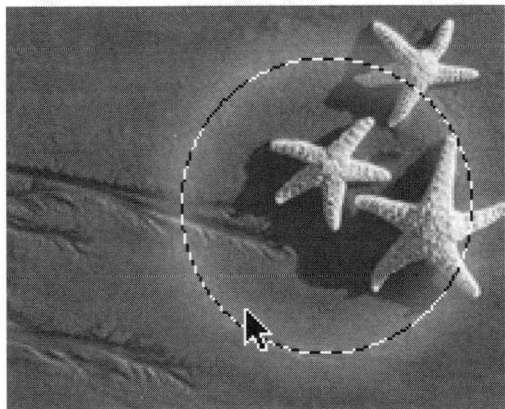

㉓ *Press on the marching ants to see a glow that indicates the area that is feathered.*

Once you have selected a certain area with the Magic Wand, you might not want to keep clicking to select similar colors.

To use the Similar command:

With an area selected, choose **Select > Select Similar**. This selects all the areas of the image that have the same color **㉑**.

TIP The Select Similar command uses the tolerance set for the Magic Wand.

TIP You can also use the Select Similar command on selections created by the Marquee or Lasso tools.

Even if you have not applied a feather to the original selection tool, you can still feather the selection afterwards. This allows you to create a softer edge to the selected area.

To feather a selection:

1. With the area selected, choose **Select > Feather** to open the Feather Selection dialog box **㉒**.

2. Enter the number of pixels that you want to blur along the edge of the selection and then click OK.

TIP To see the feathering, position the Pointer tool over the marching ants and press the mouse button. The feathering is displayed as a glow in the image **㉓**.

Selecting Pixels

Once you have made a selection, you can change the size or shape of the marching ants using the Marquee commands.

TIP Even though these commands use the term "Marquee," they can be used on selections created with any of the selection tools.

To expand the size of a selections:

1. With an area selected, choose **Select > Expand Marquee**. This opens the Expand Marquee dialog box **24**.

2. Set the size (in pixels) of how much to increase the marquee area.

3. Click OK. The size of the selection increases **25**.

To contract the size of a selections:

1. With an area selected, choose **Select > Contract Marquee**. This opens the Contract Marquee dialog box **24**.

2. Set the size (in pixels) of how much to decrease the marque area.

3. Click OK. The size of the selection decreases **25**.

To create a border around a selections:

1. With an area selected, choose **Select > Border Marquee**. This opens the Border Marquee dialog box **24**.

2. Set the size (in pixels) of the radius of the border.

3. Click OK. The selected area is converted into a border **25**.

To smooth the edges of a selections:

1. With an area selected, choose **Select > Smooth Marquee**. This opens the Smooth Marquee dialog box **24**.

2. Set the size (in pixels) of how big an area should be smoothed.

3. Click OK. The shape of the selection changes **25**.

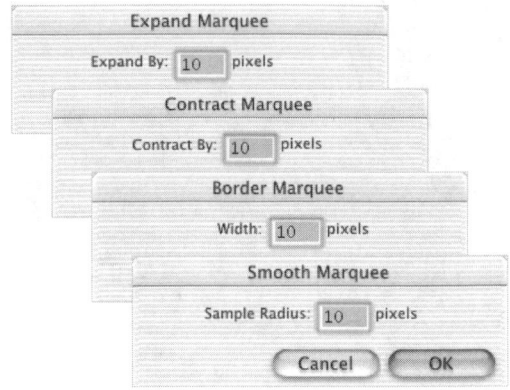

24 *The* Expand Marquee, Contract Marquee, Border Marquee, and Smooth Marquee *dialog boxes.*

Original selection

Expand Marquee   Contract Marquee

Border Marquee   Smooth Marquee

25 *The results of applying the* **Expand Marquee, Contract Marquee, Border Marquee,** *and* **Smooth Marquee** *commands to a selection.*

Move Selection cursor

㉖ A selection can be moved *without disturbing the pixels of the image inside the selection.*

Cut Selection cursor

㉗ A selection and its contents can be cut *from its image.*

Copy Selection cursor

㉘ *A selection can be moved while making a* **copy** of the contents.

Working with Selections

Once you made a selection, there are all sorts of things you can do with it. For instance, you might want to move the selection so that it is exactly over a certain area, without disturbing the pixels beneath it. Conversely, you can move both the selection and the image. Finally, you can simultaneously move the selection and copy the image.

To move a selection:

1. With one of the bitmap selection tools chosen, move the cursor within the marching ants selection. The cursor changes to the Move Selection cursor **㉖**.

2. Drag the selection to a new position.

To move a selection and the image:

1. With one of the bitmap selection tools chosen, hold the Cmd/Ctrl key and move the cursor within the marching ants selection. The cursor changes to the Cut Selection cursor **㉗**.

2. Drag the selection and image to the new position.

To move a selection and copy the image:

1. With one of the bitmap selection tools chosen, hold the Cmd+Opt (Mac) or Ctrl+Alt (Win) keys and move the cursor within the marching ants selection. The cursor changes to the copy selection cursor **㉘**.

2. Drag the selection and image to the new position.

TIP Copying a selection adds it to the currently chosen bitmap so that all the pixels merge together into one image. *(See the next page for how to copy a selection as a separate bitmap.)*

You can delete the image within a selection.

To delete the image inside a selection:

◆ With the selection active, press the Delete (Backspace) key.

Using a combination of the selection commands, you can create a vignette (faded cropping) of an image. This is a great way to quickly add interest to an ordinary photograph.

To create a vignette:

1. Use any of the bitmap selection tools to select the area that should appear inside the vignette. For example, use the Lasso tool to select an area around the focus of the image **29**.

2. Choose **Select** > **Feather** to apply a soft blur to the edge of the selection.

TIP You can also apply the feather to the selection using the Property Inspector for the selection tool.

3. Choose **Select** > **Select Inverse**. This selects the area that should be deleted **30**.

4. Press Delete/Backspace to delete the area outside the original selection **31**.

You can also copy the image inside a selection and then paste it into a separate bitmapped image in the same Fireworks document or a new document.

To copy a selection into a new bitmapped image:

1. Use any of the bitmap selection tools to select the area that should appear inside the vignette.

2. Choose **Edit** > **Copy**.

3. Click the Add Layer icon in the Layers panel.

4. Choose **Edit** > **Paste**. The area inside the selection appears on the new layer.

29 *To vignette an image, create a feathered selection of the final vignette shape.*

30 *Use the Inverse command to select the other portions of the image.*

31 *Press the Delete/Backspace key to delete the selected area from the image.*

32 *Intricate selection shapes can be saved using the* **Save Bitmap Selection** *command.*

Save the Pixel!

I hate to lose pixels. They're much too valuable to just throw away.

So instead of permanently destroying the pixel data by deleting a selection, I'd rather use a mask to hide the area inside a selection. *(See the exercise on the next page.)*

Saving and Restoring Selections

Those marching ants, which indicate your selections, are fragile little creatures. If you deselect the selection, or exit the bitmap mode, you lose the marching ants that you worked so hard to shape just so. Fortunately, you can save the shape of the selection. Once you have saved a selection, you can reapply it at any time.

To save a selection shape:

1. Use any of the selection techniques to select a part of an image.

2. Choose **Select** > **Save Bitmap Selection**. The shape of the selection is stored with the document **32**.

TIP Only one selection is saved at a time. If you save another selection you delete the previously saved selection.

To reapply a stored selection shape:

1. Use the Pointer tool to select a bitmap image or use any of the bitmap tools to switch to the bitmap mode.

2. Choose **Select** > **Restore Bitmap Selection**. The shape of the selection is reapplied.

TIP The saved selection is stored inside the document and can be applied even after the document is closed and reopened.

Another way to save a selection is to convert the shape into a mask. This converts the shape of the marching ants into a grayscale mask. *(For more information on working with masks, see Chapter 12, "Masks.")*

To save a selection as a mask:

1. Create a selection around the area that you want to show.

2. Click the Add Mask icon at the bottom of the Layers panel ③. A mask is created that follows the contours of the marching ants ④.

   or

   Choose Add Mask from the Layers panel menu.

TIP Hold the Opt/Alt key as you click the Add Mask icon to create a mask that is the inverse of the selection, i.e. the area that is selected is hidden.

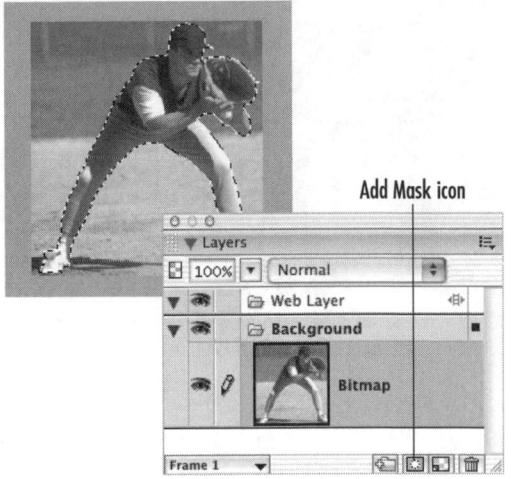

Add Mask icon

③ Click the **Add Mask icon** *to automatically convert the selection into a grayscale image that masks the original image.*

④ *A masked image shows only the area inside the white portions of the mask.*

Saving and Restoring Selections

35 *Although these two images may look like a father and son, the man on the right was created by retouching the older man on the left using Fireworks's bitmap retouching tools.*

36 *The* **Brush tool** *lets you draw bitmap strokes.*

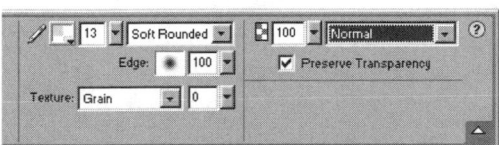

37 *The* **Brush tool** *in the Tools panel.*

Using the Bitmap Editing Tools

When should you use the bitmap tools? Not when you want to draw a simple circle, rectangle, or line. The vector drawing tools are much more flexible and should be used for those types of objects. You should use the bitmap tools when you do any sort of image retouching **35**.

The Brush tool draws bitmap strokes **36**. The look of the strokes made by the Brush tool changes depending on the settings in the Property Inspector.

To set the Brush tool options:

1. Choose the Brush tool in the Tools panel **37**. The Brush tool options appear in the Property Inspector **38**.

2. Set the controls for the brush stroke attributes. These are the same settings that are applied to vector paths. *(See pages 121 and 122 for details on setting the stroke attributes.)*

3. Set the opacity and blend mode settings for the brush stroke. These are the same as the opacity and blend modes that are applied to vector paths. *(See pages 132 and 133 for details on setting the opacity and blend modes.)*

TIP See the exercise on the page 165 for how to set the Preserve Transparency option.

TIP My favorite way to use the Brush tool is to retouch out wrinkles on faces. Choose a light facial color and then set the blend mode to lighten. This lightens just the dark areas of the wrinkles rather than painting all over the skin.

38 *The* **Brush tool options** *in the Property Inspector.*

Using the Bitmap Editing Tools

The Pencil tool is a more limited version of the Brush tool. The main benefit of the Pencil tool is to have all the Pencil stroke settings available in a tool separate from the Brush tool.

To set the Pencil tool options:

1. Choose the Pencil tool in the Tools panel 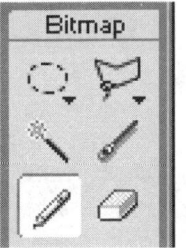. The Pencil tool options appear in the Property Inspector 39.

2. Use the Color Well to choose the color.

3. Check Anti-aliased to add a slight softness to the pencil line.

TIP The Anti-aliased option creates additional colors in artwork. This can add to the file size of the final Web graphics 40.

4. Choose Auto Erase to set the Pencil tool to erase previously drawn pencil marks by changing the Stroke color to the Fill color 41.

TIP The Auto Erase option does not actually erase pixels and may create unwanted pixels if the canvas color does not match the Fill color.

TIP Also, the Auto Erase option works best when the Anti-aliased option is turned off.

No Mode Worries

In previous versions of Fireworks, certain tools worked in either the vector or the bitmap mode. So the Brush tool could create paths or draw on bitmap images. Now, the bitmap tools automatically switch into the bitmap mode.

---

38 *The* **Pencil tool** *in the Tools panel.*

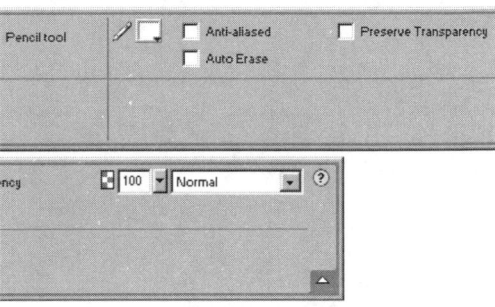

39 *The* **Pencil tool options** *in the Property Inspector.*

40 *The difference between a plain pencil stroke (top) and one set to anti-alias (bottom).*

41 *The* **Auto Erase option** *lets you cover up a pencil stroke with the Fill color.*

The Brush tool, Pencil tool, and Paint Bucket tool can be set so that they don't affect the transparent areas of the image.

To work with the Preserve Transparency setting:

1. Choose Preserve Transparency in the Property Inspector for the Brush tool, Pencil tool, Paint Bucket tool, or Gradient tool.

2. Use the tool in the document. Only those existing pixels are changed by the tool. Transparent areas remain transparent 🕸.

42 *The Brush tool set to* **Preserve Transparency** *draws only on the image.*

The Eraser tool erases pixels by deleting them and creating a transparent area in the bitmap image 🕸.

To set the Eraser tool options:

1. Choose the Eraser tool in the Tools panel 🕸. The Eraser tool options appear in the Property Inspector 🕸.

2. Use the Size control to set the size of the area erased by the Eraser tool.

3. Use the Edge control to set the softness of the Eraser edge.

4. Choose the circle or square shape of the Eraser tool.

5. Set the Opacity control to set how transparent the pixels become as the Eraser passes over them.

43 *An example of how the* **Eraser tool** *deletes pixels from an image.*

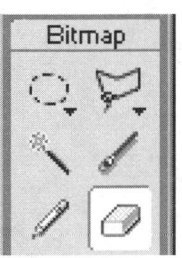

44 *The* **Eraser tool** *in the Tools panel.*

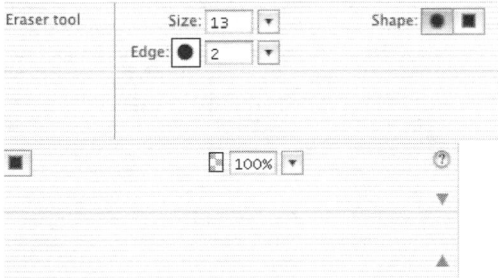

45 *The* **Eraser tool** *options in the Property Inspector.*

Using the Bitmap Editing Tools

The Rubber Stamp tool acts like a brush, but instead of painting with a solid color, you paint with an image. For example, in figure ㉟, I used the Rubber Stamp tool to paint out the apron on the younger man by sampling areas of the checkered shirt.

To set the Rubber Stamp options:

1. Choose the Rubber Stamp tool in the Tools panel ㊻. The Rubber Stamp options appear in the Property Inspector ㊼.

2. Use the Size control to set the size of the area drawn by the Rubber Stamp tool.

3. Use the Edge control to set the softness of the Rubber Stamp edge.

4. Choose Source Aligned to keep the image source positioned along with the movements of the mouse. Use this when you want to be able to release the mouse button but not lose the position you are copying.

   or

   Deselect Source Aligned to return the source to the original click point when you release the mouse. Use this when you want to make multiple copies of a part of the image.

5. Select Use Entire Document to sample images from anywhere inside the document.

   or

   Deselect Use Entire Document to sample only the pixels within the selected bitmap image.

6. Adjust the Opacity control to set how transparent the pixels become as the Eraser passes over them.

㊻ *The* **Rubber Stamp tool** *in the Tools panel.*

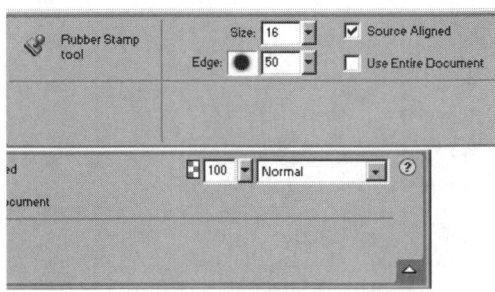

㊼ *The* **Rubber Stamp tool options** *in the Property Inspector.*

How the Rubber Stamp Works

Digital rubber stamps (such as the ones found in Fireworks or Photoshop) simply copy the image from one area and paint it onto another. This lets you paint part of one image onto another.

However, the Rubber Stamp tool does not recognize specific shapes or items. If you drag with the Rubber Stamp in a large enough area, you copy the image from one area to another.

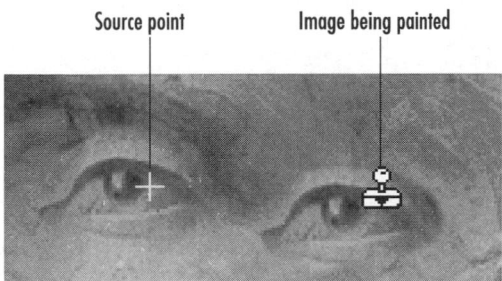

Source point — Image being painted

48 *The* **Rubber Stamp tool** *lets you sample one area and then paint it in another.*

49 *The* **Blur** *tool in the Tools panel.*

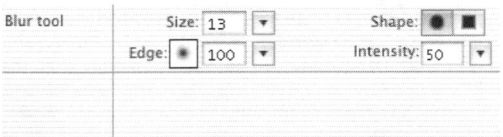

| Blur tool | Size: 13 | Shape: ● ■ |
| | Edge: ● 100 | Intensity: 50 |

50 *The* **Blur** *tool options in the Property Inspector.*

To use the Rubber Stamp tool:

1. Position the Rubber Stamp tool over the area that you want to copy.

2. Opt/Alt-click. A plus sign appears that indicates the source point.

3. Move the Rubber Stamp cursor where you want to paint with the sample and press and drag. The source point follows your movements as the Rubber Stamp paints the image where its cursor is **48**.

4. To change the sampled area, Opt/Alt-click.

5. Then paint with the Rubber Stamp tool with the new sampled area.

The Blur tool works like the blur effects except that instead of blurring the entire image, you can blur just the area where the tool passes over. In figure **35**, I used the blur tool to hide the wrinkles in the younger man's neck.

To use the Blur tool:

1. Choose the Blur tool in the Tools panel **49**. The Blur options appear in the Property Inspector **50**.

2. Use the Size control to set the size of the area blurred by the Blur tool.

3. Use the Edge control to set the softness of the Blur tool edge.

4. Choose the circle or square shape of the Blur tool.

5. Use the Intensity controls to adjust how much blur is applied with each pass of the Blur tool.

The Sharpen tool works like the sharpen effects except that instead of sharpening the entire image, you can sharpen just the area where the tool passes over. I often use the Sharpen tool to add a twinkle to the eyes or a sparkle to teeth.

To use the Sharpen tool:

1. Choose the Sharpen tool in the Tools panel ⑤. The Sharpen tool options appear in the Property Inspector ②.

2. Use the Size control to set the size of the area blurred by the Sharpen tool.

3. Use the Edge control to set the softness of the Sharpen tool edge.

4. Choose the circle or square shape of the Sharpen tool.

5. Use the Intensity controls to adjust how much sharpening is applied with each pass of the Sharpen tool.

The Dodge tool acts like electronic bleach to lighten the areas underneath it. I used the Dodge tool to lighten the teeth of the younger man in figure ㉟.

To use the Dodge tool:

1. Choose the Dodge tool in the Tools panel ㊾. The Dodge options appear in the Property Inspector ㊿.

2. Use the Size control to set the size of the area lightened by the Dodge tool.

3. Use the Edge control to set the softness of the Dodge tool edge.

4. Choose the circle or square shape of the Dodge tool.

5. Use the Range menu to select which tones in the image will be lightened.

6. Use the Exposure controls to adjust how much lightening is applied.

㊶ *The* **Sharpen tool** *in the Tools panel.*

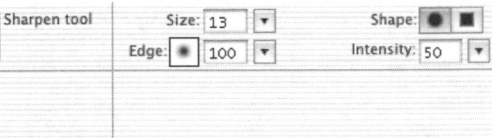

㊷ *The* **Sharpen** *tool options* *in the Property Inspector.*

㊸ *The* **Dodge tool** *in the Tools panel.*

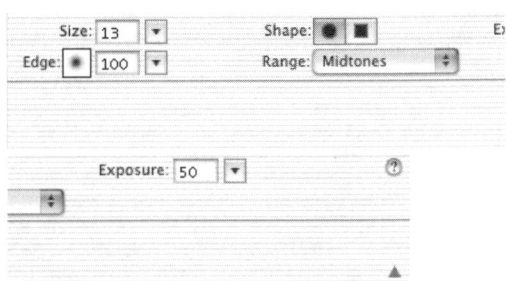

㊹ *The* **Dodge tool options** *in the Property Inspector.*

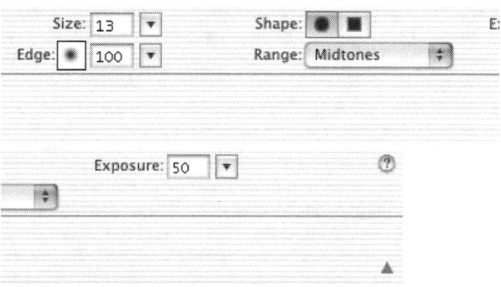

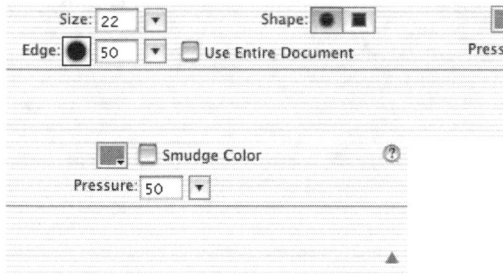

₅₅ *The* **Burn tool** *in the Tools panel.*

₅₆ *The* **Burn tool options** *in the Property Inspector.*

₅₇ *The* **Smudge tool** *in the Tools panel.*

₅₈ *The* **Smudge tool options** *in the Property Inspector.*

The Burn tool darkens the areas underneath it. I used the Burn tool to darken the skin tones of the younger man in figure **₃₅**.

To use the Burn tool:

1. Choose the Burn tool in the Tools panel **₅₅**. The Burn options appear in the Property Inspector **₅₆**.

2. Use the Size control to set the size of the area darkened by the Burn tool.

3. Use the Edge control to set the softness of the Burn tool edge.

4. Choose the circle or square shape of the Burn tool.

5. Use the Range menu to select which tones in the image will be darkened.

6. Use the Exposure controls to adjust how much darkening is applied.

The Smudge tool lets you pull the pixels in an image to distort them. The effect is similar to pulling taffy.

To use the Smudge tool:

1. Choose the Smudge tool in the Tools panel **₅₇**. The Smudge tool options appear in the Property Inspector **₅₈**.

2. Use the Size control to set the size of the area smudged by the Smudge tool.

3. Use the Edge control to set the softness of the Smudge tool edge.

4. Choose the circle or square shape of the Smudge tool.

5. Select Use Entire Document to have the smudge stroke use the pixels from all objects beneath the stroke.

6. Use the Pressure controls to adjust how long the smudge stroke lasts.

7. Check the Smudge Color option to create a smudge with a specific color.

8. If you check Smudge Color, you can then choose the color from the Color Well.

Using the Bitmap Editing Tools

Dual-Purpose Tools

Some tools work in both the bitmap mode as well as the vector mode. The Paint Bucket is one of these dual-purpose tools. It allows you to fill a bitmap area or an object with a color. *(See page 114 for how to use the Paint Bucket tool to modify gradients.)*

59 *The* **Paint Bucket tool** *in the Tools panel.*

To set the Paint Bucket tool options:

1. Choose the Paint Bucket tool in the Tools panel **59**. The Paint Bucket tool options appear in the Property Inspector **60**.

2. Set the Fill attributes for the fill color applied by the Paint Bucket tool. *(See page 108 for more information on setting the Fill attributes.)*

3. Use the Tolerance control to set the size of the area filled **61**.

TIP The Tolerance setting is unavailable for vector objects.

4. Choose the Fill Selection option to have the Paint Bucket tool completely fill a bitmap image or selection regardless of the tolerance.

5. Set an opacity and blend mode for the Paint Bucket tool. *(See page 132 and 133 for setting opacity and blend modes.)*

6. Choose Preserve Transparency to have the Paint Bucket tool only change existing pixels. *(See figure* **42** *for an example of working with the Preserve Transparency option turned on.)*

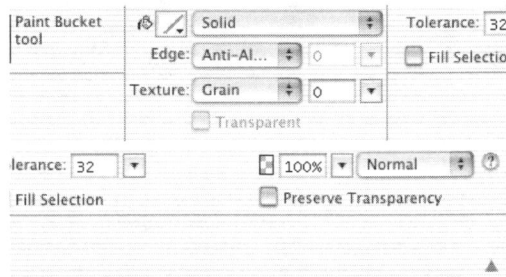

60 *The* **Paint Bucket tool options** *in the Property Inspector.*

61 *At a tolerance of 50, the Paint Bucket fills a small area of color. At a tolerance of 100, the Paint Bucket fills a larger area of color.*

To use the Paint Bucket tool:

1. Choose the Paint Bucket tool in the Tools panel.

2. Click the Paint Bucket tool inside the image to apply the fill.

TIP You can also use the Paint Bucket tool to apply the settings to a vector object.

Dual-Purpose Tools

Original image | Gradient Applied

 *Drag with the **Gradient tool** to apply a gradient to a bitmap image. In this example the Gradient tool was set to 50% opacity in the Multiply mode.*

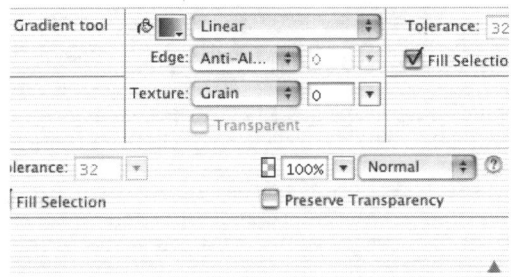 *The **Gradient** tool in the Tools panel.*

*The **Gradient tool** options in the Property Inspector.*

You can use the Gradient tool to apply a gradient within a bitmap image ⬤. *(See page 114 for how to use the Gradient tool to modify gradients.)*

To set the Gradient tool options:

1. Choose the Gradient tool in the Tools panel ⬤. The Gradient tool options appear in the Property Inspector ⬤.

2. Set the Fill attributes for the Gradient. *(See page 111 for more information on setting the Fill attributes for gradients.)*

3. Use the Tolerance control to set the size of the area filled with the gradient.

TIP The Tolerance setting is unavailable for vector objects.

4. Choose the Fill Selection option to have the Gradient tool completely fill a selection or bitmap image regardless of the tolerance.

5. Set an opacity and blend mode for the Gradient tool. *(See page 132 and 133 for setting opacity and blend modes.)*

6. Choose Preserve Transparency to have the Gradient tool change only existing pixels in bitmap images. *(See figure ⬤ for an example of working with the Preserve Transparency option turned on.)*

To use the Gradient tool:

1. Choose the Gradient tool in the Tools panel.

2. Drag the Gradient tool over the image to fill the area with the gradient.

TIP You can also use the Gradient tool to apply the settings to a vector object.

Dual-Purpose Tools

The Eyedropper tool allows you to choose colors by sampling them from images or objects. This makes it easy to match the color of a vector object in a bitmap image.

To set the Eyedropper tool options:

1. Choose the Eyedropper tool in the Tools panel . The Eyedropper tool options appear in the Property Inspector ⑥.

2. Use the Eyedropper Tool Options panel to set the size of the area the Eyedropper uses to judge the color ⑥.

   - **1 Pixel** picks up the color from the single pixel directly underneath the Eyedropper.
   - **3x3 Average** picks up the color averaged from 9 pixels within the 3x3 pixel area.
   - **5x5 Average** setting picks up the color averaged from the 25 pixels within the 5x5 pixel area.

To sample colors with the Eyedropper tool:

1. Choose either the Fill or Stroke in the Tools panel.

2. Position the Eyedropper tool over the color you wish to sample.

3. Click. The sampled color appears as either the Fill or Stroke.

⑥ *The* **Eyedropper tool** *in the Tools panel.*

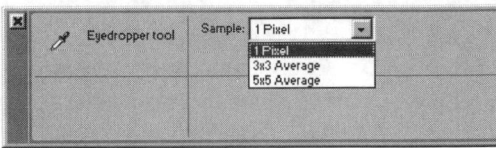

⑥ *The* **Eyedropper tool options** *in the Property Inspector.*

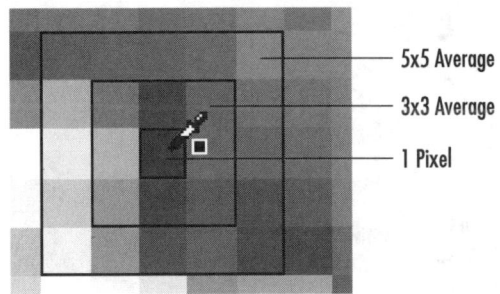

⑥ *Change the Sample area for the Eyedropper tool to* **increase the area used to choose a color.**

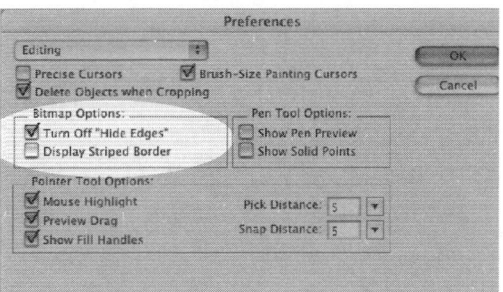

68 *The* **Bitmap Options** *in the Editing area of the Preferences dialog box.*

69 *The* **striped border** *indicates you are working with a bitmap image.*

Setting Bitmap Preferences

Fireworks also lets you customize the preferences for how you work with bitmap images.

To set the preferences for editing bitmap images:

1. Choose **Edit** > **Preferences**.

or

(Mac OS X) Choose **Fireworks** > **Preferences**.

2. Choose Editing from the Preference menu. The Bitmap Options appear **68**.

3. Choose each of the options as described below.

To change the status of the Hide Edges command:

◆ Select Turn off "Hide Edges" to display the marching ants when you create a new selection even if you have chosen the Hide Edges command.

TIP When this setting is not chosen, you do not see the marching ants even when you create a new bitmap selection. This makes it possible to confuse your students as you demonstrate Fireworks commands.

To change the bitmap display border:

◆ Select Display Striped Border to show the striped border when working with a bitmap image **69**.

TIP It was more important in previous versions of Fireworks to know when you were or were not in the bitmap mode. Because Fireworks MX automatically changes depending on the tool chosen, that distinction is less important.

Applying Filters

Filters are essentially the effects that are applied to objects and images . However, unlike effects, filters cannot be edited or removed once they have been applied to an image. Instead, they can only be changed using the Undo command *(see page 37)*.

To apply Filters to bitmap images:

1. Use the Pointer tool to select the bitmap image.

   or

   Use any of the bitmap selection tools to select an area within the bitmap image. *(see pages 153–158)*.

2. Choose a Filter from the Filters menu.

3. If the Filter has a dialog box, adjust the settings as desired. *(For details as to how to use the settings for each of the Filters, see Chapter 9, "Effects.")*

4. Click OK to apply the settings.

To apply Filters to vector objects:

1. Select one or more vector objects.

2. Choose a Filter from the Filters menu. A dialog box appears indicating that the image will be converted into a pixel image 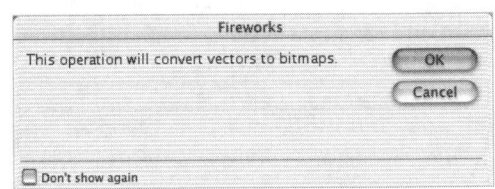.

3. Click OK. The object is converted and the Filter is applied.

To reapply Filters quickly:

◆ With an object selected, choose **Filters** > **Repeat** [**Name of Filter**] to reapply the previously chosen filter.

70 *The outside area of this image was selected by creating a feathered ellipse and then inverting the selection. The Gaussian Blur and Brightness/Contrast Filters were then applied to the selection.*

71 *This* **dialog box alert** *warns you that applying a filter to a vector object will convert it to a bitmap image.*

Using Filters Instead of Effects?

Unlike effects, which can be edited or turned off, once you apply Filters, you can't go back later to change the values or remove the results. So why would anyone want to use Filters?

Filters allow you to apply an effect to only a portion of an image object.

They require less computer processing than effects and do not have to be redrawn every time a document is opened or manipulated.

Some third-party plug-ins work only as Filters.

TEXT 11

Whoever said a picture is worth a thousand words underestimated by several hundred kilobytes. Picture and graphics create much bigger Web files than ordinary HTML text. This means that pages with graphics take much longer to appear on viewers' computer screens.

All text created in Macromedia Fireworks is eventually exported onto Web pages as graphics. So why would someone want to create text in Fireworks if it has to be exported as slow-downloading graphics?

There are loads of reasons.

One reason is that, unlike HTML text, you have much more control over the appearance of text when it is converted into graphics. You also don't have to worry about whether or not the viewer has the same font as you. With text as graphics you can also create banner ads that can appear anywhere in many different Web browsers. You can also apply special effects to graphic text that would be impossible with HTML text. Whatever your reasons for using graphic text, Fireworks has many features for working with it.

Working with Text Blocks

You access text in Fireworks by using the Text tool. You should find working with text similar to the methods you have used in any graphics or page-layout program.

To type text:

1. Choose the Text tool in the Tools panel **1**.

2. Click inside the document area. This creates a text block that expands as you type text.

   or

   Drag to define the size of the text block. Both techniques display the Text options in the Property Inspector **2**.

3. Type the text inside the text block.

TIP If you have clicked to create the text block, the text block automatically expands as you type **3**. This is indicated by a hollow circle at the top right corner of the text block.

TIP If you have dragged to define the size of the text, the text wraps inside the block **4**. This is indicated by a hollow square at the top right corner of the text block.

TIP You can resize any text block to rewrap the text **5**.

1 The **Text tool** *in the Tools panel.*

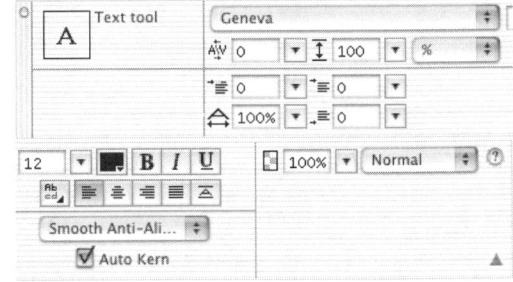

2 The **Text tool options** *in the Property Inspector.*

3 An **Auto-sizing text block** *expands horizontally as you type.*

4 A **Fixed-width text block** *expands vertically as you type.*

5 *You can manually resize any text block by dragging the corners.*

Working with Text Blocks

⑥ Double click the indicator to toggle between auto-expanding and fixed-width text blocks.

Using Specialty Fonts

Even when you work with editable text, the final images posted on the Web do not actually contain any text information at all.

That's because when you convert a Fireworks file to a GIF or JPEG, there are no longer any fonts used in the file. The text shapes are all converted into pixels.

This means that you can use a special font, such as Bonnie Bold, in your Fireworks document without worrying if your viewers will have the font when the graphic is posted to the Web.

You can easily convert a fixed-width text block to an auto-sizing text block and vice versa.

To convert the type of text block:

1. Click with the Text tool or double click with the Pointer tool to place an insertion point inside the Text block.

2. Move the cursor over the top right corner.

3. Double click. This toggles between the two types of text blocks ⑥.

TIP When you change from a fixed-width text box to an auto-expanding text box, the text box changes. However, when you change back to a fixed-width text box, the dimensions won't go back to the original box you created.

To select text in a text block:

♦ Use any of the following techniques to select the text in a text block:

- Drag the Text tool across the text inside the text block.
- Double click to select a word.
- Click inside the text block and choose **Select > Select All**. This selects all the text in the block.
- Use the Pointer tool to select the text block. This selects all the text in the block.

TIP Double click with the Pointer tool inside a text block to place an insertion point inside the block.

Setting the Text Attributes

Once you have clicked with the Text tool, you can control various text attributes. You can change the font or point size. You can apply bold or italic styling. You can also apply more sophisticated attributes such as kerning, tracking, and baseline shift.

To set the font:

◆ Use the font pop-up list in the Property Inspector to choose the typeface. A preview area appears next to the font list that displays a representation of the selected typeface **⑦**.

TIP If you change the font list with no text selected, the next text you type will appear in that font.

To set the point size:

◆ Use the point size slider or type in the field to change the point size **⑧**.

To add a type style:

◆ Click the bold, italic, or underline buttons to apply those styles to text **⑨**.

TIP The style buttons add fake styles to text. These fake styles may not be the same as using the actual bold or italic typefaces.

TIP When text is converted to paths, it uses the normal style of the text and not the fake styling that was added afterwards *(see page 192)*.

⑦ *The* **Font list and the font preview** *in the Property Inspector.*

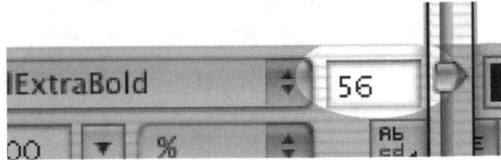

⑧ *The* **Point size controls** *in the Property Inspector.*

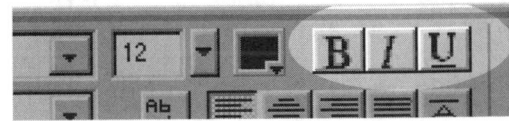

⑨ *The* **Type style buttons** *in the Property Inspector.*

People Inc.
People Inc.

10 *The result of* **kerning** *to close up the space between the letters* Pe, pl, *and* le.

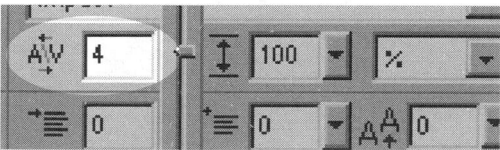

11 *The* **kerning controls** *in the Property Inspector.*

People Inc.
People Inc.

12 *The result of applying* **range kerning** *to increase the spaces between the characters.*

Subtleties of Kerning and Range Kerning

Why are there two controls for kerning and range kerning? When you set the kerning between two letters, you set the relative spacing between just those two letters. When you apply range kerning, you apply it to the text as a whole.

This means that all the text may spread apart, but any kerning set between two specific letters is still applied.

Kerning is adjusting the space between two letters. You can adjust the kerning to nicely move one letter closer to another **10**.

To kern the text:

1. Click to place an insertion point between the two letters you want to kern.

2. Use the Kern slider or type a value in the field to kern the text closer together or further apart **11**. Negative values decrease the space; positive values increase the space.

TIP Click Auto Kern in the Property Inspector to use the built-in kerning pairs from the typeface.

Range kerning is kerning applied to a selection of text. (Range kerning is sometimes called *tracking* in other programs.) You can use range kerning to spread out a selection of text **12**.

To set the range kerning:

1. Drag across a selection of the text.

2. Use the Range Kerning slider or type a value in the field to change the range kerning for the text. Negative values decrease the space; positive values increase the space.

TIP The Range Kerning controls looks the same as the Kerning controls in the Property Inspector. If the insertion point is blinking between two letters, then you are applying kerning. If more than two characters are selected, then you are applying range kerning.

Leading (pronounced "ledding"), or line spacing, is the space between multiple lines of text. (Leading is so called after the metal pieces of lead that were inserted in early typesetting equipment.) If your text consists of only a single line you don't have to worry about setting the leading.

To set the leading:

1. Use the Leading slider or type in the field to change the leading for the text **⑬**.

2. Use the Leading Units menu to choose how the leading should be set **⑭**.

   - % sets the leading as a percentage of the point size. So a setting of 120% on 10-point text creates a leading of 12 points.
   - **px** sets the leading as an absolute pixel measurement. This setting may be easier to use when fitting text into a specific pixel dimension.

   TIP Leading is applied to an entire paragraph, not individual characters.

Baseline shift is the technique of raising or lowering text from its baseline, or the line that the text sits on **⑮**. Baseline shift is often used to raise or lower the numbers in fractions.

TIP You must click inside the text block to see the baseline shift controls. The baseline shift controls are not available if the text block is selected with the Pointer tool.

To add a baseline shift:

◆ Use the baseline slider or type in the field to raise or lower the text in points from the baseline **⑯**. Positive numbers raise the text. Negative numbers lower the text.

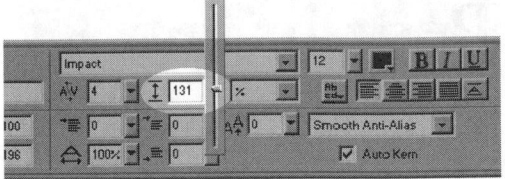

⑬ *The* **Leading controls** *in the Property Inspector.*

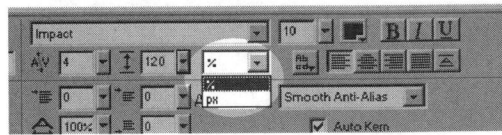

⑭ *The* **Leading Units menu** *in the Property Inspector.*

People Inc.
People Inc.

⑮ *The results of applying a* **positive baseline shift** *to the characters* **nc**. *(The baseline is indicated by the dashed line.)*

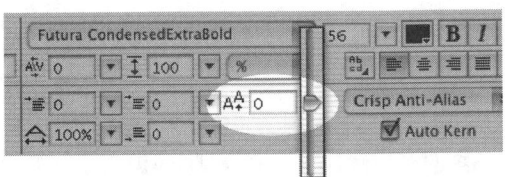

⑯ *The* **Baseline shift controls** *in the Property Inspector.*

Setting the Text Attributes

People Inc.
People Inc.

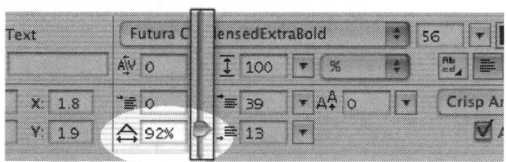

⑰ *The result of applying horizontal scale to the letter* **P.**

⑱ *The* **Horizontal scale controls** *in the Property Inspector.*

E T **⑲** *An example of the distortions that happen with extreme amounts of horizontal scale.*

Text can also be distorted using a technique called horizontal scaling. This changes the width of the text without changing the height **⑰**.

To change the horizontal scale:

◆ Use the Horizontal Scale slider or type a value in the field to increase or decrease the horizontal scaling **⑱**. Amounts lower than 100% make the text width smaller. Amounts higher than 100% make the text wider. *(See the sidebar on this page for a discussion on the wisdom of using the horizontal scale controls.)*

Should You Use Horizontal Scale?

Typography purists (such as your outspoken author) disdain the look of electronically scaled type. We say it causes ugly distortions to the look of the original typeface **⑲**.

Look at what happens if you apply a 200% horizontal scale to a sans serif typeface such as Helvetica or Arial. Letters such as E or F are distorted so that the vertical line becomes very thick while the horizontal lines are very thin. That's not what the typeface is supposed to look like.

Look at what happens if you apply a 30% horizontal scale to a serif typeface such as Times or Times New Roman. The top serifs on the capital letter T become so horribly elongated that they begin to resemble two vampire teeth hanging off the letter. If you need to fit text into a specific area you should use the proper condensed or expanded typeface.

So, why would Macromedia (and other software developers) provide such a feature? Because even the purists cannot always tell if small amounts of scaling have been applied to text. This makes it possible to squeeze text into a space where it might not always fit.

You can also align text within a text block in a wide variety of ways.

To set the horizontal alignment:

◆ Click one of the alignment settings in the Property Inspector ②⓪:

- **Left alignment** sits on the left side of the block and creates irregular line breaks along the right side of the text.
- **Right alignment** sits on the right side of the block and creates irregular line breaks along the left side of the text.
- **Centered alignment** positions the middle of the line of text in the middle of the text block. There are irregular line breaks on both the left and right sides of the text.
- **Justified alignment** sits on both the left and right side of the text block. Justified alignment increases the range kerning so the line fills the width of the text block ②①.
- **Stretched alignment** sits on both the left and right side of the text block. Stretched alignment increases the horizontal scale, so the line fills the width of the text block ②②. This could cause typographic purists to cringe *(see the sidebar on the previous page)*.

Ordinarily, text reads horizontally—from left to right. However, you can change the text direction so the letters flow from top to bottom or from right to left.

To set the text direction:

1. Click the Direction icon to open the Direction menu ②③.

2. Choose one of the horizontal and vertical options for text.

TIP Vertical left to right text reads from top to bottom. Vertical right to left reads from bottom to top.

TIP Vertical alignment does not show in the Text Editor *(see page 186)*. Use the Apply button to see the vertical alignment.

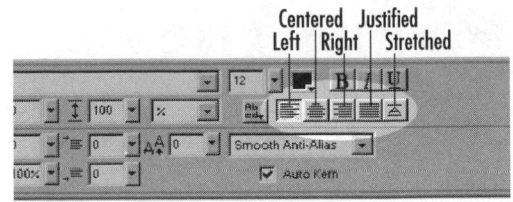

Centered   Justified
Left   Right   Stretched

②⓪ *The* **Alignment options** *for text.*

People Inc.

People Inc.

②① *The results of the* **justified alignment**.

People Inc.

People Inc.

②② *The results of the* **stretch alignment**.

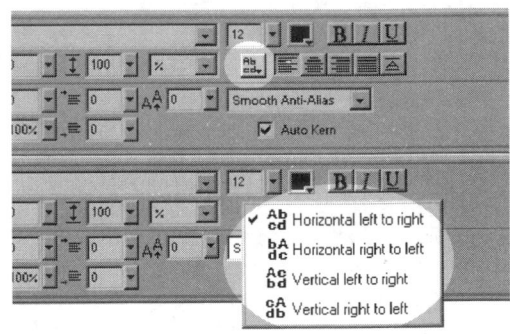

②③ *Click the* **Direction icon** *to open the* **Direction menu** *for text.*

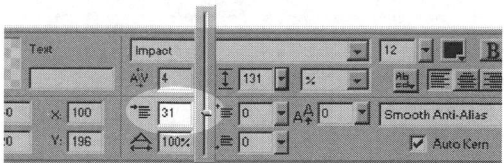

㉔ *The* **First Line Indent controls** *in the Property Inspector.*

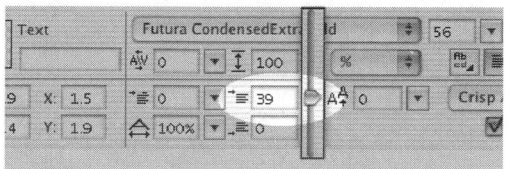

㉕ *The* **Space Before Paragraph controls** *in the Property Inspector.*

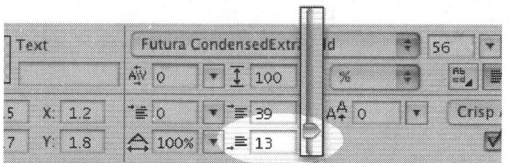

㉖ *The* **Space After Paragraph controls** *in the Property Inspector.*

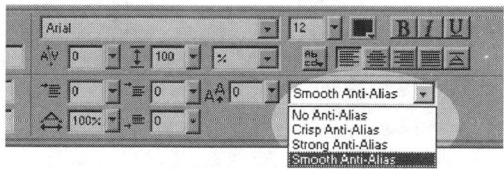

㉗ *The* **Anti-Aliasing menu** *in the Property Inspector.*

No Anti-Alias
Crisp Anti-Alias
Strong Anti-Alias
Smooth Anti-Alias

㉘ *The effects of the anti-alias settings on text.*

If you create multiple paragraphs of text, you may want to create spaces that visually separate one paragraph from another. Fireworks offers you three ways to separate one paragraph from another. For instance, you may want to create an indent for the first line of a paragraph.

To set the first line indent:

◆ Set the amount of the indent (in pixels) using the First Line Indent controls **㉔**.

You can also add space before or after a paragraph.

To add space before a paragraph:

◆ Set the amount of the space (in pixels) using the Space Before Paragraph controls **㉕**.

To add space after a paragraph:

◆ Set the amount of the space (in pixels) using the Space After Paragraph controls **㉖**.

Text that is displayed as part of Web pages may need to be softened around the edges so it appears less jagged. This is called anti-aliasing.

To set the Anti-Alias amount:

1. Select the text.

2. Choose the Anti-Alias setting from the pop-up menu **㉗**.

TIP Anti-aliasing does not show in the Text Editor. Use the Apply button to see the effect **㉘**.

TIP You can also select multiple text blocks and apply changes to them all.

Text Fills, Strokes, and Effects

In addition to the text attributes in the Property Inspector, you can also apply fills, strokes, and effects to the text.

To apply fills to text:

1. Select the text to which you want to apply the fill.

2. Click the Fill Color Well in the Property Inspector. The Fill Color Swatches appear ㉙.

3. Choose the color for the fill.

4. Click the Fill Options button. This opens the additional controls for the fill ㉚.

5. Use the Fill Options to set the type of fill, edge settings, or texture. *(See Chapter 7, "Fills" for more information.)*

TIP You can also apply a fill color by clicking the Fill Color Well in the Tools panel or the Swatches panel.

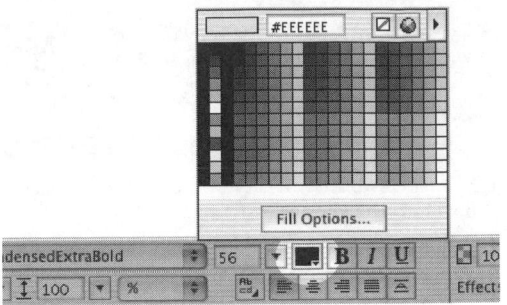

㉙ *Click the* **Fill Color Well** *in the Property Inspector to open the* **Fill Swatches**.

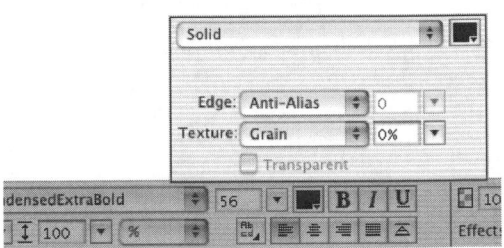

㉚ *The* **Fill Options** *for text.*

You can also apply a stroke to text.

To apply a stroke to text:

1. Select the text frame. The text attributes in the Property Inspector change so that the Stroke Color Well replaces the Baseline Shift controls.

TIP The stroke for text must be applied to all the text within a text block. If you need two different types of stroke on text, the text must be in two separate blocks.

2. Click the Stroke Color Well. The Stroke Color Swatches appear ㉛.

3. Choose the color for the stroke. *(See the next exercise for how to set the stroke position.)*

4. Click the Stroke Options button to set the type of stroke, texture, and advanced stroke options. *(See Chapter 8, "Strokes," for more information.)*

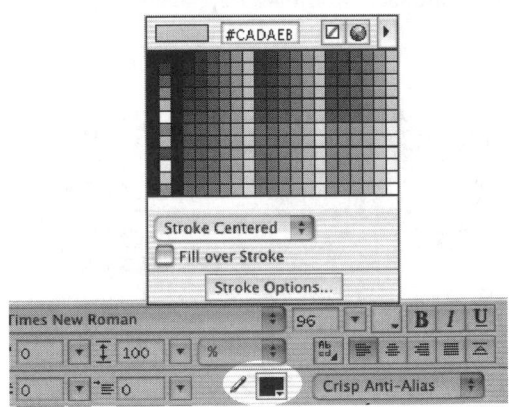

㉛ *Click the* **Stroke Color Well** *in the Property Inspector to open the* **Stroke Swatches**.

Text Fills, Strokes, and Effects

32 The **Stroke Position** menu *in Stroke Swatches panel.*

Stroke Outside
Stroke Centered
Stroke Inside

33 *Examples of the* **three different stroke positions** *on text. The circled areas show the text distortions.*

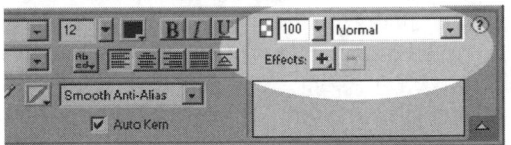

34 *The* **Effects, Opacity, and Blend Mode controls** *for a text frame in the Property Inspector.*

You can also choose the position of the stroke around the text characters.

To set the position of the text:

1. Select the text frame. The Stroke Color Well becomes visible in the Property Inspector.

2. Click the Stroke Color Well to open the Stroke Swatches panel.

3. Choose one of the following from the Stroke Position menu **32**:
   - **Outside Path** positions the stroke so that it is completely outside the character shape. This is the most acceptable way to stroke text **33**.
   - **Centered on Path** positions the stroke so that half is outside the character shape, and half is inside the shape. This can cause text to become deformed **33**.
   - **Inside Path** positions the stroke so that it is completely inside the character shape. This can cause text to become deformed **33**.

4. Select Fill over Stroke to force the fill color to cover any stroke that is inside the character shape. *(See page 122 for more information on working with this command.)*

You can also apply effects, opacity, and blend modes to text.

To apply effects to text:

1. Select the text frame.

2. Use the Property Inspector to apply effects, opacity, or blend modes **34**. *(See Chapter 9, "Effects," for more information on setting these features.)*

Using the Text Editor

I feel sorry for software engineers. They spend all their time improving software with brand new features, but then they have to leave in older features because people are used to them. The Text Editor is a perfect example. The only reason the Text Editor is still in Fireworks is that some people don't want to edit text directly on the page.

To use the Text Editor:

1. Create a text block on the page.

2. With the text selected, choose **Text > Editor**. The Text Editor appears ③⑤.

3. Use any of the Text Editor formatting buttons to format the text.

TIP Not all the formatting options in the Property Inspector are in the Text Editor.

TIP Turn off the Show Font and Show Size & Color options if you find it difficult to read the text within the Text Editor. For instance, the text may be too small to be read in the Text Editor. The text will appear at a default size making it easier to edit.

4. Click Apply to see the formatting changes without leaving the Text Editor.

5. Click OK to apply the changes and close the Text Editor.

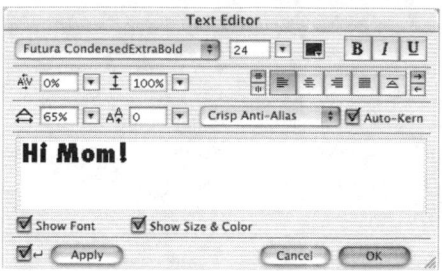

③⑤ *The* Text Editor.

The Missing Text Editor Attributes

The Text Editor in the current version of Fireworks is actually a time machine. When you open the Text Editor you go back in time to Fireworks 4.

What the Fireworks engineers did when they added onscreen text editing was take all the formatting controls from the Text Editor and put them in the Property Inspector. They then added new formatting controls such as First Line Indent, Space Before Paragraph, and Space After Paragraph.

At that point, there must have been some people who wanted to still work with the Text Editor. So the engineers dusted off the old code for the Text Editor, and put it back in the program.

The only problem is that the old Text Editor never had the new features. So, using the Text Editor is like a trip back in time. You may not see all the current text formatting options.

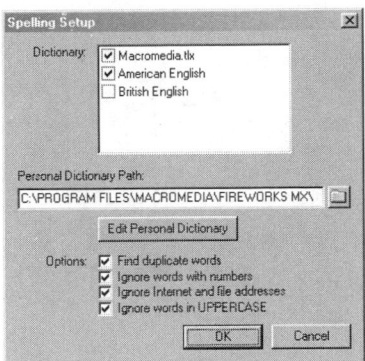

36 *The* Spelling Setup dialog box.

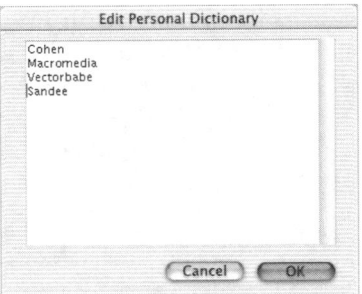

37 *You can add your own custom words for spell checks in the* Edit Personal Dictionary *dialog box.*

Using the Spell Check

Nothing is more frustrating than publishing a Web site and finding a misspelled word. That's why it's terrific that Fireworks has a spell-check feature. Before you run the first spell check, you need to use the Spelling Setup.

To set up the spell check command:

1. Choose **Text > Spelling Setup**. The Spelling Setup dialog box appears **36**.

2. Choose the dictionary that you want to use for the spell check.

TIP The Macromedia.tlx file is the custom dictionary you create. It is automatically selected.

3. Check the options for the spell check as follows:
    - **Find duplicate words** finds errors such as "the the".
    - **Ignore words with numbers** skips entries such as July 22nd (my birthday).
    - **Ignore Internet and file addresses** skips entries such as www.vectorbabe.com.
    - **Ignore words in UPPERCASE** skips entries such as NYC.

4. Click OK to finish the setup.

You can also add your own words to the personal dictionary.

To add your own words:

1. Choose **Text > Spelling Setup**.

2. Click Edit Personal Dictionary. The Edit Personal Dictionary dialog box appears **37**.

3. Type words into the field separated by a paragraph return.

4. Click OK to save the changes to the personal dictionary.

TIP You can also get to Spelling Setup through the Check Spelling dialog box.

Once you have set up the spell check options, you're ready to check the spelling.

To check spelling:

1. Select the text that you want to check.

TIP If you have multiple text blocks, you can use the Pointer tool to select the multiple blocks.

2. Choose **Text > Check Spelling**. The Check Spelling dialog box appears ⬤.

3. If the spell check finds a misspelled word, it highlights the word. You can then choose one of the following:

   • **Add to Personal** adds the word to your personal dictionary. This avoids flagging the word in future sessions of Fireworks.
   • **Ignore** skips the one instance of the word.
   • **Ignore All** skips all the instances.
   • Choose a word in the **Suggestions** list that you think is more correct.
   • If you have chosen a suggested word, click **Change** to change the one instance of the word or click **Change All** to change all the instances.
   • **Delete** removes the word from the text.

4. Click the Close button to exit the Check Spelling dialog box.

TIP Fireworks will also close the dialog box when it finishes checking all the text in the document.

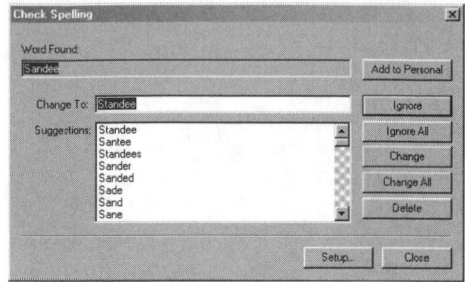

⬤ *The* **Check Spelling dialog box**.

The Limitations of the Spell Check

Every once in a while, I read an article about how the use of spelling checkers in computers is contributing to the death of proper writing and language.

It's true: too many people run a spell check and don't bother to actually read their document. Consider the following text:

Their is knot any thing wrung with using a spell cheque on a sent tents in a doc you mint. Ewe just haft to clique the write butt ends.

Obviously the paragraph is utter nonsense. Yet Fireworks's Spell Check (as well as the Spell Check in most other programs) wouldn't flag a single word as being incorrect.

A Spell Check only flags words it doesn't recognize; but since everything in the paragraph is an actual word, Fireworks doesn't see any problems.

So, please, don't skip a session with a proofreader just because you've run a spell check.

Using the Spell Check

39 *The result of applying the skew distortion to text.*

The result of **attaching text to a path**. **40**

Keeping Text Editable

Why is it so important that Fireworks lets you edit text—even after it's been transformed or attached to a path?

The primary reason is that you can make changes, run the spell check, or even use the Find and Replace features *(see page 218)* on editable text.

Transforming Text

The transformation tools create spectacular results when applied to text. In fact, this is one of the primary reasons I like Fireworks over its competition. Not only can you apply all sorts of effects to text, but the text remains editable.

To transform text in a text block:

1. Select the text block.
2. Use any of the the Transform tools *(see pages 87–92)* to distort the text within the block **39**.

TIP The transformation tools change the size of the text by distorting the text, not by changing the point size.

TIP Choose **Modify > Transform > Remove Transformations** to restore the text to its original formatting.

Text on a Path

Another text effect that separates Fireworks from its competition is the ability to place text on a path. This allows you to create the effect of text that curves up and down a path.

To attach text to a path:

1. Select the text block.
2. Select the path.
3. Choose **Text > Attach to Path**. The text automatically aligns to the path **40**.

TIP Text attached to a path can still be edited using the Text tool.

Once you have text on a path you can change the alignment, or the position where the text appears on the path. This creates the effect that the text is warped as it travels along the path.

To change the alignment of text on a path:

1. Select the path that has the text attached to it.

2. Choose **Text** > **Align** and then choose one of the alignment settings from the submenu. This changes where the text is positioned on the path ❹❶.

TIP Use the alignment settings in the Property Inspector.

You can also control the distance of the text from the beginning of the path. This is called the text offset.

To change the text offset along a path:

1. Select the text that has been attached to the path.

2. Change the amount in the Text Offset field in the Property Inspector ❹❷. The text moves along the path ❹❸.

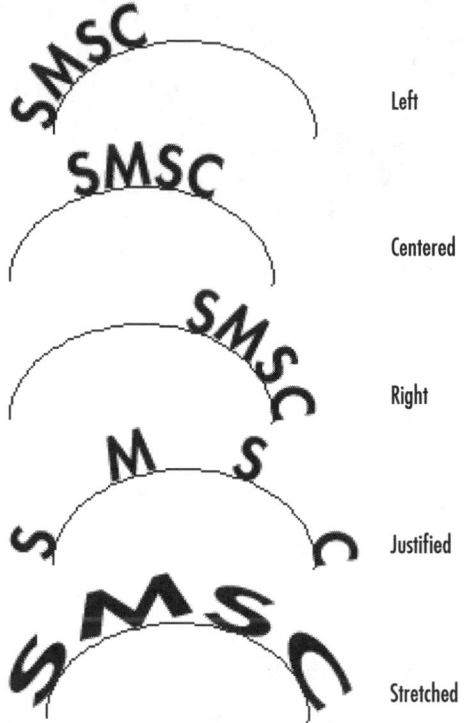

Left

Centered

Right

Justified

Stretched

❹❶ *The results of applying the different alignment settings to text on a path.*

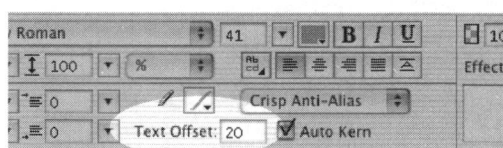

❹❷ *The* **Text Offset** *field in the Property Inspector.*

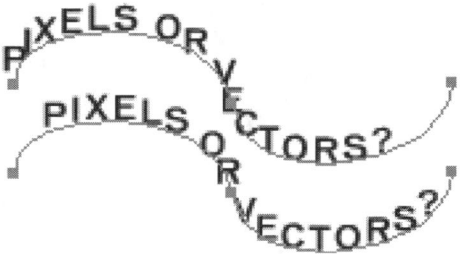

❹❸ *The result of adding a 20-pixel Text Offset to shift the text along a path (bottom).*

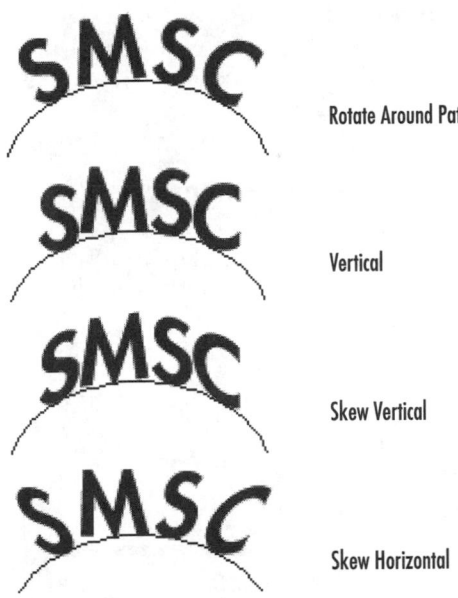

Rotate Around Path

Vertical

Skew Vertical

Skew Horizontal

④④ *The results of applying the different orientation settings to text on a path.*

④⑤ *The results of applying the Reverse Direction command settings to text on a path.*

You can also change how the individual characters of the text are positioned in relation to the angle of the path. This is called the orientation of the text.

To change the orientation of the text:

◆ Choose **Text > Orientation** and then choose one of the orientation settings in the submenu to change how the text is angled in relation to the path **④④**.

- **Rotate Around Path** keeps the text in a perpendicular orientation as it moves around the path.
- **Vertical** makes each character stand up straight no matter how the path curves.
- **Skew Vertical** maintains a vertical rotation but distorts the characters' shapes as the text follows the path.
- **Skew Horizontal** exaggerates the text's horizontal tilt up to a 90° rotation and distorts the characters' shapes as the text follows the path.

You can also flip the text to the other side of the path.

To reverse the direction of text on a path:

◆ Choose **Text > Reverse Direction** to flip the text so that it flows on the other side of the path **④⑤**.

TIP If you are like my editor who wants the text to be positioned below the path, but still read correctly, use the Baseline Shift setting to lower the text below the path.

Font Management

You may receive a Fireworks document from someone who uses fonts different from the ones in your system. If so, you need to handle the missing fonts.

To change missing fonts:

1. If the file contains missing fonts a dialog box appears that gives you two options 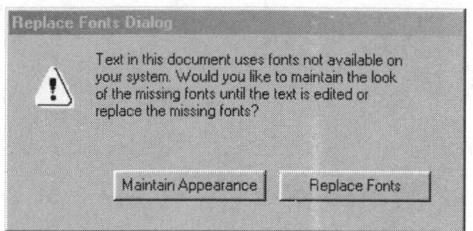:

   • **Maintain Appearance** opens the document but changes the text into an image so that it keeps the look of the original font. If you try to edit the text, you will lose the appearance of the font.
   • **Replace Fonts** opens the Replace Fonts dialog box to change the missing fonts.

2. In the Replace Fonts dialog box, use the Change Missing Font list to choose the font or fonts that you want to replace.

3. Choose the font you want to substitute from the To: list on the right side of the dialog box 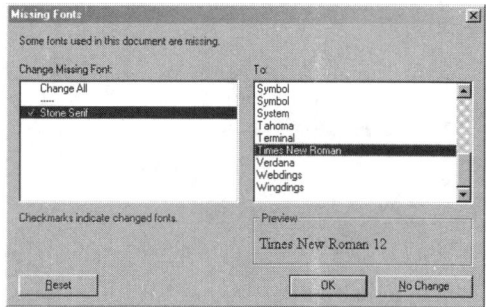.

4. Click OK to make the changes.

*The **Replace Fonts dialog box** alerts you that fonts are missing and asks how you would like to handle the file.*

*The **Missing Fonts dialog box** allows you to substitute installed fonts for the ones that are missing from the document.*

Converting Text to Paths

The text in a text block or attached to a path is called editable text. This means that you can work with the text—change the font or the letters—at any time. However, there are some effects—such as changing the shapes of letters—that require that the text be converted into paths.

To convert text to paths:

1. Select the text block or text on a path.

2. Choose **Text > Convert to Paths**. This converts the text into grouped paths.

3. Use the Subselection tool to manipulate the paths.

TIP Once you convert text to paths, you can no longer edit it in the Text Editor; you can then edit it only as path objects.

People Inc.
People Inc.

The results of converting text to paths and then manipulating the converted paths.

MASKS 12

When most people see the term *masks*, they think of scary Halloween or festive Mardi Gras masks. As much as I would love to show you those types of masks, that's not what this chapter is all about.

Instead of rubber faces or cardboard adorned with sequins and feathers, the masks in Macromedia Fireworks are more like what happens when you use masking tape or a stencil to protect or hide one part of a wall. You put the stencil or tape on the wall leaving a hole inside the tape. Whatever is inside the mask you can see; whatever is outside the mask, you can't. You can then paint inside the mask without affecting what's outside the mask.

If you have created masks in Adobe Illustrator, Macromedia FreeHand, or Adobe Photoshop, you should quickly pick up the techniques for creating masks in Fireworks.

Creating Vector Masks

The first type of mask in Fireworks is a vector mask. Vector masks use one or more vector paths as the masking objects. For instance, the Ellipse tool can be used to create a circular frame around a bitmap image. You can also use text as a vector mask for other objects. *(See page 198 for information on creating bitmap masks.)*

The Paste as Mask command takes whatever object is on the clipboard and turns it into a mask. *(For a summary of all the mask commands and their settings, see pages 204–205.)*

To paste an object as a mask:

1. Select the object to be used as the mask **①**. If you are using text, select the text block.

TIP Masks are not limited to single objects. Use the Join command *(see page 94)* to allow multiple paths to act as a single mask.

2. Choose **Edit > Cut**. The object disappears from the document.

3. Select the object or objects to be masked. If there is only one object, you can skip the next step.

4. Choose **Modify > Group**. This combines all the objects onto one thumbnail in the Layers panel **②**.

5. Choose **Edit > Paste as Mask**.

TIP This command sets the mask object to Path Outline with Show Fill and Stroke deselected **③**.

TIP The pen symbol inside the mask thumbnail indicates that the mask is a vector mask **④**.

TIP Apply a feather to the edge of the vector mask to create a soft-edged mask.

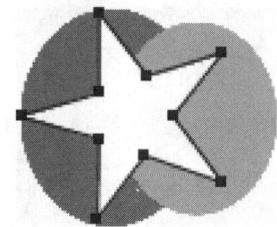

① *Select and cut the topmost object to be pasted as a mask.*

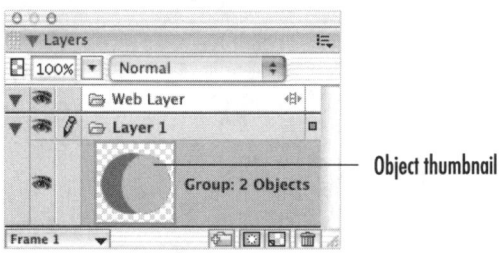

Object thumbnail

② *Group the objects to be masked by the Paste as Mask command.*

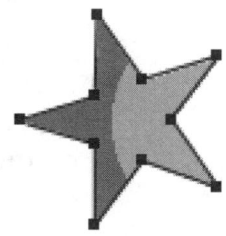

③ *The* **Paste as Mask command** *turns the cut object into a mask for the grouped objects.*

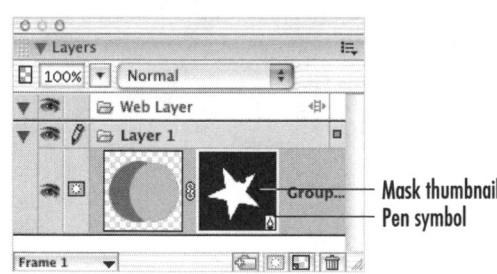

Mask thumbnail
Pen symbol

④ *The* **Mask thumbnail** *shows the object used as the mask.*

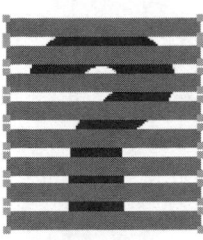

5 *Select and cut the objects to be masked by the Paste Inside command—in this case the stripes.*

6 *Select the object to be used as a mask—in this case the text block that holds the question mark character.*

7 *The* **Paste Inside** command *displays the cut objects—the stripes—within the contours of the text mask.*

Another simple way to create a mask is to use the Paste Inside command. This command is used when it is easier to select and cut the objects to be masked, rather than the masking object.

To paste objects into a mask:

1. Position the objects to be masked above the object that is to act as the mask.

2. Select the objects that are to be masked **5**.

3. Choose **Edit** > **Cut**. The objects disappear from the document.

4. Select the object to be used as the mask **6**.

5. Choose **Edit** > **Paste Inside**.

TIP This command sets the mask object to Path Outline with Show Fill and Stroke selected **7**.

TIP If you have selected multiple objects, they are automatically grouped inside the mask **8**.

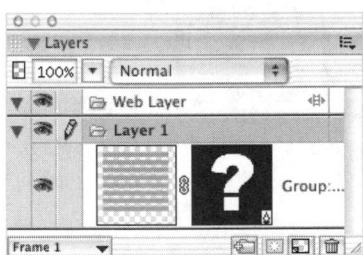

8 *Notice that the multiple objects pasted inside the mask are listed as a Grouped item in the Layers panel.*

You can also create a mask using the Group as Mask command. This command requires that the object that is the mask be positioned above the other objects. It also creates a mask based on the grayscale values of the mask.

TIP A grayscale mask allows you to use a gradient to create a mask that fades away.

To group objects into a mask:

1. Position the objects to be masked below the object that is to act as the mask **9**.

TIP If you want multiple objects to act as a mask, choose **Modify > Group** to group the objects.

2. Select all the objects.

3. Choose **Modify > Mask > Group as Mask**. The top object or group of objects become the mask for the objects below **10**. The Layers panel shows the mask thumbnail **11**.

TIP This command sets the mask object to grayscale.

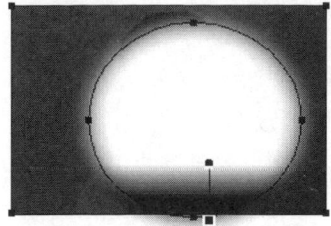

9 *To use the* **Group as Mask command**, *an object filled with a gradient was placed over a bitmap image.*

10 *After the Group as Mask command is applied, the image fades along the gradient inside the mask.*

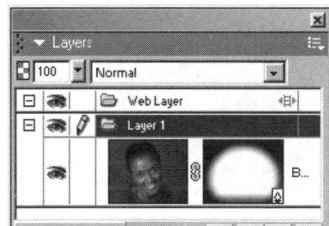

11 *The Layers panel shows the thumbnails for the original image and the vector mask.*

Creating Vector Masks

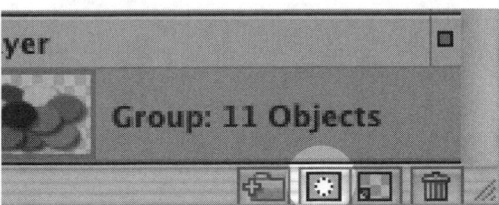

⑫ *Click the* **Add Mask icon** *in the Layers panel to add a Mask thumbnail.*

⑬ *The* **Mask symbol** *in the Layers panel indicates you can paste the object as a mask.*

Using Vector Masks

The vector masks in Fireworks are similar to the clipping masks in Adobe Illustrator or the vector masks in Adobe Photoshop. If I had to choose between working with vector masks or bitmap masks, I'd always choose the vectors. I find it easier to edit and reshape vector objects instead of painting bitmap images.

However, as you will see in the next section, there are some special effects that are possible only with bitmap masks. Bitmap masks are similar to the layer masks in Adobe Photoshop.

You can also create a mask using the Layers panel. This approach makes it easier to visualize what happens when objects are masked. It is also more familiar for anyone who has created a Layer Mask in Adobe Photoshop.

To mask objects using the Layers panel:

1. Select and cut the object to be used as the mask.

2. Select the objects to be masked. If they are not grouped, choose **Modify > Group**. This combines all the objects onto one thumbnail in the Layers panel.

TIP You can also select the grouped objects by clicking the Object Thumbnail in the Layers panel.

3. Click the Add Mask icon in the Layers panel to add an empty Mask thumbnail next to the Object Thumbnail **⑫**.

TIP A yellow square around the Mask thumbnail indicates that you are now working on the mask. In addition, the mask icon appears in the Layers panel **⑬**.

4. Choose **Edit > Paste**. The cut object or group appears in the Mask thumbnail.

TIP This command sets the mask object to Path Outline with Show Fill and Stroke deselected.

Bitmap Masks

You can also use bitmap images as the masks for objects or other bitmap images. This allows you to use the bitmap drawing tools to create the outlines for masks. It also lets you combine images together. *(For more information on working with bitmap images, see Chapter 10, "Working with Bitmaps.")*

The Paste as Mask command takes whatever object is on the clipboard and turns it into a mask. *(For a summary of all the mask commands and their settings, see pages 204–205.)*

To paste a bitmap image as a mask:

1. Use the Pointer tool to select the bitmap image to be used as the mask.

2. Choose **Edit > Cut**. The object disappears from the document.

3. Select the object to be masked. If there are multiple objects, choose **Modify > Group**.

4. Choose **Edit > Paste as Mask**. The bitmap image appears in the mask thumbnail ⓭.

TIP This command sets the bitmap mask to Grayscale ⓯.

TIP The absence of the pen symbol in the mask thumbnail indicates that the mask is a bitmap mask ⓰.

To group objects and a bitmap image into a mask:

1. Position the object or group to be masked below the bitmap image that is to act as the mask.

2. Select the objects and bitmap image.

3. Choose **Modify > Mask > Group as Mask**. The bitmap image becomes the mask for the objects below ⓱.

TIP This command sets the mask object to Grayscale.

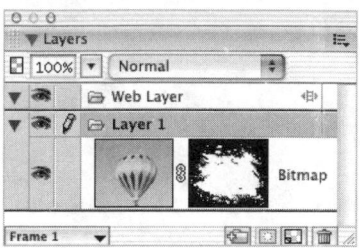

⓮ *A **bitmap mask** is indicated by a plain thumbnail (without a pen symbol) in the Layers palette.*

⓯ *A bitmap mask allows you to create freeform mask outlines.*

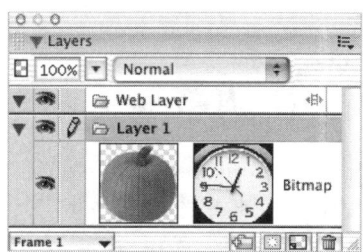

⓰ *The image used as a mask appears in the mask thumbnail in the Layers palette.*

⓱ *A **grayscale mask** uses the values of a bitmap image to mask a second image.*

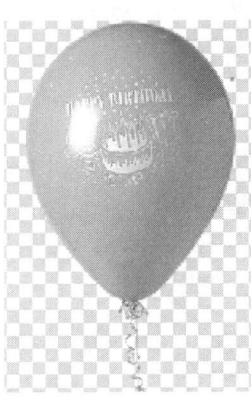

18 *The alpha channel of a bitmap image is indicated by the outline of the image against a transparent canvas.*

19 *A bitmap mask set as an alpha channel mask appears as a thumbnail in the Layers palette.*

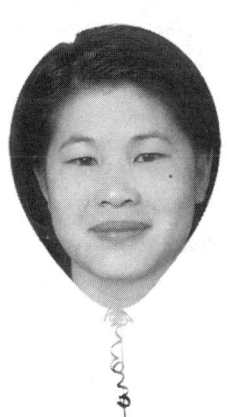

20 *A bitmap image is seen only inside the shape of the bitmask mask set to an alpha channel.*

The Paste Inside command takes whatever object is on the clipboard and pastes it into the alpha channel outline of a bitmap image.

TIP An alpha channel mask is very useful when you have a bitmap image with a unique shape on a transparent background **18**.

To paste a bitmap image as a mask:

1. Select the object to be masked. If there are multiple objects, choose **Modify** > **Group**.

2. Choose **Edit** > **Cut**. The object or group disappears from the document.

3. Use the Pointer tool to select the bitmap image to be used as the mask.

4. Choose **Edit** > **Paste Inside**. The objects appear inside the alpha channel outline of the bitmap image **19**.

TIP This command sets the bitmap mask to Alpha Channel **20**.

Stop Destroying Innocent Pixels

One of the most important reasons to mask a scanned image, rather than cutting, erasing, or cropping, is that you preserve the original pixels in the image. The benefit of the mask is that you still have the original image to go back to—not so if you cut, erase, or crop the image.

Bitmap Masks

Ordinarily I don't repeat exercises from one chapter to another. But the next technique, which also appears in Chapter 10, is so important, I feel it is necessary to repeat it here. So rather than make you switch back to Chapter 10, here's how to convert a selection into a bitmap mask. This converts the shape of a selection into a grayscale mask. *(For more information on working with selections, see pages 153–158.)*

To save a selection as a mask:

1. Create a selection around the area that you want to show.

2. Click the Add Mask icon at the bottom of the Layers panel **㉑**. A mask is created that follows the contours of the marching ants that define the selection **㉒**.

   or

   Choose Add Mask from the Layers panel menu.

TIP Hold the Opt/Alt key as you click the Add Mask icon to create a mask that is the inverse of the selection, i.e. the selected area is hidden.

㉑ *Click the* **Add Mask icon** *to automatically convert the selection into a grayscale image that masks the original image.*

㉒ *A selection converted into a mask hides the pixels outside the selection without deleting them.*

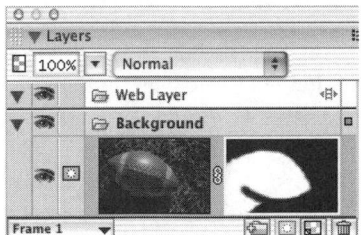

23 *When you* **paint with white on a bitmap mask,** *you erase the image or object being masked.*

24 *A masked image shows only the area inside the white portions of the mask.*

One of the advantages of using the bitmap drawing tools is that you can use them to paint a mask around an image. This technique is easier to control than working with the lasso to create a selection.

To paint a mask around an image:

1. Select the bitmap image that you want to mask.

TIP Although this technique is primarily used to mask bitmap images, you can use it to mask vector objects.

2. Click the Add Mask icon at the bottom of the Layers panel. An empty mask thumbnail is created in the Layers panel.

   or

   Choose Add Mask from the Layers panel menu.

3. Use the Brush tool or any of the other bitmap drawing tools to paint on the mask as follows **23**:

   - Black areas in the mask hide the image.
   - White areas in the mask allow the image to be seen.
   - Shades of gray in the mask show the image with shades of opacity.

TIP Watch the mask thumbnail in the layers panel to make sure all the areas are filled in with black **24**.

TIP Set the stroke color to black and the fill color to white. You can then tap the X key to easily flip between hiding and showing the image as you paint.

Setting the Mask Options

As you have seen, how you create a mask affects how the mask interacts with other objects. Vector masks have three different settings. Bitmap masks have two settings. Fortunately, none of the mask settings are permanent and you can change them at any time.

To set the vector mask settings:

1. Choose any of the techniques *(described on pages 194–197)* to create a vector mask.

2. Click the Mask thumbnail in the Layers panel to select the mask. This displays the Vector Mask settings in the Property Inspector 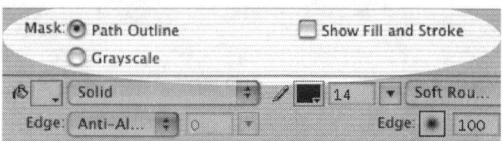.

3. Select the mask settings as follows:

   • **Path Outline** uses the shape of the path as the mask. Any feather or anti-alias settings are used as the mask outline 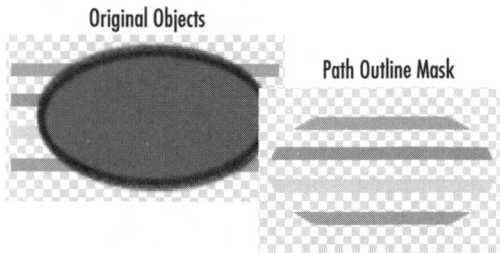.

   • **Grayscale** uses the grayscale values of the fill and stroke as the mask. White or lighter colors let you see the objects inside the mask. Black or darker colors hide the objects inside the mask 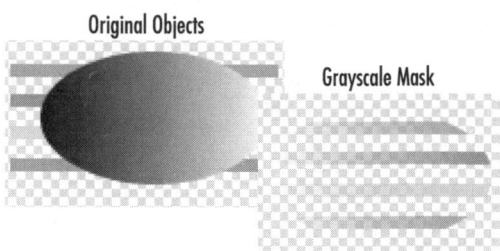.

4. If you set the vector mask to Path Outline, you can then choose Show Fill and Stroke. This lets you see any stroke color applied to the path. The fill color is visible only where there is a gap in the objects being masked 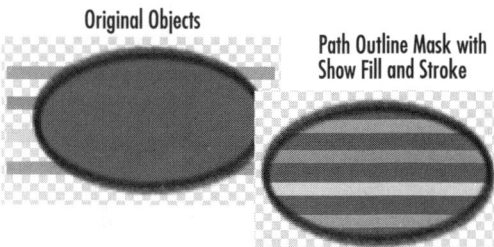.

*The **Vector Mask settings** in the Property Inspector.*

Original Objects

Path Outline Mask

*A **mask set to Path Outline** shows only the area inside the path shape of the mask.*

Original Objects

Grayscale Mask

*A **mask set to Grayscale** shows the area inside the mask based on the black and white areas of the mask.*

Original Objects

Path Outline Mask with Show Fill and Stroke

*A **mask set to Path Outline with Show Fill and Stroke** shows the area inside the path shape of the mask and any fill and stroke applied to the mask.*

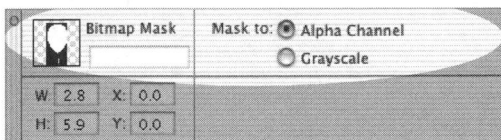

Original Objects

Alpha Channel Mask

⓴ *A* **bitmap mask set to Alpha Channel** *shows the masked object only inside the visible areas of the mask.*

Original Objects

Grayscale Mask

㉛ *A* **bitmap mask set to Grayscale** *shows the masked object according to the black and white values in the mask.*

Just as you can set the options for vector masks, so can you set the options for bitmap masks.

To set the bitmap mask settings:

1. Choose any of the techniques *(described on pages 198–201)* to create a bitmap mask.

2. Click the Mask thumbnail in the Layers panel to select the mask. This displays the Bitmap Mask settings in the Property Inspector ⓳.

3. Select the mask settings as follows:
   - **Alpha Channel** defines the mask using the shape of the pixels against the transparency grid ⓴.
   - **Grayscale** uses the grayscale values of the bitmap image as the mask ㉛. White or lighter colors let you see the objects inside the mask. Black or darker colors hide the objects inside the mask.

Grayscale Masks

The settings for grayscale masks are similar to the layer masks in Adobe Photoshop.

Pure white areas of the mask allow you to see the objects being masked. Solid black areas of the mask hide the objects inside the mask. Gray areas act like opacity settings for the mask.

One way I remember which does which is to think of the mask as a window. If the window is clean (white), then you can see through the window to the objects inside.

The dirtier the window gets, the harder it is to see through the window. If the window is solid black, you can't see anything through the window.

Setting the Mask Options

Masking Summary

As you have seen, there are many different ways to create masks. Depending on which command you choose, you will get different settings for the mask object. The following chart contains a summary of the different types of masks and how they are created.

Desired Result	Items Selected	Command	Mask Setting	Notes
Top object becomes the mask for the single object below.	Vector object on top. Single object below.	**Modify > Mask > Group as Mask**	Grayscale mask.	
Top object becomes the mask for the objects below.	Vector object on top. Multiple objects below.	**Modify > Mask > Group as Mask**	Grayscale mask.	Objects within the mask are automatically grouped.
Object becomes the mask for the selected object.	Vector object cut from page. Single object selected.	**Modify > Mask > Paste as Mask**	Path Outline. Show Fill and Stroke deselected.	
Object becomes the mask for the grouped items below.	Vector object cut from page. Grouped items selected.	**Modify > Mask > Paste as Mask**	Path Outline. Show Fill and Stroke deselected.	Items must be grouped in order for the Paste as Mask command to be available.
Object becomes the mask for the grouped items below.	Vector object cut from page. Single object or grouped items selected.	Click Add Mask icon. **Edit > Paste**	Path Outline. Show Fill and Stroke deselected.	Pasting the vector object changes the mask from the bitmap mode to the vector mode.
Object becomes the mask for the pasted item.	Single object to be masked cut from page. Vector object selected.	**Edit > Paste Inside**	Path Outline. Show Fill and Stroke selected.	

Desired Result	Items Selected	Command	Mask Setting	Notes
Object becomes the mask for the pasted items.	Multiple objects to be masked cut from page. Vector object selected.	**Edit > Paste Inside**	Path Outline. Show Fill and Stroke selected.	Objects within the mask are automatically grouped.
Bitmap image is created as the mask.	Object selected.	Click Add Mask Icon. Use any of the bitmap tools on the mask.	Grayscale bitmap mask.	Tool options indicate type of mask.
Bitmap mask is created from the image.	Bitmap image on top. Single object below.	**Modify > Mask > Group as Mask**	Grayscale bitmap mask.	
Bitmap mask is created from the image.	Bitmap object cut from page. Single object selected.	**Modify > Mask > Paste as Mask**	Grayscale bitmap mask.	
Bitmap image is converted into a bitmap mask for the object.	Object to be masked is selected and cut from page.	Select a bitmap image. **Edit > Paste Inside**	Alpha Channel bitmap mask.	
Bitmap image is converted into a bitmap mask for the grouped objects.	Multiple objects to be masked are selected and cut from the page.	Select a bitmap image. **Edit > Paste Inside**	Alpha Channel bitmap mask.	Objects within the mask are automatically grouped.
Grouped bitmap images are converted into a vector mask.	Object to be masked selected and cut from the page.	Two grouped bitmap images selected. **Edit > Paste Inside**	Path Outline with Show Fill and Stroke selected.	All objects must be ungrouped in order to use any of the bitmap tools on the images.
Bitmap images are grouped and converted into a vector mask.	Multiple bitmap objects cut from page. Single object selected.	**Modify > Mask > Paste as Mask**	Path Outline with Show Fill and Stroke selected.	Bitmap images are automatically grouped. All objects must be ungrouped in order to use any of the bitmap tools on the images.

Editing and Manipulating Masks

Once you have created a mask, you can still make changes to both the mask and the object(s) being masked. The Layers panel makes it easy to select either the mask or the objects being masked.

To edit the mask:

1. Click the Mask thumbnail of the Layers panel to select the mask. The mask icon in the Layers panel indicates you are editing the mask ⏹.

    or

    Choose Edit Mask from the Layers panel menu.

2. Use the vector tools to edit a vector mask.

    or

    Use the bitmap tools to modify a bitmap mask.

Sometimes it is easier to edit objects if you don't have a mask to deal with. Fortunately, you can temporarily disable a mask.

To temporarily hide a mask:

1. Click the listing for the mask and the masking object in the Layers panel.

2. Choose Disable Mask from the Layers panel menu. A red X appears over the Mask thumbnail ⏹. The effects of the mask are disabled.

⏹ Use the Disable Mask command if you need to edit multiple items that have been grouped together and then masked. Disabling the mask allows you to select the individual items in the group.

To re-enable a mask:

◆ Click the Mask thumbnail. This re-activates the effects of the mask.

Object thumbnail   Mask thumbnail

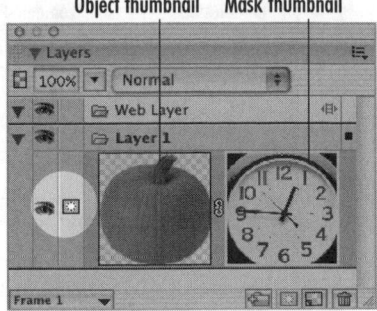

⏹ *The* **Mask icon** *in the Layers panel indicates that the mask is being edited.*

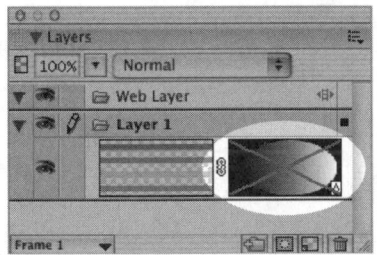

⏹ *The* **red X through the Mask thumbnail** *indicates that the mask has been disabled.*

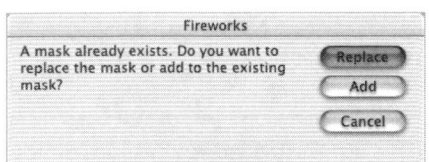

34 *The dialog box that allows you to* **replace or add an object to a mask***.*

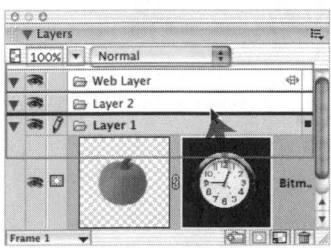

35 **Drag the mask thumbnail** *up to convert it from a mask to an ordinary object.*

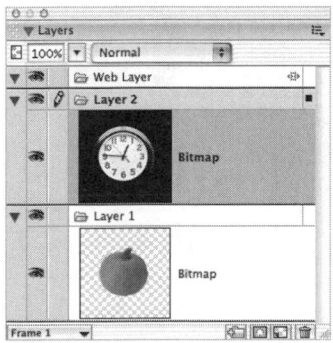

36 *After dragging the mask thumbnail upward, it appears as an object in the Layers panel.*

You can add to or replace the objects in a vector mask at any time.

To replace or add an object to a vector mask:

1. Create the object you want to add to the mask in the position where it should be when added to the mask.

2. Select the object and choose **Edit** > **Cut** to send the object to the clipboard.

3. Click the Object Thumbnail in the Layers panel to select the object being masked.

4. Choose **Edit** > **Paste as Mask**. A dialog box appears asking if you want to replace the current mask or add to it **34**.

5. Click Replace to delete the current mask and replace it with the object on the clipboard.

   or

   Click Add to add the object on the clipboard to the mask.

As I've mentioned before, part of the beauty of masks is that you don't permanently alter objects. So you can easily release a mask and restore the objects to their original appearance.

To release a mask:

1. Select the mask and the objects being masked.

2. Choose **Modify** > **Ungroup**. This releases the mask and leaves it positioned on top of the objects that were being masked.

TIP You can also drag the Mask thumbnail to another listing in the Layers panel **35**. This removes the mask and places it as an object on the document **36**.

There may come a time when you want to apply the mask to permanently change the appearance of the masked objects. For instance, you might want the effects of one masked object to be used as the mask for a different object. In that case, you need to decide what to do with the objects being masked.

To discard a mask:

1. Drag the Mask thumbnail into the Layers panel trash can 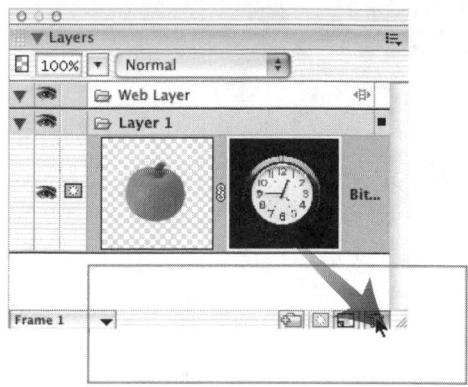. A dialog box appears asking you how you would like to dispose of the mask 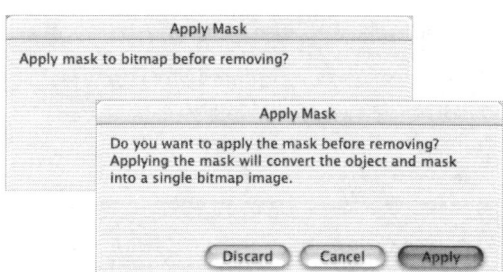.

   or

   Choose Delete Mask from the Layers panel menu.

2. Choose Apply to cause the objects being masked to retain their appearance after the mask is removed.

   or

   Choose Discard to remove the mask and leave the objects as they were before the mask was applied.

TIP If the mask contains vector objects, the dialog box will state that applying the mask will convert the objects into a bitmapped image. If you do not want a bitmapped image, do not apply the mask. Instead, you can ungroup the mask and the contents and then use the Crop command as described on page 93.

37 Drag a mask thumbnail *into the Layers panel trash can to apply or discard the mask.*

38 *The two* Apply Mask dialog boxes.

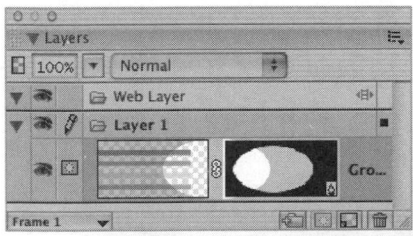

39 Drag the cloverleaf handle *to move the contents of the mask separately from the mask.*

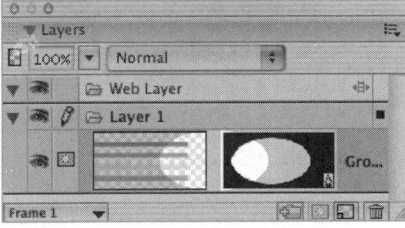

40 Clicking the Link icon *allows you to move or transform the mask without disturbing the contents of the mask.*

Ordinarily, a mask and the contents of the mask will move together. However, you may want to move the items separately to reposition either the mask or the objects being masked.

To move only the objects being masked:

1. Click the Object Thumbnail to select just the objects being masked. A cloverleaf mask handle appears.

2. Drag the cloverleaf mask handle **39**. This moves the objects being masked without disturbing the position of the mask.

To move only the mask:

1. Click the Link icon between the Object Thumbnail and the Mask thumbnail. This unlinks the mask from the objects being masked **40**.

2. Use any of the object selection tools to move the mask.

TIP Once a mask has been unlinked from its objects, you can use any of the transformation tools or commands to change the objects being masked.

Editing and Manipulating Masks

Fading Images

One of the most requested looks in Fireworks is to fade an image from top to bottom, left to right, or outwards from the middle. As you already know from reading this chapter, you can easily do this by drawing a rectangle over an image, filling the rectangle with a gradient, and then setting the gradient to be a grayscale mask for the image. However, you might find all those steps cumbersome. Fortunately, there is a handy command called Fade Image that does all those steps for you, automatically.

To use the Fade Image Command:

1. Use the Pointer tool to select the image that you want to fade.

TIP You can also apply the Fade Image command on a single vector object or grouped vector objects.

2. Choose **Commands > Creative > Fade Image**. The Fade Image dialog box appears **41**.

3. Choose one of the Fade Image pictures. Each picture shows a sample of the type of fade that will be applied to the image.

4. Click OK. A gradient mask is created over the image **42**.

TIP Once you have applied the Image Fade, you are left with an ordinary grayscale mask *(as described on pages 202–203)*. You can then use any of the gradient features to change the style of gradient, the gradient handles, or the position of the gradient **43**.

TIP Click the Information icon in the Fade Image dialog box to see the two people who created this command **44**.

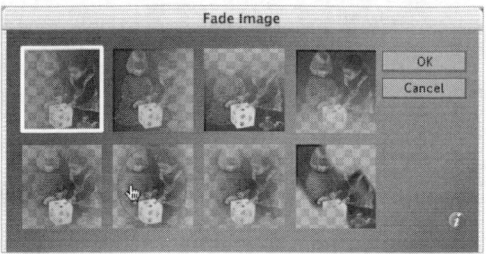

41 *The* **Fade Image dialog box** *lets you choose the type of fade from the proxy pictures.*

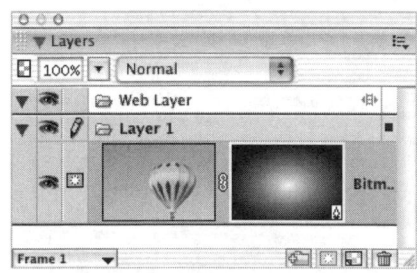

42 *The* **Fade Image command** *creates a grayscale vector mask over the image.*

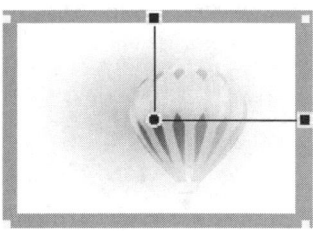

43 *The grayscale vector mask can be modified like any other gradient.*

44 *The credits for the Fade Image command.*

Fading Images

AUTOMATION FEATURES 13

One of the challenges of creating Web graphics is that a typical Web site has hundreds of different images, graphics, buttons, and navigational elements. Once you've created those items, you may find it necessary to repeatedly change the look of many different elements.

Sure, you could open each file for the different elements and make the changes manually, but would you want to? Maybe if you were being paid by the hour, but not if you're trying to get the job done quickly.

Fortunately, Macromedia Fireworks provides you with many ways to automate creating objects and making changes. Some of these automation features, such as styles, should be prepared before you do too much work. Others, such as Find and Replace, are useful in making changes to existing artwork. But no matter when you use these features, they all help you work faster and more efficiently.

Paste Attributes

If you have created an object with a certain set of intricate fill settings—for instance a special gradient fill, feathering, and fill texture—it might be cumbersome to reapply all those settings to another object created later. Rather, you can copy the settings from one object to another.

TIP Paste Attributes include stroke, fill, and effect settings. Paste Attributes from text objects will include font, size, style, and range kerning.

To paste attributes from one object to another:

1. Select the object with the attributes you want to copy.

2. Choose **Edit > Copy**.

3. Select the object with the attributes you want to change.

4. Choose **Edit > Paste Attributes**. The second object takes on all the settings of the first ❶.

TIP Changes made to gradients or patterns using the vector controls *(see page 114)* are not saved when copying and pasting attributes.

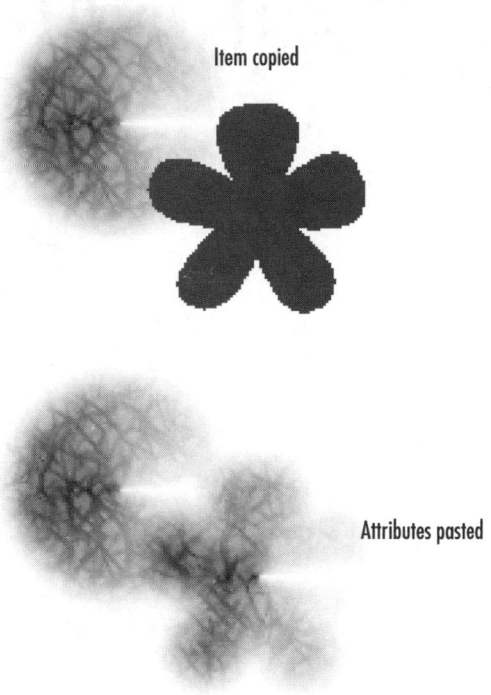

Item copied

Attributes pasted

❶ *The result of* **applying the Paste Attributes command** *of the circle object's fill attributes to the flower shape.*

Choosing Automation Features

Fireworks offers several different types of automation features. You should choose the one that makes the most sense for your workflow.

Paste Attributes is the easiest to apply, but can only be used on one object at a time. Use it if you don't have many objects to modify. Styles *(see the next page)* require a little bit more advance preparation. Once they have been defined they can be quickly applied to many objects. Find and Replace features *(see page 217)* can be applied to hundreds of objects located on many different documents. However, they can only be applied to objects with known sets of features. Script commands *(see page 224)* need quite a bit of advanced planning, but can be used to apply multiple sets of commands to objects. Batch Processing *(see page 228)* lets you combine Find and Replace and Script commands together into more powerful commands that can be applied to entire folders of documents.

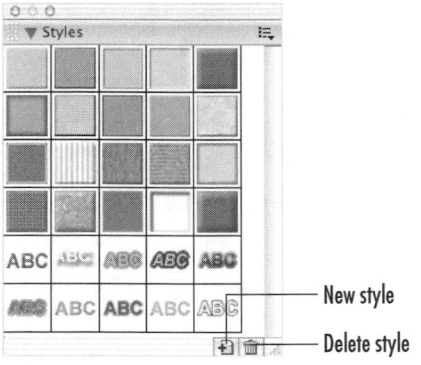

New style

Delete style

② *The* **Styles panel** *stores previews of the styles. These styles all come preset with Fireworks.*

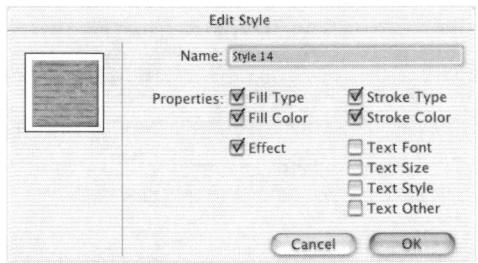

❸ *The* **Edit Style dialog box** *lets you name the style and select which properties are included as part of the style.*

Using Styles

Styles are simply a way to store all the information about the fill, stroke, effect, or text settings. You can then easily apply the style to other objects without applying all the settings one by one. The Styles panel comes with an assortment of object and text styles that you can use. There are still more styles located on the Fireworks CD. However, most likely you will want to define your own styles.

To define an object style:

1. Open the Styles panel by choosing **Window > Styles ②**.

2. Select an object and use the Fill, Stroke, and Effect panels to give the object any look you want.

3. With the object selected, click the New Style button at the bottom of the Styles panel. The Edit Style dialog box appears **❸**.

4. Name the style.

5. Check the boxes for the properties you want the style to control.
   - **Fill Type** controls a pattern, gradient, or Web dither.
   - **Fill Color** controls the color of a fill.
   - **Effect** controls the effect.
   - **Stroke Type** controls the size and type of stroke.
   - **Stroke Color** controls the color of a stroke.

6. Click OK to store the style in the Styles panel.

TIP The preview in the Styles panel is always a square, regardless of the shape that was used to define the style.

Using Styles

In addition to styles for objects, you can also define styles that apply text properties. Once you have defined a style, it is easy to apply that style to objects.

To define a text style:

1. Select a text block and use the Text Editor as well as the Fill, Stroke, and Effect panels to format the text.

2. With the formatted text block selected, click the New Style icon at the bottom of the Styles panel. The Edit Style dialog box appears ❹.

3. Use the Name field to name the style.

4. In addition to the object properties, check the boxes for which text properties you want the style to control.
   - **Text Font** controls the font.
   - **Text Size** controls the point size ❺.
   - **Text Style** controls styling such as Bold, Italic, or Underline.
   - **Text Other** controls attributes such as alignment, anti-aliasing, auto-kerning, horizontal scale, range kerning, or leading.

5. Click OK to store the style in the Styles panel.

TIP The preview of text in the Styles panel is always **abc**, regardless of the characters that were used to define the style.

To apply a style to objects:

1. Select the object or objects to which you want to apply the style.

2. Click the preview of the style ❻. The object changes according to the definition of the style.

TIP Unlike the styles in Macromedia Free-Hand or other programs, Fireworks styles can't be used to update objects. Changing the definition of the style doesn't change the objects that have had the style previously applied to them.

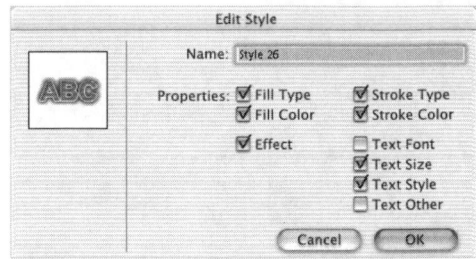

❹ *When a text block is selected, the* **Edit Style** **dialog box** *lets you control the text properties for the style.*

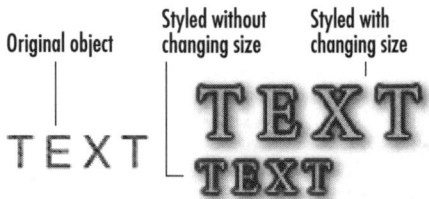

❺ *The difference between applying a style that affects the text size and one that does not.*

❻ *Click the style preview* **to apply a style to a selected object.**

❼ *The* **Styles** *panel menu.*

Managing Styles

As you create more styles, the Styles panel can get pretty crowded. You can use the Export Styles, Delete Styles, and Import Styles commands to help manage your styles.

For instance, use the Export Styles command for all the styles that relate to a specific project. Then use the Delete Styles command to delete those styles from the Styles panel.

Later, when you are working on that project, use the Import Styles command to add those styles back to the Styles panel.

This method helps keep your styles focused on your current project.

Once you define a style, it continues to appear in the Styles panel where you can access it for other documents. You can also save styles and export them into a separate file that you can share with other people working on the same project.

To export styles:

1. In the Styles panel, select the style you want to export.

2. Select additional styles by holding the Command/Ctrl key and clicking the styles.

TIP To select adjoining styles, select the style at one end of the group, hold down the Shift key, and click the style at the other end of the group. All styles between the first and last style are selected.

3. Choose Export Styles from the Styles panel menu **❼**. A dialog box appears.

4. Use the dialog box to name the document that contains the styles and click Save.

To import styles:

1. Choose Import Styles from the Styles panel menu **❼**.

2. Navigate to find the document that contains the styles you want to import.

3. Choose Open. The styles appear in the Styles panel.

If you have many styles in the panel, you can delete the ones you do not need.

To delete styles:

1. Select the styles you want to delete.

2. Click the Delete Styles button at the bottom of the Styles panel.

    or

    Open the Styles panel menu and choose Delete Styles.

Using Styles

Once you have defined a style, you can edit which properties of the style are applied to objects. For instance, you can turn off the effect and only have the fill and stroke applied to objects.

To edit styles:

1. Choose Edit Style from the Styles menu. This opens the Edit Style dialog box.

2. Make whatever changes you want and click OK.

You have two choices as to how the styles are displayed in the Styles panel. The large icons show more details in the styles but take up more room than the small icons.

To change the Styles panel views:

1. Choose Large Icons from the Styles panel menu. This increases the size of the preview in the Styles panel.

2. If Large Icons is already chosen, choose it again to change the previews to the small icons 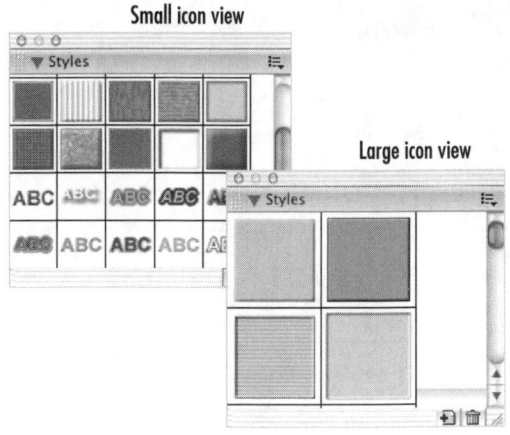 .

If you have added and deleted styles, you can reset the Styles panel to the original styles that shipped with Fireworks.

To reset the styles to the defaults:

1. Choose Reset Styles from the Styles panel menu.

2. Click OK when the dialog box asks for confirmation.

TIP The Reset Styles command deletes any custom styles you may have created.

Small icon view

Large icon view

8 *The difference between the small icons and the large icons in the Styles panel.*

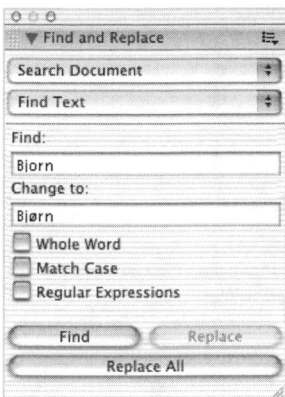

⑨ *The* **Find and Replace panel.**

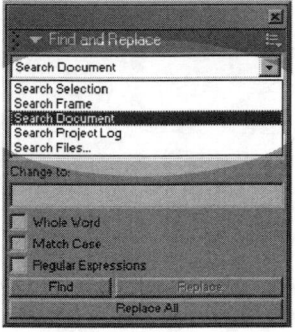

⑩ *The* **Search choices** *for Find and Replace.*

Working with Find and Replace

The Find and Replace panel lets you quickly change the formatting of vector and text objects.

TIP Find and Replace does not work with bitmap images.

To use the Find and Replace panel:

1. Choose **Window** > **Find and Replace** to open the Find and Replace panel **⑨**.

2. Use the Search list as described below to specify the locations where the Find and Replace commands should search.

3. Choose which type of attributes you want to find, as described on the next page.

4. Use the Find, Replace, and Replace All buttons as described on page 221 to control which elements should be replaced.

To set the Find and Replace search location:

1. Choose **Window** > **Find and Replace** to open the Find and Replace panel **⑨**.

2. Open the Search list and choose a place for the Find and Replace to occur as follows **⑩**:

   - **Search Selection** searches among the currently selected items.
   - **Search Frame** searches in the current frame of the document. *(For more information on working with frames, see Chapter 16, "Animations.")*
   - **Search Document** searches throughout the current document.
   - **Search Project Log** searches within all the files listed in the Project Log. *(For information on adding files to the Project Log, see page 223.)*
   - **Search Files** searches within a specific list of files.

3. If you choose Search Files, use the operating system dialog box to add files from different locations.

To set the search attributes:

◆ Choose one of the five attributes from the Find list ⓫.

- **Find Text** searches for specific words and changes them to others.
- **Find Font** searches and changes text attributes such as font, style, and point size.
- **Find Color** searches and changes colors of Fireworks objects.
- **Find URL** searches and changes the URLs within a document. *(For more information on working with URL links, see Chapter 17, "Hotspots and Links.")*
- **Find Non-Web 216** searches and changes colors so that they are part of the Web 216 palette.

TIP You can only search for one attribute at a time. So you can search and change all red objects and change them to green, but you can't search for red Courier text and change it to green Helvetica.

To find and replace text attributes:

1. Choose Find Text from the Attribute list. The text attributes appear ⓬.

2. In the Find field, type the text you want to locate.

3. In the Change to field, type the replacement text.

4. Check Whole Word to make sure the text only appears as a whole word and not part of another word.

5. Check Match Case to make sure the upper-case and lower-case letters match the text exactly as typed.

6. Check Regular Expressions to use special control characters in your find and replace text strings.

TIP For instance, entering the regular expression tag s$ searches for the letter **s** that appears only at the end of a word or line (indicated by $).

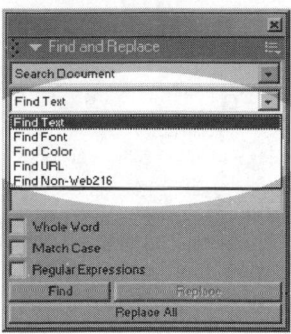

⓫ *The **Find list** in the Find and Replace panel allows you to specify the type of search.*

⓬ *The **Text attributes** in the Find and Replace panel.*

Regular Expressions

Regular expressions are special symbols that can be added to change how the Find and Replace commands work. They work like the special symbols and wild card characters in word processing and page layout programs. There are hundreds of different regular expressions—more than can be covered here. You can find an excellent article on regular expressions at http://zez.org/article/articleview/11/.

Symbol	Looks for	Example
^	The beginning of the input or line	^H finds the H in Help but not FreeHand
$	The end of the input or line	s$ finds the s in Fireworks but not wish
*	The preceding character that appears zero or more times	es* finds the es in best or the ess in mess or finds the e in bet
+	The preceding character that appears one or more times	es+ finds the es in best or the ess in mess but does not find the e in bet
?	The preceding character that appears zero or one times	st?on finds the ston in Redstone or the son in Davidson but does not find anything in Littleton or Emerson
.	Any single character except for the newsline character	.ealthy finds both healthy and wealthy
|	Either the characters before the | or the characters after the |	www|http finds both www or http
(n)	The preceding character when it occurs n number of times	e(2) finds ee in sleep or keep but not kept
(n,m)	The preceding character when it occurs at least n times but not more than m times	FF(2,4) finds FF in FF0000, FFF000 or FFFF00
[abc]	Any of the characters in the brackets	[abc] finds a, b, or c
[a-c]	Any of the characters in the range of the characters between the hyphen	[a-e] finds a, b, c, d, or e
[^abc]	Any character not enclosed in the brackets	[^aeiou] finds the d in adapt and the c in ouch
[^a-c]	Any of the characters not in the range of characters between the hyphen	[a-s] finds the t in text or u in ugly, but not the a in apple
\d	Any numerical character from 0 to 9	\d finds the 2 in H20 or the 7 in 7th Heaven
\D	Any non-numerical character (same as [^0-9])	\D finds the th in 7th or the rd in 3rd
\n	Line feed character	
\r	Carriage return	
\s	Any white space character such as a tab, form feed or line feed	\spress finds the press in Peachpit press but not depressed
\S	Any single non–white-space character	\Spress finds the press in depressed but not Peachpit press
\t	A tab character	
\W	Any non-alphanumeric character	\W finds characters such as the & in Big & Tall or the @ in @mindspring.com

To find and replace Font attributes:

1. Choose Find Font from the Attribute list. The font attributes appear 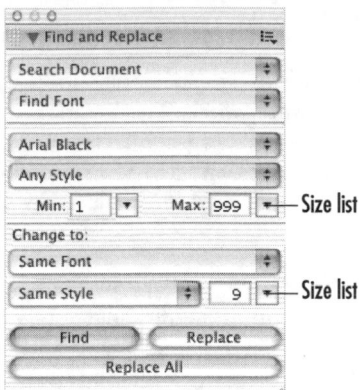.

2. Choose the typeface to search for from the Font list in the Find controls.

3. Set the replacement typeface from the Font list in the Change controls.

4. Set the type style to locate from the Style list in the Find controls.

TIP Use Any Font or Any Style to include all fonts or all styles in the search.

5. Set the replacement type style from the Style list in the Change controls.

TIP Use Same Style to retain the type style in the replacement.

6. Set a range of point sizes to be changed by entering minimum and maximum amounts in the Min and Max fields in the Find controls.

TIP To set a single point size to change, delete any amount in the Min field and enter an amount in the Max field.

7. Set the point size to be changed by entering the amount in the Size list in the Change controls.

⑬ *The* **Find Font attributes** *in the Find and Replace panel.*

To set the Color attributes:

1. Choose Find Color from the Attribute list. The color attributes appear ⑭.

2. Use the Find Color Well to select the color to change.

3. Use the Change to Color Well to set the replacement color.

4. Use the Apply to list to set which properties should change ⑮.

   - **Fills & Strokes** changes the fills and strokes but not effects.
   - **All Properties** changes the fills, strokes, and effects.
   - **Fills, Strokes,** or **Effects** changes just one of those attributes.

⑭ *The* **Find Color attributes** *in the Find and Replace panel.*

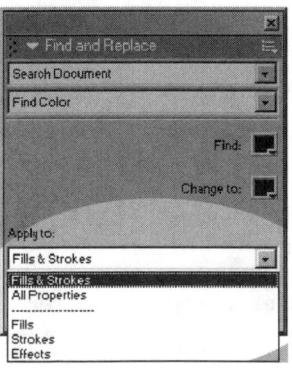

⑮ *The* **Apply to list** *for the attributes changes.*

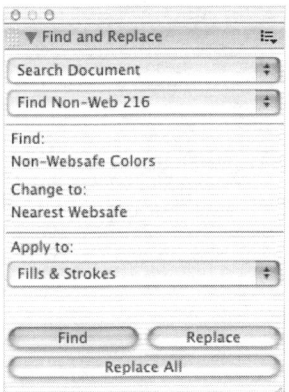

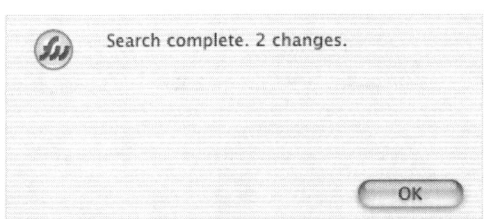

16 *The* **URL attributes** *in the Find and Replace panel.*

17 *The* **Non-Web 216 attributes** *in the Find and Replace panel.*

18 *The* **Search complete dialog box** *tells you the results of the Find and Replace command.*

To find and replace URL attributes:

1. Choose Find URL from the Attribute list. The URL attributes appear **16**.

2. In the Find field, type the URL to search for.

3. Type the replacement URL in the Change to field.

TIP Set the Whole Word, Match Case, and Regular Expressions as described on page 218.

You can also use the Find and Replace controls to change all non-Web-safe colors to their closest Web-safe equivalent.

TIP This command only works on native Fireworks objects, not scanned or bitmap images.

To search for Non-Web 216 Colors:

1. Choose Find Non-Web 216 from the attribute pop-up list. The Non-Web 216 attributes appear **17**.

2. Use the Apply to list to set which properties should change *(see the description on the previous page).*

Use the buttons in the Find and Replace panel to change the objects **17**.

To use the Find, Replace, and Replace All buttons:

1. Click Find to select the first object that meets the search criteria.

2. Click Replace to change that one instance.

   or

   Click Replace All to change all the elements that meet the search criteria.

TIP If you choose Replace All, a dialog box appears telling you when the search is complete and how many changes were made **18**.

It's not enough to make changes to multiple files. You also need to control what happens to the original files when you make those changes. To do so, you need to set the Replace Options.

To set the Replace Options:

1. Choose Replace Options from the Find and Replace panel menu ⓳. This opens the Replace Options dialog box ⓴.

2. Choose Save and Close Files to automatically save and close the files as they are changed.

3. Choose one of the options from the Backup Original Files list:
   - **No Backups** overwrites the original file with the changed file.
   - **Overwrite Existing Backups** makes a backup copy of the file, but then further changes will overwrite those backup files.
   - **Incremental Backups** makes backup files each time the changes are made, numbering each of the backups.

You can keep a record of what files have been changed and when the changes were made by adding the files to the Project Log.

To add the changed files to the Project Log:

◆ Choose Add Files to Project Log from the Find and Replace panel menu.

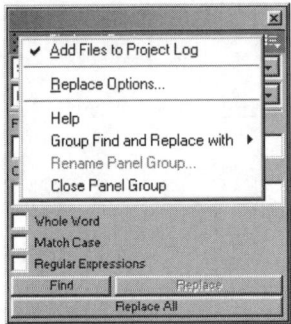

⓳ *The* **Find and Replace panel menu**.

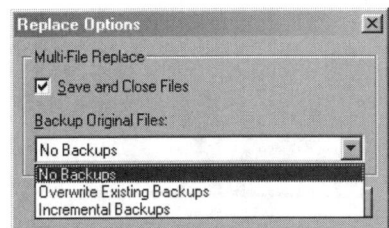

⓴ *The* **Replace Options dialog box**.

Frame

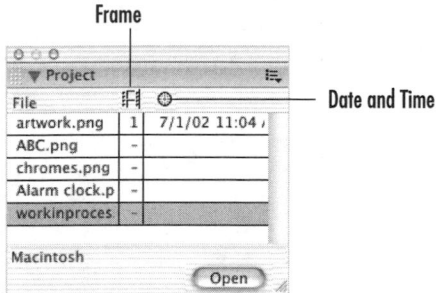

Date and Time

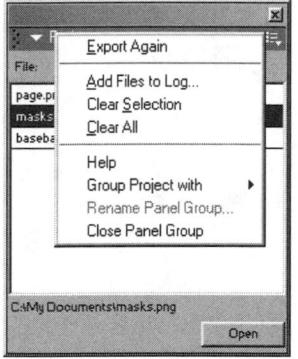

㉑ *The* **Project Log** *panel.*

㉒ *The* **Project Log** *panel menu.*

Using the Project Log

It may be difficult to remember all the files associated with a Web site or project. The Project Log gives you an easy way to organize these files into groups. You can also use the Project Log as part of a Find and Replace routine *(see the previous page)*.

To add or delete Project Log files:

1. Choose **Window** > **Project Log** to open the Project Log panel **㉑**.

2. Choose Add Files to Log from the Project Log menu **㉒**.

3. Use the operating system dialog box to select the Fireworks PNG files to be added to the Project Log.

4. Select an item or items in the Project Log and then choose Clear Selection to delete the selected files from the Project Log.

   or

   Choose Clear All to delete all the files from the Project Log.

TIP The Project Log frame and date columns show which frames have been altered and the most recent modification date using Find and Replace.

The files in the Project Log can also be exported using the current export settings.

To export files from the Project Log:

1. Set the Export defaults as desired. *(For more about setting the Export defaults, see Chapter 20, "Exporting.")*

2. Select the files in the Project Log that you want to export.

3. Choose Export Again from the Project Log menu. This lets you save each of the exported files.

Using the Project Log

History and Scripting Commands

At its simplest function, the History panel acts as a list from which you can undo and redo commands *(see page 37)*. It can also be used as part of JavaScript commands that can automate complex actions.

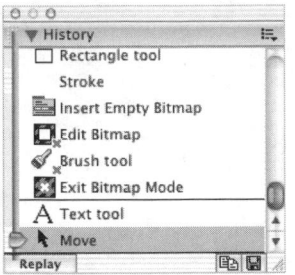

To replay a set of actions:

1. If the History panel is not visible, choose **Window** > **History** to open the History panel ㉓.

2. Use the Shift key to select the range of actions you want to replay. Use the Cmd/Ctrl key to select non-contiguous actions.

TIP The History panel displays a red x or separator line between actions that cannot be replayed together.

3. Click the Replay button.

   or

   Choose Replay Selected Steps from the History panel menu ㉔.

㉓ *The **History panel** allows you to replay actions and turn them into scripts.*

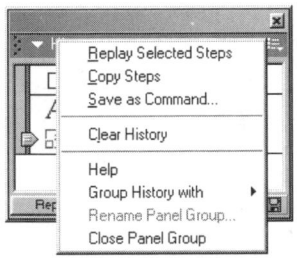

㉔ *The* **History panel menu**.

To store actions as a script:

1. Select a range of actions in the History panel.

2. Use the Shift key to select the range of actions you want to replay. Use the Cmd/Ctrl key to select non-contiguous actions.

3. Click the Save as Command button.

   or

   Choose Save as Command from the History panel menu ㉔.

4. Use the Save Command dialog box to name the command ㉕. The command automatically appears under the Commands menu.

TIP Commands are JavaScript (.jsf) files stored in the folder Fireworks MX: Configuration: Commands.

㉕ *The* **Save Command dialog box**.

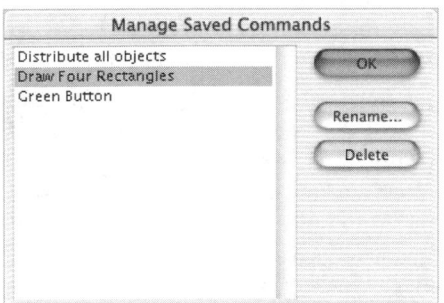

26 *The* **Manage Saved Commands dialog box.**

Sharing Commands with Dreamweaver

Macromedia Dreamweaver also uses .jsf commands. This makes it possible to have a command in Dreamweaver that also controls actions in Fireworks.

Many of these commands are available as free downloads at the Macromedia Dreamweaver Exchange site at www.macromedia.com/exchange/dreamweaver. This includes commands such as Joseph Lowery's BulletBuilder which converts the bullets of an unordered list to a graphic, generated by Fireworks.

Once you save a command, it appears under the Command menu in the menu bar. You can run these commands any time.

To play back commands:

◆ Choose the command listed under the Commands menu.

TIP Fireworks ships with many commands that make it easier to perform several commonly used tasks. These commands are listed under the Commands menu.

TIP One of the commands that is most useful is the Reset Warning Dialogs command. Run this command to bring back all the dialog boxes that you banished by selecting Don't Show Again.

Once you save many commands, you may want to rename or remove the command. For instance, if you no longer use a specific command, you may want to delete it from the list.

To edit the commands list:

1. Choose **Commands > Manage Saved Commands**. The Manage Saved Commands dialog box appears **26**.

2. Select the command you want to edit.

3. Click Rename to rename a command.

4. Click Delete to delete commands you no longer want on the list.

TIP The Delete command cannot be undone so make sure you have chosen the right command.

As mentioned, the Fireworks commands are written in a Web-scripting language called JavaScript. This is the same language many people use to program commands for Web sites. This means you can write your own commands for Fireworks actions.

TIP Learning the JavaScript necessary to write your own Fireworks commands is well beyond the scope of this book. However, the following exercise gives you the steps you need to take to write the JavaScript command.

To write your own JavaScript command:

1. Start a new document in a text editor or word processing program.

2. Open one of the commands that ship with Fireworks or type your own commands.

3. Make any changes to the command.

   or

   Type your own JavaScript commands.

4. Save the file as a text file with the extension .jsf.

5. Place the file in the Fireworks MX: Configuration: Commands folder. The command will then be available under the Fireworks Commands menu.

TIP You can create a sub-folder in the Commands folder to hold your own scripts.

Understanding a Command JavaScript

One way to learn how to write Java-Scripts is to examine the commands that ship with Fireworks. Here's what happens during the "Center in Document" command.

The first part checks to make sure there is a selected object. If not, the script won't run.

```
if (fw.selection != null && =fw.
selection.length>0) {
```

The script then gets the document size.

```
var docWidth = fw.getDocumentDOM
().width; var docHeight = fw
.getDocumentDOM().height; var
docLeft = fw.getDocumentDOM().
left; var docTop = fw.getDocument
DOM().top;
```

This section does the math to find the coordinates of the middle of the document. Notice it uses values obtained in the previous section.

```
var middleWidth = docWidth/2; var
middleHeight = docHeight/2;
```

Next, the script finds the size of the selected objects.

```
var selectBounds = fw.get
DocumentDOM().getSelection
Bounds(); var selectLeft =
selectBounds.left; var selectTop
= selectBounds.top; var
selectRight = selectBounds.right;
var selectBottom =
selectBounds.bottom;
```

The script then does the math to find the middle of the selection.

```
var selectMiddleWidth =
(selectRight - selectLeft)/
2; var selectMiddleHeight =
(selectBottom - selectTop)/2;
```

Next the script finds where to move the selection.

```
var moveToX = docLeft +
middleWidth - selectMiddleWidth
- selectLeft; var moveToY
= docTop + middleHeight -
selectMiddleHeight - selectTop;
```

Finally, the script moves the selection!

```
fw.getDocumentDOM().moveSelection
By({x:moveToX, y:moveToY}, false,
false);}
```

History and Scripting Commands

Download Extension

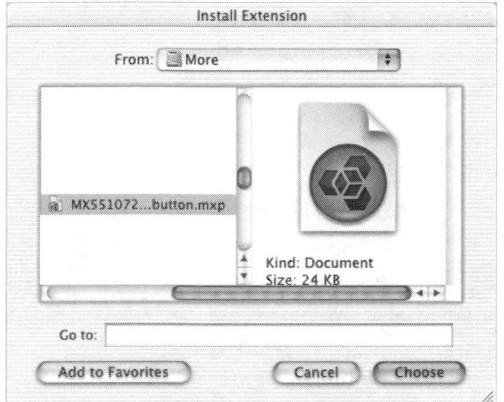

macintosh | 22.105 K
MX551072_Macbutton.mxp

windows | 22.105 K
MX551072_Macbutton.mxp

Installation instructions

㉗ *An excerpt from the* **Macromedia Exchange** Web site *to download a file.*

㉘ *A downloaded MXP Extension file.*

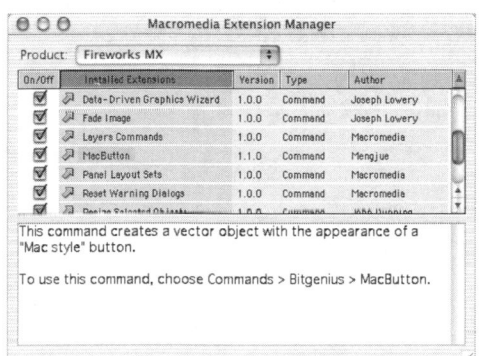

㉙ *The* **Macromedia Extension Manager.**

Adding Fireworks Extensions

JavaScript commands let people create their own features for Fireworks. Fireworks also allows programmers to create Flash (SWF) movies that provide an interface for JavaScript commands.

To download and use extensions:

1. Use a Web browser to go to www.macromedia.com/exchange.

2. Register and go to the Dreamweaver area.

3. Download the extension you want to add to Fireworks **㉗**.

4. In Fireworks, choose **Commands** > **Manage Extensions**. This opens the separate Macromedia Extension Manager application.

5. Choose Fireworks MX from the Product menu.

6. Choose **File** > **Install Extension** and then choose the extension package you downloaded **㉘**. This installs the extension into the Fireworks program.

TIP Click the name of the program in the Macromedia Extension Manager to see how to launch the extension **㉙**.

Create Your Own Extensions

Do you know JavaScript? Are you comfortable moving around Flash? Well, then you can amaze your friends by creating your own Fireworks Extensions. Look in the Fireworks CD for the folder Extending Fireworks MX. In there you'll find documentation, sample Flash files, and the Fireworks components.

Batch Processing Changes

Batch processing allows you to combine exporting, scaling, find and replace, renaming, and commands together into one super-command that can be applied to many files at once.

To set the batch processing options:

1. Choose **File > Batch Process**. The first Batch Process (Mac) or Batch (Win) dialog box appears **30**.

2. Set the files for batch processing as described in the next exercise.

3. Click the Next button to set the Batch Options as described on the next page.

4. Click the Next button to set the renaming controls as described on page 230.

5. Click the Next button to set the destination controls as described on page 231.

TIP You can batch process any native Fireworks file as well as any other file that Fireworks can open. This includes scans or FreeHand files.

There are several different ways to set which files should be part of batch processing.

To choose the files for batch processing:

1. In the Batch Process dialog box, use the navigation controls to select the files for batch processing.

2. Click the Add, Add All, or Remove buttons to add or delete the files for batch processing.

3. Choose Include Files from Project Log to batch process those files listed in the Project Log.

4. Choose Include Current Open Files to batch process the files that are currently open.

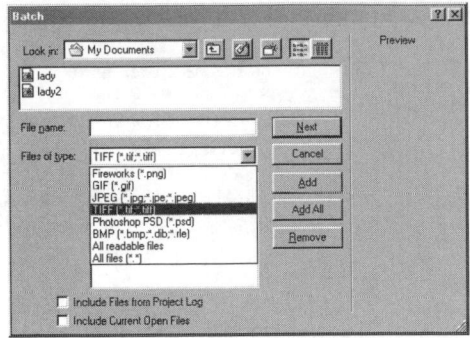

30 *The first* **Batch Process dialog box** *lets you select the files for batch processing.*

The Power of Batch Processing

A typical Web site can contain hundreds, even thousands, of images. When you need to make changes, you don't want to have to open and modify each file one by one.

Combining the different options together makes Fireworks's batch processing commands a very powerful tool. You choose the files you want to change, pick the changes you want to make, and let Fireworks do the rest.

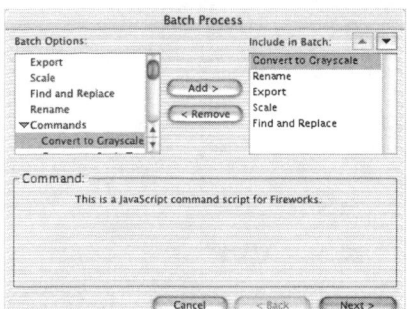

⑪ *The second* **Batch Process dialog box** *lets you choose which of the Batch Options should be included in the batch processing.*

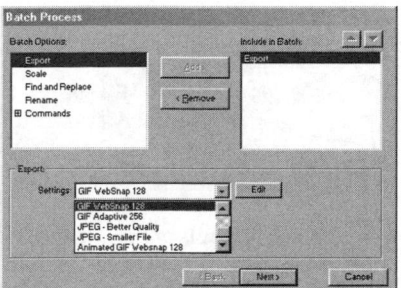

⑫ *The* **Export controls** *of Batch Options.*

Once you have selected the files for batch processing, you can choose what commands you want to apply to the files.

To set the commands for batch processing:

1. Click the Next button in the Batch Processing dialog box to open the second dialog box **⑪**. This is where you can set which commands should be made part of the batch processing.

2. Choose an option from the list under Batch Options.

3. Use the Add button to add that option to the Include in Batch list on the right.

4. Select each option under the Include in Batch list, and set the controls for the option. *(These options are described in the following exercises.)*

5. Repeat steps 2, 3, and 4 to add more options to the process.

6. Use the up or down arrows to set the order that the option should run.

The export controls let you choose how the file should be optimized for viewing on the Web. *(For more information on the export commands, see Chapter 20, "Exporting.")*

To set the controls for the Export option:

♦ Use the Settings list to choose one of the export options **⑫**.

or

Click the Edit button to open the Export Preview dialog box which lets you create a new set of export options.

The Batch Processing Scale controls let you choose the final size of the images.

To set the controls for the Scale option:

◆ Use the Scale list to choose one of the scaling options **33**.

- **No Scaling** leaves the images at their original size.
- **Scale to Size** lets you set specific pixel dimensions.
- **Scale to Fit Area** lets you set a maximum height or width.
- **Scale to Percentage** lets you set the percentage of change.

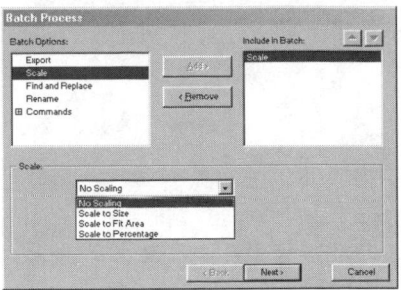

33 *The* **Scale controls** *of the Batch Options.*

The Batch Replace controls of the Batch Processing let you look for certain attributes in a file and replace them with others.

To set the Batch Replace controls:

◆ Use the Batch Replace panel to change the various options in the file **34**. *(These are the same controls found in the Find and Replace panel covered on page 217.)*

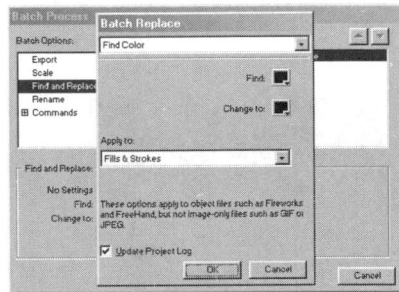

34 *The* **Batch Replace controls** *of the Find and Replace section of the Batch Options.*

You can also control the naming conventions used for the new files. For instance, you may want to add a suffix to indicate the new files are different from the old ones.

To set the Rename controls:

◆ Use the Rename pop-up list to add a prefix or suffix to the changed files **35**.

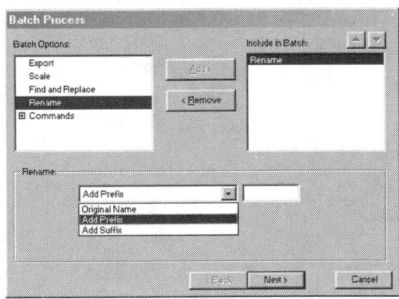

35 *The* **Rename controls** *of the Batch Options.*

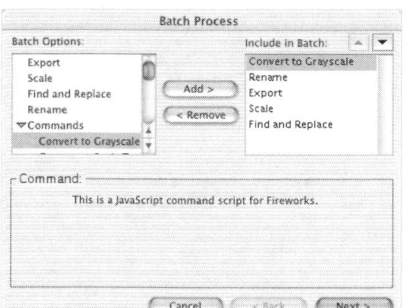

36 *The* **Commands controls** *of the Batch Options.*

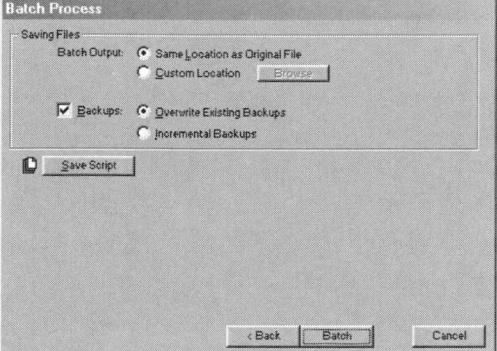

37 *The* **third Batch Processing dialog box** *lets you set the destinations for the saved files.*

The Batch Process Commands controls let you add your own custom JavaScript commands as part of the batch processing.

To set the Commands controls:

◆ Choose one of the JavaScripts listed under the Commands section **36**.

Finally, you use the Saving Files controls to set where you want the new files to be saved **37**.

To set destination options for batch processing:

1. Set the Batch Output for the Same Location as Original File.

   or

   Choose Custom Location and then click the Browse button to choose a new location for the files.

2. If desired, check the Backups option to make backups of the original files.

3. If you choose Backups, you can choose Overwrite Existing Backups to have any new backups erase older ones.

   or

   You can choose Incremental Backups to add to the backups by making numbered copies of the originals.

4. Click the Batch button to run the complete batch processing.

Batch Processing Changes

Once you have made all the settings for the batch processing, you can then save them as a JavaScript that can be run over and over. For instance, if you receive a large number of scans every month that need to be scaled and exported, you can run the batch process script rather than have to reset the batch options.

To save the batch settings as a script:

◆ Click the Save Script button. A dialog box lets you choose where to save the .jsf file.

IMPORTING 14

As the poet John Donne wrote, "No man is an island, entire of itself." So, too, with Macromedia Fireworks. Although it boasts a wealth of tools, fills, and effects, it is not a software island unto itself. It is very likely that you will need to work with other programs alongside Fireworks.

For instance, you probably have scanned images into pixel-based programs such as Adobe Photoshop directly from scanner software. Or you may have used Procreate Painter to create artwork with special effects.

You might have logos and other artwork created in vector-drawing programs such as Macromedia FreeHand, CorelDraw, or Adobe Illustrator.

Fortunately, Fireworks can open or import files created in all of these programs.

Working with Scanned Artwork

If you have a scanner, you can scan images directly into Fireworks. You can also open or insert scans created by other programs into existing Fireworks documents. The scans can be TIFF, GIF, JPEG, PNG, BMP, or PICT (Mac) files.

To scan an image directly into Fireworks:

1. Choose **File** > **Scan** and then use the TWAIN module or Photoshop Acquire plug-in that matches your scanner.

2. Follow the scanner software instructions to scan the image. The image opens as a native Fireworks document.

To open a scanned image:

1. Choose **File** > **Open** and then choose the scan you want to open.

2. Click OK. The scan opens ready for image editing ➊.

You can also import images into existing files.

To import scans as image objects:

1. Choose **File** > **Import** or **Insert** > **Image** and then find the scan you want to import. Click OK. The L-shaped pointer indicates the file is ready for placing on the currently selected Fireworks layer.

2. Drag the import pointer to draw a rectangle that scales the image to fit.

   or

   Click to place the scanned image at the original size.

3. The scan appears as bitmap image on the currently selected object layer ➋. *(For more information on importing bitmap images, see Chapter 10, "Working with Bitmaps.")*

➊ *A scan opened in the* **Bitmap mode** *on the background layer of a Fireworks document.*

➋ *A scan imported as a* **bitmap image** *on a layer of a Fireworks document. Notice the extra canvas area around the bitmap image.*

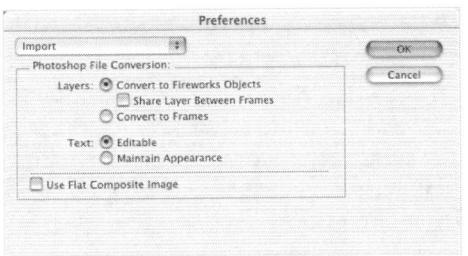

③ *The **Photoshop File Conversion Preferences** control how Photoshop documents are imported.*

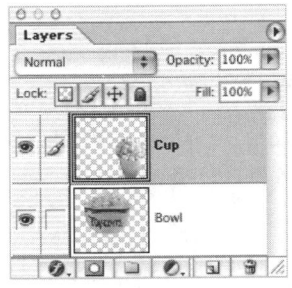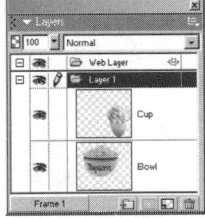

④ *The layers from a Photoshop document (left) can be converted into Fireworks bitmapped objects (right).*

Importing Photoshop Files

Macromedia knows how popular Adobe Photoshop is. So Fireworks lets you import and open Photoshop files in their native PSD format. You can control how features such as layers, masks, and effects are imported.

Use the Photoshop File Conversion options to control how Photoshop files are opened in Fireworks.

To set the Photoshop File Conversions:

1. Choose Edit > Preferences.

   or

   (Mac OS X) Choose **Fireworks > Preferences**.

2. Choose Import from the pop-up menu (Mac) or click the Import tab (Win) to show the Photoshop File Conversion settings **③**.

3. Use the following exercises to control how Photoshop elements are converted.

To set the Layer options:

◆ Set the Photoshop File Conversion options for Layers as follows:

- **Convert to Fireworks Objects** converts Photoshop layers into individual bitmap objects **④**. This is the most common option.
- **Share Layer Between Frames** sets the Photoshop layers as Fireworks shared layers. This can be useful in creating animations. *(For more information about creating animations, see Chapter 16, "Animations.")*
- **Convert to Frames** converts each layer into a Fireworks frame. This is another option that can help when creating animations.
- **Use Flat Composite Image** imports Photoshop files as an image with only one layer.

You use the Text settings to control how text is converted from Photoshop into Fireworks.

To set the Text options:

◆ Set the Photoshop File Conversion options for Layers as follows:

- **Editable** converts the Photoshop text into Fireworks text.
- **Maintain Appearance** converts the Photoshop text into a Fireworks bitmapped image.

TIP When Photoshop 6 and 7 files are opened in Fireworks, any text in the file is displayed as it looked in Photoshop. If you need to edit the text, it is converted into editable Fireworks text. This may cause the text to change appearance.

Photoshop allows you to add layer masks, shadows, glows, and bevels to images. Wherever possible Fireworks tries to maintain these effects.

To open Photoshop files with layer effects:

◆ In the Photoshop File Conversion Preferences choose Maintain Layers. Photoshop layer effects are converted into the nearest Fireworks effect.

TIP Although Fireworks can convert effects such as Drop Shadow and Bevel, other Photoshop features such as Satin or Pattern Overlay do not have an equivalent in Fireworks and are discarded when imported. *(See the sidebar on this page.)*

Working with Photoshop

Fireworks lets you move files from Photoshop to Fireworks as easily as possible. However, there are some features in Photoshop 6 and 7 that have no equivalent in Fireworks.

For instance, there is no equivalent to the Satin, Pattern, Gradient Overlay, and Stroke layer effects. Fireworks discards these effects when opening Photoshop files. Adjustment layers are also discarded.

Fireworks converts Photoshop's layer clipping paths into bitmapped masks. However, if a layer has both a layer mask and a clipping path, Fireworks cannot convert both and only converts the layer mask.

Finally, although Fireworks does have an equivalent to Photoshop's Drop Shadow, there are controls in the Photoshop Drop Shadow that that do not exist in Fireworks. Those features are discarded when the file is opened in Fireworks.

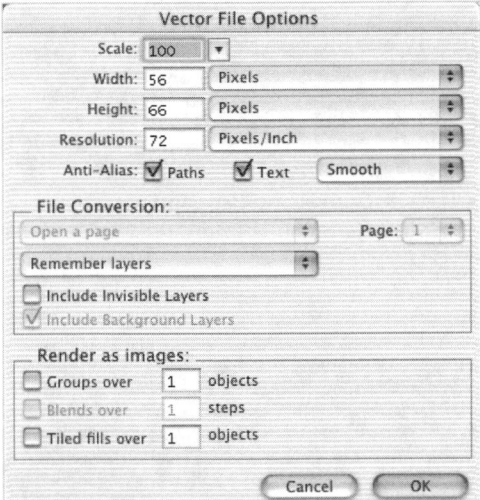

⑤ *The* **Vector File Options dialog box***.*

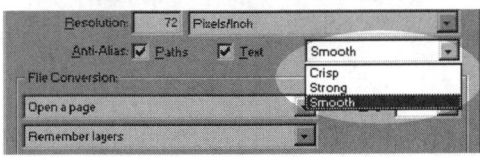

⑥ *The* **Anti-Alias options** *let you control the look of paths and text separately.*

Working with Anti-Aliasing

Anti-aliasing adds to the number of colors in GIF images. Turning off the anti-aliasing helps keep the file size down.

Also, at very small point sizes, text with anti-aliasing set to Smooth or Strong may become difficult to read. Using the Crisp setting or turning off anti-aliasing entirely may improve the legibility of the text.

Remember, regardless of how you set the anti-aliasing of imported artwork, you can always change those settings later in the Fill panel or Text Editor.

Importing Vector Objects

Fireworks can also open artwork created in vector-drawing programs such as Macromedia FreeHand or Adobe Illustrator. This lets you use the more sophisticated tools in the vector-drawing programs; the vector artwork you then import into your Fireworks document retains its editability.

To set the size of imported vector artwork:

1. Choose **File > Open** and navigate to choose the vector file. The Vector File Options dialog box appears **⑤**.

2. Use the Scale control to import the art at a specific size relative to its original size.

   or

   Adjust the width and height fields to change the size of the art to fit a space.

   or

   Change the resolution from the default setting of 72 pixels per inch to change the size of the art.

TIP The same choices are available if you choose **File > Import** to add vector files into an existing Fireworks document.

The Vector File Options let you control the anti-aliasing around paths and text.

To set the Anti-Alias options for paths and text:

1. Check Anti-Alias: Paths to set a soft edge around the paths **⑥**. *(See page 118 for an illustration of how anti-aliasing affects paths.)*

2. Check Anti-Alias: Text to set a soft edge around text **⑥**.

3. If you set text to Anti-Alias, choose Crisp, Strong, or Smooth in the pop-up menu **⑥**. *(See page 183 for an illustration of each of these settings.)*

Importing Vector Objects

If your artwork has multiple pages or layers, you can specify how those pages or layers are opened.

To set which pages of vector artwork to open:

◆ In the Vector File Options dialog box, choose the following file conversion options for opening multi-page documents:

- **Open a page** opens a specific page. If you choose this option, use the Page list to choose which page is imported **7**.

  or

- **Open pages as frames** from the Open As list to open each of the pages as a Fireworks frame.

TIP Open pages as frames was designed to allow you to import FreeHand pages as Fireworks frames. This is useful for creating animations. *(For more information on working with animations, see Chapter 16, "Animations.")*

To set the layers of opened vector artwork:

1. In the Vector File Options dialog box, choose the following layer options **8**:

   - **Remember layers** imports the layers as Fireworks layers.
   - **Ignore layers** imports the artwork onto one Fireworks layer.
   - **Convert layers to frames** opens each of the layers as a Fireworks frame **9**.

2. Check **Include Invisible Layers** to bring in artwork on the layers that are not visible in the vector program.

3. Check **Include Background Layers** to bring in artwork on the background layers in FreeHand.

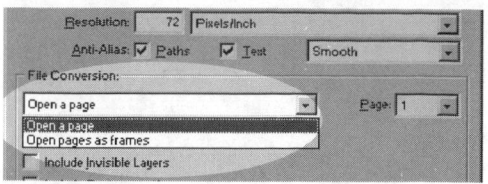

7 *The* **File Conversion Page options** *for importing vector artwork from a program that lets you specify multiple pages.*

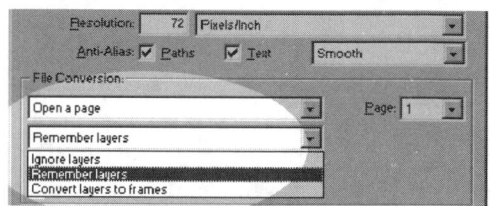

8 *The* **Layer options** *for importing vector artwork.*

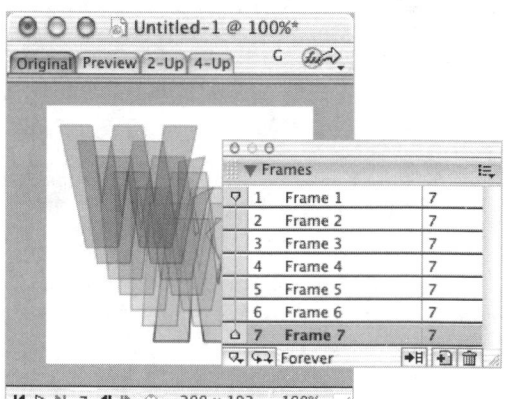

9 *Individual layers in vector artwork can be converted into individual frames in Fireworks.*

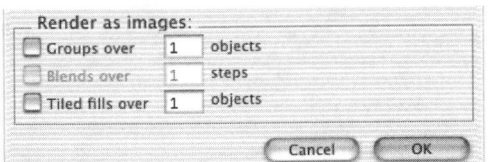

① *The* **Render as images** *controls for converting vector files.*

① *The difference between importing artwork as vector objects or pixel-based images. Notice that the bitmap image has a rectangle defining its boundary.*

Fireworks lets you convert those elements in a vector file that contain hundreds of elements into bitmap images. This helps avoid importing files that create hundreds of individual Fireworks objects.

To convert imported vector art into pixel images:

◆ In the Vector File Options dialog box, choose one of the following option for Render as images **①**:

- **Groups over_ objects** controls how groups should be converted.
- **Blends over_steps** controls how blends are converted.
- **Tiled fills over_objects** controls how tiled fills or patterns are converted.

TIP Rendering vectors as pixels turns all the objects into a single bitmapped image **①**.

When to Rasterize Vector Objects?

As you have guessed by now, this vectorbabe would much rather work with vector objects than bitmap images. So when might I want to convert groups, blends, or patterns into bitmap images?

If I have grouped artwork for simple logos, maps, or illustrations I usually turn off the option to convert groups into bitmap images for groups. I want the ability to edit the individual elements in the group.

With blends, I usually leave the number at the default setting of 30. This lets me use morphing blends for animations but rasterizes the blends that are simply gradients into bitmaps.

Finally, I always rasterize tiled fills. I've yet to find the need to edit pattern elements in Fireworks.

Importing Vector Objects

Importing EPS Files

Fireworks can open EPS files. If the files are rasterized EPS images, such as those created by Photoshop, the EPS File Options dialog box appears.

To open EPS files:

1. Choose **File** > **Open** and then find the EPS file you want to open. Click OK. The EPS File Options dialog appears ⑫.

2. Set the Width and Height fields.

3. Set the Resolution amount.

4. Check Constrain Proportions to keep the width and height in proportion to each other.

5. Check Anti-aliased to soften the edges of the artwork.

TIP Vector EPS files created in programs such as FreeHand and CorelDraw will be rasterized when they are opened. Save the original file without the EPS information to open it in Fireworks as a vector file.

TIP Some vector EPS files created by Adobe Illustrator are opened using the vector options covered in the previous section. *(See the sidebar on this page for a discussion of which vector EPS files can be opened.)*

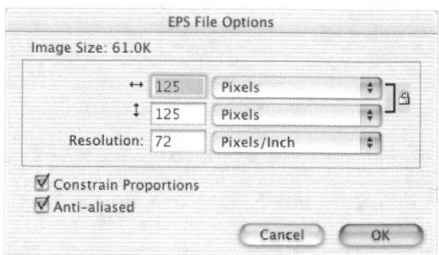

⑫ *The* **EPS File Options** *let you open EPS files as rasterized images.*

What about Vector EPS Files?

Vector EPS files are those files created by Macromedia FreeHand, Adobe Illustrator, or CorelDraw. They are actually vector drawings with a special EPS header that allows them to be placed in print page layout programs such as QuarkXPress or Adobe InDesign.

For the most part, Fireworks will open these vector EPS files as if they are rasterized EPS files. That is, Fireworks will convert all the vectors into one solid bitmap image — most likely *not* what you want to happen!

If you want to open these files as vectors, you need to open them in the program they were created in and re-save the file as a native FreeHand or CorelDraw file.

The exception is Adobe Illustrator EPS files. Thanks to John Ahlquist and Jeff Doar, Fireworks is able to open some versions of Illustrator EPS files using the vector file options. These are usually files saved in early versions of Illustrator such as Illustrator 88 or Illustrator 3.

⓭ *GIF Animations are imported into Fireworks as animation symbols with each of the animation images in its own Fireworks frame.*

Importing GIF Animations

Fireworks can open and convert GIF animations into Fireworks frames. This makes it easy to convert your old GIF animations into new Fireworks animations. *(For more information on creating animations in Fireworks, see Chapter 16, "Animations.")* There is a difference between opening Animated GIF files as their own document and importing Animated GIF files into another document.

To open animated GIF files:

1. Choose **File** > **Open** and then navigate to find the Animated GIF you want to open.

2. Click OK. The animation opens with each image frame of the animation on its own Fireworks frame **⓭**.

To import animated GIF files:

1. Choose **File** > **Import** and then find the Animated GIF you want to open.

2. Click OK.

3. If there are not enough frames in your document, an dialog box alert appears asking if you want to add more frames to the file.

4. Click OK to add the frames. The cursor changes to the L-shaped import corner pointer *(see page 234)*.

TIP GIF animations are imported into Fireworks as animation symbols.

Importing Text

You can also import text saved in the ASCII or RTF formats into Fireworks documents. This is much easier than retyping long documents.

To open text as Fireworks files:

1. Choose **File** > **Import**. Navigate to find an RTF (Rich Text Format) or ASCII text file.

TIP You can also choose **File** > **Open** to open text files as their own Fireworks documents.

2. Click to place the text file in a text block the same width as the document **14**.

   or

   Drag to set a specific width for the text block.

TIP RTF text maintains all the font attributes that are in the Fireworks Property Inspector for text. The character color comes from the color of the first character in the text file.

3. Use the Property Inspector to make any changes to the text.

14 **RTF or ASCII text** *can be imported into Fireworks documents.*

OPTIMIZING 15

People who create Web graphics are obsessed — not necessarily with the look of the graphics (although that would be nice) — but with file sizes. They can spend *hours* working to reduce the size of a graphic from 5.1K to 4.9K.

Why the obsession? While two-tenths of a kilobyte may not seem like much to a single graphic, multiply it across all the graphics on a page and it adds up. The accumulated kilobytes add to the time that it takes the page to download — time that viewers don't want to waste sitting around waiting for a page to come into view.

Optimizing refers to setting all the controls so that graphics are created in the proper format and in the smallest possible file size. It is often a juggling act to balance reducing the file size while at the same time maintaining the original quality of the image.

Fireworks gives you specialized tools that make it easy to reduce files while maintaining their appearance.

Following the Optimizing Steps

There are several different parts to optimizing files. Use the steps below as a guide to optimizing files using the document window controls. *(For the equivalent steps using the special Export Preview controls, see page 262.)*

To optimize and export files:

1. Use the tab controls in the Document Window to control the onscreen preview of the file *(see the next page).*

    TIP The onscreen preview allows you to compare different optimization settings as well as judge how long it will take the file to download.

2. Use the Optimize panel to set the type of file, its compression, and other file characteristics *(see pages 247 and 252).*

    TIP Most Web graphics are saved in either the GIF or JPEG formats. *(For more information as to which format to choose, see page 257.)*

3. If you are optimizing a GIF file, control the colors in the file using the Color Table panel *(see page 251).*

4. Set the transparency options *(see page 258).*

5. Choose **File** > **Export** to export the file at the optimization settings. *(For more information about export settings, see Chapter 20, "Exporting.")*

The Optimize Panel or Export Preview?

When Fireworks was first released you could only optimize files in the Export Preview dialog box. Many people complained that if you needed to make a change as you were setting the optimization controls, you had to switch out of the Export Preview, make the change, and then come back to the document page.

So Fireworks made it possible to set the optimization controls and preview the results while still working on the document—a better way to work.

However, Macromedia didn't throw out the Export Preview dialog box. You can still use it to optimize Fireworks images.

While there may be some old-time Fireworks users who still use the Export Preview dialog box for optimization, I'd rather use the Optimize panel.

❶ *The* **Preview tab** *in the document window.*

Active Panel

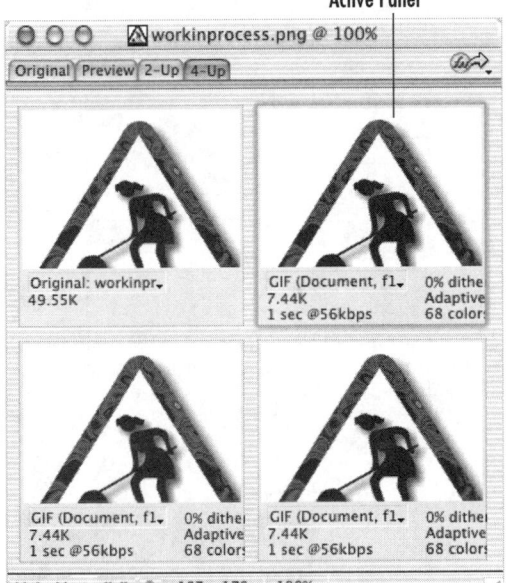

❷ *The* **4-Up Preview tab** *lets you compare different optimization settings of the image.*

❸ *The* **panel information** *shows basic information about the export settings, file size, and download time.*

Controlling the Onscreen Preview

As you optimize images, their appearance can drastically change from the original artwork. The Preview tabs allow you to see how the optimization settings affect the image.

To use the preview tabs:

◆ Click the Preview tab in the document window to see a full-screen preview of the optimized artwork **❶**.

or

Click the 2-Up tab to split the window into two sections so you can compare the original artwork to the artwork at the current optimization settings.

or

Click the 4-Up tab to split the window into four sections so you can compare the original artwork to the artwork at three different optimization settings **❷**.

TIP Although you can use the zoom and magnification controls to change the size or position of the preview, it is usually better to optimize an image at the 100% view. This lets you see the image without exaggerating or minimizing the effects of the optimization.

The active panel shows the results of the current settings of the Optimize panel. You can select each panel and create different optimization settings for them.

To change the active panel:

◆ Click inside one of the panels. A highlight color appears around the panel. This indicates that panel is active **❷**.

TIP Each of the preview panels shows the type of file, output size, download time, and settings details **❸**.

By default, Fireworks displays the original file in the left-hand panel in the 2-Up tab and the top-left panel in the 4-Up tab. If you want, you can change that panel so that it displays a preview setting.

To change a panel to show the original file:

1. Press the panel control under the preview image in the panel.

2. Choose Original (No Preview) to see the original image ❹.

TIP When a panel has been set to Original (No Preview), you can use any of the Fireworks editing tools or commands to make changes to the file.

❹ *The* **panel control** *under the preview image lets you switch between showing the original image and the export preview.*

To change a panel to show the export preview:

1. Press the panel control under the preview image in the panel.

2. Choose Export Preview to see the effects of the optimization settings.

TIP When a panel has been set to Export Preview, you can not make changes to the file within that panel.

There is a difference between the brightness, or gamma, of Macintosh and Windows monitors. Fireworks lets you switch your monitor display so you can simulate the gamma of another operating system. Subtle differences in light colors tend to be harder to see on Macintosh monitors ❺. Subtle differences in dark colors tend to be harder to see on Windows monitors ❻. *(See the color pages for a display of this effect.)*

To change the preview gamma display:

♦ Choose **View > Windows Gamma** or **View > Macintosh Gamma** to see how your image will appear using a different operating system.

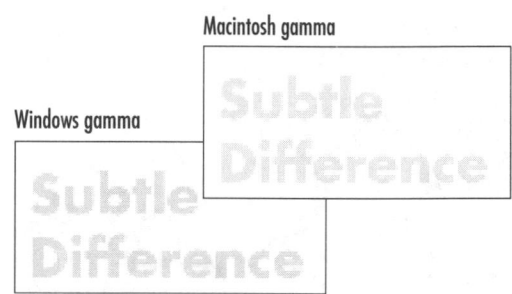

❺ *An example of the difference between the* **Windows and Macintosh Gamma displays** *for light colors.*

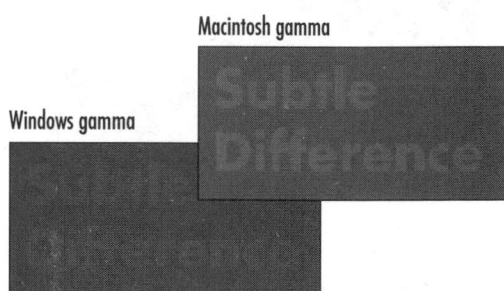

❻ *An example of the difference between the Windows and Macintosh Gamma displays for dark colors.*

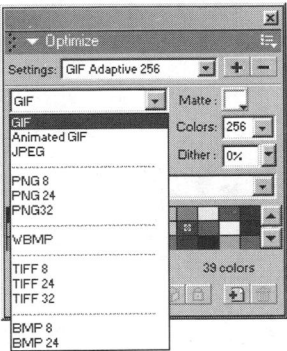

❼ *The* **Format menu** *in the Optimize panel.*

❽ *The* **Palette menu** *for GIF colors.*

When Should You Use the GIF Format?

Use the GIF format for images with flat or solid areas of color. Type, cartoons, and flat-color logos usually look best when saved as GIF images. GIF images are limited to 256 colors; but you can use fewer colors to reduce file size.

You must use GIF images if you need the area around the image to be transparent or for animations. *(See the color pages for a display of the type of images that look best as a GIF.)*

Although some people pronounce this format as "jif," I prefer "gif" since I don't like peanut butter on the Web.

Optimizing GIF Files

The GIF (Graphic Interchange Format) is generally used for graphics with lots of flat color areas.

To choose GIF as the optimize format:

1. If the Optimize panel is not visible, choose **Window > Optimize.**

2. Choose GIF from the Format menu **❼**. This changes the panel to the GIF options.

3. Set the GIF options as described in the following exercises.

GIF files are limited to a maximum of 256 colors. The color palette determines what kinds of colors are included in the file.

To choose a GIF color palette:

◆ Choose one of the following from the Palette list **❽**:

- **Adaptive** samples the colors in your file whether or not they're Web-safe.
- **Web Adaptive** (Mac) or **WebSnap Adaptive** (Win) uses the Adaptive palette, but any color that's within 7 units of a Web-safe color gets shifted to the nearest one.
- **Web 216** uses only Web-safe colors, replacing non-Web-safe colors with the closest Web-safe color.
- **Exact** uses the Adaptive palette but automatically finds the exact number of colors in the graphic.
- **Macintosh** or **Windows** limits the colors to those in the Macintosh or Windows operating systems.
- **Grayscale** shifts the colors to the range of 256 grayscale values.
- **Black & White** uses just those colors.
- **Uniform** uses a mathematical palette based on RGB pixel values. There is little use for this on the Web.
- **Custom** lets you open a swatches palette saved from Fireworks *(see page 251)* or from Adobe Photoshop.

Most Web designers make GIF files smaller by reducing the number of colors in the image below the maximum number of 256.

To reduce the number of colors in a file:

◆ Use the Number of Colors in the Optimization panel to lower the number even further ⑨.

TIP Fireworks eliminates colors from the palette based on how often the color appears in the image. You can also use the Color Table panel to delete specific colors in the file *(see the next page)*.

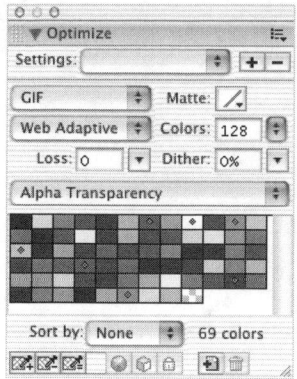

⑨ *The Optimize panel set to* **GIF** *options.*

Dithering is a technique that mixes two colors in a dot pattern to create the illusion of a third. Dithering helps maintain the look of GIF files when reducing colors.

To set the dithering of an image:

◆ Use the Dither control to change how much dithering is applied ⑩.

TIP Most people don't like the look of dithering. Use the smallest amount of dithering you can.

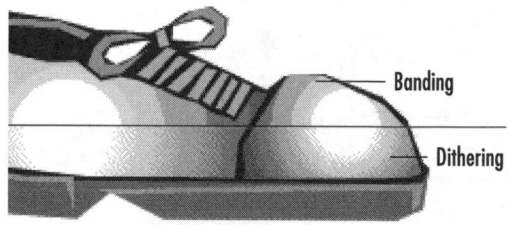

⑩ *The result of* **applying dithering** *to a banded graphic.*

Another way to lower the file size is to apply a Loss compression which is similar to the compression used on JPEG images *(see page 252)*. This lowers the file size by throwing away some of the details and distorting the image.

To apply Loss to a GIF image:

◆ Use the Loss control to increase the amount of Loss compression in the image ⑪. The higher the Loss values the more distortions will be created in the image.

TIP Use low values of the Loss setting to shave small amounts from the file. Higher Loss settings create ugly distortions in the flat colors.

⑪ *The effect of* **applying Loss compression** *to a graphic.*

Optimizing GIF Files

⑫ *The* **Color Table area** *of the Optimize panel.*

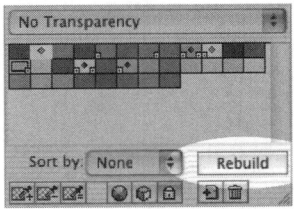

⑬ *The* **Rebuild button** *of the Optimize panel.*

Swatch Status	Swatch Appearance
Plain	
Locked	
Edited	
Edited and Locked	
Web-Safe	
Locked and Web-Safe	
Shifted to Web-Safe	
Locked and Shifted to Web-Safe	

⑭ *The* **Swatch feedback symbols** *in the Color Table tell you the status of each swatch.*

In addition to lowering the number of colors for a GIF image, you can control each individual color in the file with the Color Table area of the Optimize panel **⑫**. *(See the color pages for how the Color Table changes images.)*

To control the colors in the Color Table:

1. If necessary, click the Rebuild button to update the colors **⑬**.

TIP The Rebuild button updates the colors in the Color Table. The button is available if you have changed the optimization settings when the Preview tab is not chosen.

2. Click the swatch in the Color Table to select the color. A highlight appears around the swatch.

3. Select additional colors by holding the Command/Ctrl key as you click the color swatch.

   or

   Hold the Shift key to select a range of colors.

4. Use the exercises that follow to change the colors in the table.

TIP Colors that have been locked or modified can be identified by the swatch feedback symbols in the Color Table area **⑭**.

TIP Deselect Show Swatch Feedback in the Optimize panel menu to hide the swatch feedback symbols.

To display colors in the image:

◆ Press a swatch in the Color Table. The corresponding color appears highlighted in the image.

Optimizing GIF Files

To edit colors in the table:

◆ Click the Edit icon at the bottom of the Optimize panel ⑮. This opens the color picker.

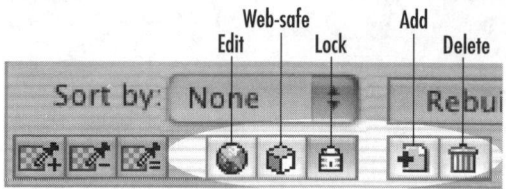

⑮ *The* swatch editing icons *in the Optimize panel.*

To change the color to a Web-safe color:

◆ Click the Web-safe icon ⑮ at the bottom of the Optimize panel. This forces the color to the closest Web-safe color.

To delete colors from the table:

◆ Click the Delete icon at the bottom of the Optimize panel ⑮.

To lock the color:

◆ Click the Lock icon at the bottom of the Optimize panel ⑮.

TIP Apply the Lock color command again to unlock colors.

TIP Use the Unlock All Colors command from the panel menu to unlock all the colors in the table ⑯.

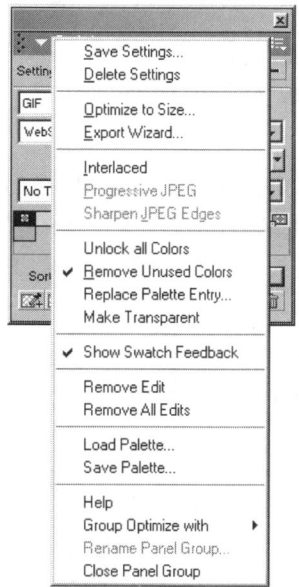

To add colors to the table:

◆ Click the Add icon at the bottom of the Optimize panel ⑮. This opens the color picker.

⑯ *The* Optimize panel menu.

To clear color changes in the table:

◆ Choose Remove Edit from the Optimize panel menu ⑯. This restores the swatch to its original value.

TIP Use Remove All Edits to restore all modified swatches to their original values.

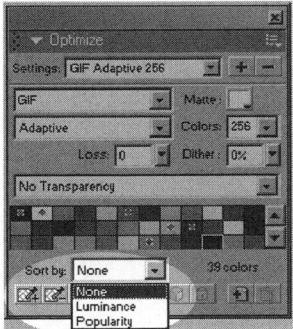

⑰ *The* **swatch Sort by menu** *in the Optimize panel.*

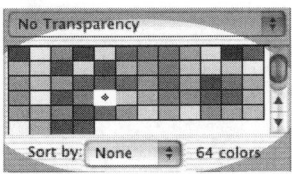

⑱ *Color swatches* **displayed without sorting.**

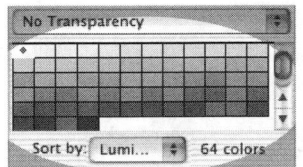

⑲ *Color swatches* **sorted by luminance.**

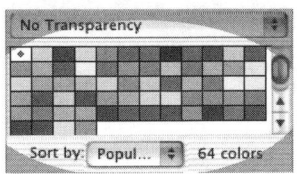

⑳ *Color swatches* **sorted by popularity.**

You can change the order in which colors appear in the Color Table.

To sort the colors in the Color Table:

◆ Choose one of the following from the Sort by menu **⑰**:

- **None** to leave the colors unsorted **⑱**.
- **Luminance** to arrange the colors from light to dark **⑲**.
- **Popularity** to arrange the colors from most-used to least-used **⑳**. This usually forces the background color to the first position.

If you have spent some time modifying a Color Table, you can save it for later use.

To save the colors in the Color Table:

1. Select Save Palette from the Optimize panel menu. This opens the standard Save As dialog box.

2. Use the Save As dialog box to name and save the palette to a location.

To load colors into the Color Table:

1. Select Load Palette from the Optimize panel menu.

2. Navigate to a saved palette. The palette replaces the swatches in the current Color Table.

TIP You can also load .act files created by Adobe Photoshop or Adobe ImageReady into a Fireworks Color Table.

Optimizing GIF Files

Optimizing JPEG Files

JPEG is another popular file format for Web graphics. Instead of throwing away colors, JPEG files are compressed by throwing away some information. *(See the color pages for an illustration of various compression settings.)*

To choose JPEG as the optimization format:

1. If the Optimize panel is not visible, choose **Window > Optimize**.

2. Choose JPEG from the Format list. This changes the panel to the JPEG options **㉑**.

3. Set the JPEG options as described in the following exercises.

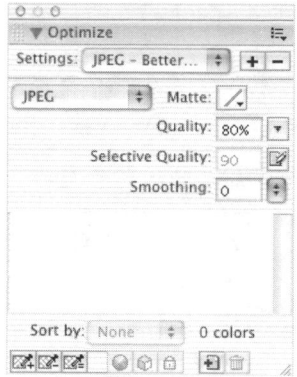

㉑ *The* **JPEG settings** *in the Optimize panel.*

You control the file size by changing the Quality setting. As you lower the quality, more compression is applied to the image, resulting in a smaller file.

To change the file size of the JPEG image:

◆ Use the Quality field to change the file size—the lower the quality, the smaller the file **㉒**.

TIP Setting the Quality control too low can make the image look coarse or filled with blocks.

TIP There are no industry standards for what the amount of compression stands for. So a Quality setting of 50% in Fireworks may not look the same as the same amount applied in ImageReady or another program.

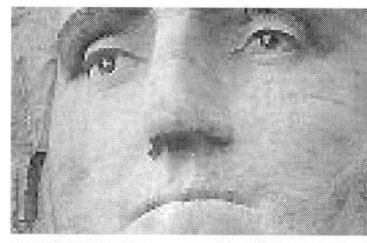

80% Quality

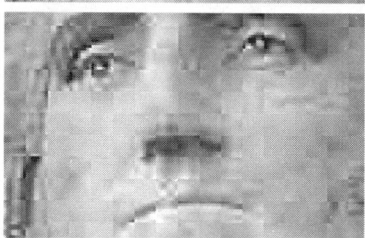

20% Quality

㉒ Lowering the quality of a JPEG image *degrades the image by deleting details and creating square blocks in the image.*

When Should You Use the JPEG Format?

Because JPEG images can display millions of colors, they are used for photographic images or images with subtle blends. (See the color pages for a display of the type of images that look best as a JPEG.)

The art of setting the JPEG controls lies in making the compression artifacts less noticeable.

Without Smoothing

With Smoothing

The more you lower the JPEG quality the more you may notice coarse or blocky areas in the image. Fireworks gives you several tools to reduce that coarseness.

Smoothing works by slightly blurring the details in the image.

To smooth a JPEG image:

◆ Set the Smoothing control to the numbers 0 through 8. The higher the number, the greater the blur applied to the image ㉓. *(See the color insert for examples of the different JPEG settings.)*

㉓ Adding Smoothing *to a JPEG can reduce the coarseness by adding a slight blur.*

Sharpen JPEG Edges off

Sharpen JPEG Edges on

You can also improve the appearance of a JPEG image by applying the Sharpen JPEG Edges command. This setting looks for areas of flat color and sharpens the edges ㉔.

To sharpen the edges of a JPEG image:

◆ Choose Sharpen JPEG Edges from the Optimize panel menu.

TIP Sharpen JPEG Edges does not affect the entire image, just where there is a flat area of color against a different colored background.

TIP The Sharpen JPEG Edges command is particularly useful for enhancing text that is part of a scanned image. However, if you have text created in Fireworks, the Selective JPEG Compression works even better to improve the look of the image *(see the next page).*

㉔ *The* **Sharpen JPEG Edges** *setting helps keep the flat areas of color, such as type, crisp against the background of an image.*

Optimizing JPEG Files

Revealing Images

You can set graphics so they reveal themselves gradually as they download . This lets visitors quickly decide if they want to wait to see the complete image.

To create images that appear gradually:

◆ For GIF images, choose Interlaced from the Optimize panel menu.

or

◆ For JPEG images, choose Progressive JPEG from the Optimize panel menu.

Creating Selective JPEG Files

Another way to improve the look of a JPEG image is to create a Selective JPEG. This allows you to have a low quality for certain parts of the image and a higher quality for areas that you want to look good. For example, you can set a high quality around someone's face but use a low quality for the background.

Creating a Selective JPEG is a two-step process. First you mask the part of the image you want to maintain at high quality, then you set the amount of compression to apply to that area.

To create the Selective JPEG mask:

1. Use the bitmap selection tools to select the area to act as the mask.

2. Choose **Modify > Selective JPEG > Save Selection as JPEG Mask**. A color appears inside the marching ants. This indicates the mask area of the Selective JPEG ㉖.

3. After setting the mask, you can deselect the bitmap selection. The mask is saved as part of the document.

㉕ *How* interlaced or progressive images *appear as they are downloaded into a file.*

㉖ *The* **Selective JPEG mask** *is shown inside the selection of marching ants. This indicates which area of the image will be compressed by the Selective Quality control.*

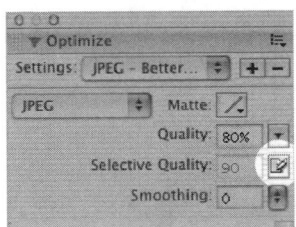

① *Click the* **Selective Quality icon** *to open the Selective JPEG Settings dialog box.*

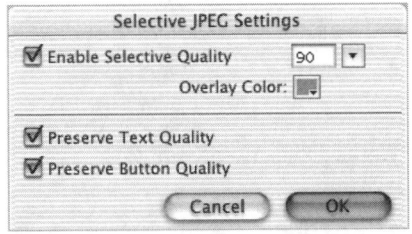

② *The* **Selective JPEG Settings** *dialog box.*

To set the amount of Selective JPEG compression:

1. Click the Selective Quality icon in the Optimize panel **①**.

   or

   Choose **Modify** > **Selective JPEG** > **Settings**. The Selective JPEG Settings dialog box appears **②**.

2. Select Enable Selective Quality.

3. Enter an amount between 1 and 100 in the Quality field. The higher the amount the larger the file size.

TIP Once you have enabled the Selective JPEG Quality you can also change the quality from the Optimize panel.

You can modify the mask by converting it back into a selection.

To modify the mask:

1. Choose **Modify** > **Selective JPEG** > **Restore JPEG Mask as Selection**. The mask is converted into marching ants.

2. Move or modify the selection using any of the bitmap selection tools *(as covered in Chapter 10, "Working with Bitmaps")*.

3. Choose **Modify** > **Selective JPEG** > **Save Selection as JPEG Mask** to apply the new selection as the mask.

To remove the Selective JPEG mask:

◆ Choose **Modify** > **Selective JPEG** > **Remove JPEG Mask**.

Creating Selective JPEG Files

You can also apply Selective JPEG compression to text and buttons.

To apply a Selective JPEG to text or buttons:

◆ Set the following in the Selective JPEG Settings dialog box:

- **Preserve Text Quality** applies the Selective JPEG Quality to text created in Fireworks .
- **Preserve Button Quality** applies the Selective JPEG Quality to symbols that act as buttons. *(For more information on creating buttons, see Chapter 19, "Buttons and Behaviors.")*

㉙ *The* **Preserve Text Quality and Preserve Button Quality** settings *maintain a high quality for the Fireworks text and buttons over the low-quality JPEG background.*

You can also change the color that indicates the mask.

To change the Selective JPEG overlay color:

◆ Use the Overlay Color Well in the Selective JPEG dialog box to set the color of the Selective JPEG mask.

TIP Changing the mask color has no effect on your final image but can help you see the mask over colors in the image.

TIP If you are extremely organized, you can change the color according to the amount of compression applied.

Working with Selective JPEGs

When you first apply Selective JPEG you may see an increase in the file size. This is because the area under the Select JPEG has less compression applied.

However, you can lower the total file size even further because you can then increase the compression applied outside the mask.

If you set Selective Quality for text or buttons you may see some additional compression outside the text or buttons.

The amount of compression remains constant even if you apply feathering to the selection.

Swatches Palettes

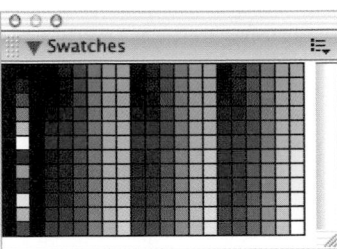

The Swatches panel set to display the Web-safe colors in the **Color Cubes** arrangement.

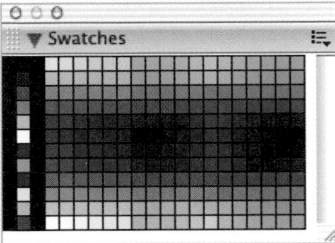

The Swatches panel set to display the Web-safe colors in the **Continuous** arrangement.

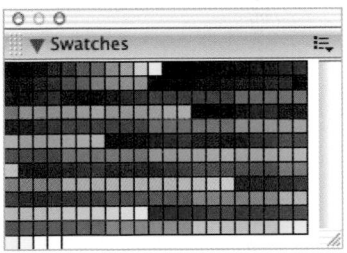

The Swatches panel set to display the **Macintosh** colors.

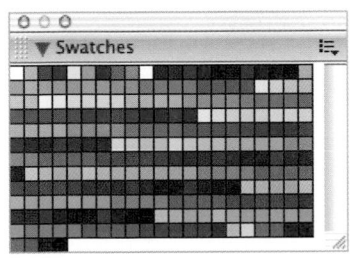

The Swatches panel set to display the **Windows** colors.

Choosing GIF Optimization

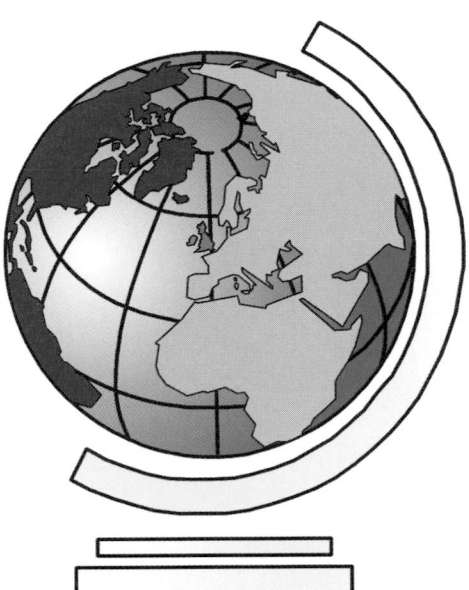

The flat colors and limited blends in this image should be exported as a **GIF** image.

Choosing JPEG Optimization

The continuous tones in this photo should be exported as a **JPEG** image.

Adding Dithering to Maintain Colors

The Adaptive palette always is the closest to the original image. As you lower the number of colors, you may need to add dithering to maintain blends.

Using the Web-safe palette almost always changes the look of the artwork. Adding dithering can help maintain blends, but can distort the look of flat colors.

*The **original art** contains more than 256 colors. These colors are easily reproduced in print.*

*Using all **256 Adaptive colors** provides the closest equivalent of the original art.*

*Using **32 Adaptive colors without dithering** some of the subtle colors have shifted. The blend in the left block is slightly banded.*

*Using **32 Adaptive colors with a small amount of dithering** restores an indication of the blend. Notice, though, some dithering in the flat colors.*

*Using **32 Web-safe colors without dithering** many of the colors have been shifted, noticeably in top block. There is no indication of the blend.*

*Using **32 Web-safe colors with dithering** restores an indication of the blend but requires much more dithering in the flat colors than the Adaptive palette.*

Handling GIF Blends

GIF images with blends need special handling to avoid banding, or the abrupt transition from one color to another.

Using 256 colors, there is some banding in the colors of the blend.

Switching to the Web-safe palette creates unacceptable banding.

Adding dithering helps reduce the banding with the 256 colors, and the dithering is hardly noticeable.

Adding dithering to the Web-safe palette helps reduce the banding but is very noticeable.

Color Table

The settings of the Color Table change the look of a GIF image.

The original color table for this image consists of mostly blue, red, and off-white gray colors.

When a new color table is loaded, the colors of the image changes to match the new combination of blue colors.

JPEG Comparisons

As you lower the file size of a JPEG image, the image quality decreases. Notice that a small amount of compression is hardly noticeable while the file size is reduced greatly. Notice also how smoothing blurs the image.

JPEG at 100% Quality *creates a 16.58 K image.*

JPEG at 80% Quality *creates a 5.00 K image.*

JPEG at 40% Quality *creates a 2.80 K image.*

JPEG at 40% Quality, Smoothing of 4 *creates a 2.52 K image.*

GIF Loss

The Loss control in the GIF Optimize panel decreases the file size while keeping the number of colors constant. However, it can cause distortions in the image.

The original GIF image with **no Loss applied** *has a file size of 9.10K.*

With a **Loss setting of 10,** *the file size is reduced to 8.18K. The disortion is hardly noticeable.*

With a Loss setting of 50, the file size is reduced to 5.92K, but the distortion is now very noticeable around the shadow of the bevel.

Web Palette or Adpative Palette

The differences between an Adaptive palette or a Web palette.

An **Adaptive palette** *maintains as many of the original colors as possible. Notice the subtle shade for the face and hands.*

A **Web 216 palette with dithering on** *creates a pattern of dots in the shirt, face, and hands to simulate non-Web colors. This is unacceptable for flat color art.*

The **Web 216 palette with dithering off** *shifts the colors in the shirt, face, and hands to the closest Web-safe color.*

Gamma Correction

Use the View menu to compare the effect of choosing the Windows or Macintosh gamma on artwork.

*Artwork as seen in the **Windows Gamma**. Notice that the dark letters on the dark background are difficult to read.*

*Artwork as seen in the **Macintosh Gamma**. Notice that the light letters on the light background are difficult to read.*

Web Dither Fill

The Web Dither Fill allows you to use two colors in a checkerboard pattern to create the illusion of a third color.

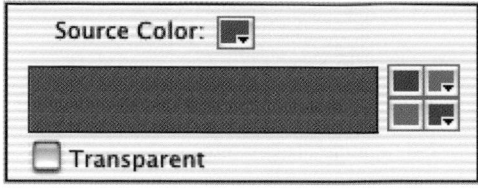

The Fill controls set to Web Dither shows the mixture of the two colors.

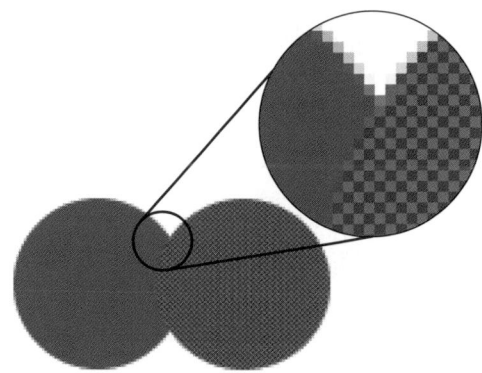

*The **Web Dither fill** in the right circle approximates the purple in the left circle. The blow up shows the color on the right is actually a pattern.*

The Blending Modes

The blending modes control how one color interacts with the colors below it.

*The **Normal** blending mode.*

*The **Multiply** blending mode.*

*The **Screen** blending mode.*

*The **Darken** blending mode.*

*The **Lighten** blending mode.*

*The **Difference** blending mode.*

*The **Hue** blending mode.*

*The **Saturation** blending mode.*

*The **Invert** blending mode.*

*The **Tint** blending mode.*

*The **Color** blending mode.*

*The **Luminosity** blending mode*

*The **Erase** blending mode.*

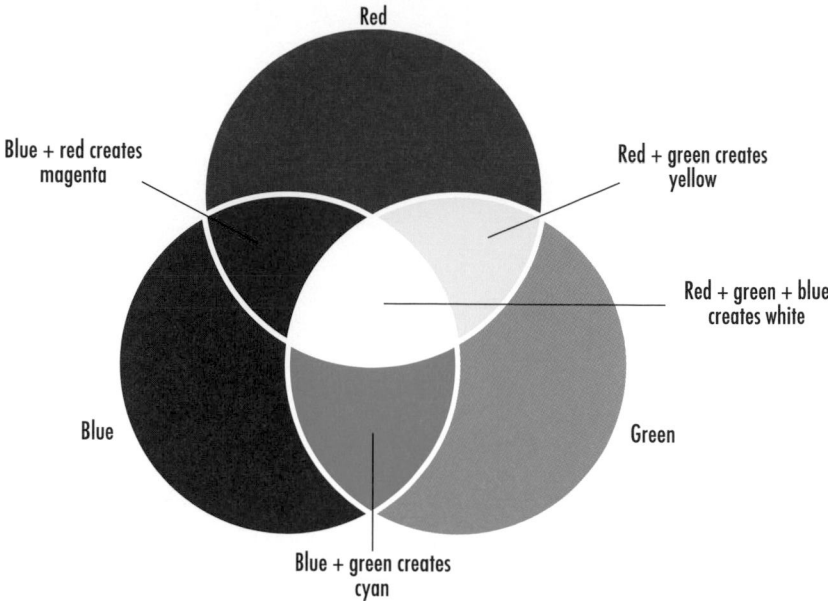

*An example of **additive** colors, sometimes called RGB.*

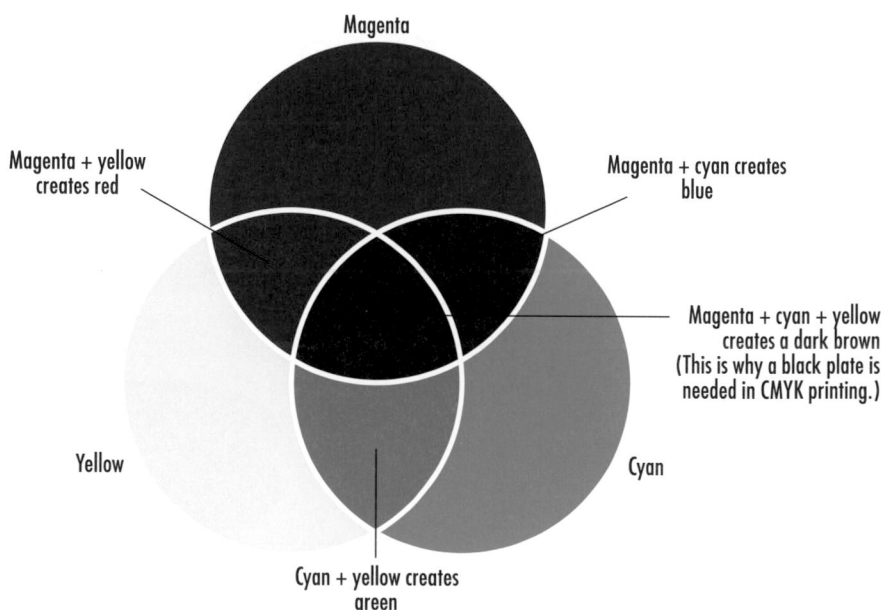

*An example of **subtractive** colors, sometimes called process colors.*

❸⓿ Optimizing as a GIF (top) *maintains the look of the flat colors in a photograph.* **Optimizing as a JPEG (bottom)** *can create distortions in the flat colors.*

❸① *The details against a flat background in a monochromatic image may look better when optimized as a GIF (top) rather than as a JPEG (bottom).*

Choosing GIF or JPEG

As a general rule, most people use JPEG for photos and GIF for flat-color artwork. But there are times when that rule does not apply.

Working with Flat Colors

For instance, if you have a photograph with very flat colors, such as a road sign on a white background, you may find that optimizing as a GIF allows you to keep the appearance of the flat colors **❸⓿**.

The same image, optimized as a JPEG, may require high amounts of smoothing to overcome distortion in the JPEG compression **❸⓿**. Even then, the flat colors may still look distorted.

You may also find that monochromatic images with text, such as the face of a clock, look better when optimized as a GIF **❸①**. The monochrome colors in the image allow you to use a palette of colors without sacrificing the look of the numbers of the clock.

You may also want to optimize as a GIF since GIF images can support transparency *(see the next page).*

GIF or JPEG? The lady or the tiger? The choices are not always simple.

Setting Transparency

One of the main advantages of the GIF format is that certain areas of an image can be made transparent. This allows you to have a Web graphic that blends into the background of the page.

To create transparency in a GIF image:

1. Choose GIF in the Optimize panel.

TIP The Preview tab must be active in order to see the effects of the transparency settings.

2. Choose either Index Transparency or Alpha Transparency from the Transparency list 32.

TIP See the exercise on the next page to understand the difference between the two types of transparency settings.

3. Use the Transparency Eyedropper to click the color in the image that you want to make transparent 33. The transparent area is indicated with a checkerboard grid 34.
4. Use the Eyedropper with the plus (+) sign to select additional colors to make transparent.
5. Use the Eyedropper with the minus (–) sign to deselect colors.

TIP You can also select colors in the Color Table and click the Transparency icon to make those colors transparent.

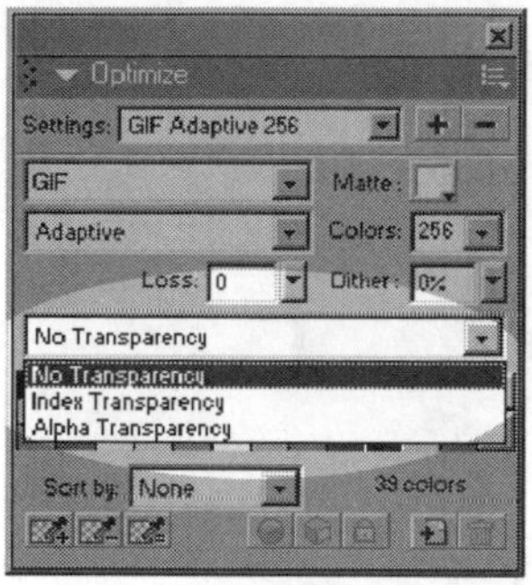

32 *The* **Transparency list** *lets you add transparency to GIF images.*

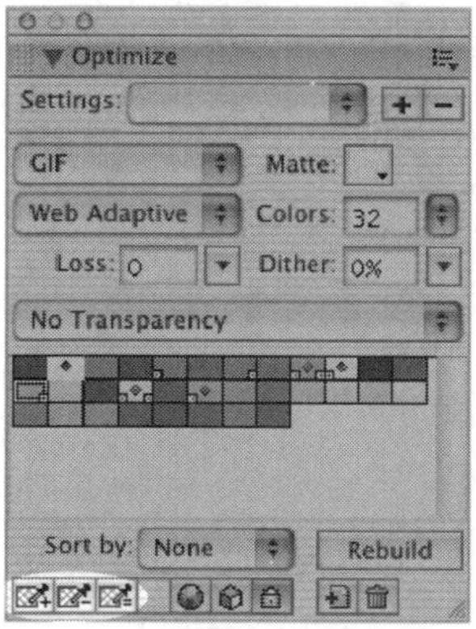

33 *The* **Transparency Eyedropper** *lets you select which colors should be made transparent.*

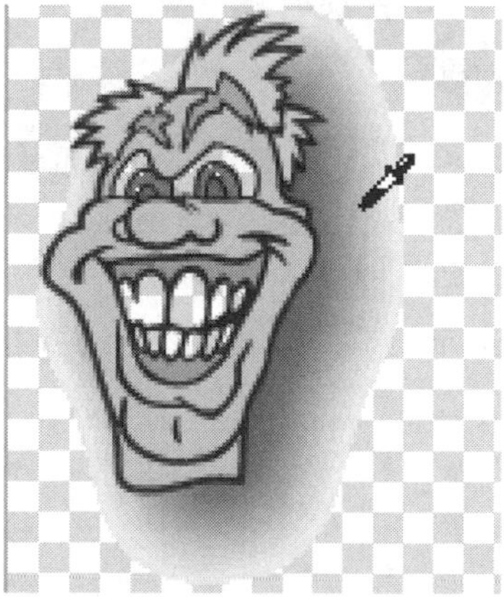

34 *The Eyedropper allows you to select colors in the image that should be transparent.*

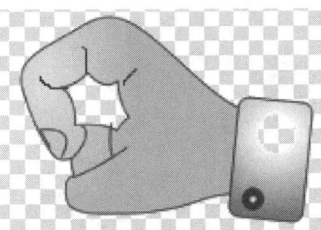

35 *An* **Index Transparency** *using the color white created a transparent background but also caused the white in the cuff to become transparent.*

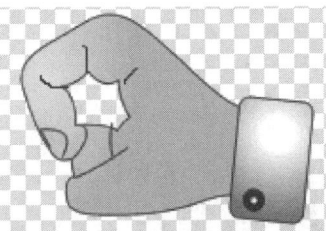

36 *An* **Alpha Transparency** *used the outline of the objects as the transparency without causing the white in the cuff to be transparent.*

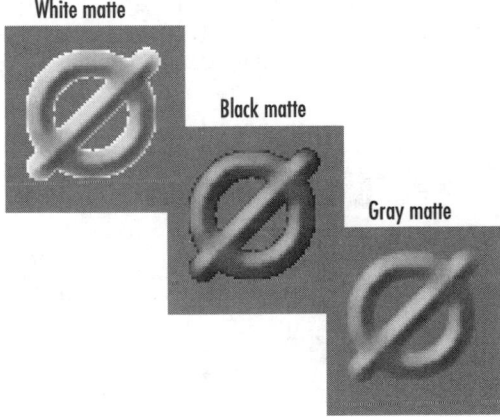

White matte

Black matte

Gray matte

37 **Different matte colors** *change how images appear over backgrounds. In this case the gray matte looks best over the gray background.*

Fireworks lets you choose between Index Transparency and Alpha Transparency. Index Transparency makes specific colors transparent. Alpha Transparency uses the outline of the objects on the canvas as the shape of the transparency.

To choose the type of transparency:

◆ Set the Transparency pop-up list as follows:

- **Index Transparency** sets a specific color as transparent.

TIP Index Transparency can create undesirable effects if the transparency color appears within the image itself **35**.

- **Alpha Transparency** sets the transparent areas of the canvas as transparent **36**.

TIP The Alpha Transparency is seen only if the canvas color of the image has been set to transparent.

TIP You must first reset the Transparency list to No Transparency before you choose Alpha Transparency.

A matte color changes the edges of transparent images so that they look better as they pass over background colors **37**.

To choose a matte color:

◆ Click the Matte Color Well in the Optimize panel to choose the color closest to the backgrounds or images that you expect the file to be placed over.

TIP If possible, use the Eyedropper to sample the color from another document.

TIP If you don't know the color of the background, click the None icon in the panel to specify no matte.

TIP Although there is no actual transparency for JPEG images, you can use the Matte color to set the background color for JPEG images.

Setting Transparency

Creating WBMP Images

In the future, most people will view Web pages on WAP (Wireless Application Protocol) devices such as cellular telephones or personal digital assistants such as Palm Pilots.

Instead of GIF or JPEG, these devices will display WBMP (Wireless BitMap) images. WBMP images display images using only black or white pixels. (My cat, Pixel, is a WBMP image!)

To save files in the WBMP format:

1. Choose WBMP from the format list in the Optimize palette ❸❽.
2. Set the amount of dithering applied to the image ❸❾. Dithering simulates colors and shades in images. *(For more information on dithering, see page 248.)*

Optimizing Other Formats

Although Fireworks was designed for Web graphics, Fireworks does convert images for use in print and onscreen presentations.

To export other file formats:

1. Choose among the other file formats in the Optimize panel format list.
   - **Animated GIF** is used for animations. *(See Chapter 16, "Animations.")*
   - **PNG** is used for Web graphics that can be seen with specialized plug-ins. PNG is also used for onscreen presentations such as those created in Microsoft PowerPoint, Macromedia Director, or Macromedia Authorware.
   - **TIFF** is used for graphics inserted into page layout programs such as QuarkX-Press or Adobe PageMaker.
   - Choose **PICT** (Mac) or **BMP** (Win) for applications that cannot read any of the other formats.
2. Set the number of colors and matte color according to the previous exercises.

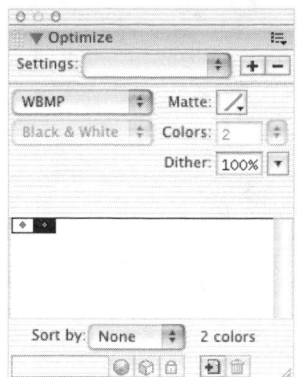

❸❽ *The* WBMP Optimization settings.

❸❾ *A* **WBMP image** *is displayed in black and white with dithering to show shading.*

The Web on a Telephone?

Yes, many communications experts agree that in the future most people will access the Web via their cellular telephone. Think about it—a cellular phone is cheaper and more portable than a computer. In fact, I already get text-only Web pages and e-mail on my cell phone.

Of course the Web on a cell phone will be much different from the Web you access on a computer. The colors will be much more limited and there will be far less text.

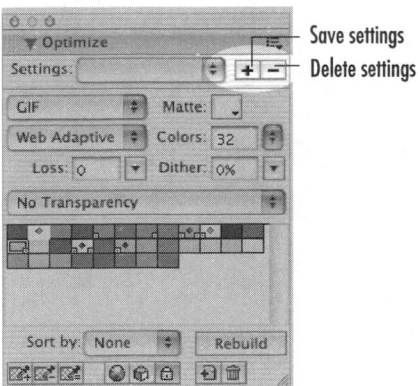

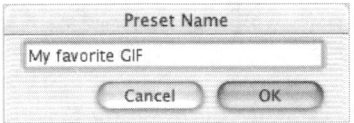

❹ *The* **Save Settings and Delete Settings icons** *in the Optimize panel.*

❹ *The* **Preset Name dialog box**.

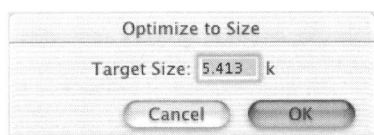

❹ *The* **Settings list** *in the Optimize panel.*

Optimize to Size

Target Size: 5.413 k

Cancel | OK

❹ *The* **Optimize to Size dialog box** *lets you set a target size that the optimization settings should be set to.*

Working with Optimization Settings

Fireworks lets you save the settings in the Optimize panel so they can be applied later.

To save optimization settings:

1. Set the Optimize panel to the settings you want to save.

2. Click the Save Settings icon (plus sign) **❹**. The Preset Name dialog box appears **❹**.

3. Give the settings a name and then click OK. This adds the settings to the default settings in the Settings list **❹**.

TIP Saved settings automatically appear in the Settings list of the Optimize panel.

TIP Saved settings are text files stored in the Export Settings director. They can be moved from one machine to another.

If you no longer want to use a preset, you can delete it from the Settings list.

To delete saved settings:

1. Choose the setting you want to delete.

2. Click the Delete Settings icon (minus sign).

Instead of juggling with the settings in the Optimize panel, Fireworks also lets you optimize files to a specific size.

To optimize a file to a target size:

1. Set the file type in the Optimize panel.

2. Choose Optimize to Size from the Optimize panel menu. A dialog box appears **❹**.

3. Enter an amount in the Target Size field.

4. Click OK. Fireworks changes the optimization settings so that the file is as close as possible to the target size.

Optimizing in the Export Preview

As mentioned earlier, you can also optimize images in the Export Preview dialog box. You can also export files directly from the Export Preview.

To optimize using the Export Preview:

1. Choose **File** > **Export Preview**. This opens the Export Preview dialog box ㊹.

2. Use the Preview Window controls to split the preview area into sections ㊺.

3. Use the Format list to choose the type of file format.

4. Set the format options.

5. Use the Transparency options to set any transparency for the file.

6. Click OK to set the optimization and return to the document window.

   or

   Click Export to export the file. *(For more information on exporting files, see Chapter 20, "Exporting.")*

To save settings using the Export Preview:

1. Click Save Current Settings in the Export Preview ㊻.

2. Name the settings file.

3. Click OK. The setting appears in the Export Preview Saved Settings list as well as the Optimize panel settings.

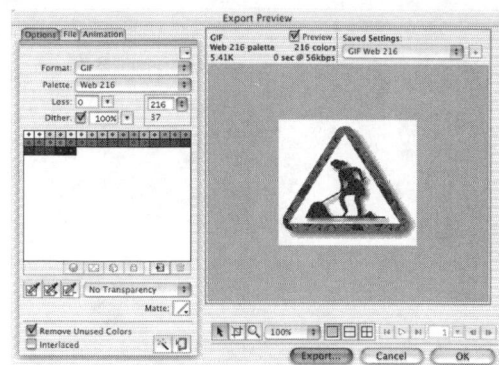

㊹ *The* **Export Preview dialog box** *allows you to optimize and export files.*

㊺ *The* **Preview Window controls** *in the Export Preview dialog box function like the 2-Up and 4-Up tabs in the document window.*

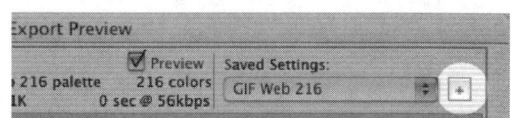

㊻ *The* **Save Current Settings button** *adds the current optimization settings to the Saved Settings list in the Export Preview dialog box.*

ANIMATIONS 16

It's hard to believe that, just a few years ago, there were very few Web pages with animated images. Today it's hard to find a Web page that doesn't have some type of animated image. Words move up and down or from side to side. One picture turns into another. Images zoom in and out.

Any animation—a cartoon, a Web graphic, or a motion picture—is basically a series of still images that appear in quick succession, giving the illusion of motion. They're just like the flip books you played with as a child.

Fireworks gives you an extensive collection of tools and commands to create GIF animations. Fireworks does not create Flash (SWF) animations. However, you can export Fireworks artwork into Macromedia Flash to use in SWF movies *(see Chapter 20, "Exporting")*.

I remember how excited I was when I created my first Web animation. Even though I have written and produced many television commercials, it was a real thrill to see my own artwork move around the page. If this is your first experience creating animations, enjoy it!

Working with Frames

Before you can create animations, you need to understand how to work with frames. Each frame of your Fireworks document becomes an image of the animation.

To open the Frames panel:

◆ Choose **Windows** > **Frames**. The Frames panel appears **❶**.

Each document contains at least one frame. You can add more frames at any time.

To add individual frames:

1. Click the New/Duplicate icon in the Frames panel. A new frame appears.

TIP The new frame created by clicking the icon does not contain any artwork.

2. Click the name of the frame to make it the active frame. Any artwork created appears only on that frame.

To add multiple frames:

1. Choose Add Frames from the Frames panel menu. The Add Frames dialog box appears **❷**.

2. Use the number control to set how many frames will be added.

3. Click one of the four radio buttons to choose where to insert the new frames.

4. Click OK. The new frames appear.

You can duplicate frames and their artwork by using the Frames panel.

To duplicate frames:

1. Select the frame or frames you want to duplicate.

2. Drag the frames onto the New/Duplicate icon **❸**.

Frame number
Frame name

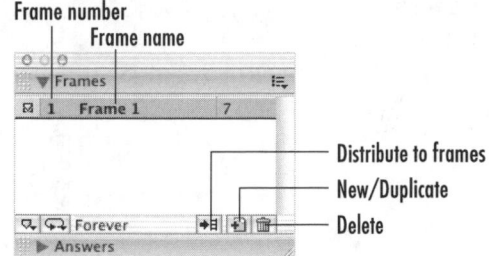

❶ *The* **Frames panel**. *Every new Fireworks document begins with a single frame.*

Distribute to frames
New/Duplicate
Delete

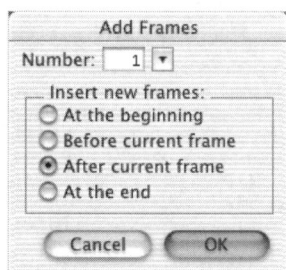

❷ *The* **Add Frames dialog box** *allows you to add many frames at once.*

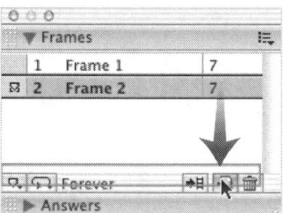

❸ *Drag selected frames onto the* **New/Duplicate icon** *to duplicate those frames.*

Working with Frames

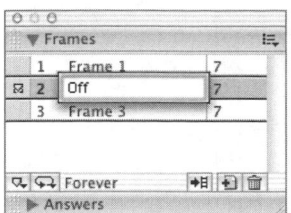

④ *Double-click to* **rename a frame.**

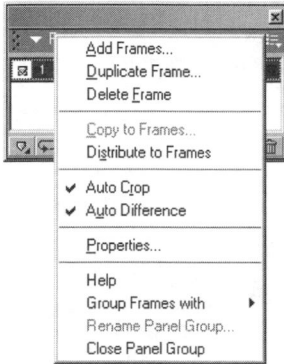

⑤ *Use the* **Frames** *panel menu or the Delete icon to delete a frame.*

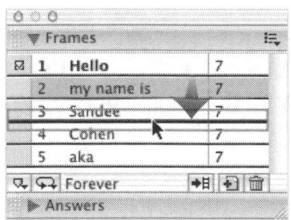

⑥ **Drag the selected frame** *to a new position to reorder a frame.*

Frames are created with the default names Frame 1, Frame 2, and so on. You can change the default names at any time.

To rename a frame:

1. Double-click to highlight the name of the frame **④**.

2. Type the new name.

3. Press the Return/Enter key to apply the new name.

TIP If you reorder frames (as discussed below), the default names automatically re-number as you change the frame position. Custom names do not change when you reorder frames.

To delete frames:

1. Click to select one frame.

2. Hold the Shift key and click another frame. All the frames between are selected.

   or

   Hold the Command/Ctrl key and click individual frames.

3. Click the Delete icon in the Frames panel.

   or

   Choose Delete Frame from the Frames panel menu **⑤**.

To reorder frames:

1. Drag the frame to the new position **⑥**.

2. Release the mouse. The frame appears in the new position.

Creating Frame-by-Frame Animations

The most rudimentary way to create animations is to manually place objects on each frame of the document. If you have many objects it may be easier to arrange all the objects on one frame and then let Fireworks automatically place the objects onto new frames.

TIP You can preview how your animation will appear by using the preview controls *(see page 281)*.

To place objects on separate frames:

1. Place the objects on one frame.
2. Add a new frame using the Frames panel *(see previous page)*.
3. Select the new frame.
4. Create the artwork on the new frame.
5. Repeat these steps as many times as is necessary to create the animation.

To automatically distribute objects onto frames:

1. Create a file with all the objects on a single frame.

TIP The order that the objects appear in the Layers panel is the order that they will appear in the Frames panel.

TIP Group objects that you want to keep together.

2. Select all the objects and choose Distribute to Frames from the Frames panel menu **7**. New frames are created with each of the objects in the selection on its own frame **8** and **9**.

   or

   Click the Distribute to Frames icon at the bottom of the Frames panel.

TIP The number of objects determines the number of frames.

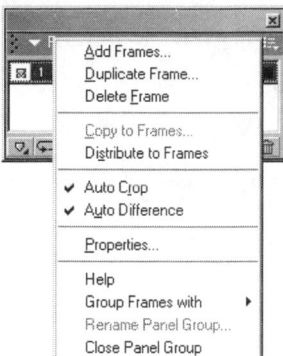

7 *The Distribute to Frames command in the* **Frames panel menu.**

8 **Before the Distribute to Frames command** *is applied, there are three grouped objects on one frame.*

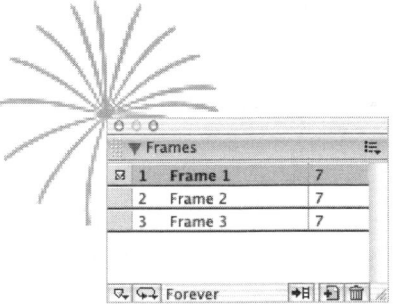

9 **After the Distribute to Frames command** *is applied each object is on its own frame.*

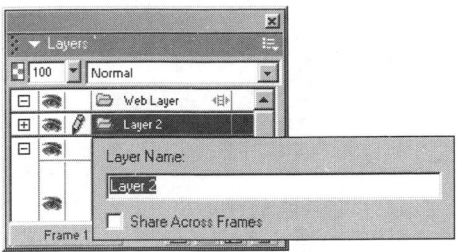

⑩ *The* **Share Across Frames** *command sets a layer to be visible on all frames.*

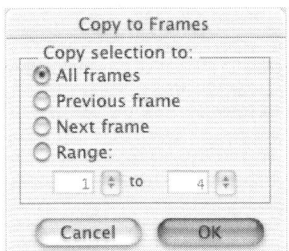

⑪ *The* **Share This Layer** *icon indicates that the artwork on that layer is seen when any frame is visible.*

Copy to Frames
Copy selection to:
● All frames
○ Previous frame
○ Next frame
○ Range: 1 to 4
Cancel   OK

⑫ *The* **Copy to Frames** *dialog box.*

You may want an image to appear on every frame. Rather than copy the image onto each frame, you can place it on a layer that is shared across frames.

To share a layer across frames:

1. Select the layer that you want to share.
2. Double-click the layer name to open the pop-up dialog box **⑩**.
3. Choose Share Across Frames. The Shared This Layer icon appears next to the layer name **⑪**.

TIP When a layer is shared across frames, editing an object on that layer changes the object's appearance on all the frames.

You can also copy an object onto all the frames, or a selected range of frames, of a document.

To copy an object onto frames:

1. Create a file with multiple frames.
2. Place an object on one of the frames that you want to appear on all the frames.
3. With the object selected, choose Copy to Frames from the Frames panel menu. The Copy to Frames dialog box appears **⑫**.
4. Choose All Frames to copy the selected object onto all the frames of the image.

   or

   Use the other selections in the Copy to Frames dialog box to copy an object to a specific frame or a range of frames.

TIP After you copy an object to frames, editing the object changes its appearance only on the frame where you make the changes.

Importing onto Frames

Although Fireworks has a robust set of drawing tools, you may want to create artwork in programs such as Macromedia FreeHand or Adobe Illustrator . For instance, you can use the blend commands in those porgrams to morph one shape into another. You can then import the artwork and distribute it to frames in Fireworks.

⓭ *A blend created in a vector drawing program can be imported into Fireworks to create an animation.*

TIP Use the Release to Layers command in FreeHand or Illustrator to distribute the blends onto layers.

To distribute vector layers onto frames:

1. Choose **File** > **Import** or **File** > **Open** and find a vector file with objects on separate layers. The Vector File Options dialog box opens.

2. Use the Layers pop-up list to assign objects on each layer to frames **⓮**.

3. Click the OK button to import or open the file.

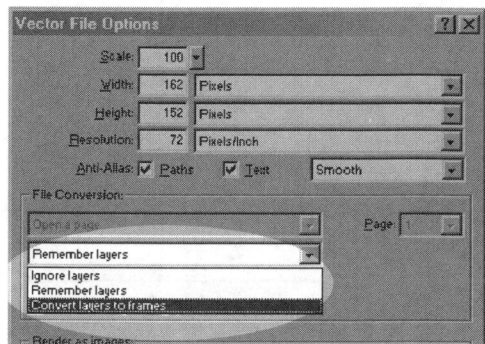

⓮ *The **Layers pop-up list** lets you move the objects on layers in a vector file onto frames in Fireworks.*

You can also distribute objects on FreeHand's multiple pages onto frames.

To distribute pages onto frames:

1. Choose **File** > **Import** and find a FreeHand file with objects on separate pages. This opens the Vector File Options dialog box.

2. Use the Pages pop-up list to assign objects on each page to frames **⓯**.

3. Click the OK button to import or open the file.

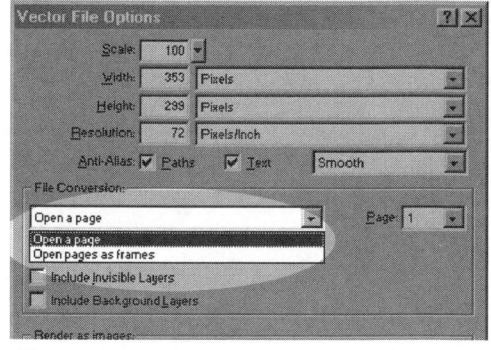

⓯ *The **Pages pop-up list** lets you move objects from pages to frames.*

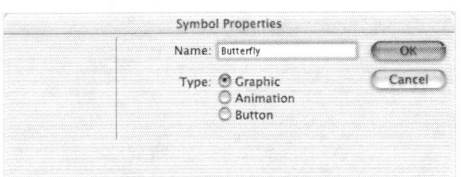

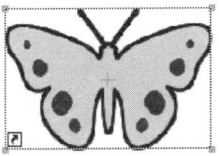

16 *The* **Symbol Properties dialog box** *lets you name and choose the type of symbol.*

17 *The* **Instance of a symbol** *is indicated by the arrow icon.*

Symbol Preview

Symbol List

18 *The* **Library panel** *holds the symbols for a document.*

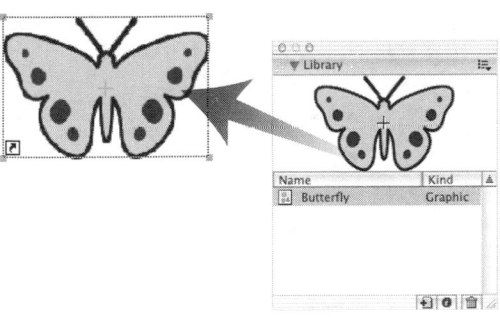

19 *Drag a symbol from the Library panel to create a new instance.*

Creating Graphic Symbols

Symbols are objects or groups of objects that control copies of themselves. Copies created from symbols are called *instances*.

There are three types of symbols in Fireworks. Graphic symbols are single-frame symbols that can be animated using a technique called *tweening*. (*Animation symbols are covered later in this chapter. Button symbols are covered in Chapter 19.*)

To create a graphic symbol:

1. Select the object or objects that you want to make into a symbol.

2. Choose **Modify** > **Symbol** > **Convert to Symbol**. The Symbol Properties dialog box appears **16**.

3. Enter the name for the symbol.

4. Choose Graphic as the type of symbol.

5. Click OK. The object or objects on the canvas are converted into an instance of the symbol **17**. The symbol appears in the Library panel **18**.

You can have as many instances of a symbol as you want on a canvas.

To create additional instances of a symbol:

◆ Copy the instance and paste it on the canvas.

or

Opt/Alt-drag the first instance to create a new instance.

or

Drag the preview or the listing of the symbol from the Library panel onto the canvas **19**.

TIP You can drag instances from one Fireworks document into another. This adds the symbol to the new document's Library panel.

Changes made to a symbol are automatically applied to all of its instances.

To edit a symbol:

1. Double-click an instance of the symbol. This opens the Symbol Editor ⓩ.

   or

   With an instance selected, choose **Modify** > **Symbol** > **Edit Symbol**.

   or

   Double-click the Symbol Preview or Symbol Listing in the Library panel.

2. In the Symbol Editor, make whatever changes you want to the symbol.

3. Close the window. All instances of the symbol are updated.

TIP Notice that the Symbol Editor does not show the tabs for the Preview options.

TIP If you find it difficult to see the symbol in its window, choose **Modify** > **Canvas Color** to set a separate background color for the symbol.

To create a blank Symbol Editor:

1. Choose **Edit** > **Insert** > **New Symbol**. This opens the Symbol Properties dialog box.

2. Name the symbol.

3. Choose Graphic for the type of symbol.

4. Click OK. A blank Symbol Editor appears.

TIP You can also click the New Symbol icon in the Library panel *(see page 276)* to create a blank Symbol Editor.

To break the link to a symbol:

1. Select the instance.

2. Choose **Modify** > **Symbol** > **Break Apart**. This converts the instance into an ordinary object, no longer controlled by the symbol.

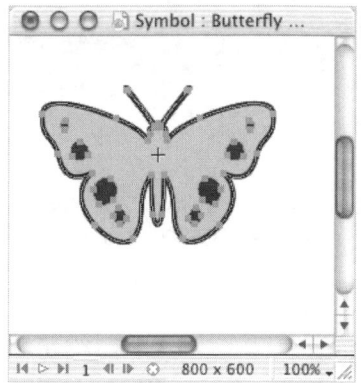

ⓩ *The* **Symbol Editor** *is where you can edit the appearance of a symbol.*

Other Uses for Symbols

Although graphic symbols are very helpful in creating animations, their uses aren't limited to just creating animated images.

You can also use graphic symbols for elements that appear many times in your artwork. Since each instance is governed by the symbol, any changes to the symbol will change all the instances.

For example, if you create a page with the name of a company repeated many times, you can change the typeface or color of the name and see those changes reflected in the instances of that symbol throughout the document.

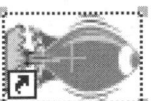

㉑ *The instances created by a graphic symbol can be modified before tweening.*

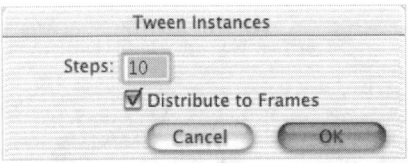

㉒ *The* **Tween Instances dialog box** *lets you set the number of steps between the instances.*

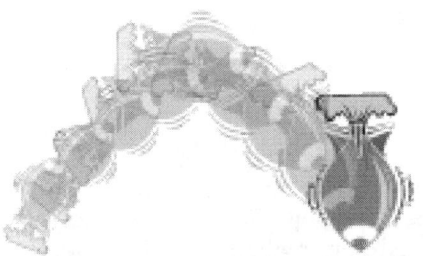

㉓ *Tweened instances create frame-by-frame animation.*

A Bit of History

The term tweening comes from film animation. The artists who drew the animations would draw the main frames of an action. They would then hand the job over to lower-ranking artists, called tweeners, who would fill in the artwork between the frames of the action.

Tweening Instances

You can modify two or more instances so that their appearance changes over a series of frames. This is called tweening.

To animate instances by tweening:

1. Position the first instance.

2. On the same frame, position additional instances where you want the instances to move **㉑**.

TIP Although the instances will eventually be on different frames, they are all on the same frame as you prepare the animation.

3. Make any changes you want to the instances.

TIP You can scale, rotate, or skew the instances. You can also change the opacity of the instances.

4. Select all the instances and choose **Modify > Symbol > Tween Instances**. The Tween Instances dialog box appears **㉒**.

5. Set the number of new instances that will be added between the current symbol instances.

6. Select Distribute to Frames to create new frames with each instance on its own frame.

TIP If you do not select Distribute to Frames in the Tween Instances dialog box, you can use the Distribute to Frames command in the Frames panel *(see page 266)*.

7. Click OK. The new instances fill in the space between the original instances **㉓**.

One important advantage that tweening has over animation symbols *(see the next page)* is the ability to tween effects. This allows you to change an object's color or apply any of the other effects as part of the animation.

To tween effects:

1. Select an instance of a graphic symbol.

2. Use the Effect panel to add an effect to the instance ㉔. For example, to change the color of an object, you would use the Color Fill effect.

3. Apply the same type of effect to another instance of the same symbol. For example, select a second color in the Color Fill effect.

TIP You must apply the effect to both instances. For example, you must have the color effect set for both instances to see a color change.

4. Apply the Tween command. The effect changes across the intermediate steps of the tween ㉕.

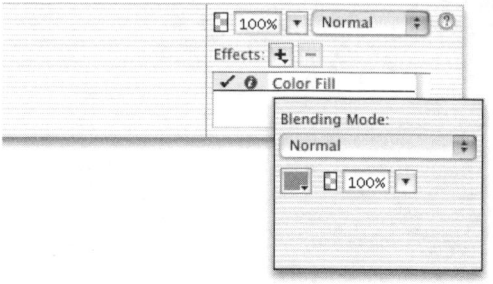

㉔ *Use the Color Fill effect to change the color of an instance.*

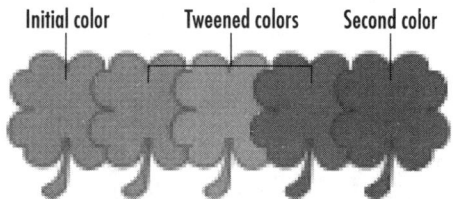

Initial color   Tweened colors   Second color

㉕ *Tweening two instances with the Color Effect applied lets you change the color of an object as part of an animation.*

Tweening versus Animation Symbols

Tweening the instances created by graphic symbols offers some advantages over using animation symbols. (See the opposite page for more information on working with animation symbols.)

You can tween multiple objects to move them in different directions. You can apply effects such as changing color. Or you can apply skewing to change the shape of an instance.

However, unlike animation symbols, tweened instances are discrete objects on multiple frames and cannot be easily modified later.

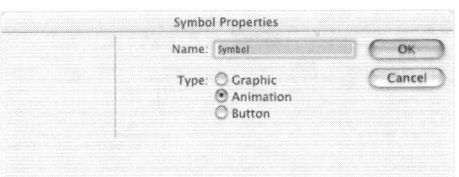

㉖ *The* **Symbol Properties dialog box** *lets you set an animation symbol.*

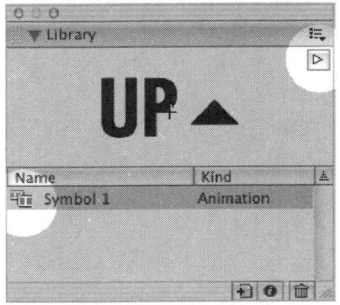

㉗ *This frame-by-frame animation symbol has the Up graphic on one frame of the symbol and the Down graphic on the second.*

㉘ *An* **animation symbol in the Library panel** *displays a special animation symbol icon and the Play button.*

Creating Animation Symbols

Animation symbols make it easier to animate objects and make changes later. You can create an animation symbol that contains frame-by-frame animation.

TIP You can preview how your animation will appear by using the preview controls *(see page 281)*.

To create a frame-by-frame animation symbol:

1. Choose **Edit** > **Insert** > **New Symbol**.

2. In the Symbol Properties dialog box, name the symbol and set the type for Animation **㉖**.

3. Click OK to open the Symbol Editor.

4. In the Symbol Editor, use the tools and commands to create the artwork *(see page 269)*.

TIP To use existing artwork in the animation, cut the artwork from the document window and then paste it into the Symbol Editor.

5. Use the Frames panel to add the frames to the animation Symbol Editor.

6. Create the artwork for each frame of the animation.

TIP For instance, to animate text that changes, you would put one text block on the first frame and another text block on a second frame **㉗**.

7. Close the Symbol Editor. The new symbol you just created appears in the Library panel **㉘**.

TIP Click the Play button in the Library panel to see a preview of the animation.

8. Drag the symbol from the Library panel to add it to your document.

TIP If you see a dialog box asking you to add frames, click OK. The animation symbol will not play properly without the extra frames.

The Animate selection command automatically converts an object into an animation symbol. These automatic controls let you set the motion, direction, scaling, opacity, and rotation of the symbol.

To set the automatic animation controls:

1. Select the artwork you want to animate.

2. Choose **Modify** > **Animation** > **Animate Selection**. This opens the Animate dialog box 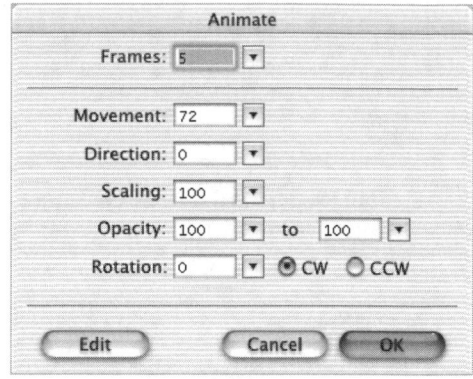.

3. Use any combination of the settings to control the animation as follows 𝟛𝟘:
   - **Frames** sets the number of frames that the animation will use.
   - **Movement** sets the distance (in pixels) that the object will move. This creates a motion controller that extends out from the instance 𝟛𝟙. *(See page 280 for how to manually adjust the control.)*
   - **Direction** sets the angle that the object will move.
   - **Scaling** sets the final size of the object.
   - **Opacity** sets the beginning and end opacity of the object.
   - **Rotation** sets the degrees that the object will rotate and the direction of rotation as clockwise (**CW**) or counterclockwise (**CCW**).

4. Click OK to return to the document window. The symbol is added to the Library panel and an instance of the symbol replaces the artwork originally selected.

To edit the settings of an animation symbol:

1. Select the instance.

2. Change the animation settings in the Property Inspector 𝟛𝟚.

   or

   Choose **Modify** > **Animation** > **Settings** to reopen the Animate dialog box.

𝟚𝟡 *The **Animate dialog box** lets you set the controls for automatic animation.*

𝟛𝟘 *Using a combination of the animation controls, this text was set to move, fade in, scale up, and rotate over ten frames.*

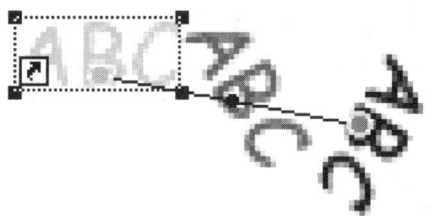

𝟛𝟙 *The Movement control extends out from the animation symbol.*

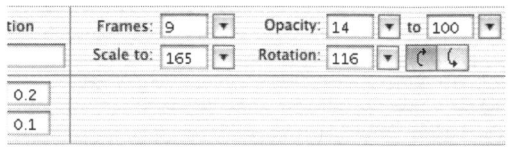

𝟛𝟚 *The Property Inspector contains the controls for an animation symbol.*

Creating Animation Symbols

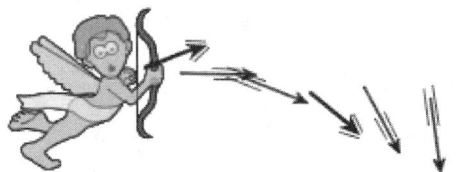

③ *Automatic animation controls moved and rotated the arrow. Frame-by-frame animation created the motion lines around the arrow.*

Nesting Symbols

If you have used graphic and animation symbols in Macromedia Flash, you should be familiar with the concept of nesting symbols—using the instance of a graphic symbol as the artwork for an animation symbol.

For example, let's say you create a graphic symbol of a star.

You can then drag an instance of that star from the Library panel into the Symbol Editor of a frame-by-frame animation.

Next, you can use two or more frames to create the effect of the star blinking on and off or changing color.

Finally, you can add the automatic animation controls to make the blinking star rotate and move across the page.

The benefit of all this is, if you want to change the shape or color of the star, you only need to edit the original graphic symbol and all the other instances will update.

You can also convert existing artwork into a frame-by-frame animation symbol.

To convert artwork into a frame-by-frame animation symbol:

1. Select the artwork you want to animate.

2. Choose **Modify** > **Symbol** > **Convert to Symbol**. This opens the Symbol Properties dialog box.

3. Name the symbol and set the type for animation and click OK. This opens the Animate dialog box.

4. Click Edit in the Animate dialog box. This opens the Symbol Editor which contains the selected artwork.

5. Use the techniques described on pages 266–267 to create the animation.

6. Close the Symbol Editor. The new symbol appears in the Library panel. An instance of the symbol replaces the artwork that was selected.

You can create an animation symbol that uses a combination of automatic animation and frame-by-frame techniques **③**.

To create a combination of animation controls:

1. Select the artwork you want to animate.

2. Choose **Modify** > **Animation** > **Animate Selection**.

3. Set the Animate options as described on the previous page.

4. Click Edit to open the Symbol Editor and set the frame-by-frame animation.

5. Close the Symbol Editor. The new animation symbol appears in the Library panel and the animation instance replaces the selected artwork.

TIP Combining the two types of animation allows you to move artwork on the page while at the same time changing the image inside the artwork.

Working with Symbols

Creating symbols isn't enough; you will also want to edit them. You can change the name of a symbol or convert it to a different type of symbol by opening the Symbol Properties dialog box ③④.

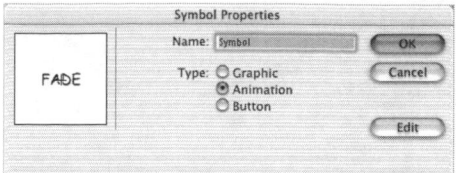

To open the Symbol Properties dialog box:

◆ Double-click the name of the symbol in the Library panel ③⑤.

or

Click the Symbol Properties icon in the Library panel .

or

Choose Properties from the Library panel menu ③⑥.

③④ *The* **Symbol Properties dialog box** *for an existing symbol.*

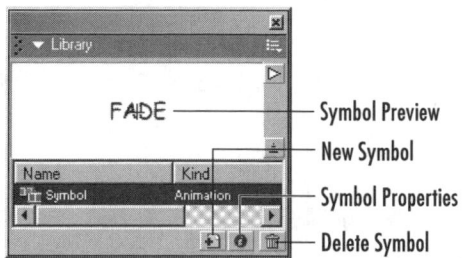

③⑤ *The* **Library panel** *displays and controls the symbols in a document.*

— Symbol Preview
— New Symbol
— Symbol Properties
— Delete Symbol

You can edit the artwork or frames of a symbol by opening the Symbol Editor.

To open the Symbol Editor:

◆ Double-click a graphic or animation symbol.

or

Click the Symbol Properties icon in the Library panel ③⑤. Then click the Edit button in the Symbol Properties dialog box.

or

Double-click the symbol preview in the Library panel.

or

Choose Edit Symbol from the Library panel menu ③⑥.

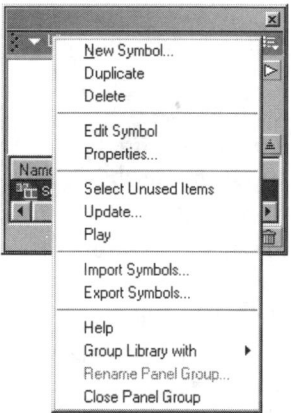

③⑥ *The* **Library panel menu.**

WARNING: Saving Symbols

The Save command does not work when you are working inside the Symbol Editor. You must close the window and then apply the Save command to save your work.

Exporting and Importing Symbols

You may notice two commands in the Library panel for Exporting Symbols and Importing Symbols.

This makes it possible for you to use symbols throughout many different Fireworks documents. Then, if you change the appearance of a symbol in the main document, you can update all the instances in other documents.

Although it is perfectly fine to use these commands with graphic and animation symbols, it's more likely that you will want to export button symbols to other documents. Exporting and importing symbols are covered in Chapter 19, "Buttons and Behaviors."

Of course, the techniques described here for editing, naming, duplicating, deleting, and managing graphic and animation symbols also apply to button symbols.

To create a blank Symbol Editor:

◆ Click the New Symbol icon in the Library panel **35**.

or

Choose New Symbol from the Library panel menu **36**.

To duplicate a symbol:

◆ Drag the symbol listing onto the New Symbol icon in the Library panel **35**.

or

With the symbol selected choose Duplicate from the Library panel menu **36**.

To delete a symbol:

1. Select the symbol or symbols you want to delete.

2. Click the Delete icon in the Library panel **35**.

or

Drag the symbols onto the Delete Symbol icon in the Library panel.

or

Choose Delete from the Library panel menu **36**.

TIP If you delete a symbol that is in use you will see a dialog box alerting you that this will also delete any instances of that symbol in the document.

TIP You may also want to clean up your files by deleting symbols that are not in use. Use the Select Unused Items command in the Library panel menu so you can then delete them.

Modifying Animations

Fireworks uses a technique called *onion skinning*, which allows you to see a lower opacity version of the objects on other frames **37**.

TIP I turned on onion skinning to create the animation images in this chapter.

To turn on onion skinning:

1. Open the Onion Skinning controls in the Frames panel **38**.

TIP You can also turn on onion skinning in either the Document window or a Symbol Editor.

TIP If you turn on onion skinning in the Document window, you need to turn it on separately in a Symbol Editor.

2. Choose one of the following options:
   • **Show Next Frame** displays the frame after the selected frame.
   • **Before and After** shows the frames before and after the selected frame.
   • **Show All Frames** displays all the frames in the document.

TIP Onion skinning also shows the individual steps of automatic animation symbols.

37 *An example of how onion skinning lets you see multiple frames of an animation.*

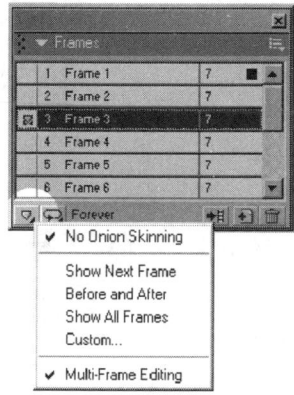

38 *Click the* Onion Skinning icon *in the lower left corner to open the* Onion Skinning *menu.*

Still More History

Once again a term in computer animation comes from traditional film animation. Onion skinning comes from the days when film animators used vellum sheets to plot their animations. When the sheets were layered, the artists could see through them like the layers of an onion.

Modifying Animations

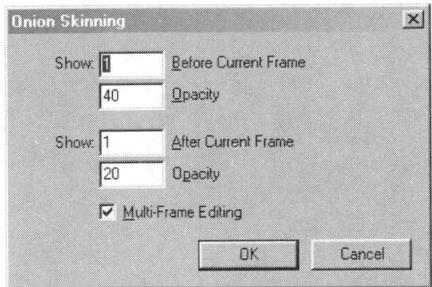

39 *The* **Onion Skinning dialog box**.

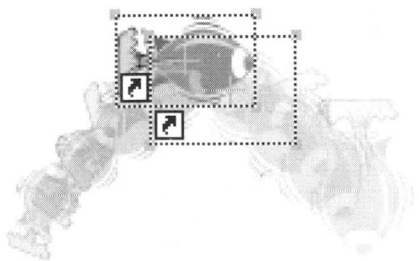

40 *The* **Onion Skinning controls** *in the Frames panel show which frames are displayed. Here frames 1–6 have onion skinning turned on.*

41 *Multi-frame editing allows you to select and modify objects on different frames.*

You can also customize the onion skinning to specific frames or opacity levels.

To customize onion skinning:

1. Choose Custom from the Onion Skinning controls menu. The Onion Skinning dialog box appears **39**.

2. Use the Show fields to change the number of frames that should be visible.

3. Use the Opacity fields to change the opacity of the visible frames.

TIP Click in the Frames panel to move the onion skinning icons to the frames you want displayed. The onion skinning icons indicate which frames are displayed **40**.

Multi-frame editing allows you to work with objects that are on different frames. This is very helpful if you need to move several elements of a frame-by-frame animation.

To edit multiple frames of a window:

1. Make sure onion skinning is turned on.

TIP The frames available for multi-frame editing are limited to the frames visible through onion skinning.

2. Check Multi-Frame Editing from the Onion Skinning menu of the Frames panel.

3. Use any of the tools or commands to select objects on any of the visible frames **41**.

You can change the length and direction of an animation by changing its motion path.

To edit an animation symbol motion path:

1. Drag the green dot of the motion path to position the start of the animation ⓫.

2. Drag the red dot to position the end of the animation.

TIP If there is no motion path, only a green dot, you need to add frames using the Object panel or choose **Modify** > **Animation** > **Settings**.

The number of frames assigned to an animation symbol can be extended. This allows you to create a symbol that loops or repeats during the animation ⓭.

To create a repeating animation symbol:

1. Create a frame-by-frame animation symbol *(see page 273)*.

2. Place the instance of the symbol on the canvas.

3. Use the Object panel to increase the number of frames for that instance of the symbol ⓭.

Two instances of the same symbol can start on different frames. Each instance displays the images on staggered frames ⓮.

To stagger the animation display:

1. Create a frame-by-frame animation symbol.

2. Place one instance of the symbol on the first frame of the document.

3. Use the Object panel to extend the number of frames.

4. Place another instance on the next frame. When the animation plays, each instance displays a different image in each frame.

Green dot (start)   Red dot (end)

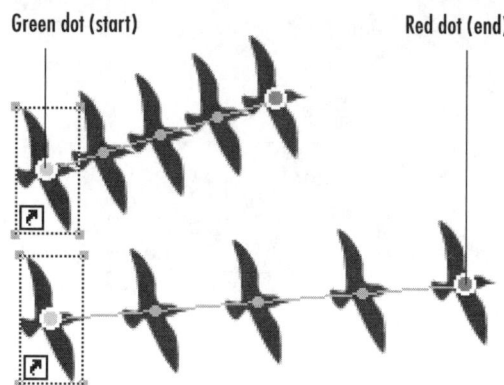

⓫ **Drag the motion path** *to change the length and direction of an animation symbol.*

⓭ *Increase the frames for an animation symbol to repeat the animation. Here the two frames of the blinking star repeat three times across six frames.*

Starts on frame 1   Starts on frame 2

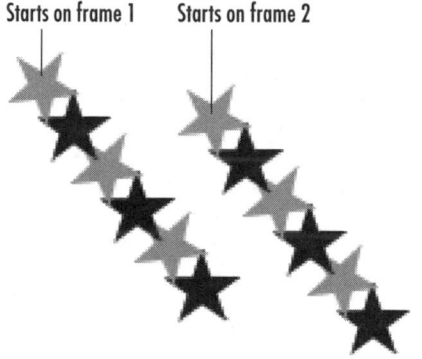

⓮ *Place the start point of an animation symbol on different frames to* **stagger the appearance of the animation**.

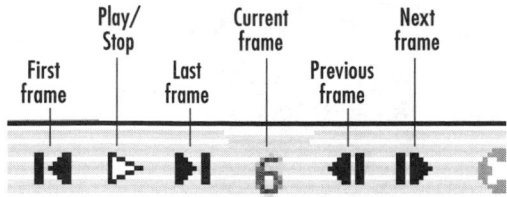

First frame | Play/Stop | Last frame | Current frame | Previous frame | Next frame

45 *The* Animation controls in the Document window.

46 *The* Animation controls in the Export Preview dialog box.

Don't Overload Your Animations

As exciting as it is to create an animation, watch out. If you create a large image with many colors and many frames your animation will take too long to download.

For instance, the total number of colors in the document comes from all the colors in each frame. If each frame is colored differently from the other frames, it will add to the number of colors in the document.

Previewing Animations

As you create animations, you may want to see how the frames look when played together. Fireworks lets you preview animations in the Document window.

To preview animations in the document window:

◆ Use the animation controls at the bottom of the Document window **45**.

- **First frame** or **Last frame** jump to the beginning or end of the animation.
- **Play** runs the animation.
- **Stop** halts the play of the animation.
- **Next frame** or **Previous frame** move one frame at a time.

TIP If you try to play the animation with the Preview tab selected, make sure you have set the Optimize panel to Animated GIF. If not, the animation will play extremely slowly. *(For more information on using the Optimize panel and Preview tab, see Chapter 15, "Optimizing.")*

You can also preview animations in the Export Preview dialog box, although it is much easier to preview in the Document window.

To preview animations in Export Preview:

1. Choose File > Export Preview.
2. Use the animation controls at the bottom of the preview area **46**.

Frame Controls

Just as in comedy, in animation timing is everything. Fireworks lets you control the frame timing, or how long each frame remains visible.

To set the frame timing in the document window:

1. Double-click the number in the Frame Delay column of the frame in the Frames panel. This opens the Frames Properties controls **47**.

   or

   Select the frame and choose Properties from the Frames panel menu.

   TIP Use the Shift key to select more than one frame at a time.

2. Enter a number in the Frame Delay field. The higher the number, the longer the frame remains visible.

3. Press the Return/Enter key to apply the changes and close the Frames Properties controls.

If you use the Export Preview dialog box to optimize and export your images, you can set the animation timing using the animation controls in the Export Preview.

To set the frame timing in Export Preview:

1. Choose **File** > **Export Preview**.

2. Click the Animation tab to display the Frame list.

3. Enter a number in the Frame Delay field **48**.

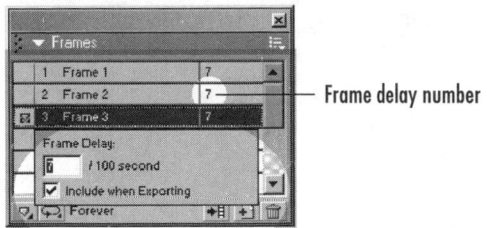

Frame delay number

47 *The* **Frames Properties controls** *let you set the frame delay for each frame.*

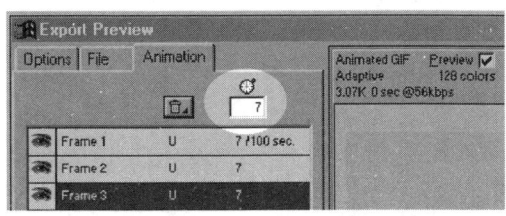

48 *Set the frame delay in the Export Preview to control how long a frame is visible during an animation.*

Timing Secrets

Here are a few of my favorite timing tricks for animations:

- If you set the animation to loop many times, set the last frame of an animation to run longer than the other frames. This gives your viewer's eyes a chance to rest on the final frame.

- If objects move in the animation, increase the frame delay as the animation progresses. This gives the effect of the objects slowing down as they move.

- Decrease the frame delay as the animation progresses to give the effect of speeding up the motion.

- Stagger the timing of frames to make the object's motion more natural looking.

Frame Controls

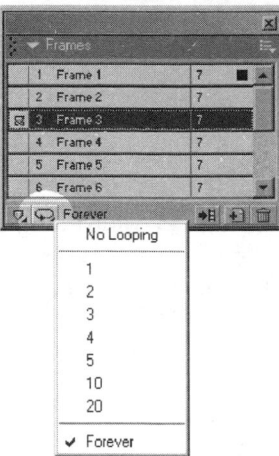

49 *Click the* **Looping icon** *in the Frames panel to open the* **Looping menu**.

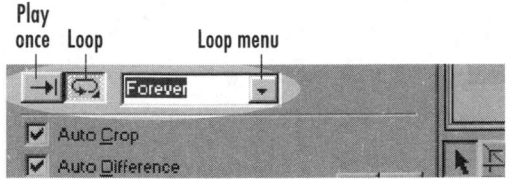

50 *The* **Looping controls** *in the Export Preview.*

Looping Trick

Normally, GIF animations start on frame 1 and end on the last frame of the animation. If the first frame of your animation contains the most important information, here's how to have an animation stop on the first frame:

Duplicate the first frame and position it at the end of the animation. Set the timing for the duplicate of the first frame to a very small amount.

When the animation runs, it appears to run full circle and stop on the first frame. It actually stops on the last frame—the duplicate of the first frame.

You can set how many times the animation repeats using the looping controls.

TIP Some Web sites require banner ads to repeat only a certain number of times and then stop.

To set looping in the document window:

1. Click the Loop icon to open the Loop list **49**. Set the list as follows:
   - **No Looping** sets the animation to play once.
   - The **numbers** specify how many times the animation repeats.
   - **Forever** plays the animation endlessly.
2. Press Return/Enter to apply the setting.

TIP The first time the animation plays is not counted in the Loop control. So, to play the animation four times, set the loop number to three.

To set looping in the Export Preview:

1. Choose **File > Export Preview**.
2. Click the Animation tab to display the Loop controls at the bottom of the Animation Frames list **50**.
3. Click the Play once icon to have the animation play one time and then stop.
4. Click the Loop icon.
5. Open the Numbers list and choose how many times the animation should play.

Fireworks also lets you control frame disposal. This is a sophisticated way to control the transition of the pixels on one frame to the next frame or the background. Frame disposal can help speed the download of a GIF animation.

To set the transition of the frames:

1. Select a frame in the animation options panel of the Export Preview.

2. Use the Disposal method list to control the blends between frames.

   • **Unspecified** has Fireworks choose the most efficient disposal method.
   • **None** leaves any pixels that are not covered by the next frame visible. This option is useful when objects are revealed in different areas of the frames.
   • Select **Restore to Background** when transparency is turned on so that each frame changes from one to another.
   • Select **Restore to Previous** when objects appear over a frame created earlier.

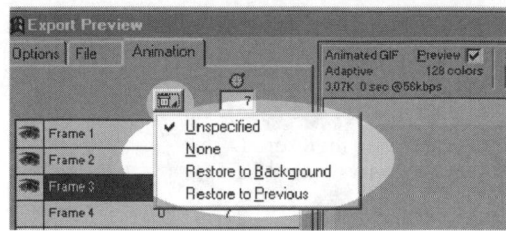

⑤ *The* **Disposal icon** *and the* **Disposal menu** *in the Export Preview dialog box.*

Fireworks is Disposal Smart

You don't have to worry about the disposal settings. As Macromedia says, Fireworks is "disposal smart"—that is, the Unspecified setting automatically chooses the most efficient disposal method.

For example, when the Unspecified setting is chosen and the background is transparent, Fireworks automatically uses the correct disposal method which is Restore to Background.

So, unless you have an overwhelming reason to change the disposal setting, leave it set to Unspecified.

Frame Controls

52 Auto Crop *and* Auto Difference *are on by default to create the smallest possible files.*

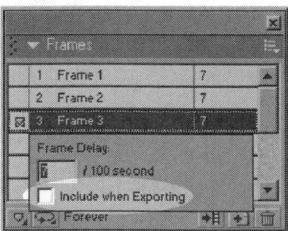

53 *Uncheck* Include when Exporting *to stop a frame from being exported.*

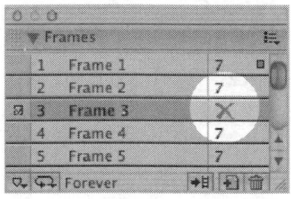

54 *The X marks the frame excluded from export in the Frames panel.*

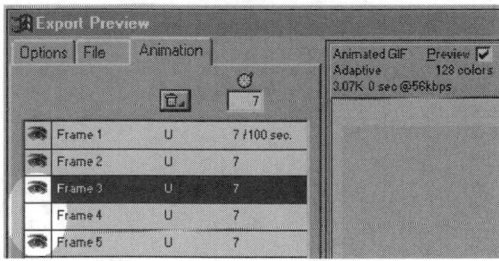

55 *The* visibility settings for frames in the Export Preview. *In this example, all the frames except frame 4 are set to export.*

The Export Preview has another way to control the final size of the animation: the Auto Crop and Auto Difference settings.

TIP These settings are on by default to give you the smallest possible files. If you export animations to other applications, such as Macromedia Director, you may need to turn off these settings.

To set the Auto Crop and Auto Difference:

1. Choose the Animation tab of the Export Preview dialog box. The Auto Crop and Auto Difference settings are at the bottom of the Animation panel **52**.

2. Check Auto Crop to automatically crop the image instead of sending the same information over and over.

3. Check Auto Difference to use a transparency to make the file size even smaller.

You don't have to export all of the frames in the final animation.

To set the frames to export in the Frames panel:

1. Double-click the number of the frame to open the Frames Properties control for the frame you want to omit (*see page 282*).

2. Deselect Include when Exporting **53**.

3. Close the control. A red X next to the frame indicates that the frame will not export as part of the animation **54**.

To set the frames to export in Export Preview:

1. Choose File > Export Preview.

2. Click the Animation tab to display the Frame list.

3. Double-click the Show/Hide icon in the Animation tab **55**. If the icon is visible, the frame exports. If the icon is not visible, the frame does not export.

Frame Controls

Optimizing Animations

After you have finished the frames of the animation, you use the Optimize panel or Export Preview to fine tune the settings and export the file.

To set the animation export options:

1. Open the Optimize panel **56**.

   or

   Choose **File > Export Preview** to open the Export Preview window **57**.

2. Choose Animated GIF from the Format list.

3. Set the GIF color and transparency options as desired *(see Chapter 15, "Optimizing")*.

4. Use the Export commands to export the file *(see Chapter 20, "Exporting")*.

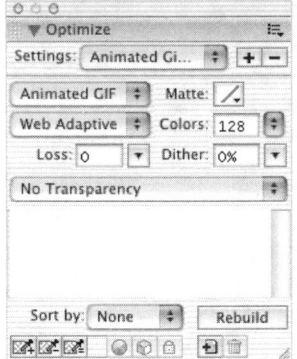

56 *Choose Animated GIF from the* **Optimize panel** *before exporting an animated GIF.*

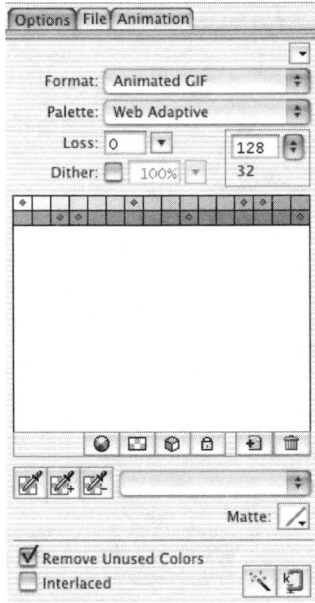

57 *Choose Animated GIF from the* **Options** *tab of the* **Export Preview** *dialog box to export an animation.*

HOTSPOTS AND LINKS 17

Imagine you create a magical machine that transports people all over the world. How would you design the controls? One way might be to start with a map of the world. Your passengers would simply touch a certain part of the map and they would be instantly transported to where they wanted to go.

That's the idea behind image maps for Web graphics. You embed different areas of an image with information that sends the viewer to different Web pages or performs a certain action. All the viewer needs to do is click inside each area of the image to be transported to a new Web page.

The special areas on the image are created using the Fireworks hotspot tools. The embedded information that sends you to a new Web page or performs the action is called a link.

Creating Hotspots

You can draw hotspots directly on your image using one of the three hotspot tools: the Rectangle, Circle, and Polygon hotspot tools.

To draw a rectangular or circular hotspot object:

1. Choose the Rectangle or Circle Hotspot tool in the Tools panel **①**.

2. Drag to create a rectangle or circle that defines the hotspot area **②**.

TIP Hold the Shift key to constrain the rectangle to a square.

TIP Hold the Opt/Alt key to drag from the center outward.

TIP Hotspots are automatically placed on the Web layer even if that layer is not the selected layer.

To draw a polygon hotspot object:

1. Choose the Polygon hotspot tool in the Tools panel **①**.

2. Click to set the first point of the polygon.

3. Click the next corner of the polygon to make the first line segment.

4. Continue clicking to set more points.

5. Close the hotspot object by clicking again on the first point.

Rather than try to match the size or shape of a path, you can convert paths into hotspots.

To convert objects into hotspots:

1. Select the path or paths.

2. Choose **Edit > Insert > Hotspot**. This converts a single path into a hotspot.

3. If you have multiple objects selected, a dialog box appears **③**.
   - Choose **Single** to create one hotspot for all the objects.
   - Choose **Multiple** to create an individual hotspot for each object.

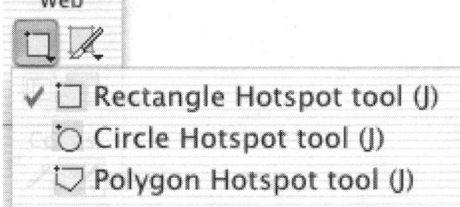

① *The* **three Hotspot tools** *in the Tools panel.*

② **Hotspots** *can be rectangular, circular, or irregular polygons.*

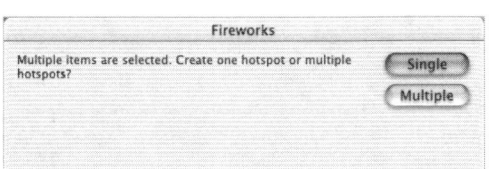

③ *You can choose to create one hotspot or multiple hotspots from multiple selected paths.*

Creating Hotspots

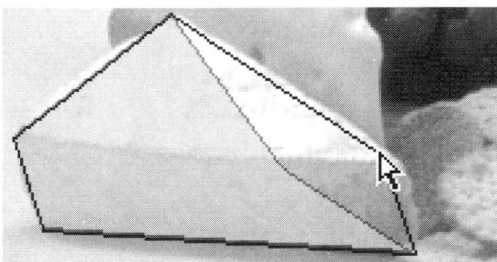

④ *Use the Selection or Subselection tools* **to modify hotspot objects.**

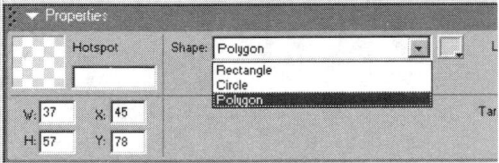

⑤ *The* **Shape menu of the Hotspot controls** *in the Property Inspector.*

Show/Hide All Web objects

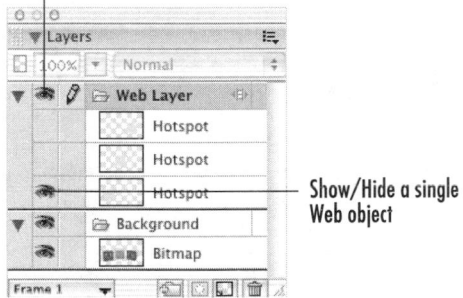

Show/Hide a single Web object

⑥ *The* **Show/Hide icons** *for the Web layer.*

Show Web objects

Hide Web objects

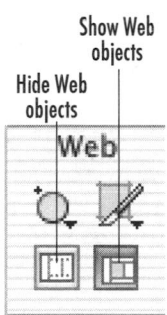

⑦ *Click the* **Web visibility icons** *in the Tools panel to show or hide Web objects.*

Modifying Hotspots

Once you have created hotspot objects, you can still modify them.

To move and modify hotspot objects:

1. Choose either the Selection or the Subselection tools in the Tools panel.

2. Drag inside a hotspot object to move it to a new positon.

3. Drag one of the anchor points of the hotspot object to change its shape **④**.

You can also convert hotspot objects from one shape to another.

To change hotspot shapes:

1. Choose the hotspot object you want to convert.

2. Choose a shape from the Hotspot Object panel Shape list **⑤**.

The Layers panel allows you to control the visibility of hotspots. This makes it easier to modify paths below the hotspots.

To show and hide each hotspot object:

◆ To show or hide each individual hotspot object, click the Show/Hide icon area next to the object **⑥**.

To show and hide all the hotspot objects:

◆ To show or hide all the the hotspot objects, click the Show/Hide icon area next to the Web layer.

or

Click the Show/Hide controls at the bottom of the Tools panel **⑦**.

TIP Use any of the hotspot tools on the image. The Web layer automatically becomes visible.

Assigning Hotspot Attributes

Once you have created hotspot objects, you can then apply URL links to them. If you need to apply only one or two links you can easily type them directly into the Object panel.

To link a hotspot to a URL:

1. Select the hotspot object.
2. Type the URL in the Link field in the Property Inspector ❽.

As you apply or create URL links a record of each link is retained as the Link list. You can use the list to reapply a URL link without having to type it.

To apply links from the Link list:

1. Select the hotspot object you want to apply a URL link to.
2. Choose a link from the Link menu in the Property Inspector ❾.

TIP Only the links that have been applied to objects are kept in the Link list. Other links are discarded when you quit Fireworks. If you want a permanent record of all the URL links, you can add the list to a URL library *(see page 293)*.

Hotspots don't have to have URL links. A hotspot can also be used as the trigger for a behavior. *(See Chapter 19, "Buttons and Behaviors.")*

To detach a URL link from a hotspot:

1. Select the hotspot.
2. Choose **No URL (no HREF)** from the Link list.

TIP The **No URL (no HREF)** is the default entry for new hotspots.

❽ *The **Link field** for a hotspot in the Property Inspector.*

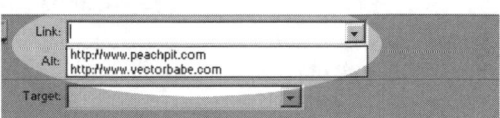

❾ *The **stored links menu** for the hotspots in the Property Inspector.*

> ### Understanding URLs
>
> URL stands for **uniform resource locator**. It contains information for the browser to perform an action. The most common types of URLs are http, mailto, and ftp.
>
> **http** stands for **HyperText Transfer Protocol**. These are the links that send visitors to new Web pages.
>
> **mailto** is used to send e-mail.
>
> **ftp** stands for **File Transfer Protocol**. It directs the browser to download a file located in a specific location.
>
> Fireworks supports all these types of links. For more information on working with URLs, you can read *HTML 4.0: No Experience Required* by Stephen Mack and Janan Platt.

Assigning Hotspot Attributes

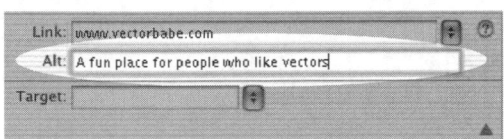

⑩ *The* **Alt tag field** *for a hotspot in the Property Inspector.*

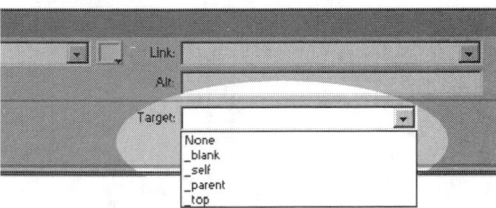

⑪ *The* **Target field and list** *for hotspot objects in the Property Inspector.*

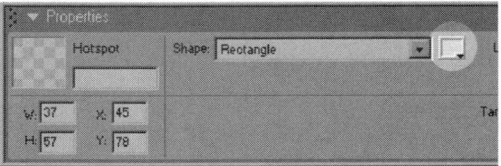

⑫ *The* **Color Well** *for a hotspot object in the Property Inspector.*

In addition to the URL links, there are other settings for hotspot objects. The (alt) tag contains the text that is displayed while the image is loading or if the image can't be found. In some browsers, the (alt) tag will pop up when you mouse over the image. In text-to-speech browsers the (alt) tag will be read as a substitute for the image *(see page 332)*.

To set the (alt) tag:

◆ Type the text in the Alt field **⑩**.

The Target field controls where the Web page requested by a link appears. Targets are usually used as part of framesets.

To set the target:

◆ Use the Target list or type in the field the window or frame you want the link to open to **⑪**.

- **None** and **_self** open the destination page in the same location that the button was in.
- **_blank** opens the destination page in a new browser window.
- **_parent** opens the destination page in the parent frameset of the link.
- **_top** replaces all the frames in the current browser window and opens the destination page in that window.

Hotspots are displayed with a see-through overlay. You can change the overlay color to help organize different links.

To change the hotspot color:

◆ Use the Hotspot Color Well to set the color for different hotspots **⑫**.

TIP Darker colors make it easier to see through the overlay.

Managing Links

Typing URL links is fine if you only have a couple of links to add. However, complicated Web sites can have hundreds of links. Fireworks offers you many features for working with large numbers of links. Rather than type links one by one you can import URLs from any HTML file, Netscape Navigator bookmarks, or Internet Explorer favorites.

To import links:

1. If the URL panel **⑬** is not visible, choose **Window** > **URL**.

2. Choose Import URLs from the panel menu **⑭**.

3. Navigate to select an HTML file, Navigator bookmarks file, or Internet Explorer favorites file. The URLs appear as a list in the panel **⑮**.

You can also create libraries, or groups of URLs. This allows you to group all the URLs for a certain Web site or client.

To create a URL library:

1. Choose New URL Library from the URL panel menu. This opens the New URL Library dialog box **⑯**.

2. Type the name of the library and click OK. This adds the library to the library list.

TIP Libraries can be used by multiple documents.

TIP To delete a library from the list, delete the library file located in the folder Fireworks MX: Configuration: URL Libraries.

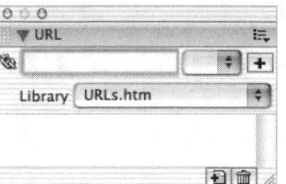

⑬ *The* **URL panel** *allows you to manage links.*

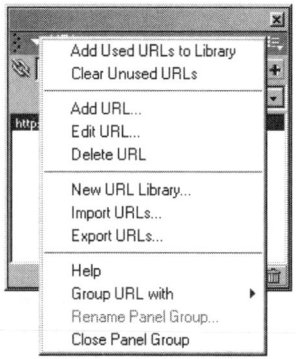

⑭ *The* **URL panel menu.**

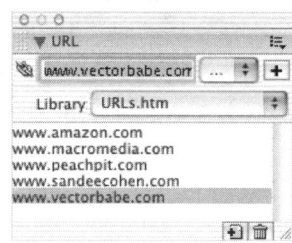

⑮ **Imported URLs** *appear in the URL panel.*

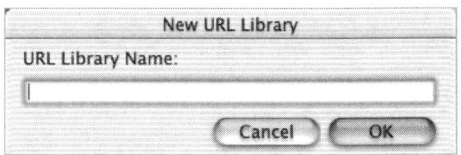

⑯ *Name a new URL library using the* **New URL Library dialog box.**

⓱ *The currently assigned URL appears in the* **Current URL** *list*.

⓲ *The* **Add Current URL** *icon to add the URL of a selected object to the URL Library*.

⓳ *Click the* **Add New URL to Library** *icon to open the Add URL dialog box*.

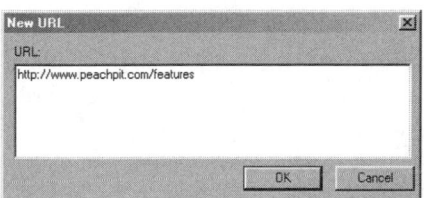

⓴ *Use the expansive area in the* **New URL** *dialog box to type in new URLs*.

You can add the current URL assigned to an object to a URL Library.

To add the current URL to a Library:

1. Select the object that contains the URL. The URL appears in the Current URL list **⓱**.

2. Create a new library or choose a library from the list.

3. Click the Add Current URL icon **⓲**. The URL appears as part of the URL Library.

The URL panel keeps a list of used URLs in all the documents for that session of Fireworks. This list is erased when you quit Fireworks. You can make the list permanent by adding the used URLs to a library.

To add used URLs to a Library:

1. Create a new library or choose a library from the list.

2. Choose Add Used URLs to Library from the URL panel menu.

You don't have to type URLs only in the cramped Links field. You can add them directly to a Library using an expansive dialog box.

To add a new URL link to a Library:

1. Select the library that you want to add the URL link to.

2. Choose Add URL from the URL Manager menu or click the Add URL icon **⓳**. This opens the New URL dialog box **⓴**.

3. Type the URL in the field and then click OK. This adds the URL to the library.

To delete URL links:

1. Choose a link in the library.

2. Choose Delete URL from the URL panel menu.

   or

   Click the Delete URL icon 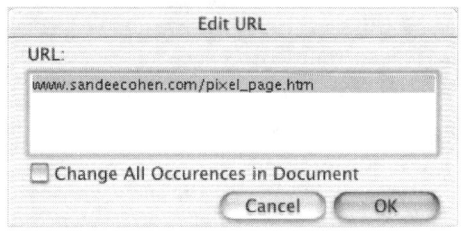.

㉑ *Click the* **Delete URL icon** *to remove a URL from a Library.*

URL links change continually. Fortunately, Fireworks provides a simple way to edit URL links in a document.

To edit URL links:

1. Click the URL you want to edit.

2. Choose Edit URL from the URL panel menu. This opens the Edit URL dialog box **㉒**.

3. Make whatever changes you want to the URL.

4. Check **Change All Occurrences in Document** to automatically change the links in all objects that use that URL.

㉒ *Make changes to URLs in the* **Edit URL** *dialog box.*

SLICES 18

Why would anyone spend hours creating an intricate Web graphic and then cut it up into different pieces? Well, the technique is called slicing and it allows you to define regions of an image that you can set to behave differently.

For instance, you might want to slice an image so that each slice has its own optimization settings. If you have a photo next to an object with text, for example, the two parts of the total file need to be exported as different types of images. A slice lets you define one area as a JPEG and the other as a GIF.

Sliced images appear to download faster. Also, the first time visitors view images those images are cached, or stored, on their computers. The next time visitors come to that image, even if it's on a different page, it appears faster because it is already downloaded.

You might want to slice an image into sections so that you can easily update new products or news stories. Instead of changing the entire image, you can just update the slice. You can also slice an image so that it contains plain HTML text rather than an image.

You also need to slice images to assign JavaScript behaviors such as rollovers and Swap Images. *(For more information on working with behaviors, see Chapter 19, "Buttons and Behaviors.")*

Working with slices is the heart and soul of creating Web graphics in Fireworks.

Using Ruler Guides to Slice

If you're in a hurry, and don't need to set any different optimization settings or links, the easiest way to slice an image is to use ruler guides.

To slice using ruler guides:

1. Drag a guide from a ruler around the side of the area you want to slice *(see pages 30–31)*.

2. Drag additional guides until you have defined all the slices for the image **❶**.

3. When you export the file, set the slicing to Slice Along Guides *(see Chapter 20, "Exporting")*.

TIP Fireworks opens Adobe Photoshop files with the Photoshop ruler guides in place. They can then be used as ordinary slices in Fireworks.

TIP Use hotspot objects *(see Chapter 17, "Hotspots and Links")* to add links to slices created by guides.

Creating Slice Objects

Ruler guides do not provide enough control to slice all the areas of the image. For instance, a ruler guide placed around one area of the image may cut through another area that you don't want sliced **❷**. You can create slices around specific areas of your image with slice objects. Other areas are sliced only if necessary.

TIP Slice objects create slice guides that create the minimum amount of slices necessary to slice the rest of the image **❸**.

❶ Ruler guides *can be used to define slices.*

❷ *When ruler guides are used to slice an image they may cut into other images that you don't want sliced, such as the slices through the images of the statue and Washington.*

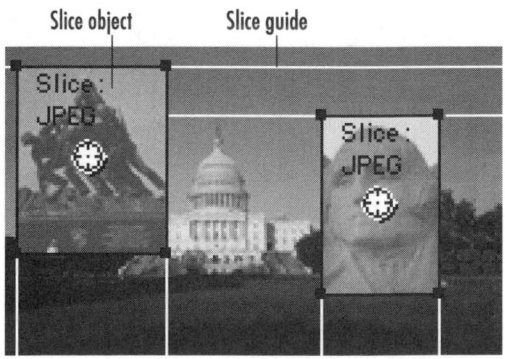

❸ *Slice objects create slice guides that keep the slices to a minimum and avoid cutting through other slice objects.*

④ *The* **Rectangular Slice tool** *in the Tools panel.*

⑤ **Drag the Slice tool** *to create a Slice object.*

⑥ *The* **Polygon Slice tool** *in the Tools panel.*

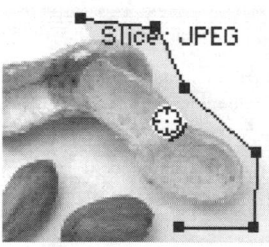

⑦ *Click to create segments of a polygon slice.*

When Should You Use Polygon Slices?

The area under a Polygon Slice is actually a hotspot image with as many rectangular sub-slices as necessary to create the irregular shape.

Many slices means more images that need to be handled as your Web page loads. This can slow down the display of your page. **Bottom line:** Use the Polygon Slice tool not because you *can*, but when you *must!*

To use the Rectangular Slice tool:

1. Choose the Rectangular Slice tool from the Tools panel **④**. (Be careful, it's sharp.)

2. Drag a rectangle around the area that you want to slice **⑤**. This creates a rectangular slice object.

TIP If slice objects overlap, the top object will be used to control optimization, behaviors, and actions.

3. Use the Selection tools to move or modify slice objects.

TIP Slice objects can be copied, pasted and duplicated just like ordinary objects (*see Chapter 6, "Working with Objects"*).

To use the Polygon Slice tool:

1. Choose the Polygon Slice tool from the Tools panel **⑥**.

2. Click to create a point that defines each segment of the polygon that defines the slice **⑦**.

3. Use the Selection tools to move or modify slice objects.

To create slices from objects:

1. Select the object or objects you want to slice. This includes placed images.

2. Choose **Edit > Insert > Slice**. This creates a slice object around the selected object.

TIP If you select multiple objects, a dialog box will ask if you want to create multiple slices or a single slice.

Viewing Slice Objects and Guides

You may find it difficult to select or work with objects that have slices over them. You can control whether or not the slices or the slices guides are displayed.

To show and hide slice objects:

◆ Click the Show/Hide icon for the Web Layer in the Layers panel **8**.

or

Click the Show or Hide Web Layer icons at the bottom of the Tools panel **9**.

To show and hide slice guides:

◆ Choose **View > Slice Guides**. This displays and hides the guides that extend out from a slice.

Setting the Slice Options

You set the options for slice objects using the Slice Object panel. Its controls are similar to the Hotspot options. *(For more information working with the URL settings, see Chapter 17, "Hotspots and Links.")*

To set the slice options:

◆ Select a slice object. The Slice object controls appear in the Property Inspector **10**.

To set the link for a slice object:

1. Use the link list to choose a link from either the current Link list or the Library selected in the URL Manager.

2. To enter a link not in the list, type the link directly into the Link field.

TIP The no URL (no HREF) setting lets you slice an image without a URL link.

Hidden slice

8 *Use the* **Web Layer Show/Hide icon** *to control the display of slice objects.*

Show Web objects

Hide Web objects

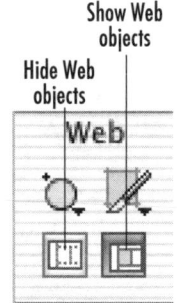

9 *Use the* **Show/Hide Web Layer icons in the Tools panel** *to control the display of slice objects.*

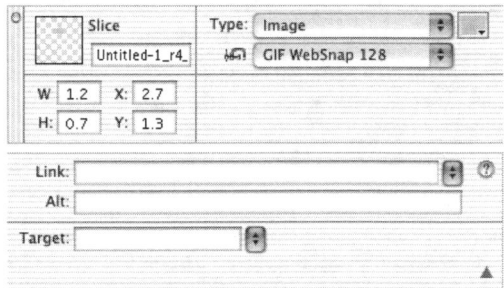

10 *The* **Slice controls** *in the Property Inspector.*

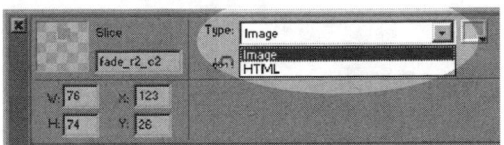

⓫ *The* Type *menu for a Slice menu in the Property Inspector.*

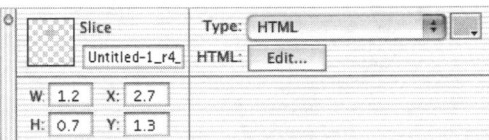

⓬ *The* HTML Slice object options *in the Property Inspector.*

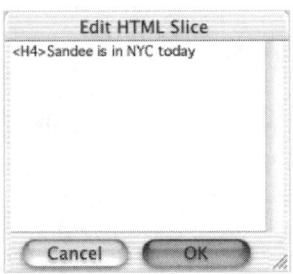

⓭ *The code for an HTML slice in the* Edit HTML Slice dialog box.

⓮ *The information in a HTML slice is shown inside the selected slice object.*

⓯ *Use the* Preview in Browser command *to see an actual preview of a text slice.*

Like hotspot objects, slice objects let you enter the (alt) tag and target information. *(For a description of the (alt) tag and target fields, see page 291.)*

To set the (alt) tag and target:

1. Type the text in the (alt) field.
2. Use the Target field or list to set a specific frame or window for the link.

You can also control the color of the slice object.

To set the slice object display color:

◆ Use the Color Well to set the display color for the Slice object.

You can set a slice so that it displays ordinary HTML text in the sliced area.

To create a text slice:

1. Select the slice object and set the Type list in the Property Inspector to HTML **⓫**.
2. Click the Edit button in the Property Inspector **⓬**. This opens the Edit HTML Slice dialog box **⓭**.
3. Type the HTML code. Use HTML codes to set the style, color, size, and other attributes of the text **⓮**.

TIP The area inside a text cell uses the canvas color as its background.

You need to preview HTML slices in a browser in order to see the effect of any HTML formatting you put into the text slice field **⓯**.

To preview the text slice in a browser:

◆ Choose File > Preview in Browser and then choose either the primary or secondary browser listing in the menu.

Setting the Slice Options

Optimizing Slices

One of the most important reasons to slice images is so you can set separate optimizations for the areas under each slice object. This allows you to set different optimization settings within an image.

To optimize slices:

1. Select one or more slice objects.

2. Use the Optimize panel to set the optimization for the area under the slice object. *(For more information on working with the Optimize panel, see Chapter 15, "Optimizing.")*

TIP Hold the Shift key to select multiple slice objects. You can then set the optimization for all the selected slice objects.

TIP Each slice object is labeled with its optimization setting **16**.

Empty areas—areas not covered by slices—can be optimized separately from the slices.

To optimize the empty areas:

1. Make sure no slice objects are selected.

2. Use the Optimize panel to set the optimization. This setting will be applied to all empty areas in the document.

16 *Select individual slice objects to create different optimization settings.*

Optimizing Strategies

Setting different optimization settings for the slices can help you lower the file size.

For instance, you can set a photograph to be a JPEG and flat art to be a GIF image.

You can set the critical areas of an image to a higher JPEG quality and the background to a lower quality to create smaller images.

You can use different GIF palettes for separate areas. This lets you set a limited number of colors individually for different images.

Watch out, though! Slices have to be reassembled using HTML tables and the table code can take up its own space and add to the download time.

Putting Slices Back Together

Once you set the slices for an image, you need some way to reassemble the slices on your Web page. That is the function of an HTML table.

When you export the images, Fireworks creates the HTML table necessary to reassemble the slices. *(See Chapter 20, "Exporting," for more information on exporting slices and HTML code.)*

BUTTONS AND BEHAVIORS 19

People expect Web pages to do more than just display information. They want to click onscreen buttons that whisk them away to new pages. And they expect those buttons to light up or do something when the mouse passes over them or look like they're in the up or down position.

With Macromedia Fireworks you can easily create interactive elements using behavior commands. For instance, a simple rollover behavior changes the appearance of a button as the mouse passes over it. A more complex behavior gives users four different looks as the user moves over the area and clicks the button. Behaviors also let visitors move the cursor over one area to display pictures or animations else-where on the page. Behaviors also let you create pop-up menus with a list of choices.

Interface designers know that adding behaviors to Web pages is a great way to give visual feed-back to the navigational elements. (They're also lots of fun to play with!)

Understanding the Rollover States

How do you let people know where to click on your Web page? A hotspot *(see Chapter 18, "Hotspots and Links")* is too primitive. It hardly gives any feedback that there is something to click ❶.

Rollovers are more sophisticated. You can create a rollover so that it changes dramatically when the viewer passes the cursor over the button area ❷.

Fireworks gives you four different choices for the appearance of a rollover ❸:

- **Up** is the appearance of the rollover when there is no cursor inside the image area. This is also called the normal state of the rollover.

- **Over** is the appearance of the rollover when the cursor is moved inside the area of the rollover. The Over state alternates with the Up state when the cursor moves in and out of the rollover.

- **Down** is the appearance of the rollover after the mouse clicks inside the area. The Down state is "sticky" in that it stays down after you click it.

- **Over While Down** is the appearance of the rollover when the cursor passes over a rollover that is in the Down state. This Over While Down state alternates with the Down state when the cursor moves in and out of the rollover.

TIP The Down and Over While Down states are best used with framesets so that the rollover is seen in one frame while the new page appears in another.

❶ *When the mouse **passes over an image map**, it changes from an arrow to a simple hand cursor.*

❷ *When the mouse **passes over a rollover**, it not only shows the hand cursor but the image also changes to the Over state. In this case the image changed its size and color and added a beveled edge and a drop shadow.*

❸ *The **four rollover states** can be set for whatever looks you want. Each state can display a distinct image in response to the action of the mouse.*

Understanding the Rollover States

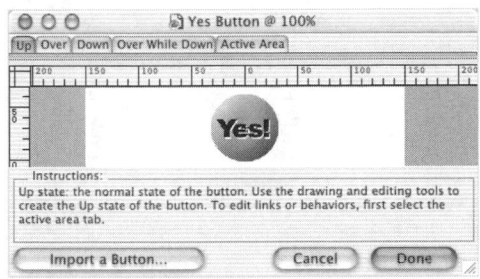

❹ *The Button Editor in the* **Up** *state.*

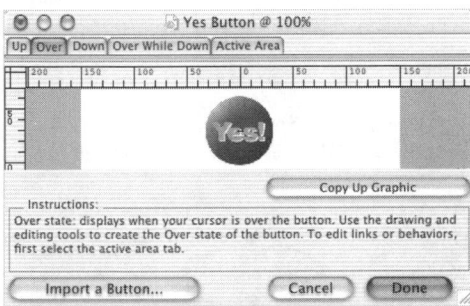

❺ *The Button Editor in the* **Over** *state.*

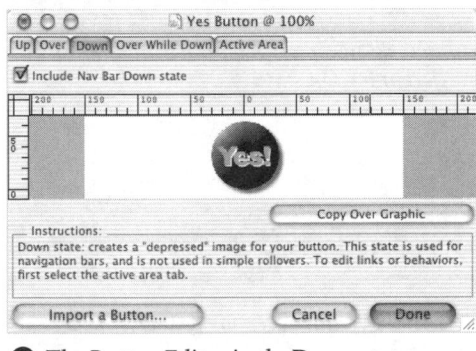

❻ *The Button Editor in the* **Down** *state.*

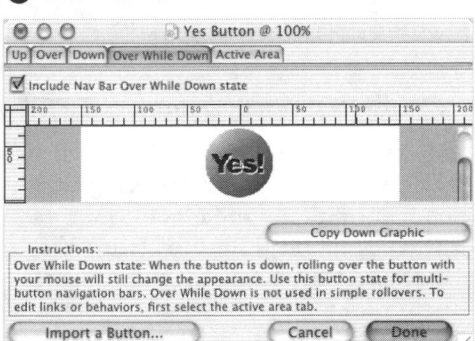

❼ *The Button Editor in the* **Over While Down** state.

Creating a Button Symbol

The easiest way to create a rollover is to create a Button symbol. *(For information on graphic and animation symbols, see Chapter 16, "Animations.")*

To create a button symbol:

1. Choose **Edit** > **Insert** > **New Button**. This opens the Button Editor.

2. Click the tabs to create the artwork for each of the states *(see the following exercise)*.

TIP You create all the artwork for each of the states within the Button Editor. You don't use the regular document window.

3. Set the active area for the rollover *(see the following page)*.

To create the button symbol artwork:

1. With the Up tab selected, create the artwork for the Up state **❹**.

2. Click the Over tab to switch to the work area that controls the appearance of the Over state of the button **❺**.

3. Click the Copy Up Graphic button to bring the artwork from the Up window into the Over window. You can then make any adjustments as desired.

   or

   Use any of the Fireworks tools and commands to create a new graphic for the Over state of the button.

4. Repeat steps 2 and 3 for the Down and Over While Down states **❻** and **❼**.

TIP You can create a simple button with just the Up and Over states.

The active area is a slice object that defines the area of the button that responds to the presence of the cursor. It is also the area that sets the link for a button.

To set the active area and link for a button:

1. Select the Active Area tab ❽.

2. Use either of the selection tools to increase or decrease the size of the green rectangle that covers the button.

TIP Don't make the active area slice smaller than the artwork for any of the states. If the artwork lies outside the active area rectangle, that artwork will not be seen during the rollover.

3. With the slice object selected, set any of the link attributes using the slice object controls in the Property Inspector.

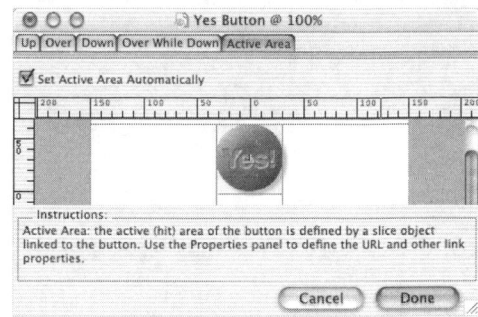

❽ *The* **Active Area** *in the Button Editor.*

As you work on a button symbol, you may want to see how one state relates to another.

To view multiple states of a button:

1. Select Onion Skinning in any of the button states.

2. Use the Onion Skinning controls in the Frames panel to change which states are visible ❾. *(See pages 278 for working with the Onion Skinning controls.)*

TIP The Up, Over, Down, and Over While Down states corresponds to frames 1, 2, 3, and 4 of the Frames panel.

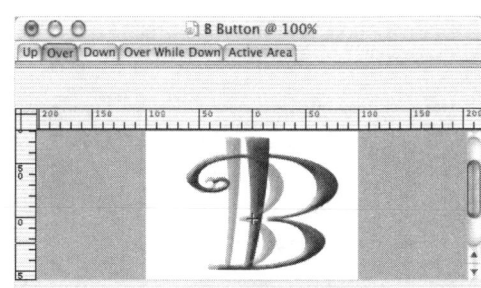

❾ *Onion skinning lets you see a combination of the different button states.*

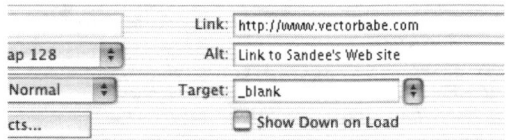

❿ *The* **Links controls** *in the Property Inspector for a button.*

Ordinarily a button is first displayed with the Up state visible. However, you can set the button so the Down state is displayed first.

To control the opening display of a button:

1. Select button in the document window—not the Button Editor.

2. Select Show Down on Load in the Property Inspector.

Behaviors in Fireworks or Dreamweaver?

Those of you who know Macromedia Dreamweaver may be wondering why not create buttons and other behaviors in that program instead of Fireworks. There's no reason not to. The behaviors in Fireworks are there as a convenience for the graphic designers who don't layout their own Web pages.

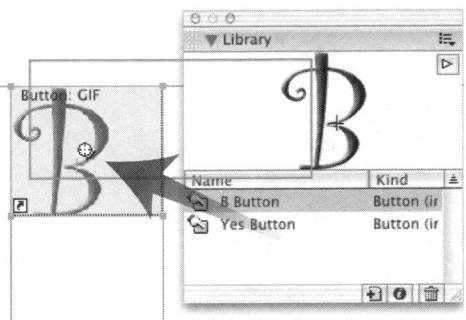

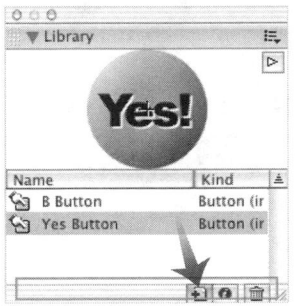

Working with Button Symbols

It's a rare Web site that only has one button on a page. So you're going to want to duplicate and modify instances of buttons.

To add a button from the Library:

◆ Drag the button symbol from the Library panel onto the canvas ⑪.

TIP The instances of button symbols automatically create slice areas. This is so they can display the different rollover states.

⑪ *Drag buttons from the Library panel to the canvas to* **create the buttons for a Nav Bar**.

To duplicate an instance on the canvas:

1. Select the button on the canvas.

2. Use any duplication commands or Opt/Alt-drag to create a second instance of the button.

⑫ **Duplicate a button** *by dragging it onto the New Symbol icon.*

Rather than create new buttons from scratch, button symbols can begat other buttons. These new buttons can be modified as desired.

To duplicate a symbol in the Library:

1. Drag the symbol onto the New Symbol icon in the Library panel ⑫.

    or

    Choose Duplicate from the Library panel menu.

2. Edit the button in the Button Editor.

TIP The new symbol will have the same name as the original button plus a numerical suffix. Use the Symbol Properties dialog box to change the name.

Save Outside the Button Editor

The Save command does not work when you are working inside the Button Editor. You must close the Editor and then choose the Save command to save your work. Other commands such as Revert also don't work while in the Editor. However, commands, such as Align, Arrange, Group, and so on, are all available while you're in the Button Editor.

Working with Button Symbols

Once you create a button, you most likely are going to want to edit it. There are several ways to change button symbols in a document.

To edit a button symbol:

◆ Double-click an instance of the button symbol on the canvas. This opens the Button Symbol editor.

or

Double-click the preview of the button symbol in the Library panel.

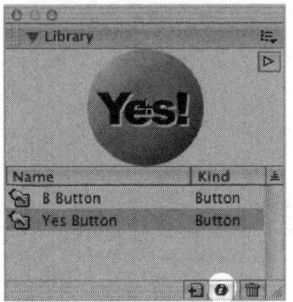

⑬ *The* **Symbol Properties** *icon in the Library panel.*

To edit the button symbol properties:

◆ Double-click the name of a button symbol in the Library panel. This opens the Symbol Properties dialog box.

or

Select the button symbol in the Library panel and then click the Symbol Properties icon in the Library panel **⑬**.

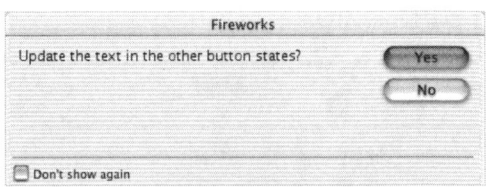

⑭ *You have a choice whether or not to update all the text in the button states.*

There are two ways to edit the text in a button. The first way lets you edit the text for all the instances of that symbol.

To edit text for all instances of a button symbol:

1. Open the Symbol Editor for the button *(see the first exercise on this page).*

2. Use the Text tool to edit the text on any of the button states.

3. Click the Done button in the Symbol Editor. A dialog box appears asking if you would like to change the text on the other button states **⑭**.

4. Click Yes to update the text for all the states of the button.

or

Click No to leave the text on the other button states unchanged.

Designing Buttons

As you create the artwork for buttons, keep in mind you're actually designing an application that visitors use to navigate to the different pages on your Web site.

Try to design your Web page interface so that it's clear to your visitors where the buttons are, what will happen if they click a particular button, and whether or not they have in fact clicked that button. Probably the most obvious way to indicate the presence of a button is to have color changes in the different rollover states.

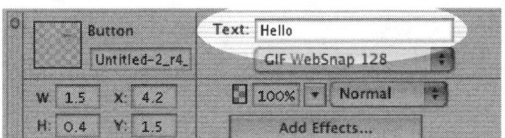

⑮ *The* **Text field** *for a button symbol in the Property Inspector.*

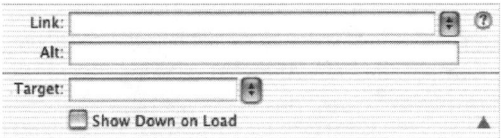

⑯ *The* **Link, Alt tag, and Target fields** *for a button symbol in the Property Inspector.*

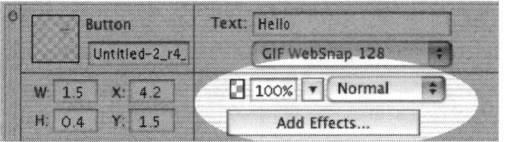

⑰ *Use the* **opacity, blend modes, and effects controls** *for a button.*

Adding Buttons and Behaviors to Web Pages

All the buttons and other behaviors, described in this chapter need to be exported from Fireworks as HTML code and images. You then can import that HTML code into a program such as Macromedia Dreamweaver to use in your Web pages. *(For more information on exporting documents, see Chapter 20, "Exporting.")*

The second way to edit text in a button symbol is to edit the text on just that instance. This allows you to have one button act as the symbol for many different instances.

To edit text for one instance of a button symbol:

1. Select the instance of the button symbol on the canvas .

2. Change the text in the Text field in the Property Inspector **⑮**. The text automatically changes for all the states of that one instance of the button symbol.

You may also want to change the link properties of a button. The first way is to change the link properties for all instances of the button symbol.

To change links for all instances of a button:

1. Open the Symbol Editor for the button by double-clicking it.

2. Click the Active Area tab.

3. Select the slice object that covers the button.

4. Set the links controls in the Property Inspector **⑯**.

You can also set the link properties for just one instance of a button.

To change links for one instance of a button:

1. Select the instance.

2. Set the links controls in the Property Inspector.

TIP You can also use the Property Inspector to add effects and set the opacity of a single instance of a button **⑰**.

Creating a Nav Bar

A Nav Bar (from the term navigation bar) is
a set of button symbols that work together to
link to different Web pages. You first create a
button symbol and then assemble them into
a graphic symbol that acts as the Nav Bar.

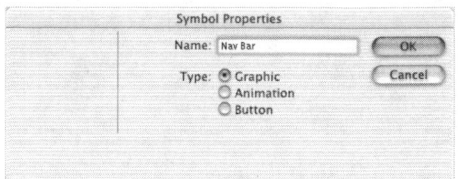

⓲ *A Nav Bar is created as a Graphic symbol.*

To create a Nav Bar:

1. Create the button symbol you want to
   serve as the style for all the buttons in the
   Nav Bar. The symbol should appear in
   the Library panel.

2. Choose **Edit** > **Insert** > **New Symbol**. This
   opens the Symbol Properties dialog box.

3. Set the Symbol type as Graphic **⓲**. Name
   the Symbol and click OK. This opens the
   Symbol Editor.

   TIP Although a Nav Bar contains button
   symbols, it is actually a graphic symbol
   with nested button symbols.

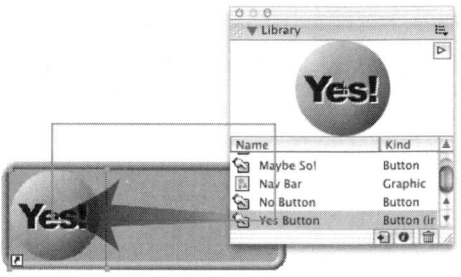

⓳ *Drag buttons from the Library panel onto the
artwork for the Nav Bar graphic symbol*

4. Use any of the tools to create background
   artwork for the Nav Bar.

5. Drag instances of the button symbols
   from the Library panel into the Symbol
   Editor **⓳**. Each instance is used as one of
   the buttons in the nav bar.

6. Use the Property Inspector to change
   the text and links for each of the button
   instances.

7. Choose Share Across Frames from the
   Layers panel menu **⓴**.

   TIP The Share Layer setting ensures that the
   buttons change their states without white
   areas around them.

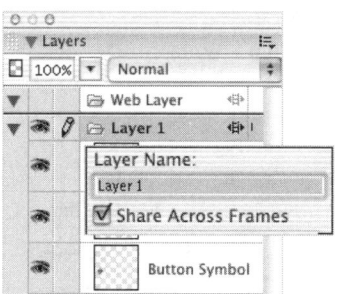

⓴ *The artwork for a Nav Bar must be on a
shared layer.*

8. Close the Symbol Editor. An instance
   of the Nav Bar appears in the Library
   panel **㉑**.

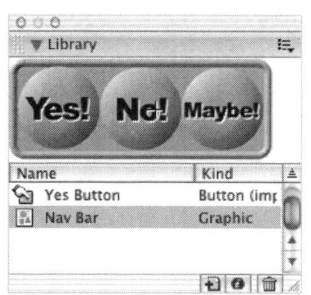

㉑ *The Graphic symbol for the Nav Bar appears
in the Library panel.*

Creating a Nav Bar

❷❷ *A Nav Bar appears on the document page as a symbol.*

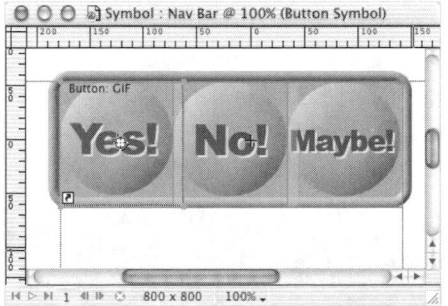

❷❸ *The Symbol Editor for a Nav Bar contains the buttons for the Nav Bar buttons.*

Plan, Plan, Plan!

The biggest mistake designers make has nothing to do with file sizes or HTML — it's not planning ahead.

Before you create your buttons and Nav Bars make sure you know what your page names are going to be.

You can't believe what a pain in the neck it is to redo your Nav Bar just because you didn't make your buttons big enough to accommodate the word or phrase with the most characters!

To use a Nav Bar:

1. Drag the graphic symbol for the Nav Bar from the Library panel onto the canvas.

2. The Nav Bar appears on the canvas as a single instance containing both the background and the buttons **❷❷**.

To edit a Nav Bar:

1. Double-click the instance of the Nav Bar on the page.

   or

   Double-click the preview of the Nav Bar in the Library panel. Either way this opens the Symbol Editor.

2. Make whatever changes you want in the background artwork for the Nav Bar.

3. Close the Symbol Editor to apply the changes to the Nav Bar in the document.

4. Double-click the instances of the button symbol used in the Nav Bar to open the Symbol Editor for each button **❷❸**.

   or

   Use the Property Inspector to change text and link attributes for each specific instance of the button symbol.

TIP The Nav Bars you create for one document can be used in other documents *(see the next page)*.

Many designers want Nav Bars to look like a radio button — when the page that the button is linked to appears, the button for that page is displayed in its down state.

To control the opening display of a button:

1. Select the button in the document window.

2. Select Show Down on Load from the Property Inspector.

Sharing Symbols

You can reuse button symbols created for one document in other documents as well. (*These techniques for sharing and editing symbols apply equally well to the graphic symbols and animation symbols covered in Chapter 16.*)

To place a symbol in a document:

1. Open the document that contains the button symbol you want to use.
2. Open the document in which you want to use the button.
3. Drag the button symbol from the Library panel into the new document.

   or

   Copy and paste (or drag and drop) an instance of the button symbol from one document to another.

You can also import many symbols from one document to another.

To import symbols into a document:

1. Choose Import Symbols from the Library panel menu 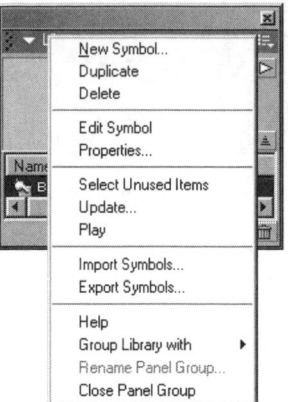.
2. Navigate to find the file from which you want to import the symbols.
3. Click OK. This opens the Import Symbols dialog box **㉕**.
4. Select the symbols you want to import.

   TIP Hold the Shift key to select contiguous symbols in the Import dialog box. Hold the Cmd/Ctrl key to select non-contiguous symbols in the dialog box.

5. Click Import to add the selected symbols to the document. The word imported appears after the name **㉖**.

   TIP The Symbol Properties dialog box shows a path to the original source file of an imported symbol **㉗**.

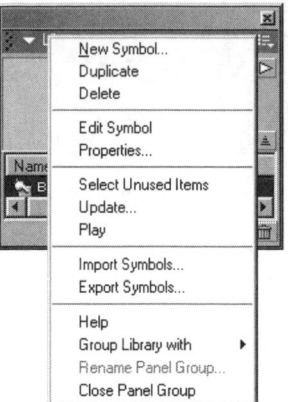

㉔ *The* **Library panel menu.**

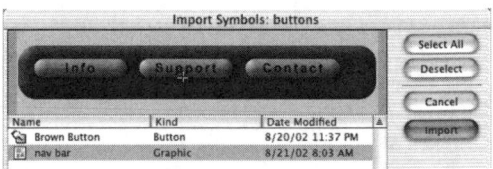

㉕ *The* **Import Symbols dialog box** *lets you select symbols used in other documents and import them into the current document.*

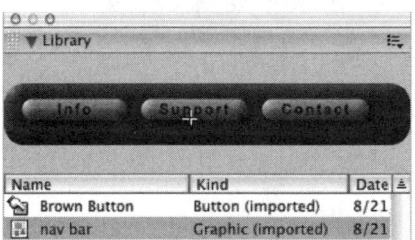

㉖ *An imported symbol is identified in the Library panel.*

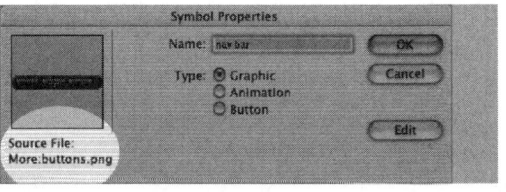

㉗ *The Symbol Properties shows the original source of an imported symbol.*

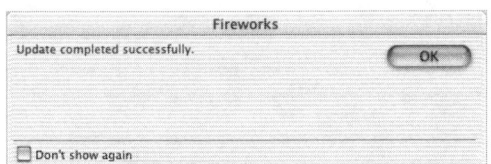

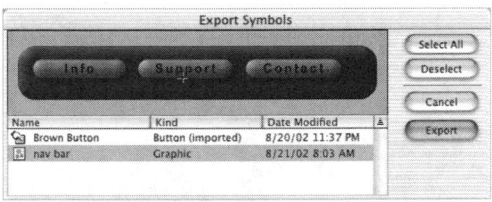

28 *You can update an imported symbol so that it matches its appearance in the original file.*

29 *The* **Export Symbols dialog box** *lets you export symbols to a new file.*

Different from Flash

If you are familiar with Macromedia Flash you know how the symbols work in that program. Fireworks symbols are slightly different.

Symbols in Fireworks do not reduce the final file size. There is no difference in final file size if a symbol is used when creating a GIF or JPEG.

That is because the final file size comes from the pixels in the graphic. Using symbols to create the image doesn't change the final pixels in the graphic.

The main benefit of using symbols in Fireworks is to make it easier to edit buttons and other graphics.

Symbols imported from other documents retain a link to the original symbol. If you edit the symbol in the original document, you can then update the imported instance.

To update an imported symbol:

1. Edit the symbol in the original document.

2. Save that file.

3. Select the imported symbol in the second document.

4. Choose Update from the Library panel menu. A dialog box appears indicating that the object was updated **28**.

TIP Imported instances of an edited symbol do not update unless you specifically apply the Update command. This allows you to edit the symbol in one document without affecting other documents.

You can also export symbols from one document into a new one.

To export symbols to a new document:

1. Choose Export Symbols from the Library panel menu. The Export Symbols dialog box appears **29**.

2. Select the symbols you want to export.

3. Click Export. This opens a standard dialog box that lets you name and save the file with the selected symbols.

TIP Exported symbols are still linked to their original file so you can update them to reflect changes in the originals, if you choose.

Sharing Symbols

Creating a Disjointed Rollover

You can use a swap image behavior to create a disjointed rollover. If you move your cursor in a disjointed rollover, it will trigger another image to appear elsewhere on your page ㉚ and ㉛.

You need to create certain elements to create a disjointed rollover. The order in which you create these elements is important.

To create the elements of a disjointed rollover:

1. Create the frames with different images under the area to be changed *(see the next exercise)*.

2. Create a slice object (not a hotspot) to define the target image—the area to be changed by the behavior *(see the exercise on the next page)*.

3. Create either a hotspot or slice object to define the trigger object—the area that triggers the behavior *(see the exercise on the next page)*.

4. Assign a swap image behavior to the trigger object hotspot or slice object *(see the exercise on page 314)*.

To create the frames for a disjointed rollover:

1. Create a frame that displays the normal state of the target image ㉜.

2. Create a second frame that displays the second state of the target image ㉝.

TIP The same area used for one disjointed rollover can be used for other target images. Simply put the artwork on other frames.

Trigger object   Target image

㉚ *When the cursor is outside the trigger object, the target image displays its normal state.*

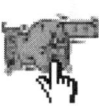 

㉛ *When the cursor is inside the trigger object, the target image displays a second state.*

 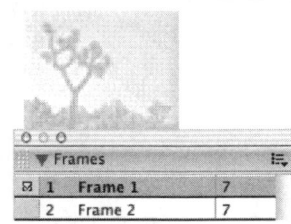

㉜ *Frame 1 displays the trigger object and the normal state of the target image.*

㉝ *Frame 2 displays the trigger object and the second state of the target image.*

Creating a Disjointed Rollover

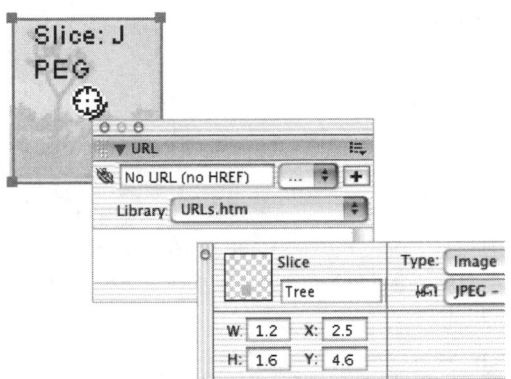

④ *The target image of a swap image behavior must be covered with a slice object.*

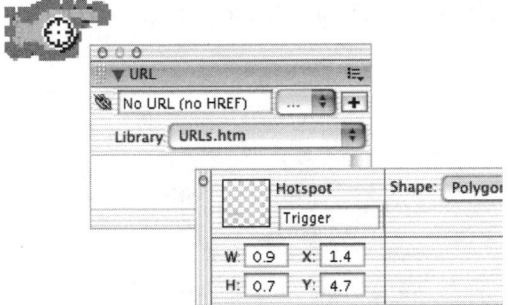

⑤ *The trigger object can be defined with either a hotspot or a slice object.*

After you create the frames, you then need to add a slice object that defines the target image for the disjointed rollover.

To define the target image:

1. Create a slice object that completely covers the area to be changed **④**.

2. In the URL panel, leave the Link as No URL (no HREF).

3. If desired, change the automatic name in the Property Inspector to a distinctive name.

TIP Although a distinctive name is not necessary, it can help as you assign the area for the disjointed rollover.

You can use either a hotspot or slice object to define the trigger object of the disjointed rollover.

To define the trigger object:

1. Select the path or object that triggers the change.

2. To create a hotspot area the same shape as the path, choose **Edit > Insert > Hotspot ⑤**.

   or

   Use any of the hotspot tools to define the area for the rollover.

   or

   To create a slice object that can trigger the change, choose **Edit > Insert > Slice.**

TIP Using a hotspot object allows you to make a non-rectangular area for the trigger object.

TIP Using a slice object to trigger the change allows you to have that area also change its appearance, for example, with another rollover effect.

Creating a Disjointed Rollover

With all the elements in place, you are now ready to actually assign the swap image behavior to create the disjointed rollover.

To assign the swap image behavior:

1. Select the hotspot or slice object that triggers the change. A Behavior Controller appears.

2. Press and drag out from the Behavior Controller. A line appears.

3. Drag the line onto the target slice area for the swap image ㊱.

4. Release the mouse. The small Swap Image dialog box appears ㊲.

5. Use the Swap Image From list to choose which frame should appear for the swap image behavior ㊳.

6. Click OK to apply the swap image behavior. A curved line connects the trigger object to the swap area. This indicates that the swap image behavior is in place ㊴.

   or

   Click More Options to modify the swap image behavior. This opens the larger Swap Image dialog box. *(See the exercise on the next page for details.)*

Trigger object   Behavior Controller   Target image

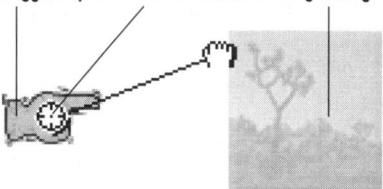

㊱ *Drag from the Behavior Controller of the trigger object to the target image of the disjointed rollover.*

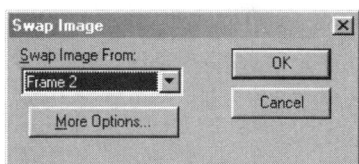

㊲ *The* **Swap Image** *dialog box.*

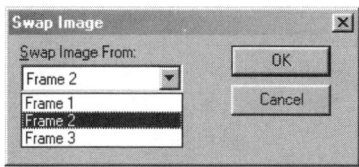

㊳ *The* **Swap Image From menu** *displays a list of the frames in the document.*

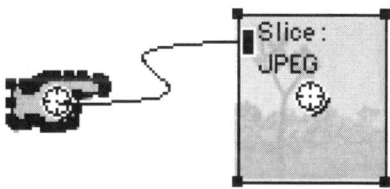

㊴ *The curved line shows there is a Swap Image behavior between the hotspot and the slice.*

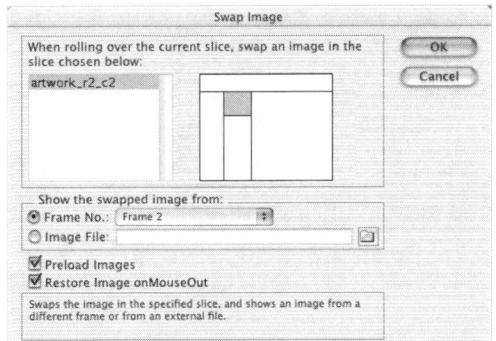

40 *The* **larger Swap Image dialog box** *gives you more controls over the settings for the Swap Image Behavior.*

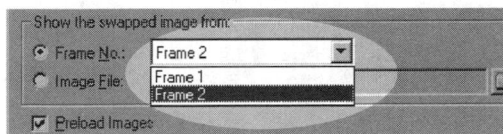

41 *Use the* **Frame No menu** *to choose the frame that contains the swap image.*

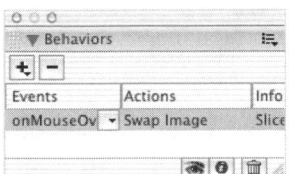

42 *A swap image action is listed in the Behaviors panel.*

If you want to refine the swap image behavior, you can use the options in the large Swap Image dialog box **40**.

To modify the swap image behavior:

1. Choose one of the following from the Show swapped image from area:
   - Select **Frame No.** to choose the frame that contains the swap image **41**.

   or

   - Select **Image File** to swap an external file instead of a frame within the document.

   TIP The external file should be the same dimensions as the slice area or the image will be distorted when it is swapped. You must also specify the correct path to that file and the path must be in the site folder.

2. Choose Preload Images to download the hidden images along with the rest of the artwork. This slows down the initial download but makes the swap occur faster. (This setting is on by default.)

3. Deselect Restore Image onMouseOut to keep the swapped image displayed after the cursor leaves the trigger area. (This setting is on by default.)

4. Click OK to return to the document. The swap image appears in the Behaviors panel **42**.

   TIP To see if the swap image behavior is working correctly, click the Preview tab. To see any external files used, you need to choose **File > Preview in Browser**.

If you want to go directly to the large Swap Image dialog box you can use the Behaviors panel.

To re-open the second Swap Image dialog box:

◆ Double-click the Swap Image listing in the Behaviors panel. This opens the large Swap Image dialog box.

Working with the Behaviors Panel

The Behaviors panel gives you still more control over behaviors. For instance, you may want a Swap Image behavior to be activated by a mouse click rather than moving the mouse over the image.

To modify the swap image events:

1. Select the hotspot or slice object that triggers the change.

2. Select the behavior in the Behaviors panel. A small triangle control appears in the Events column.

3. Click the Events triangle control. This opens the Events list 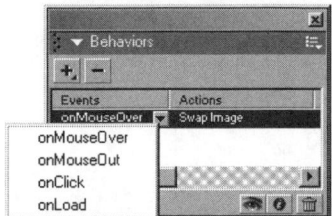.

4. Choose the type of Mouse action that should trigger the behavior from the following:

   - **onMouseOver** triggers the action as the mouse moves inside the hotspot area.
   - **onMouseOut** triggers the action as the mouse leaves the hotspot area.
   - **onClick** triggers the action when the mouse button is clicked inside the hotspot area.
   - **onLoad** automatically triggers the action as the images are loaded.

   TIP The custom event appears in the Behaviors panel 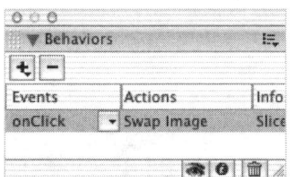.

To delete a behavior:

◆ Click the Minus (–) sign in the Behaviors panel to delete a selected behavior 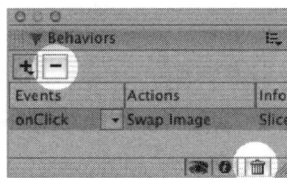.

   or

   Click the Delete icon in the Behaviors panel.

   or

   Select Delete from the Behaviors panel menu.

④③ *The* **Events** *list in the Behaviors panel allows you to choose which mouse action will trigger the behavior.*

④④ *You can set your own custom event for a Swap Image Behavior.*

④⑤ *You can delete behaviors using the* **Minus sign** *or* **Delete icon***.*

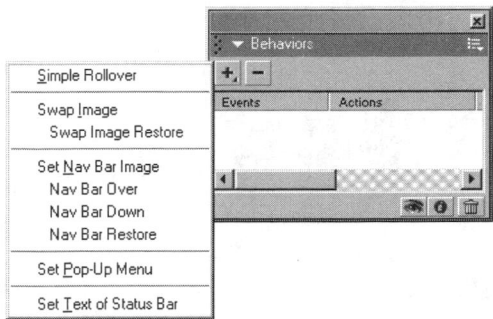

⑥ The **Behaviors** Events list *allows you to add behaviors to hotspots or slices.*

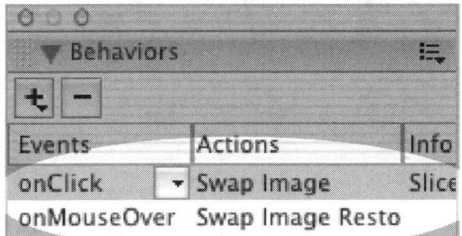

⑦ The **custom settings for a behavior** *display the event for the Swap Image and the event for the Swap Image Restore.*

You can also add a setting to control how the swap image behavior is restored when the mouse leaves the trigger object. For instance, you can add a behavior so that the image is restored when the mouse moves inside the trigger area.

To change the restore behavior:

1. Select the hotspot or slice object that triggers the change.

2. Click the Plus (+) sign in the Behaviors panel. This opens the Behaviors list **⑥**.

3. Choose Swap Image Restore. This adds a listing for the Swap Image Restore behavior **⑦**.

4. Use the Events control to change the mouse action for how the image is restored.

My Favorite Swap Image Settings

I like to create two or more trigger areas that swap images on different frames under the same slice.

Then I use onClick to swap the image rather than onMouseOver. I also use onMouseOver to apply the Swap Image Restore **⑦**.

When the mouse clicks inside the first trigger area, the image is swapped. However, when the mouse leaves the first trigger area the image is not restored.

When the mouse enters the second trigger area, that's when the onMouseOver event restores the image. A click swaps the new image.

This setup allows the trigger for one area to change the image swapped by a different trigger area.

Creating Pop-up Menus

Another type of behavior is the Pop-up Menu behavior. This allows you to create sophisticated pop-up menus that give visitors menus and submenus of destinations. These pop-up menus can be arranged in either vertical or horizontal positions ⓸ and ⓹.

To create a Pop-up menu:

1. Create the menu graphic. This is the area that is clicked to open the pop-up menu.

2. Create a hotspot or slice object to define the trigger area for the pop-up menu *(see the next exercise)*.

3. Add the Pop-up Menu behavior to either the hotspot or slice *(see the next exercise)*. This opens the Pop-up Menu Editor.

4. Use the first part of the Pop-up Menu Editor to enter the menu and submenus listings *(see the next page)*.

5. Use the second part of the Pop-up Menu Editor to format the appearance of the pop-up menu *(see pages 320–321)*.

6. Set the Advanced options for the pop-up menu *(see page 322)*.

7. Adjust the position of the pop-up menu *(see page 323)*.

To add the Pop-up Menu behavior:

1. Create the hotspot or slice to be used as the trigger for the Pop-up Menu.

2. Press the Behavior Controller and choose Add Pop-up Menu from the menu ⓾.

    or

    Choose **Modify > Pop-up Menu > Add Pop-up Menu**. This opens the Pop-up Menu Editor.

Menu graphic   Pop-up menu

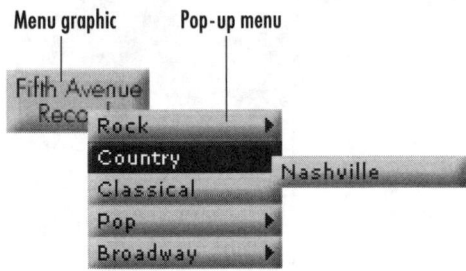

⓸ *An example of a* **vertical** *pop-up menu.*

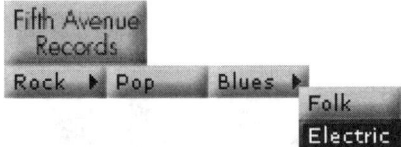

⓹ *An example of a* **horizontal** *pop-up menu.*

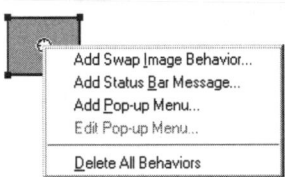

⓾ *Press the* **Behavior Controller** *to open the menu to choose Add Pop-up Menu.*

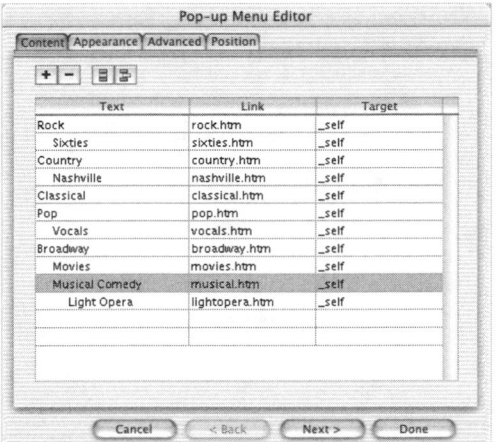

⑤ *The* **Content area of the Pop-up Menu Editor** *lets you enter the listings and sub-listings for the pop-up menu.*

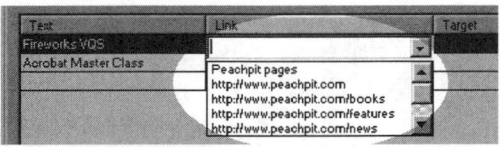

⑤ *The* **Link field** *for the Pop-up Menu Editor.*

⑤ *The* **Target field** *for the Pop-up Menu Editor.*

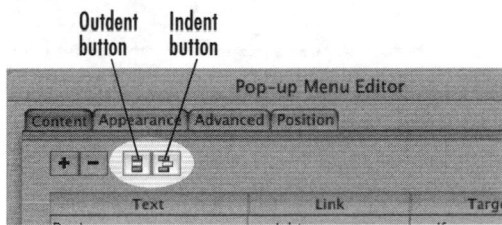

⑤ *The* **Menu controls** *Pop-up Menu Editor.*

The Pop-up Menu Editor opens with the Content tab selected **⑤**. This is where you add the menu items for the pop-up menu.

To add the menu items for a pop-up menu:

1. In the the Pop-up Menu Editor, enter a menu listing in the Text field.

2. Press the Tab key to move to the Link Field and enter the URL **⑤**.

3. Press the Tab key to move to the Target Field and choose a target where the content will appear **⑤**.

TIP You can rearrange the order of the listings by dragging items up or down in the dialog box.

4. Click the Indent Menu button to convert a listing to a submenu of the previous item **⑤**.

5. Click the Outdent Menu button to elevate a listing back to the next level up **⑤**.

6. Press the Plus (+) button or the Return/Enter key to apply the listing and clear the Text field for a new listing.

7. Repeat steps 1 through 6 as many times as necessary to create all the listings and sub-listings for the menu.

8. Click the Next button or the Appearance tab to format the appearance of the menus.

To correct errors in the listings:

1. Double-click to highlight the text.

2. Type the correct text.

3. Press Return/Enter to apply the change.

To delete a listing:

1. Select the listing that you want to delete.

2. Press the Minus (-) button.

Creating Pop-up Menus

The cells of the pop-up menus can be formatted as HTML code or as graphic images. HTML code menus tend to download faster. Graphic image menus create more sophisticated effects.

To set the HTML Appearance options:

1. Select HTML from the Cells choices. The HTML formatting appears **55**.

2. Choose Vertical Menu or Horizontal Menu from the menu **56**.

3. Choose the font from the Font list.

4. Set the point size from the Size list. As you increase the point size, the cells for each menu listing increase in size.

5. If desired, set the text style for bold or italic.

6. Use the color wells to set the text and cell colors for the Up state or Normal state of the Pop-up Menu.

7. Use the color wells to set the text and cell colors for the Over State of the pop-up menu.

8. Click the Next button or the Advanced tab to format the advanced features of the menus.

TIP Use the Events list of the Behaviors panel so that the pop-up menu is revealed by a click or onMouseOut.

TIP Watch the Preview area for an example of how the settings will affect the final menu **57**.

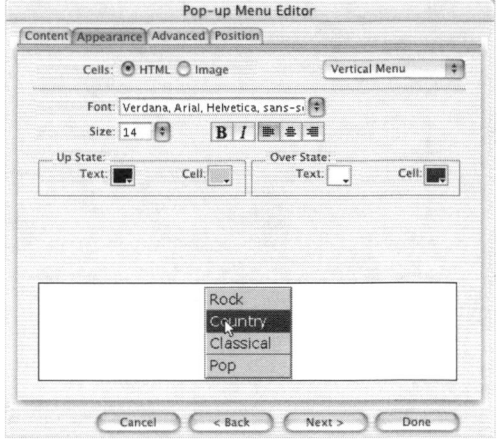

55 *The* **HTML controls** *of the Pop-up Menu Editor control the appearance of menus that are formatted using HTML code.*

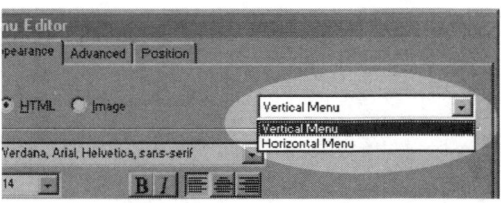

56 *Choose* **Horizontal Menu or Vertical Menu** *to change the orientation of the pop-up menu.*

57 *Use the* **Preview area** *of the Pop-up Menu Editor to see how the finished menu will appear.*

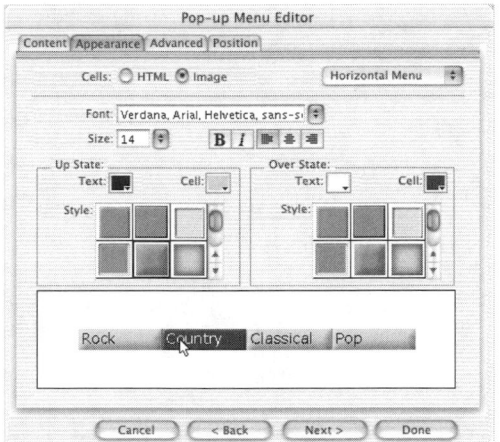

58 *The* **Image controls** *of the Pop-up Menu Editor control the appearance of menus that are formatted using graphic styles.*

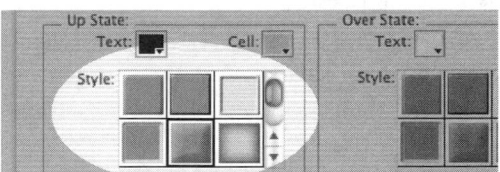

59 *The* **Style choices** *are grayscale images that are applied to the cells of the menu.*

To set the image appearance options:

1. Choose Image from the Cells choices. The Image formatting appears **58**.

2. Choose Vertical Menu or Horizontal Menu from the menu.

TIP Watch the Preview area for an example of how the settings will affect the final menu.

3. Choose the font from the Font list.

4. Set the point size from the Size list. As you increase the point size, the cells for each menu listing increase in size.

5. If desired, set the text style for bold or italic.

6. Use the color wells to set the text and cell colors for the Up state or Normal state of the Pop-up Menu.

7. Use the color wells to set the text and cell colors for the Over state of the pop-up menu.

8. Use the Style lists to choose one of the graphic styles for the Up state and the Over state.

TIP The style graphics are grayscale images that are colored using the choices in the color wells **59**.

9. Click the Next button or the Advanced tab to format the advanced features of the menus.

The Advanced options of the Pop-up Menu Editor let you refine the appearance of the pop-up menu and how it behaves when clicked **60**.

TIP Watch the Preview area to see how each of the settings affects the cells **61**.

To set the Advanced options:

1. Choose one of the following from the Cell Width menu **62**:
   - **Automatic** sets the width of all the cells to at least the length of the longest line of text.
   - **Pixels** lets you set a specific width.

TIP The amount for the Pixels setting cannot be shorter than the longest line of text.

2. Choose one of the following from the Cell Height menu:
   - **Automatic** sets the height of the cells to at least the height of the largest text character as set by the point size.
   - **Pixels** lets you set a specific height for the cell.

3. Set the Cell Padding to control the space between the text and the edge of the cell.

4. Set the Cell Spacing to control the space between cells.

5. Set the Text Indent to control the amount of space added to indent the text.

TIP The Text Indent is added in addition to the space from the Cell Padding.

6. Set the Menu Delay to control the amount of time in seconds that the menu remains visible after the cursor leaves the menu area.

7. Choose Show Borders to add border elements to the menus. *(See the next exercise for how to set the Pop-up Borders controls.)*

8. Click the Next button or the Position tab to set the position menus.

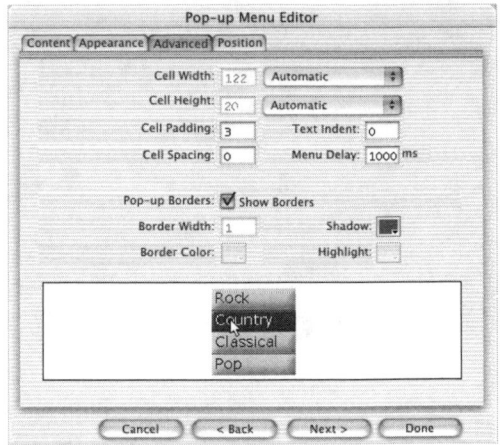

60 *The **Advanced controls** of the Pop-up Menu Editor let you refine the appearance of the menus.*

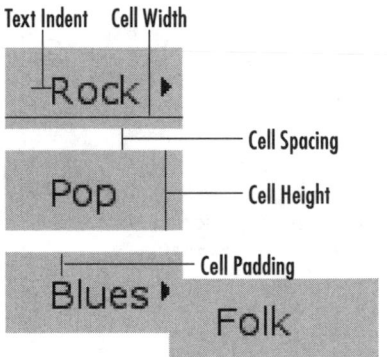

61 *A diagram of the **spacing choices** for a pop-up menu.*

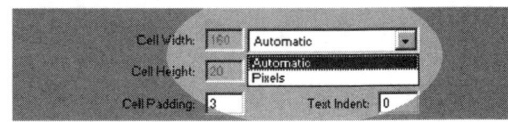

62 *Use the **Cell Width menu** to set the size of the cells in a pop-up menu.*

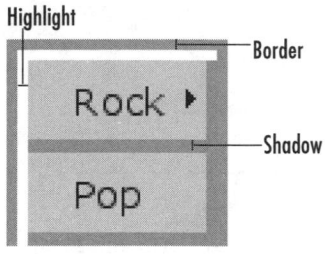

Highlight

Border

Shadow

63 *A diagram of the borders, highlights, and shadows applied to an HTML pop-up menu.*

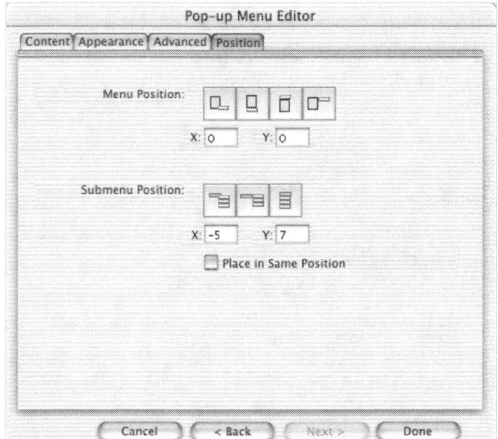

64 *The* **Position controls** *of the Pop-up Menu Editor.*

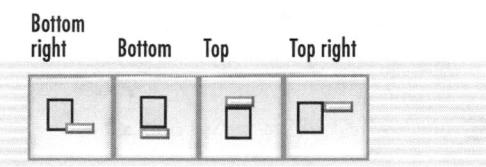

Bottom right   Bottom   Top   Top right

65 *The* **Menu Position** *presets.*

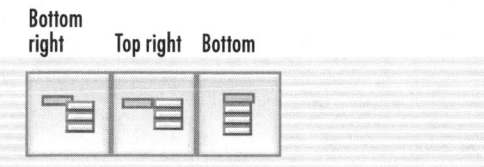

Bottom right   Top right   Bottom

66 *The* **Submenu Position** *presets.*

The Pop-up Border controls offer additional appearance options for HTML pop-up menus. These controls help you simulate the look of a three-dimensional button **63**.

To set the Pop-up Border controls:

1. Choose Show Borders to display the Pop-up Borders controls.

2. Set the Border Width. This controls the size of all the elements of the border.

3. Use each of the color wells to set the color of the border, shadow, and highlight.

TIP If you turn on Show Borders for an Image pop-up menu, only the Shadow Color Well becomes available. This becomes the color of the Cell Spacing.

The Position tab contains presets and controls that help you set where the menus and submenus appear in relationship to the slice object or hotspot object that triggers the pop-up menu **64**.

To set the Position controls:

1. Click one of the four presets for the Menu Position **65**. These presets are in relation to the original trigger object.

   or

   Enter the X and Y coordinates for the upper left corner of the pop-up menu.

2. Click one of the three presets for the Submenu Position **66**.

   or

   Enter the X and Y coordinates for the upper left corner of the submenus.

3. Choose Place in Same Position to position all the submenus in the same place as the first submenu.

Creating Pop-up Menus

The pop-up menu can also be positioned manually on the canvas area.

To manually position the pop-up menu:

1. Select the hotspot or slice that acts as the trigger area for the pop-up menu. An outline of the pop-up menu appears.

2. Press and drag the outline of the pop-up menu to a new position ⓰.

To edit an existing pop-up menu:

◆ Double-click the menu outline.

or

Double-click the Show Popup Menu label listed under Activities of the Behaviors panel ⓰.

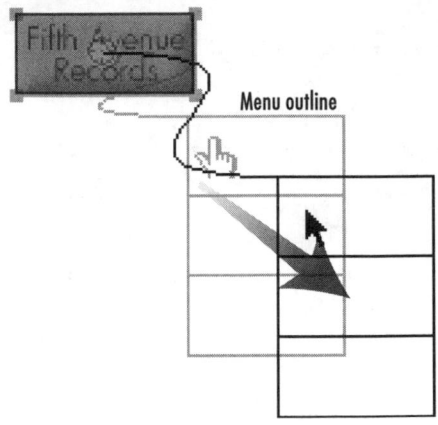

Menu outline

⓰ *You can* **reposition the pop-up menu** *by dragging the menu outline on the canvas.*

In order to see the pop-up menu, you must preview it in a browser.

To preview a pop-up menu:

◆ Choose **File > Preview in Browser** and then choose the Primary or secondary browser listed in the submenu.

Setting Other Behaviors

The Behaviors panel also lets you add text that appears in the browser's Status Bar.

To add a Status Bar message:

1. Select the hotspot or slice that you want to trigger the message.

2. Click the Plus (+) sign in the Behaviors panel to add the Set Text of Status Bar behavior. This opens the Set Text of Status Bar dialog box ⓰.

3. Type the text in the message field.

4. Click OK. The behavior is listed in the Behaviors panel ⓰.

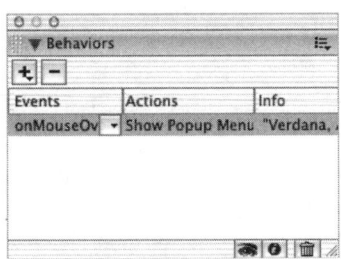

⓰ *The* **listing for a pop-up menu** *in the Behaviors panel.*

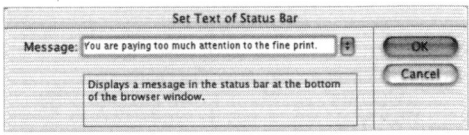

⓰ *The* **Set Text of Status Bar** *dialog box.*

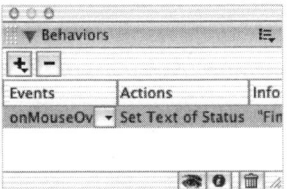

⓰ *The* **Status Bar Text** *in the Behaviors panel.*

EXPORTING 20

Unlike print images, graphics created for the Web require special handling when it comes to exporting. Not only do you have to optimize to the proper file format but you also have to make sure you use or generate the HTML code necessary to create the image maps or reassemble sliced graphics.

That's where exporting comes in. Fortunately, Macromedia Fireworks makes it easy to export your graphics together with the HTML code. It even provides special export settings that make it easy to use your Web graphics with Macromedia Dreamweaver and Macromedia Director.

Finally, Fireworks lets you export files in formats that can be used by other applications such as Macromedia Flash, Macromedia Dreamweaver, Adobe Illustrator, and Adobe Photoshop.

Understanding Exporting

There are several steps to exporting files. Each of the steps controls different aspects of the final output.

TIP You cannot use Save As command *(see page 38)* to create GIF or JPEG files. You must use the Export command.

To export files:

1. Set the optimization settings as desired *(see Chapter 15, "Optimizing.")*

2. Choose **File > Export**. This opens the Export dialog box.

3. If the file does not contain slices or image maps, export the file as a basic export ❶ *(see the following exercise).*

4. If the file contains slices, you must set the slicing controls ❷ *(see the next page).*

5. If the file contains slices, rollovers, buttons, pop-up menus, behaviors, or image maps, you must set the HTML properties *(see page 329).*

6. Navigate to set the location of the images created by slicing.

7. Name the file.

8. Click Save to export the files.

Creating a Basic Export

If the file does not contain slices or image maps, it can be exported without setting many controls. This is a basic export ❸.

To export without slices or image maps:

1. Choose **File > Export**. The Export dialog box appears.

2. Set Save As pop-up menu to Images only ❶.

TIP If you do not have slices or image maps in the file Fireworks automatically sets the Slices and HTML options to None.

❶ *The* **Export dialog box set for a plain graphic** *does not have options for slices or HTML.*

❷ *The* **Export dialog box set for a graphic that contains slices or buttons** *displays the options for slices or HTML.*

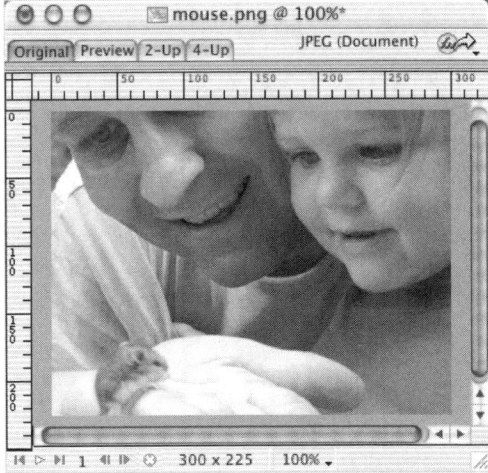

❸ *A graphic, such as this photo, that does not contain slices or buttons can be handled as a basic export.*

Understanding Exporting; Basic Export

❹ *Fireworks files with slice objects need special handling during exporting.*

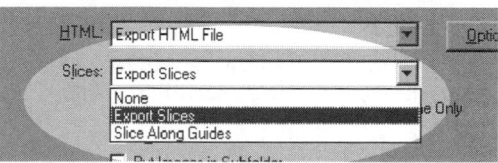

❺ *The Slices list in the Export dialog box controls how the image is sliced.*

❻ *The slices options in the Export dialog box control which slices are exported.*

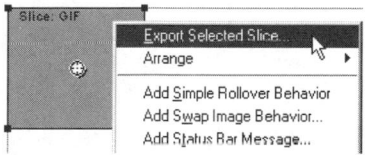

❼ *The contextual menu for a slice object lets you export a single slice.*

❽ *The Export dialog box for a single slice does not contain the HTML options.*

Setting the Slices Controls

If you have slices, buttons, or pop-up menus, you need to set the slices options **❹**.

To set the slices options:

1. In the Export dialog box use the Slices list to choose how to slice the file **❺**:
   - **None** turns off any slicing applied to the image.
   - **Export Slices** uses the slice objects to define the slices.
   - **Slice Along Guides** slices along the ruler guides.
2. Check Include Areas without Slices to also export those areas that are not covered by slice objects **❻**.

TIP If you deselect Include Areas without Slices, you create empty cells. *(See page 330 to control the appearance of empty cells.)*

You can also export only the slices you have selected in the document. This makes it easy to update only certain parts of an image.

To export selected slices:

1. Select the slice objects you want to export. (Use the Shift key to select more than one slice object.)
2. In the Export dialog box, choose Selected Slices Only **❻**.
3. Choose Current Frame Only to limit the slices to the image in the currently selected frame.

To export one slice:

1. Select the slice you want to export.
2. Control-click (Mac) or right-mouse-click (Win) and choose Export Selected Slice from the contextual menu **❼**.
3. Set the Slices options **❽**.

TIP The HTML options are not available when you export a single slice.

Setting the HTML Properties

Any document that contains slices, buttons, rollovers, pop-up menus, or image maps requires an HTML file that contains the code to assemble the images for those items.

You can create an actual HTML file or copy the HTML file to the computer clipboard.

To set the HTML destination:

◆ In the Export dialog box use the HTML list to choose the destination for the HTML code **❾**:

- **Export HTML File** creates an actual file containing the HTML information.
- **Copy to Clipboard** copies the HTML information to the computer clipboard.

TIP Copy to Clipboard allows you to switch to a program such as Dreamweaver and paste the code directly onto a page.

You can also set many options for exporting files in the HTML Setup.

To open the HTML Setup:

◆ In the Export dialog box click Options **❿**. This opens the HTML Setup dialog box **⓫**.

or

With the document window open, choose **File** > HTML Setup.

❾ *The* **HTML list** *lets you create an actual HTML file or copy the HTML to the clipboard.*

❿ *The* **Options button** in the Export dialog box *opens the HTML Setup controls.*

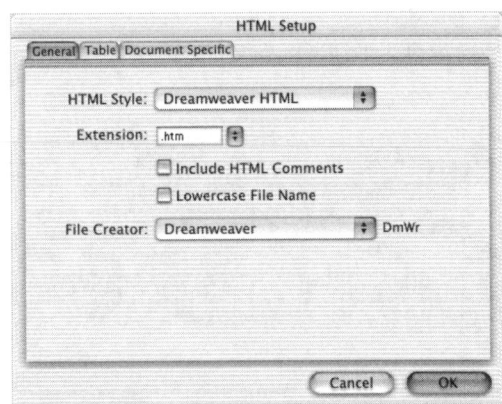

⓫ *The* **General controls of the HTML Setup.**

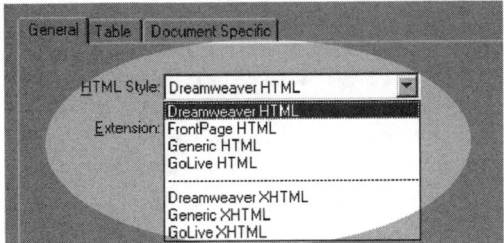

⑫ *The* **HTML Style list** *lets you match the HTML code to the application you use to create the Web page.*

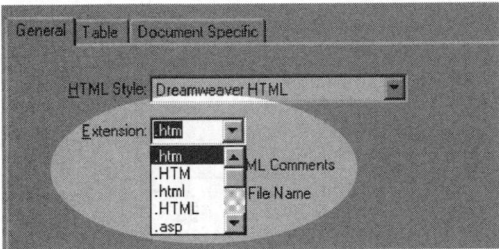

⑬ *The* **Extension list** *lets you change the extension that is added to the file.*

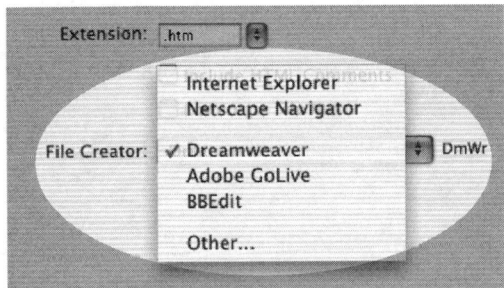

⑭ *The* **File Creator list** *(Mac) lets you assign a specific creator code to the HTML file.*

The General tab of the HTML Setup contains several options for different aspects of the exported files.

To set the HTML General options:

1. Click the General tab in the HTML Setup dialog box:

2. Use the HTML Style list to choose the program that you want the HTML code to be inserted into ⑫.
   - Choose among the programs Macromedia Dreamweaver, Microsoft FrontPage, or Adobe GoLive.
   - Choose Generic if you don't know the Web page layout program you will be using or if you will be hand coding the page.

3. Use the Extension list to set the file extension applied to the HTML file ⑬.

4. Check Include HTML Comments to add the extra comments that explain the functions of the different codes and show how to copy and paste the code into your page layout.

5. Check Lowercase File Name to insure that no capital letters are used in naming the files.

TIP The Lowercase File Name option forces Fireworks to save your files with only lowercase letters—even if you have uppercase letters in the file names. This is helpful if your Web server does not display files that contain uppercase letters.

6. (Mac) Use the File Creator list to choose which application can be used to open the HTML code ⑭.

Setting the HTML Properties

Fireworks lets you control the spacing options for the HTML tables.

To set the table spacing options:

1. Click the Table tab in the HTML Setup dialog box ⓯.

2. Use the Space with list to control the type of table ⓰:

   - **1-Pixel Transparent Spacer** creates a single table that uses a 1-pixel transparent GIF image to ensure the table cells display properly.

   TIP The transparent GIF image is called a spacer.gif and is created along with the other images for the file.

   - **Nested Tables - No Spacers** uses tables within tables to lay out the image. No spacer.gif images are used.
   - **Single Table - No Spacers** creates a single table without any spacer.gif images.

   TIP Single Table - No Spacers creates a simpler table but the result does not always display correctly in browsers.

Empty cells are are created by HTML slices *(see page 299)* and when you deselect Include Areas without Slices *(see page 327)*.

To control the empty cells:

1. In the Empty Cells area ⓱ select Use Canvas Color to use the Fireworks background color.

2. If you deselect Use Canvas Color, use the Cell Color color well to choose a specific cell color.

3. Use the Contents list to choose what should be included in the empty cells:

   - **None** adds nothing to the empty cell so that the cell remains blank. This creates the smallest possible file.
   - **Spacer Image** inserts a spacer.gif in empty cells.
   - **Non-breaking Space** inserts the HTML code for a space tag.

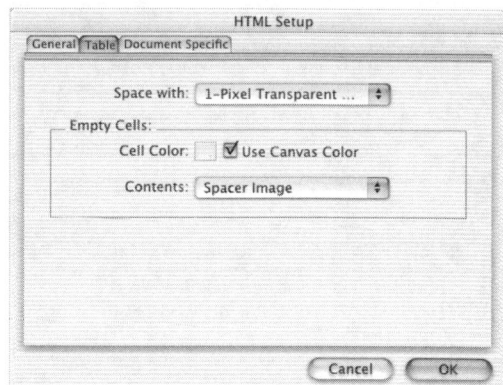

⓯ *The* **HTML Setup dialog box** *set to the Table controls.*

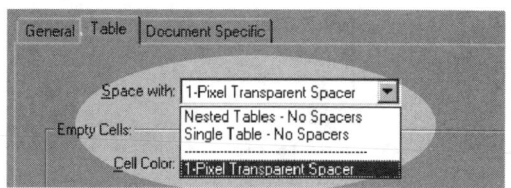

⓰ *The* **Space with list** *lets you control how the tables are created.*

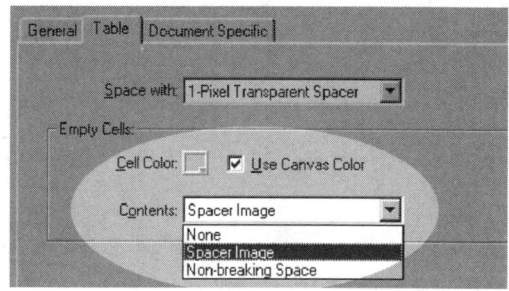

⓱ *The* **Empty Cells controls** *affect the appearance and layout of non-image slices*

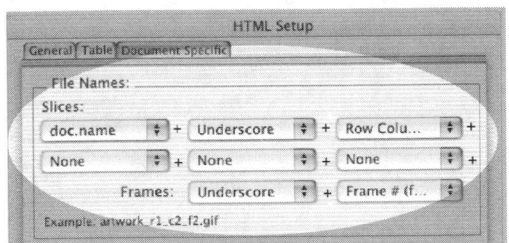

⓲ *The* **File Names options** *of the Document Specific controls.*

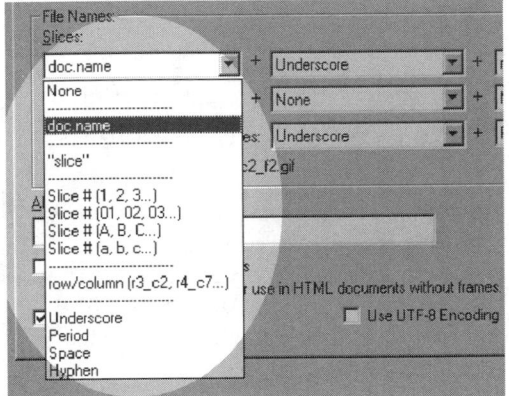

⓳ *The* **Slices pop-up menus** *let you assign the naming conventions for the files created from slicing.*

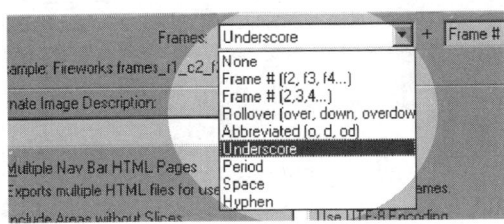

⓴ *The* **Frames pop-up menu** *lets you assign the naming conventions for the files created from frames.*

Use the Document Specific tab to set how Fireworks names the sliced images.

To set the File Names:

1. Click the Document Specific tab in the HTML Setup dialog box **⓲**.

2. Use the Slices pop-up menus under File Names to set the file naming as follows **⓳**:
    - **doc.name** sets where the name of the document should appear.
    - **"slice"** inserts the word slice into the file name.
    - **Slice#** options inserts a number for each slice.

    TIP The "slice" and Slice# options can be used together to number the slices in the table without using rows and columns.

    - **row/column** names the slice using the row and column where the slice appears in the table.
    - **Underscore, Period, Space**, or **Hyphen** adds those elements as dividers between the slice labels.
    - **None** adds no element in that space for the file name.

3. Use the Frames pop-up menu under File Names to set the file naming as follows **⓴**:
    - **Frame #** (**f2, f3, f4**) inserts the label f and the frame number.
    - **Frame #** (**2, 3, 4**) inserts just the frame number.
    - **Rollover** (**over, down, overdown**) adds the name of the rollover state of the frame.
    - **Abbreviated** (**o, d, od**) adds letter labels for the rollover state.

4. Choose **Underscore, Period, Space**, or **Hyphen** to add those elements as dividers between the slice labels.

5. Choose None to add no element in that space for the file name.

Setting the HTML Properties

You can also set the Alternate Image Description. This alt text appears on the image place holder while the image is downloading from the Web or in place of an image if it fails to download. It may also appear as a tool tip when the mouse passes over the image.

To enter the Alternate Image Description:

◆ Enter the text in the Alternate Image Description field 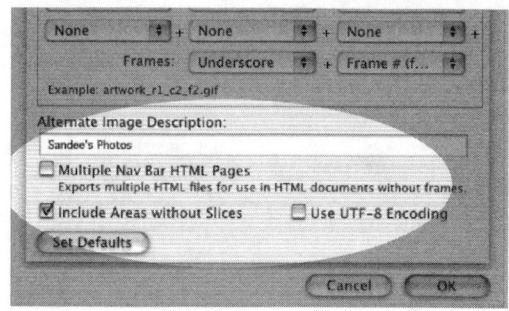.

TIP This Alternative Image Description adds an image description for documents that don't use slices.

The **Alternate Image Description options and other controls** *in the Document Specific controls.*

You can export the Multiple Nav Bar HTML as separate pages. This lets you use the Nav Bars on layouts that don't use framesets.

◆ Choose Multiple Nav Bar HTML Pages ●.

TIP If you import the code created by the Multiple Nav Bar HTML Pages into existing pages that have different file names, you'll need to fix the URLs in the Behaviors that point to those files.

You can also set the HTML so that it can display different character sets, such as English and Chinese, within the same document.

To set the text encoding:

◆ Choose UTF-8 encoding ●.

Finally, you can set the defaults for all the document specific settings.

To set the defaults:

◆ Click the Set Defaults button to convert the current Document Specific settings into defaults for new documents ●.

Setting the Alternate Image Description

The Alternate Image Description is also called the alt tag. The alt tag is the text that is displayed while an image is downloading. If the viewer has turned off viewing images the alt tag is the only indication of what the image is supposed to be.

That's why you should give the alt tag a descriptive name that explains the image instead of something generic such as "image" or "graphic."

Many screen readers, which are used by those who are blind or have vision impairments, use the alt tag as the information read aloud for their listeners. Once again you will provide more information for the visitors to your site if you use descriptive alt tags.

(sidebar, left margin) **Setting the HTML Properties**

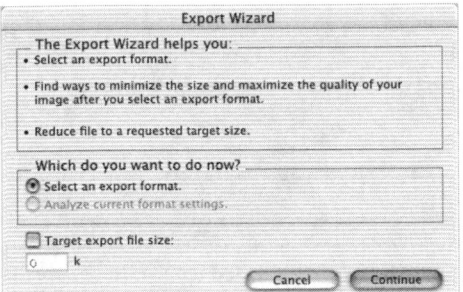

22 *The* first window of the Export Wizard *takes you through the steps necessary to export files.*

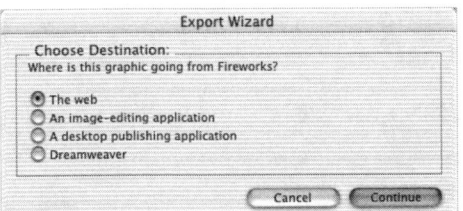

23 *The* second window of the Export Wizard *lets you choose the destination for the files.*

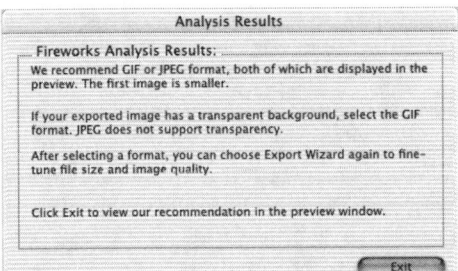

24 *The* Analysis Results window of the Export Wizard *displays the choices for the file.*

Using the Export Wizard

If you would like some help exporting files, Fireworks has an Export Wizard that can take you through the export steps.

To use the Export Wizard:

1. Choose File > Export Wizard. This opens the first window of the Export Wizard **22**.

2. Click Select an export format to have the Export Wizard choose the format that is most appropriate for your image.

TIP The option for Analyze current format settings is only available through the Export Preview dialog box *(see the next exercise).*

3. Check Target export file size to limit the size of the final exported file.

4. Click Continue to open the second window which lets you choose a destination for the image **23**.

5. Choose one of the destinations listed.

6. Click Continue to have the Export Wizard analyze the export options **24**.

7. Click the Exit button. This opens the Export Preview set with the options chosen by the Export Wizard. *(For more information on setting the optimization settings in the Export Preview dialog box, see page 262.)*

Using the Export Wizard

The Export Wizard can also help you understand the optimization settings in the Export Preview dialog box.

To analyze the Export Preview settings.

1. Choose **File > Export Preview**. This opens the Export Preview dialog box.

2. Choose the optimization settings for the file *(see page 262)*.

3. Click the Export Wizard icon in the Export Preview dialog box **25**. This opens the first window of the Export Wizard.

4. Choose Analyze current format settings **26**. A dialog box appears that explains the current optimization settings. Use this information as a guide as to how to export the file **27**.

TIP The Export Wizard doesn't actually look at the images in your file and suggest the best possible export options. It simply displays a series of pre-made dialog boxes that contain information about exporting images.

5. Click Exit to return to the Export Preview dialog box.

6. Click Export in the Export Preview.

   or

   Click OK to return to the document window. The Optimize panel will be set to the options chosen in the Export Preview.

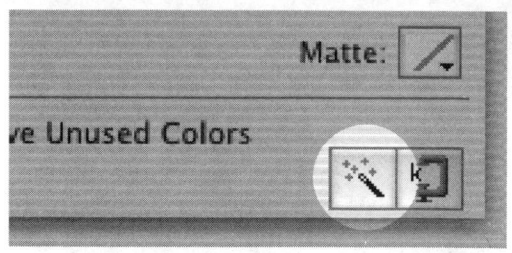

25 *Click the* **Export Wizard icon** *in the Export Preview dialog box to open the Export Wizard.*

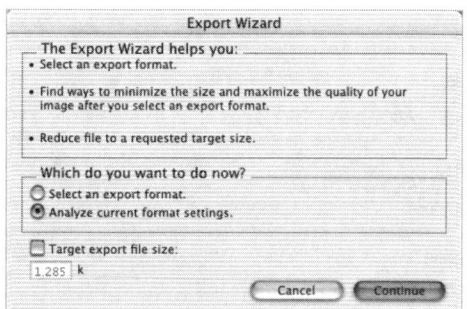

26 *The* **Analyze current format settings** *is available only when you open the Export Wizard from the Export Preview dialog box.*

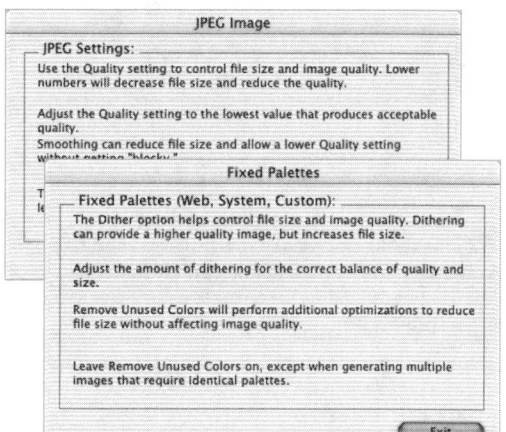

27 *Two of the Export Wizard dialog boxes that explain the current optimization settings.*

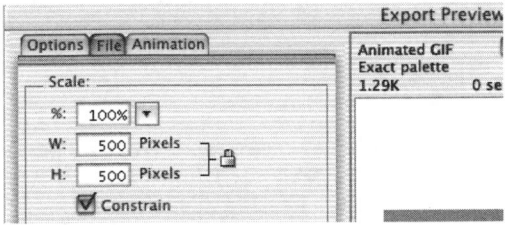

28 *The* **Scale controls** *of the File tab of the Export Preview dialog box.*

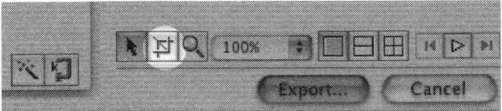

29 *The* **Export Area tool** *in the Export Preview dialog box.*

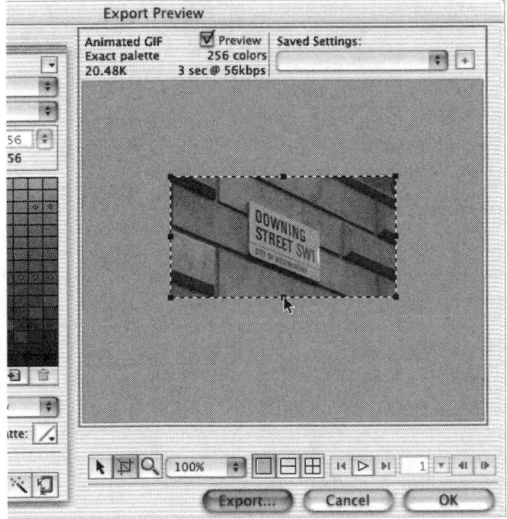

30 *Use the* **Export Area tool handles** *to define the area that you want to export.*

Cropping or Scaling Exported Images

Once you have created an image you can scale the image or crop it to export just a certain area.

To scale an image in Export Preview:

1. Choose **File > Export Preview** to open the Export Preview dialog box.

2. Click the File tab. This opens the File Scale and Export Area options **28**.

3. Use the percentage (%) slider or type in the field to scale the image to a percentage of its original size.

   or

   Enter an amount in the **W** (width) or **H** (height) fields to scale the image to an absolute measurement (in pixels).

TIP With Constrain selected, the width and height of the image keep the proportions of the original image.

You can also crop an image while you are working inside the Export Preview area. This crops the exported image but does not crop any part of the original image.

To use the Export Area tool in the Export Preview:

1. Choose **File > Export Preview**.

2. Click the Export Area tool at the bottom of the preview area **29**.

3. Adjust the handles to fit the area you want to export **30**.

4. Use the Export Preview dialog box to export the image.

You can also use the Export Area tool to select and export a portion of the image while working in the Document window.

To use the Export Area tool:

1. Choose the Export Area tool from the Tools panel ❸❶.

2. Drag to create a rectangle around the area you want to export.

3. Adjust the handles so they are around the area you want to export ❸❷.

4. Double-click inside the rectangle. This opens the Export Preview dialog box where only the selected area appears in the preview area.

5. Use the Export Preview dialog box to export the image *(see page 262)*.

You can control the size of the export area numerically using the Export Area controls of the File tab.

To crop numerically in the Export Preview:

1. Choose **File > Export Preview**.

2. Choose the File tab. The Export Area controls appear ❸❸.

3. Use the X and Y fields to set the upper left corner of the area to be exported.

4. Use the W and H fields to set the width and height of the exported area.

TIP When you set the export area numerically, you see the same handles as when you use the Export Area tool. You can drag the handles in the box that surrounds the selected portion to adjust the selection.

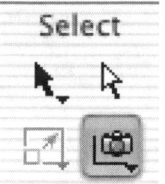

❸❶ *The* **Export Area tool** *in the Tools panel.*

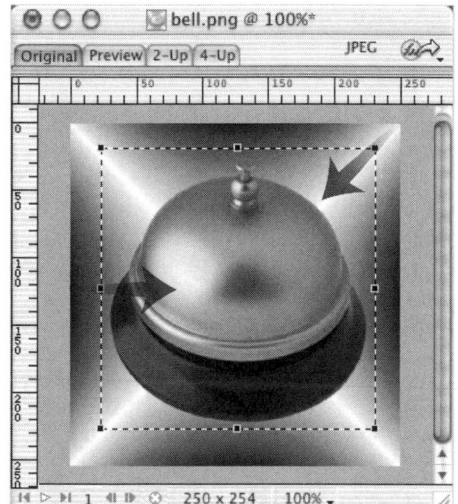

❸❷ *Adjust the* **Export Area handles** *to set the area to be exported.*

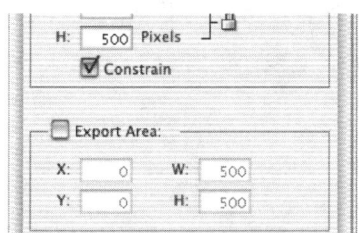

❸❸ *The* **Export Area controls** *of the File tab of the Export Preview dialog box.*

34 *The* **Insert Fireworks table icon** *in Dreamweaver's Insert panel.*

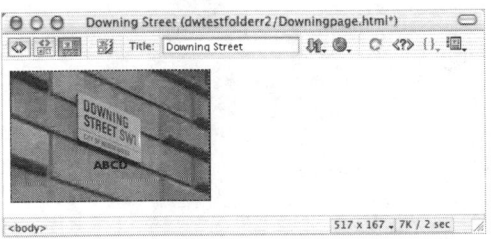

35 *Use Dreamweaver's* **Insert Fireworks HTML** *dialog box to find the Fireworks HTML file.*

[A Fireworks table imports into a Dreamweaver page — with window labeled "Downing Street (dwtestfolderr2/Downingpage.html*)", dimensions "517 x 167" and "7K / 2 sec", tag "<body>"]

36 *A Fireworks table imports into a Dreamweaver page.*

Fireworks or Photoshop?

First, let me say that I really like Adobe Photoshop. I used it to create all the screen shots in this book. However, I meet many students who use Dreamweaver with Photoshop. That's like wearing a dress shoe on one foot and a sneaker on the other. The shoes work best with their mates.

If you use Dreamweaver, you are missing out on the special advantages that you get working with Fireworks.

Working with Dreamweaver

In the world of great duos, there are Bogart & Bacall, Ben & Jerry, and, for Web graphics, Dreamweaver & Fireworks. If you use Macromedia Dreamweaver to lay out your Web pages, you have some unique benefits from using Fireworks to create your graphics. The first is how easy it is to import the HTML code that contains the table created by the Fireworks into Dreamweaver layouts. *(For more information on exporting HTML tables, see page 328.)*

TIP These Dreamweaver exercises assume you have already defined a Web site and are working on your Web page. If you need more help working with Dreamweaver, I suggest the *Dreamweaver MX Visual Quickstart Guide* by J. Tarin Towers.

To insert Fireworks HTML into Dreamweaver:

1. Place an insertion point where you would like the table to appear.

2. Click the Fireworks table icon in the Dreamweaver Insert panel **34**. This opens the Insert HTML dialog box **35**.

3. Navigate to find the HTML document created by Fireworks.

4. Click OK. The table is automatically inserted into the Dreamweaver file **36**.

Working with Dreamweaver

Once you have inserted a table from Fireworks into a Dreamweaver layout, you have several different ways to update or edit that table. The first way lets you select the table in the Dreamweaver layout and then launch Fireworks for editing.

To edit a Fireworks table from Dreamweaver:

1. In Dreamweaver, click to select the table. Dreamweaver's Property Inspector identifies it as a Fireworks table **37**.

2. Click the Edit button in the Property Inspector. This launches the Fireworks application and opens the original PNG file that was used to create the HTML table.

TIP If you do not see the Edit button, you may need to expand Dreamweaver's Property Inspector.

TIP The logos and Done button at the top of the Fireworks document window indicates that you are working in a special session launched from Dreamweaver **38**.

TIP If you have moved the Fireworks PNG since it was originally exported, you will be prompted to locate the PNG file.

3. In Fireworks, edit the PNG file using any of the normal editing tools.

4. Click the Done button at the top of the Fireworks document window. This causes all of the following to happen automatically:

   - The changes to the PNG file are saved.
   - The graphics for the file are re-exported according to the optimization settings.
   - The PNG file is closed.
   - The Dreamweaver file is opened.
   - The Dreamweaver page is updated with new exported graphics and HTML.

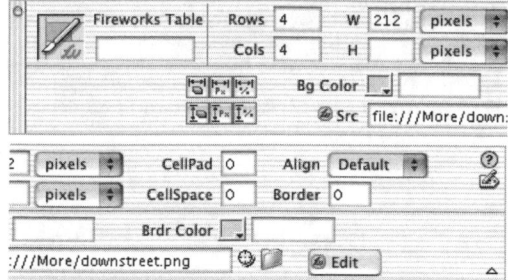

37 A **Fireworks table** *as it appears in Dreamweaver's Property Inspector.*

38 *The Done button and logos indicate that the Fireworks file is being edited through Dreamweaver.*

Keep Your Originals!

No matter what format you export your files as, don't lose the original PNG file. All the export formats rasterize the artwork into non-editable pixels. This means you will lose your text, paths, effect settings, and other parts of the artwork.

If you have to make changes to the exported artwork, it is easier to go back to the original Fireworks PNG file and then re-export. I find it easier to keep track of the Fireworks PNG file when it's in the same folder with the exported files.

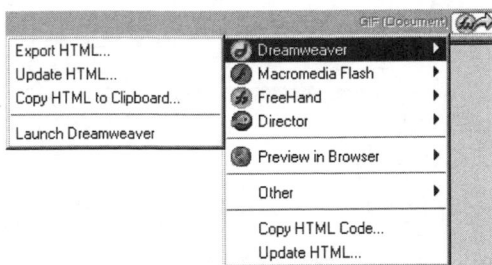

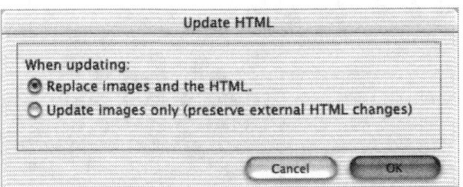

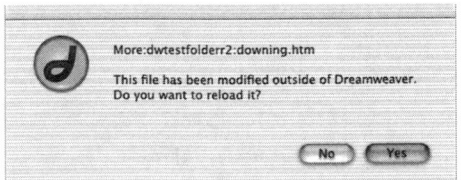

39 *Use the* **Quick Export menu** *to update the Fireworks HTML placed in a Dreamweaver file.*

40 *The* **Update HTML dialog box** *lets you choose which parts of the exported file will be updated.*

41 *An dialog box alert informs you that the Dreamweaver file has been modified.*

The flip side to the previous exercise starts in Fireworks and then updates the Dreamweaver document.

To update a Dreamweaver file from Fireworks:

1. Open and make changes to the Fireworks PNG file exported into Dreamweaver.

2. Choose **File** > **Update HTML**.

   or

   Choose **Dreamweaver** > **Update HTML** from the Fireworks Quick Export menu **39**.

3. Navigate to locate the HTML file inserted into the Dreamweaver document. The Update HTML dialog box appears **40**.

4. Choose one of the following in the Update HTML dialog box:
   - **Replace images and the HTML** changes both the images and the HTML code.
   - **Update images only** (**preserve external HTML changes**) changes the images without exporting any new HTML.

5. Open the Dreamweaver document. An alert informs you that changes were made outside of Dreamweaver **41**.

6. Click Yes to update the file.

You can also use the Quick Export menu for other features.

To export from Fireworks to Dreamweaver:

- Choose one of the following from the Dreamweaver choices:
  - **Export HTML** opens the Export dialog box set to create an HTML file (*see page 326*).
  - **Copy HTML to Clipboard** opens the Export dialog box set to copy the HTML to the clipboard.

To launch Dreamweaver from Fireworks:

- Choose Launch Dreamweaver from the Dreamweaver choices.

Working with Dreamweaver

In addition to exporting graphics and HTML code, Fireworks lets you export files in formats for use in other applications. For instance, you can export the HTML file with the special code that can be used as a Macromedia Dreamweaver Library item.

TIP Dreamweaver Library items are reusable graphics, nav bars, bits of code, and other page components that can be applied to multiple pages in a Web site.

To export as a Dreamweaver Library:

1. In Fireworks, choose **File** > **Export**.

2. Choose Dreamweaver Library from the Save as type list 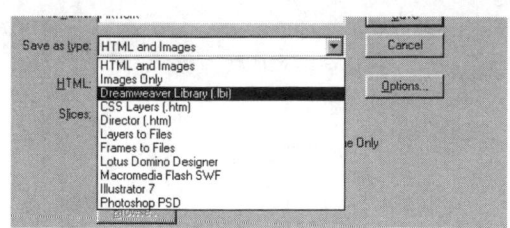.

3. Navigate to place the Library (.lbi) in the Dreamweaver Library folder.

4. Set the Slice options as described on page 331.

TIP The HTML options are not available since the Dreamweaver Library format is already a type of code.

5. Select Put Images in Subfolder to navigate to locate the subfolder where images should be stored.

6. Click Save to export the artwork.

To use a Library item in Dreamweaver:

1. In Dreamweaver, choose **Window** > **Library** to open the Assets panel in the Library mode.

2. Drag the item from the panel onto the Dreamweaver page .

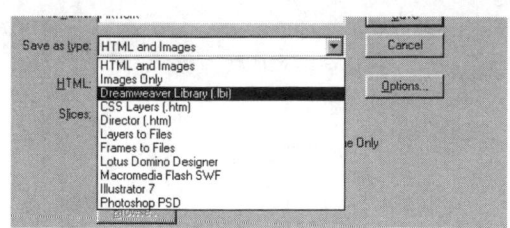

*You create a **Dreamweaver Library** by exporting it from the Save as type list.*

Drag a Dreamweaver Library element from the Library panel onto the page.

Before You Export as a Dreamweaver Library

You need to do some preparation ahead of time before you export as a Dreamweaver Library (.lbi) item.

First, you should use Dreamweaver to define the local site root folder.

Then, create a folder named Library (with a capital L) that is inside the local site root folder.

You can now use that Library folder for export Fireworks objects as Dreamweaver elements.

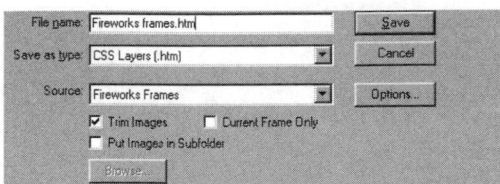

④④ *The export choices for saving files in the* **CSS Layers (.htm)** *format.*

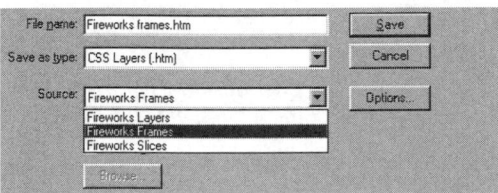

④⑤ *The* **Source** *list lets you choose what elements should be used to create the CSS elements.*

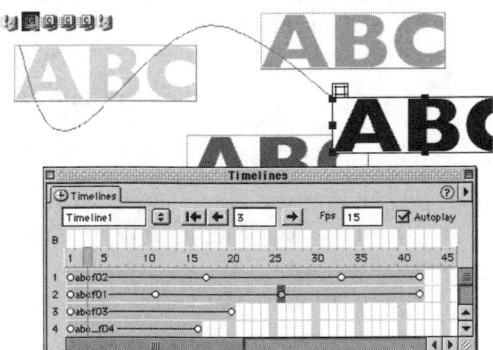

④⑥ *CSS Layers can be animated using the* Timeline in Dreamweaver.

Exporting CSS Layers

You can also export Fireworks objects as Cascading Style Sheets (CSS) Layers. This allows you to export the individual layers or frames of a Fireworks document together with the HTML code necessary to create a CSS Layer.

To export as CSS Layers:

1. Create your Fireworks objects using layers, frames, or slices.

TIP Artwork on a single frame should be separated by placing the different elements on separate layers. The elements for a button automatically appear on frames. An image that is sliced appears as a part of slices.

2. In Fireworks, choose **File > Export**.

3. Choose CSS Layers (.htm) from the Save As list **④④**.

4. Use the Source list to choose how to separate the elements **④⑤**.

5. Select Trim Images to discard any excess canvas area around the images.

6. Select Put Images in Subfolder to navigate to locate the subfolder where images should be stored.

7. Click Save to export the artwork.

To use the CSS Layers items in Dreamweaver:

1. In Dreamweaver, choose **File > Open** to open the HTML file created when you exported the artwork. The CSS elements appear inside the Dreamweaver document window.

2. Use the Timelines or other CSS options to animate the graphics **④⑥**.

Breaking Up Files

As sad as it sounds, sometimes you need to break up files. Perhaps you need to separate the frames of a rollover into individual artwork for a print ad. You may need to separate the layers of a file to use in a presentation or for video. Fireworks lets you separate layers or frames into their own files.

To convert layers to files:

1. Create your Fireworks objects using layers.
2. Set the Optimize panel to the final format.
3. Choose **File** > **Export**.
4. Choose Layers to Files from the Save as list ❹.
5. Choose Trim Images to discard any excess canvas area around the images.
6. Click OK to export the artwork.

To convert frames to files:

1. Create your Fireworks objects using frames.
2. Set the Optimize panel to the final format.
3. Choose **File** > **Export**.
4. Choose Frames to Files from the Save as list ❹.
5. Choose Trim Images to discard any excess canvas area around the images.
6. Click Save to export the artwork.

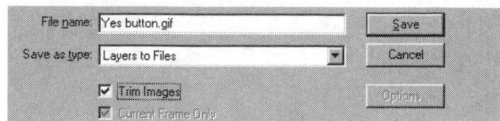

❹ *The* **Layers to Files** *option separates Fireworks frames into individual files.*

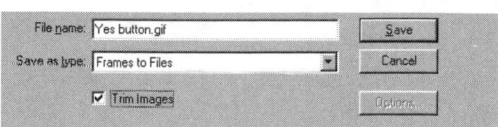

❹ *The* **Frames to Files** *option separates Fireworks frames into individual files.*

Naming Multiple Files

Fireworks automatically names each of the multiple files created when you break up layers or frames into individual files.

Layers converted to files are named with the layer name replacing the original file name.

Frames converted to files are named by adding the label_f01, _f02, and so on to the original file name.

Fireworks object | Exported as vector object

49 *Most of the Fireworks formatting is lost when you export as vectors.*

50 *Choose* **Illustrator 7** *to export files in the vector format.*

51 *The* **Illustrator Export Options** *controls how objects are converted into vector files.*

Don't Be Disappointed

You may be surprised how different your artwork looks when you export it into vectors. Anti-aliasing, feathering, effects, opacity, blending modes, textures, patterns, Web dither fills, slices, hotspots, guides, grids, canvas color, and some text formatting will be discarded. Gradient fills and bitmap images will also be discarded if the FreeHand Compatible option is chosen.

Exporting as Vector Artwork

Fireworks lets you export its vector artwork into vectors that can be opened by programs such as Adobe Illustrator or Macromedia FreeHand.

TIP Much of the formatting is lost when you export as vectors **49**. If you need to use the artwork in Illustrator, you may want to use the TIFF format which maintains the formatting. However, if you want only the path shapes, you can export as vectors.

To export as vector artwork:

1. Choose **File > Export**.

   or

   Choose **Other > Export to Illustrator** from the Quick Export menu.

2. Choose Illustrator 7 from the Save As list **50**.

3. Click the Options button to open the Illustrator Export Options dialog box **51**.

4. Select Export Current Frame Only to keep the artwork on individual layers.

   or

   Select Convert Frames to Layers. This converts each Fireworks frame into a layer.

5. Select FreeHand Compatible to discard those objects that FreeHand is unable to open. *(See the sidebar on this page to find out which elements are discarded when converting to vectors.)*

6. Click OK to return to the Export dialog box.

7. Click Save to export the artwork.

Working with Flash SWF

As mentioned in Chapter 15, you can also import the native Fireworks PNG file into Macromedia Flash. Importing PNG files into Flash keeps a link to the PNG file. This is my favorite way to use Fireworks artwork in Flash animations.

To import Fireworks PNG files into Flash:

1. Save the Fireworks file in the native PNG format *(see page 38)*.

2. In Flash, choose **File > Import to Library** and navigate to select the Fireworks PNG file. The Fireworks PNG Import Settings dialog box appears ⑤②.

3. Choose Import as a single flattened bitmap. This makes the other options unavailable.

TIP The other options in the dialog box do not keep a link to the original Fireworks document. *(See page 346 for how to set those options.)*

4. Use the imported bitmap object on the Flash page or in a symbol ⑤③.

TIP Although the bitmap image is described as flattened, that does not mean that it loses any transparency.

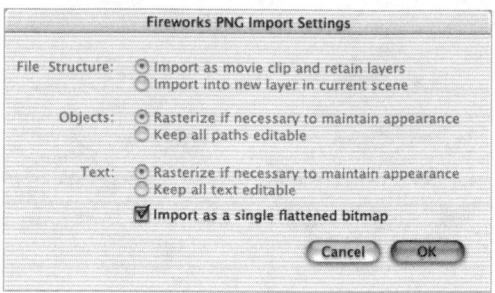

⑤② *The* **Fireworks PNG Import Settings** *dialog box set to import a Fireworks file as a single flattened image.*

⑤③ *A Fireworks PNG file imported as a bitmap into the Flash Library.*

Using Bitmaps in SWF Movies

Ordinarily I would encourage you to use all sorts of Fireworks images in Flash. Watch out! Bitmap images can cause the SWF movie to pause or play slowly. I recommend using only photographic images or objects with special effects like bevels or filter effects, such as the Eye Candy motion trail.

Working with Flash SWF

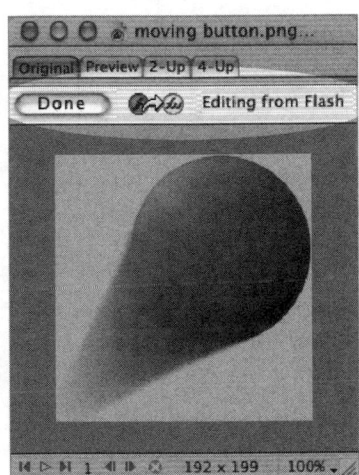

54 *Choose* **Macromedia Flash SWF** *to convert a Fireworks file into a Flash SWF document.*

55 *A* **special session of Fireworks** *is indicated by the logos and Done button at the top of the document window.*

Once you have imported a Fireworks PNG into Flash, you can edit the bitmap image and automatically update it throughout the Flash document.

To edit a Fireworks PNG imported into Flash:

1. Position the mouse cursor over the bitmap PNG listed in the Flash Library.

2. Control-click (Mac) or right-mouse-click (Win) the name of the imported PNG file in the Flash Library. A contextual menu appears **54**.

3. Choose Edit with Fireworks MX from the contextual menu. This opens Fireworks and the original PNG file.

TIP The logos and Done button at the top of the document window indicate that this is a special session of Fireworks launched through Flash **55**.

4. Make any changes to the Fireworks document.

5. Click the Done button at the top of the Fireworks window. This closes the Fireworks file and returns you to Flash. All instances of the bitmap PNG within the Flash document are automatically updated.

Working with Flash SWF

Instead of importing Fireworks files as a bitmap image, you can convert the objects into Flash objects.

To import objects into Flash:

1. Save the Fireworks file in the native PNG format *(see page 38)*.

2. In Flash, choose **File > Import to Library** and navigate to select the Fireworks PNG file. The Fireworks PNG Import Settings dialog box appears **56**.

3. Choose one of the following from the File Structure settings:
    *   **Import as movie clip and retain layers** retains the objects on the original Fireworks layers.
    *   **Import into new layer in current scene** flattens all the objects onto one layer.

4. Choose one of the following from the Objects settings:
    *   **Rasterize if necessary to maintain appearance** keeps the appearance of the Fireworks objects. This option is necessary to keep the appearance of effects such as bevels, shadows, and filters **57**. However, the paths are not editable.
    *   **Keep all paths editable** maintains the paths but discards any effects.

5. Choose one of the following from the Text settings:
    *   **Rasterize if necessary to maintain appearance** keeps the appearance of effects applied to text **57**.
    *   **Keep all text editable** maintains the text but discards any effects.

6. Leave Import as a single flattened bitmap unchecked. *(See page 344 for how to work with a flattened bitmap.)*

7. Click OK to import the file.

TIP You can copy objects in Fireworks and paste them into Flash. The objects are converted depending on the most current settings in the Fireworks PNG Import Settings.

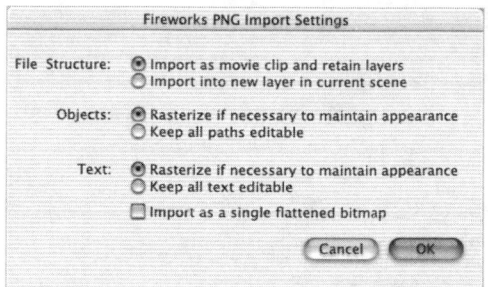

56 *The* **Fireworks PNG Import Settings** *dialog box set to import a Fireworks file as individual elements.*

Rasterized to maintain appearance

Editable paths and text

57 *The difference between rasterizing paths and text or keeping the paths and text editable.*

58 *Choose Macromedia Flash SWF to* convert a Fireworks file into a Flash SWF document.

Flash SWF Export Options

Objects: ⦿ Maintain Paths
○ Maintain Appearance

Text: ⦿ Maintain Editability
○ Convert to Paths

JPEG Quality: 100 ▾

Frames: ⦿ All
○ From 1 to 1

Frame Rate: 15 per second

For best editability in Flash, choose Maintain Paths and Maintain Editability.

To prefer appearance over editability and file size, choose Maintain Appreance and Convert to Paths.

Cancel   OK

59 *The* **Flash SWF Export Options** *dialog box lets you export a Fireworks file as a Flash SWF movie.*

Flash Replaces GIF?

Not too long ago, many companies would not use SWF animations in their Web pages. Today, more and more Web sites are integrating SWF—either by inserting Flash buttons and animations or by creating entire sites using Flash.

A small size, five-frame GIF animation can take up 5K of file space. The same animation saved in the SWF format is less than 1K.

You can also convert animations created in Fireworks into SWF animations.

To export Flash SWF files:

1. Choose **File** > **Export**. This opens the Export dialog box.

2. Choose Macromedia Flash SWF from the Save As list **58**.

TIP You can also choose **Macromedia Flash** > **Export SWF** from the Quick Export menu.

3. Click the Options button to open the Flash SWF Options dialog box **59**.

4. Set the SWF options as explained in the next exercise.

5. Click Save to export the file.

To export Flash SWF files:

1. Use the Objects controls to choose how Fireworks objects are exported to Flash SWF:
   - **Maintain Paths** converts Fireworks paths into editable Flash paths.
   - **Maintain Appearance** converts paths into bitmapped images.

2. Use the Text controls to choose how text is exported:
   - **Maintain Editability** converts Fireworks text into Flash text which can be edited.
   - **Convert to Paths** converts Fireworks text into artwork.

3. Set the JPEG quality for bitmapped images.

TIP The lower the quality, the smaller the file size.

4. Use the Frames controls to choose which frames should be exported.

5. Choose a Frame Rate to control the speed of the animation.

6. Click OK to return to the Export dialog box.

Working with Flash SWF

Exporting as Photoshop Files

It must be an indication of how popular Fireworks has become because not only can you import files from Adobe Photoshop you can also export Fireworks files back into Photoshop. This makes it easy for you to do all your work in Fireworks and then send the files back to those who have to work in Photoshop.

TIP Exporting to Photoshop always converts Fireworks paths into bitmap images.

To export as Photoshop files:

1. Choose File > Export.

2. Choose Photoshop PSD from the Save As list.

3. Choose the controls from the Settings list as follows 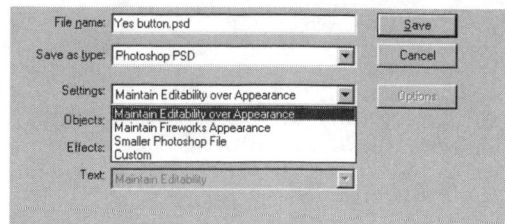:

   - **Maintain Editability over Appearance** converts objects to layers, keeps effects editable, and converts text into editable text.

TIP Only those Fireworks effects that have Photoshop equivalents will be kept. Effects such as the Eye Candy Motion Blur don't remain editable 🚱.

   - **Maintain Fireworks Appearance** converts objects into layers, renders the effects as part of the layer, and turns text into images.
   - **Smaller Photoshop File** flattens each Fireworks layer into a fully rendered image.
   - **Custom** allows you to control the individual settings for objects, effects, and text. (*See the following exercise.*)

4. Click Save to export the file.

🚰 *The export choices for saving files in the* **Photoshop format.**

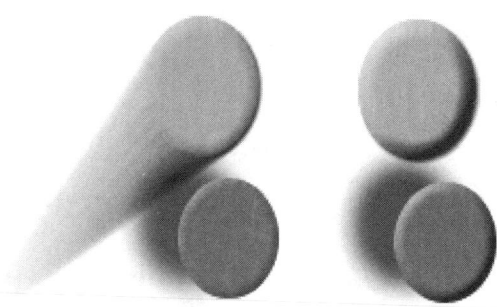

🚱 *Effects such as the Motion Trail are discarded when the file is exported in the Photoshop format.*

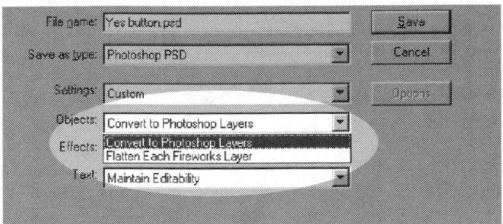

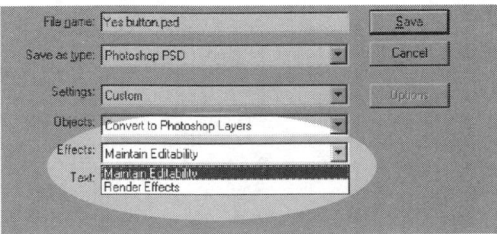

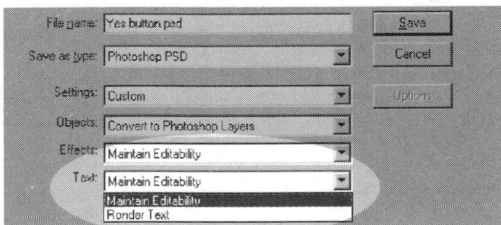

62 *The Objects list controls how objects are converted into the Photoshop format.*

63 *The Effects list controls how Live Effects are converted into the Photoshop format.*

64 *The Text list controls how text is converted into the Photoshop format.*

To set the custom Photoshop export settings:

1. Choose Custom from the Settings list.

2. Choose the controls from the Objects list as follows **62**:

   - **Convert to Photoshop Layers** creates a new Photoshop layer for each Fireworks object.
   - **Flatten Each Fireworks Layer** merges all the objects on each Fireworks layer into one Photoshop layer.

   TIP If you choose Flatten Each Fireworks Layer, you will not have any choices for Effects and Text.

3. Choose the controls from the Effects list as follows **63**:

   - **Maintain Editability** converts the Fireworks effects into the equivalent Photoshop effect. Effects that have no equivalent are discarded.
   - **Render Effects** rasterizes the Fireworks effects as part of the image.

4. Choose the controls from the Text list as follows **64**:

   - **Maintain Editability** converts the text into the equivalent Photoshop text.
   - **Render Text** rasterizes the text into a Photoshop layer.

   TIP Fireworks text on a path has no equivalent in Photoshop and will be converted into linear text.

KEYBOARD SHORTCUTS

As you become more familiar with the various Fireworks features, you should begin to use the keyboard shortcuts for the commands you use most often. For instance, rather than use the mouse to choose **File > Export**, it is much faster and easier to use the keyboard shortcut: Cmd+R on the Macintosh or Ctrl+R on Windows.

This appendix lists the shortcuts for Macromedia's standard set of Fireworks menu commands. These are the commands that ship as the default setting with Fireworks. As shown on pages 17–20, you can change these keyboard commands.

Most of these shortcuts are also displayed along with the command on the menus, so you don't have to use this list to find the shortcut for the commands you use the most.

Macintosh Keyboard Shortcuts

The following are the keyboard shortcuts for the
Macintosh platform. These are the abbreviations
used for the keys.

Cmd	Command key
Opt	Option key
Up	Up key
Down	Down key
Left	Left key
Right	Right key
Space	Spacebar

Fireworks Menu (OS X)

Preferences	Cmd+U
Quit Fireworks	Cmd+Q

File Menu

New	Cmd+N
Open...	Cmd+O
Close	Cmd+W
Save	Cmd+S
Save As...	Cmd+Shift+S
Import...	Cmd+R
Export...	Cmd+Shift+R
Export Preview...	Cmd+Shift+X
Preview in Browser	F12
Preview in Secondary Browser	Cmd+F12, Shift+F12
Print...	Cmd+P
Quit Fireworks (Mac OS 9)	Cmd+Q

Edit Menu

Undo	Cmd+Z
Redo	Cmd+Y, Cmd+Shift+Z
Insert New Button...	Cmd+Shift+F8
Insert New Symbol...	Cmd+F8

Insert Hotspot	Cmd+Shift+U
Insert Slice	Opt+Shift+U
Find and Replace...	Cmd+F
Cut	Cmd+X
Copy	Cmd+C
Copy HTML Code...	Cmd+Opt+C
Paste	Cmd+V
Clear	Delete, Delete
Paste Inside	Cmd+Shift+V
Paste Attributes	Cmd+Opt+Shift+V
Duplicate	Cmd+Opt+D
Clone	Cmd+Shift+D

View Menu

Zoom In	Cmd+=, Cmd++, Cmd+Shift+=
Zoom Out	Cmd+-
Magnification 50%	Cmd+5
Magnification 100%	Cmd+1
Magnification 200%	Cmd+2
Magnification 300%	Cmd+3
Magnification 400%	Cmd+4
Magnification 800%	Cmd+8
Magnification 1600%	Cmd+6
Fit Selection	Cmd+Opt+0
Fit All	Cmd+0
Full Display	Cmd+K
Hide Selection	Cmd+L
Show All	Cmd+Shift+L
Rulers	Cmd+Opt+R
Show Grid	Cmd+Opt+G
Snap to Grid	Cmd+Opt+Shift+G
Show Guides	Cmd+;
Lock Guides	Cmd+Opt+;
Snap to Guides	Cmd+Shift+;

Macintosh Keyboard Shortcuts

Slice Guides	Cmd+Opt+Shift+;
Hide Edges	F9
Hide Panels	F4, Tab

Select Menu

Select All	Cmd+A
Deselect	Cmd+D
Superselect	Cmd+Right
Subselect	Cmd+Left
Select Inverse	Cmd+Shift+I

Modify Menu

Trim Canvas	Cmd+Opt+T
Fit Canvas	Cmd+Opt+F
Animate Selection...	Opt+Shift+F8
Convert to Symbol...	F8
Tween Instances...	Cmd+Opt+Shift+T
Flatten Selection	Cmd+Opt+Shift+Z
Merge Down	Cmd+E
Free Transform	Cmd+T
Rotate 90° CW	Cmd+Shift+9
Rotate 90° CCW	Cmd+Shift+7
Bring to Front	Cmd+Shift+Up
Bring Forward	Cmd+Up
Send Backward	Cmd+Down
Send to Back	Cmd+Shift+Down
Align Left	Cmd+Opt+1
Align Center Vertical	Cmd+Opt+2
Align Right	Cmd+Opt+3
Align Top	Cmd+Opt+4
Align Center Horizontal	Cmd+Opt+5
Align Bottom	Cmd+Opt+6
Distribute Widths	Cmd+Opt+7
Distribute Heights	Cmd+Opt+9
Join	Cmd+J

Split	Cmd+Shift+J
Group	Cmd+G
Ungroup	Cmd+Shift+G

Text Menu

Text Size Smaller	Cmd+Shift+,
Text Size Larger	Cmd+Shift+.
Text Style Bold	Cmd+B
Text Style Italic	Cmd+I
Align Left	Cmd+Opt+Shift+L
Align Centered Horizontally	Cmd+Opt+Shift+C
Align Right	Cmd+Opt+Shift+R
Align Justified	Cmd+Opt+Shift+J
Align Stretched	Cmd+Opt+Shift+S
Attach to Path	Cmd+Shift+Y
Convert to Paths	Cmd+Shift+P
Check Spelling	Shift+F7

Filters Menu

| Repeat Plug-in | Cmd+Opt+Shift+X |
| Invert | Cmd+Opt+Shift+I |

Window Menu

New Window	Cmd+Opt+N
Minimize Window	Cmd+M
Tools	Cmd+F2
Properties	Cmd+F3
Answers	Opt+F1
Optimize	F6
Layers	F2
Frames	Shift+F2
History	Shift+F10
Styles	Shift+F11
Library	F11
URL	Opt+Shift+F10

Macintosh Keyboard Shortcuts

Color Mixer	Shift+F9
Swatches	Cmd+F9
Info	Opt+Shift+F12
Behaviors	Shift+F3
Find and Replace	Cmd+F

Tools

Pointer tool	V, 0
Select Behind tool	V, 0
Subselection tool	A, 1
Marquee tool	M
Oval Marquee tool	M
Lasso tool	L
Polygon Lasso tool	L
Crop tool	C
Export Area tool	C
Magic Wand tool	W
Line tool	N
Pen tool	P
Rectangle tool	U
Rounded Rectangle tool	U
Ellipse tool	U
Polygon tool	U
Text tool	T
Pencil tool	B
Vector Path tool	P
Redraw Path tool	P
Brush tool	B
Scale tool	Q
Skew tool	Q
Distort tool	Q
Freeform tool	O
Reshape Area tool	O
Eyedropper tool	I

Paint Bucket tool	G
Gradient tool	G
Eraser tool	E
Blur tool	R
Sharpen tool	R
Dodge tool	R
Burn tool	R
Smudge tool	R
Rubber Stamp tool	S
Knife tool	Y
Rectangle Hotspot tool	J
Circle Hotspot tool	J
Polygon Hotspot tool	J
Slice tool	K
Polygon Slice tool	K
Hand tool	H
Zoom tool	Z
Hide/Show Slices	2
Default Stroke and Fill Colors	D
Swap Stroke and Fill Colors	X
Toggle Screen Mode	F

Miscellaneous

Clone and Nudge Down	Opt+Down, Cmd+Opt+Down
Clone and Nudge Down Large	Opt+Shift+Down, Cmd+Opt+Shift+Down
Clone and Nudge Left	Opt+Left, Cmd+Opt+Left
Clone and Nudge Left Large	Opt+Shift+Left, Cmd+Opt+Shift+Left
Clone and Nudge Right	Opt+Right, Cmd+Opt+Right
Clone and Nudge Right Large	Opt+Shift+Right, Cmd+Opt+Shift+Right
Clone and Nudge Up	Opt+Up, Cmd+Opt+Up
Clone and Nudge Up Large	Opt+Shift+Up, Cmd+Opt+Shift+Up
Edit Bitmap	Cmd+E
Exit Bitmap Mode	Cmd+Shift+E
Fill Selected Pixels	Opt+Delete

Macintosh Keyboard Shortcuts

Next Frame	Page Down, Cmd+Page Down
Nudge Down	Down
Nudge Down Large	Shift+Down
Nudge Left	Left
Nudge Left Large	Shift+Left
Nudge Right	Right
Nudge Right Large	Shift+Right
Nudge Up	Up
Nudge Up Large	Shift+Up
Paste Inside	Cmd+Shift+V
Play Animation	Ctrl+Opt+P
Previous Frame	Page Up, Cmd+Page Up

Windows Keyboard Shortcuts

The following are the keyboard shortcuts for the
Windows platform. These are the abbreviations used
for the keys.

Ctrl	Control key
Alt	Alt key
Up	Up arrow key
Down	Down arrow key
Left	Left arrow key
Right	Right arrow key
Space	Spacebar

File Menu

New	Ctrl+N
Open...	Ctrl+O
Close	Ctrl+W
Save	Ctrl+S
Save As...	Ctrl+Shift+S
Import...	Ctrl+R
Export...	Ctrl+Shift+R
Export Preview...	Ctrl+Shift+X

Preview in Browser	F12
Preview in Secondary Browser	Ctrl+F12, Shift+F12
Print...	Ctrl+P
Exit	Ctrl+Q

Edit Menu

Undo	Ctrl+Z
Redo	Ctrl+Y, Ctrl+Shift+Z
New Button...	Ctrl+Shift+F8
New Symbol...	Ctrl+F8
Hotspot	Ctrl+Shift+U
Slice	Alt+Shift+U
Find and Replace...	Ctrl+F
Cut	Ctrl+X
Copy	Ctrl+C
Copy HTML Code...	Ctrl+Alt+C
Paste	Ctrl+V
Clear	Backspace, Del
Paste Inside	Ctrl+Shift+V
Paste Attributes	Ctrl+Alt+Shift+V
Duplicate	Ctrl+Alt+D
Clone	Ctrl+Shift+D
Preferences...	Ctrl+U

View Menu

Zoom In	Ctrl+=, Ctrl+Num +, Ctrl+Shift+=
Zoom Out	Ctrl+-, Ctrl+Num -
Magnification 50%	Ctrl+5, Ctrl+Num 5
Magnification 100%	Ctrl+1, Ctrl+Num 1
Magnification 200%	Ctrl+2, Ctrl+Num 2
Magnification 300%	Ctrl+3, Ctrl+Num 3
Magnification 400%	Ctrl+4, Ctrl+Num 4
Magnification 800%	Ctrl+8, Ctrl+Num 8
Magnification 1600%	Ctrl+6, Ctrl+Num 6
Fit Selection	Ctrl+Alt+0, Ctrl+Alt+Num 0

Windows Keyboard Shortcuts

Fit All	Ctrl+0, Ctrl+Num 0
Full Display	Ctrl+K
Hide Selection	Ctrl+L
Show All	Ctrl+Shift+L
Rulers	Ctrl+Alt+R
Show Grid	Ctrl+Alt+G
Snap to Grid	Ctrl+Alt+Shift+G
Show Guides	Ctrl+;
Lock Guides	Ctrl+Alt+;
Snap to Guides	Ctrl+Shift+;
Slice Guides	Ctrl+Alt+Shift+;
Hide Edges	F9
Hide Panels	F4, Tab

Select Menu

Select All	Ctrl+A
Deselect	Ctrl+D
Superselect	Ctrl+Right
Subselect	Ctrl+Left
Select Inverse	Ctrl+Shift+I

Modify Menu

Trim Canvas	Ctrl+Alt+T
Fit Canvas	Ctrl+Alt+F
Animate Selection...	Alt+Shift+F8
Convert to Symbol...	F8
Tween Instances...	Ctrl+Alt+Shift+T
Flatten Selection	Ctrl+Alt+Shift+Z
Merge Down	Ctrl+E
Free Transform	Ctrl+T
Numeric Transform...	Ctrl+Shift+T
Rotate 90° CW	Ctrl+Shift+9
Rotate 90° CCW	Ctrl+Shift+7
Bring to Front	Ctrl+Shift+Up
Bring Forward	Ctrl+Up

Send Backward	Ctrl+Down
Send to Back	Ctrl+Shift+Down
Left	Ctrl+Alt+1, Ctrl+Alt+Num 1
Center Vertical	Ctrl+Alt+2, Ctrl+Alt+Num 2
Right	Ctrl+Alt+3, Ctrl+Alt+Num 3
Top	Ctrl+Alt+4, Ctrl+Alt+Num 4
Center Horizontal	Ctrl+Alt+5, Ctrl+Alt+Num 5
Bottom	Ctrl+Alt+6, Ctrl+Alt+Num 6
Distribute Widths	Ctrl+Alt+7, Ctrl+Alt+Num 7
Distribute Heights	Ctrl+Alt+9, Ctrl+Alt+Num 9
Join	Ctrl+J
Split	Ctrl+Shift+J
Group	Ctrl+G
Ungroup	Ctrl+Shift+G

Text Menu

Text Smaller	Ctrl+Shift+,
Text Larger	Ctrl+Shift+.
Text Bold	Ctrl+B
Text Italic	Ctrl+I
Align Left	Ctrl+Alt+Shift+L
Align Centered Horizontally	Ctrl+Alt+Shift+C
Align Right	Ctrl+Alt+Shift+R
Align Justified	Ctrl+Alt+Shift+J
Align Stretched	Ctrl+Alt+Shift+S
Attach to Path	Ctrl+Shift+Y
Convert to Paths	Ctrl+Shift+P
Check Spelling...	Shift+F7

Filters Menu

Repeat Plug-in	Ctrl+Alt+Shift+X
Invert	Ctrl+Alt+Shift+I

Window Menu

New Window	Ctrl+Alt+N

Windows Keyboard Shortcuts

Tools	Ctrl+F2
Properties	Ctrl+F3
Answers	Alt+F1
Optimize	F6
Layers	F2
Frames	Shift+F2
History	Shift+F10
Styles	Shift+F11
Library	F11
URL	Alt+Shift+F10
Color Mixer	Shift+F9
Swatches	Ctrl+F9
Info	Alt+Shift+F12
Behaviors	Shift+F3
Find and Replace	Ctrl+F
Using Fireworks	F1

Tools

Pointer tool	V, 0
Select Behind tool	V, 0
Subselection tool	A, 1
Marquee tool	M
Oval Marquee tool	M
Lasso tool	L
Polygon Lasso tool	L
Crop tool	C
Export Area tool	C
Magic Wand tool	W
Line tool	N
Pen tool	P
Rectangle tool	U
Rounded Rectangle tool	U
Ellipse tool	U
Polygon tool	U

Text tool	T
Pencil tool	B
Vector Path tool	P
Redraw Path tool	P
Brush tool	B
Scale tool	Q
Skew tool	Q
Distort tool	Q
Freeform tool	O
Reshape Area tool	O
Eyedropper tool	I
Paint Bucket tool	G
Gradient tool	G
Eraser tool	E
Blur tool	R
Sharpen tool	R
Dodge tool	R
Burn tool	R
Smudge tool	R
Rubber Stamp tool	S
Knife tool	Y
Rectangle Hotspot tool	J
Circle Hotspot tool	J
Polygon Hotspot tool	J
Slice tool	K
Polygon Slice tool	K
Hand tool	H
Zoom tool	Z
Hide/Show Slices	2
Set Default Stroke/Fill Colors	D
Swap Stroke/Fill Colors	X
Toggle Screen Mode	F

Windows Keyboard Shortcuts

Miscellaneous

Clone and Nudge Down	Alt+Down, Ctrl+Alt+Down
Clone and Nudge Down Large	Alt+Shift+Down, Ctrl+Alt+Shift+Down
Clone and Nudge Left	Alt+Left, Ctrl+Alt+Left
Clone and Nudge Left Large	Alt+Shift+Left, Ctrl+Alt+Shift+Left
Clone and Nudge Right	Alt+Right, Ctrl+Alt+Right
Clone and Nudge Right Large	Alt+Shift+Right, Ctrl+Alt+Shift+Right
Clone and Nudge Up	Alt+Up, Ctrl+Alt+Up
Clone and Nudge Up Large	Alt+Shift+Up, Ctrl+Alt+Shift+Up
Edit Bitmap	Ctrl+E
Exit Bitmap Mode	Ctrl+Shift+E
Fill Pixel Selection	Alt+Backspace, Alt+Del
Next Frame	Page Down, Ctrl+Page Down
Nudge Down	Down
Nudge Down Large	Shift+Down
Nudge Left	Left
Nudge Left Large	Shift+Left
Nudge Right	Right
Nudge Right Large	Shift+Right
Nudge Up	Up
Nudge Up Large	Shift+Up
Paste Inside	Ctrl+Shift+V
Play Animation	Ctrl+Alt+P
Previous Frame	Page Up, Ctrl+Page Up

INDEX

A

actions
  display in History panel, 224
  redoing, 37
  reversing, 37
  selecting range of, 224
  undoing, 37
Add Arrowheads panel, 129
Add Frames dialog box, 264
additive colors, 40
Add URL dialog box, 293
adjust color effects, 144–147
  Auto Levels, 144
  Brightness/Contrast, 144
  Color Fill, 145
  Curves, 145
  Hue/Saturation, 147
  Invert, 146
  Levels, 146
  See also effects
Adobe Illustrator EPS files, 240
alignment
  anchor points, 77
  bitmap images, 100
  control handles, 77
  horizontal text, 182
  hotspots, 100
  justified, 182
  objects, 97-101
  slices, 100
  stretch, 182
  text on paths, 190
  vector objects, 100
Align panel, 97–101
  Anchors icon, 77, 98, 99, 100
  Distribute icons, 98
  handle control icons, 77

icon chart, 101
icons, clicking, 98
illustrated, 77
Match Size icons, 100
opening, 97, 98, 99
point alignment icons, 77
Space icons, 99
To Canvas button, 97, 98, 99
undos, 99
uses, 100
See also alignment
alpha. *See* transparency
Alpha Channel masks, 199, 203
Alpha Transparency, 258, 259
(alt) tag, 291, 299
Alternate Image Description, 332
anchor points
  adding, 69
  aligning, 299
  control handles, creating, 58
  control handles, extending, 59
  control handles, retracting, 59
  converting, 70
  creating, 57
  deleting, 69
  moving, 76
  selected, displaying, 62
  selecting, 76
  unselected, displaying, 62
Animated GIF format, 260
Animate dialog box, 274, 275
Animation controls, 16, 281
animations, 263–286
  creating, 266–267
  file size control, 285
  frames, 264–265
  frames, importing onto, 268
  frames, timing, 282
  GIF, 241

G

H

I

M

T